Women, Sex and Marriage in Early Modern Venice

For Jens Hammer

Women, Sex and Marriage in Early Modern Venice

DANIELA HACKE

ASHGATE

Published by
Ashgate Publishing Limited
Gower House, Croft Road
Aldershot, Hants
GU11 3HR
England

Ashgate Publishing Company
Suite 420
101 Cherry Street
Burlington, VT 05401–4405
USA

Ashgate website: http://www.ashgate.com

British Library Cataloguing in Publication Data
Hacke, Daniela Alexandra
  Women, sex and marriage in early modern Venice. – (St Andrews studies in
  Reformation history)
  1. Marriage – Italy – Venice – History – 16th century
  2. Women – Italy – Venice – Social conditions – 16th century
  3. Marriage law – Italy – Venice – History – 16th century
  4. Marriage – Religious aspects. 5. Venice (Italy) – social
  life and customs – 16th century
  I. Title
  306.8'1'094531'09031

Library of Congress Cataloging-in-Publication Data
Hacke, Daniela.
  Women, sex, and marriage in early modern Venice / Daniela Alexandra Hacke.
      p. cm. – (St Andrews studies in Reformation history)
  Includes bibliographical references (p.)
  (alk. paper)
  1. Marriage – Italy – Venice – History. 2. Women – Italy – Venice – History.
  3. Husband and wife – Italy – Venice – History. 4. Domestic relations
  courts – Italy – Venice – History. I. Title.
  II. Series.

  HQ630.15.V465H33 2003
  306.81'0945'31–dc21   2003041874

ISBN 0 7546 0763 1

This book is printed on acid-free paper

Typeset in Sabon by Bournemouth Colour Press, Parkstone, Poole

Printed and bound in Great Britain by TJ International Ltd, Padstow, Cornwall.

Contents

St Andrews Studies in Reformation History

*Seminary of University? The Genevan Academy and
Reformed Higher Education, 1560–1620*
Karin Maag

Marian Protestantism: Six Studies
Andrew Pettegree

Protestant History and Identity in Sixteenth-Century Europe
(2 volumes) edited by Bruce Gordon

*Antifraternalism and Anticlericalism in the German Reformation:
Johann Eberlin von Günzburg and the Campaign Against the Friars*
Geoffrey Dipple

Piety and the People: Religious Printing in French, 1511–1551
Francis M. Higman

*The Shaping of a Community: The Rise and Reformation of the
English Parish c. 1400–1560*
Beat Kümin

The Reformation in Eastern and Central Europe
Karin Maag

The Magnificent Ride: The First Reformation in Hussite Bohemia
Thomas A. Fudge

Kepler's Tübingen: Stimulus to a Theological Mathematics
Charlotte Methuen

The Reformation and the Book
Jean-François Gilmont, edited and translated by Karin Maag

'Practical Divinity': The Works and Life of Revd Richard Greenham
Kenneth L. Parker and Eric J. Carlson

Belief and Practice in Reformation England: A Tribute to
Patrick Collinson by His Students
edited by Susan Wabuda and Caroline Litzenberger

Frontiers of the Reformation: Dissidence and Orthodoxy
in Sixteenth-Century Europe
Auke Jelsma

The Jacobean Kirk, 1567–1625:
Sovereignty, Polity and Liturgy
Alan R. MacDonald

John Knox and the British Reformations
edited by Roger A. Mason

The Education of a Christian Society:
Humanism and the Reformation in Britain and the Netherlands
edited by N. Scott Amos, Andrew Pettegree and Henk van Nierop

Poor Relief and Protestantism:
The Evolution of Social Welfare in Sixteenth-Century Emden
Timothy G. Fehler

Tudor Histories of the English Reformations, 1530–83
Thomas Betteridge

Radical Reformation Studies:
Essays presented to James M. Stayer
edited by Werner O. Packull and Geoffrey L. Dipple

Clerical Marriage and the English Reformation:
Precedent Policy and Practice
Helen L. Parish

Penitence in the Age of Reformations
edited by Katharine Jackson Lualdi and Anne T. Thayer

The Faith and Fortunes of France's Huguenots, 1600–85
Philip Benedict

The Sixteenth-Century French Religious Book
edited by Andrew Pettegree, Paul Nelles and Philip Conner

William of Orange and the Revolt of the Netherlands, 1572–84
K.W. Swart, edited by R.P. Fagle, M.E.H.N. Mout and
H.F.K. van Nierop,
translated by J.C. Grayson

A Dialogue on the Law of Kingship among the Scots
A Critical Edition and Translation of George Buchanan's De Iure Regni
apud Scotos Dialogus
Roger A. Mason and Martin S. Smith

William Cecil and Episcopacy, 1559–1577
Brett Usher

List of Figures and Tables

Tables

Figures

Acknowledgements

My first debt is to Peter Burke, under whose wise guidance and support this book was started as a doctoral thesis at the University of Cambridge. I am immensely grateful for his scholarly advice, his careful reading and his patience and sensitivity in helping me to overcome the problems posed by the English language to a non-native speaker. Bob Scribner, whose premature death has deprived early modern studies of an innovative scholar, was my joint supervisor for one year. He was important in clarifying crucial questions regarding the structure of the work, while Brian Pullan and Richard Mackenney suggested ways in which I might turn the thesis into a better book. My honest thanks to all of them.

Throughout my work I have benefited immensely from the help and the support of many friends and colleagues. Claudia Opitz helped get the project started, as did Guido Ruggiero, whose initial advice on archival material was much appreciated. In Venice a number of local scholars and friends provided advice and shared their knowledge of Venetian society with me. Among them I wish to thank in particular Gaetano Cozzi (whose recent death has deprived Venetian historiography of a very distinguished scholar) and Claudio Povolo, who helped me more than they might have imagined. To Vittorio Mandelli and Filippo Paladini I owe a personal debt of gratitude for their friendship and support in the Venetian archives. Loris Menegon generously provided me with his transcription of Lorenzo Priuli's *Prattica Criminale* (a project under the supervision of Claudio Povolo) from which I benefited a lot.

Equally helpful were the staff of the Venetian Archivio di Stato and among the archivists I wish to thank Alessandra Sambo, Claudia Salmini, Alessandra Schiavon and Edoardo Giuffrida in particular. Manuela Barausse and Maria Giovanni Siet made the Archivio della Curia Patriarchale an enjoyable and friendly place to work and I am grateful for their helpful assistance.

Most of my research was carried out at a time when in Italy interest in the history of marital disputes arose. It is thanks to Silvana Seidel Menchi who, with the assistance of Francesca Cavazzana Romanelli and Diego Quaglioni, brought together an accomplished group of international legal and social scholars with shared interests in the *Cause matrimoniali*. I am grateful to have been invited to the many stimulating meetings and conferences which were held at the Istituto Storico Italiano-Germanico at the University of Trent and at the Villa I Tatti in Florence, the Harvard Center for Renaissance Studies, over a couple of years.

Throughout the writing of the book, Ulinka Rublack in particular has offered constant encouragement and advice – her commitment and the many stimulating discussions we had were invaluable. Stanley Chojnacki also deserves special thanks for the interest he took in my work, for sustaining me intellectually and for his kindness and honest thoughts. Jutta Sperling was equally helpful – she was a reliable source of support at a time when the manuscript felt apart. Victoria Avery, Nicholas Davidson, Martin Dinges, Vic Gatrell, John Henderson, David Hopkins, Mary Laven, Daniela Lombardi, Claudio Povolo, Lyndal Roper, Erik O. Ründal, James Shaw, Michael Stolberg and Jonathan Walker commented on single sections of the book. Their suggestions were invaluable. Many others, including Patricia Allerston, Sybille Backmann, Bernd Roeck and Ulrike Strasser, provided references or gave vital advice on the social and gender history of Venice and Europe.

This book would not have been written without the financial assistance I received from various institutions. I wish to thank the Evangelisches Studienwerk e.V. Villigst, the Centro Tedesco di Studi Veneziani and the DFG-Graduiertenkolleg 'Die Renaissance in Italien', Bonn, for the grants they provided. Thanks also to the editors and publishers of Truman State University Press and the Science and Research Centre of the Republic of Slovenia, Koper, for granting me permission to reproduce my articles 'Non Lo Volevo Per Marito in Modo Alcuno: Forced Marriages, Generational Conflicts, and the Limits of Patriarchal Power in Early Modern Venice, c. 1580–1680', in *Time, Space, and Women's Lives in Early Modern Europe*, ed. A. Jacobson Schutte, Th. Kuehn and S. Seidel Menchi, Kirksville 2001, 203–22 and 'Gendering Men in Early Modern Venice', in *Acta Histriae* 8 (2000), 49–68 in a revised version.

Finally I wish to thank my family Claudia, Ursula and Klaus Hacke for the confidence they have had in me and, in particular, my husband Jens Hammer. He has lived with this project for many years, has shared my work experiences and discussed many of my findings with me. Despite his own demanding professional life he has read endless drafts, set up the diagrams and even cheerfully checked every single one of my calculations when I was struggling with numbers and figures. He has steadily encouraged me to sharpen my arguments, and has given me the confidence to carry on; but equally he had taught me to let things grow with time. I dedicate this book to him.

Abbreviations and Notes

A.d.C.	Avogaria di Comun
ASPV, Curia	Archivio Storico della Curia Patriarchale, Venice
ASV	Archivio di Stato, Venice
BMC	Biblioteca del Museo Correr, Venice
BNM	Biblioteca Nazionale Marciana, Venice
b.	busta
C.M.	Causarum Matrimoniorum
F.C.	Filicae Causarum
m.v.	more veneto
Misc. pen.	Miscellanea penale
q.m (q.)	the former (the deceased)
Reg.	registro
S.U.	Sant'Uffizio

The quotations from archival sources retain original spellings and punctuation, although the letters 'u' and 'v' have not been distinguished. First names are standardised were possible and have, moreover, been Italianised (for example, Zuane to Giovanni). Unless stated otherwise, all translations are by the author.

In Venice the year ran from 1 March to the end of February (*more veneto*), although the Holy Office and the Patriarchal Court used the Roman calendar with the new year starting on 1 January.

CHAPTER ONE

Introduction

In Mattäus Merian's engraving from 1630 Venice looks like a peaceful and tranquil city, with just a few people walking on the *fondamenta*, and rather more gondolas plying the Canal Grande. Great care was devoted to depicting the city's splendours, such as the Ducal Palace, and, in particular, the urban topography: its palaces, churches, gardens and many small streets. At the far eastern end the cathedral church of S. Pietro di Castello – the ecclesiastical centre of Venice – stands out among the other buildings (see Figure 1.1).

Castello was one of the most populous of Venice's 71 parishes (see Figure 1.2), with more than 9000 inhabitants in the 1580s, most of them humble people such as simple labourers working for the nearby arsenal, fishermen and washerwomen. The seaman Alessandro Franchi and his young wife Elena Bottera formed one of the many households of this parish. But they did not live in conjugal harmony. They had quarrelled soon after their marriage, and ever since their lives were overshadowed by marital discord. Neighbours would hear Elena yelling and crying and believed that Franchi, far from being a good companion, battered his wife 'without any reason'. By about 1582 Elena had abandoned the marital home and had moved in with her mother near S. Sofia, a parish on the northern side of Venice. One day the peace in the neighbourhood was disturbed by loud screaming. Attracted by the noise, a woman looked down from her balcony to discover a man standing below, insulting Elena's mother and threatening to make mincemeat of her. This curious neighbour later learned that the furious man was Alessandro Franchi, whose wife had deserted him.

In April 1583 this case of marital discord came to the attention of Venice's secular authorities, the Avogadori di Comun. Mother and daughter accused Franchi of 'unnatural' sexual intercourse, 'cruelty' and 'tyranny'. He had treated Elena so badly and had beaten her so severely, they alleged, that she had lost her unborn child. Franchi denied these allegations; in return he accused his wife Elena of laziness and disobedience, maintaining that she had refused to obey his orders and had not wanted to lift a finger, not even to prepare his dinner for his return from work. He argued that he had therefore simply corrected her behaviour and given her a few slaps. Elena and her mother, however, could call on 12 witnesses to support their

1.1   View of the city of Venice (Matthäus Merian, 1630)

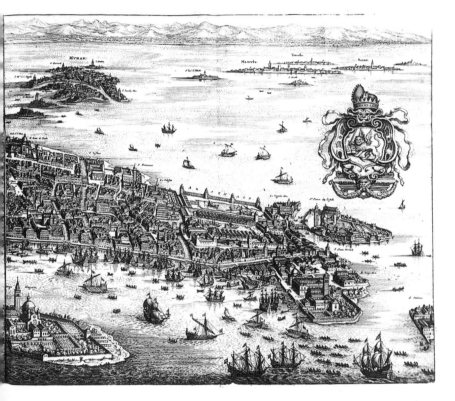

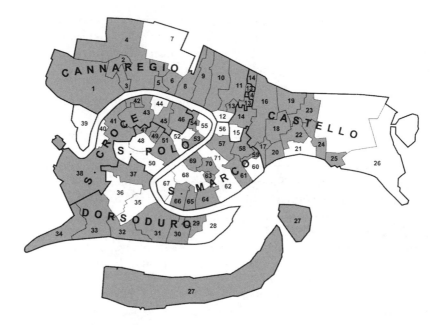

VENETIAN PARISHES
Shading indicates areas represented in the status animarum. Michael Feeney

CANNAREGIO
1. S. Geremia
2. Ghetto
3. S. Leonardo
4. S. Marcuola
5. S. Maria Maddalena
6. S. Fosca
7. S. Marcilian
8. S. Felice
9. S. Sofia
10. SS. Apostoli
11. S. Canciano
12. S. Giovanni Grisostomo
13. S. Maria Nova

CASTELLO
14. S. Marina
15. S. Lio
16. S. Maria Formosa
17. S. Giovanni Novo
18. S. Severo
19. S. Giustina
20. S. Provolo
21. S. Giovanni in Bragora
22. S. Antonin
23. S. Ternità
24. S. Martino
25. S. Biagio
26. S. Pietro di Castello

DORSODURO
27. S. Eufemia
28. S. Gregorio
29. S. Vio
30. S. Agnese
31. S. Trovaso
32. S. Basegio
33. S. Anzolo Raffael
34. S. Nicolò
35. S. Barnaba
36. S. Margherita
37. S. Pantalon

S. CROCE
38. S. Croce
39. S. Lucia
40. S. Simeon Piccolo
41. S. Simeon Grande
42. S. Zuan Degolà
43. S. Giacomo dall Orio
44. S. Stae
45. S. Maria Mater Domini
46. S. Cassiano

S. POLO
47. S. Boldo
48. S. Stin
49. S. Agostin
50. S. Tomà
51. S. Polo
52. S. Aponal
53. S. Silvestro
54. S. Mattio
55. S. Giovanni
Elemosinario

S. MARCO
56. S. Bortolomio
57. S. Salvador
58. S. Zulian
59. S. Basso
60. S. Marco
61. S. Giminian
62. S. Moisè
63. S. Fantin
64. S. Maria Zobenigo
65. S. Maurizio
66. S. Vidal
67. S. Samuele
68. S. Angelo
69. S. Beneto
70. S. Paternian
71. S. Luca

1.2   Map of Venetian parishes

case. The pair wanted to live 'in peace' – and to get the dowry back.[1]

Marriage culture, gender and social order

This is just one example of numerous cases of domestic disputes and marital discord that lay at the heart of early modern Venice, belying the city's apparent tranquillity. As this study will show, scenarios like this one permeated the city to the point of threatening the very fabric of early modern Venetian society, as many women, both single and married, filed lawsuits on domestic and marital matters at the Venetian secular and ecclesiastical courts. Through the use and analysis of contemporary case studies this book presents and examines the dynamics of domestic society, focusing in particular on marital disputes, ideas of gender and the role of the courts in Counter-Reformation Venice. An important aim is to explore the internal dynamics of Venetian households by looking at contested meanings of domestic patriarchy. This book is not so much about normative texts emphasising ordered households, but rather about the implementation of patriarchal authority in daily life – its abuse, acceptable limits and related problems. It examines what patriarchy meant to the people living in the fascinatingly heterogeneous parishes of early modern Venice.

What, then, do cases of marital dysfunction tell us about marriage culture, conjugality and patriarchy in early modern Venice? As this study will show, gender was crucial to the legal dynamics and patterns of accusation. Both men and women, husbands and wives referred to contemporary understandings of dominant gender roles and behaviour when attacking the head of the household's use or abuse of authority. Allegations of cruelty and tyranny made by wives against husbands figure prominently in marital disputes: these were quite familiar and potent images in early modern Venice, and they were elaborated copiously. Wives would complain about cruel and lazy husbands who battered them, neglected family members and wasted household resources. Counter-allegations by husbands would then focus on the wives' refusal to perform their household tasks, to care for their husbands and to fulfil their sexual commitment to them. Men and women thus fought not only over proper gender behaviour within marriage, but also over the *meaning* of conjugality and domestic patriarchy. Legal depositions of the time give complex and telling

---

[1] ASV, AdC., Misc. pen. 416.6, Franchi, Alessandro.

insights into contemporary ideas of how the conjugal household was expected to work. While various authors of prescriptive literature expressed their vision of ordered households and ordered society, numerous legal depositions from litigants and both male and female witnesses provided a unique window onto the appropriation of these dominant gender ideologies. While husbands, in ruling over their wives, defined conjugality and the way households should be run, unhappy and mistreated women underscored the limits of male authority when they filed requests in court for separation or annulment.

Marital disputes therefore expose the challenges posed to domestic patriarchy – by husbands who abused their authority or were unable to consummate a marriage and by wives who abandoned the conjugal home or betrayed the holy sacrament of matrimony. Adultery was the most manifest expression of a husband's loss of control over his wife. A wife's desertion of her husband then marked the final breakdown of household order and was, moreover, perceived as endangering neighbourhood peace and civic harmony. As cases discussed in this book will show, there was a strong connection between the breakdown of marriage and the abuse of male authority. Patriarchy, then, was not a stable concept but one that had to be enforced and implemented in daily life.

When disputes between men and women, husbands and wives, or parents and children overshadowed the peace of Venice's densely populated neighbourhoods, the parishioners would stop to observe quarrelling couples from their balconies or windows. When they later were summoned to court as witnesses they had to reflect on their understanding of domestic hierarchy, proper female or filial conduct and marital conjugality. Before the city's secular and ecclesiastical authorities they would be asked to form and express moral judgements that were linked intrinsically to questions concerning the daily conduct of husbands and wives or parents and children. They thus had to reflect on domestic patriarchy, gender differences and the way these differences operated in daily life.

Marital and household disputes also had wider implications: because society was based on stable marriages and household order, disputes threatened the peace and harmony not only of the neighbourhood but that of society as a whole. From the fifteenth century onwards good household rule was considered crucial for the maintenance of household order and social stability, and the importance of the family as the foundation of social order was increasingly stressed. The *cittadino* (citizen) Giovanni Caldiera (c. 1400–74), for example, emphasised in *De oeconomia veneta* (c. 1463–64) the head of the household's responsibility to govern his family in a well-balanced way, promoting desirable virtues in his children, the future citizens of the republic. Caldiera's views on the household were unsurprisingly hierarchical, but his vision of domestic patriarchy was tempered by virtues befitting each household member. The main characteristics of a *boun economo* (good household manager) were virtue and the ability to make sound decisions. Above all he had to be 'wise and prudent'. His rule had to be strict but righteous, caring for the physical and spiritual well-being of the household members.[2]

Since gender relations and household hierarchy in early modern society were understood more broadly in their relation to social order, household rule had to be well balanced and judicious. Indeed, in the early fifteenth century the patrician Francesco Barbaro (1390–1454) established a connection between the well-being of the republic and ordered households. In his *De re uxoria* he insisted that 'well-ordered families maintain the stability of the state'. The conjugal household was, moreover, perceived as a diminutive image of the state, a political metaphor often expressed in connection with noble households. It was the aforementioned Giovanni Caldiera who developed the fullest expression of the family as a political metaphor when he wrote, '[a]nd just as every economy resembles a polity, so also the home is in the likeness of the city.'[3] In this analogy of city and household, family life was seen as mirroring the order of the state. Household rule embodied symbolic meaning because it paralleled the rule of the city magistrate and thus the relationship between ruler and ruled. As Dennis Romano has argued, in Renaissance Venice this political metaphor altered servant–master relationships and influenced profoundly the way in which masters responded to acts of disobedience.[4]

Use of the analogy between household and social order was widespread among Italian humanists. For example, in 1560 Alessandro Piccolomini could claim bluntly that 'a house ... is none other than a small city; and a city a big house.'[5] It was also during the sixteenth century that the perception of Venetians' well-balanced rule found its fullest expression. In his *De magistratibus et Republica Venetorum* the renowned sixteenth-century Venetian patrician Gasparo Contarini praised the city's unique balance between monarchy, aristocracy and democracy in the Venetian constitution. Contarini articulated the myth

---

2 On Caldiera see Romano, 1996, pp. 13–15; King, 1975, p. 557; on household management in general see the seminal work of Frigo, 1985, here pp. 84, 155–6.

3 Quoted in Romano, 1996, p. 14. See also King, 1975, pp. 535–74, and 1976, pp. 19–50.

4 Romano, 1996, p. 16.

5 Ibid. For other late sixteenth-century examples (Lantieri, Gaggio) see Frigo, 1985, pp. 86–7. For a similar analogy in early modern France see Hanley, 1989, pp. 4–27.

of Venice as a city of stable government in which a perfectly formed constitution prevented opportunities for self-interest and dissension through a system of a 'mixed constitution'. In his view monarchical rule was limited by the control of the magistracies and by the laws that safeguarded public welfare, so that 'all dangerous inconveniences, whereby the commonwealth might sustain harm, are thereby removed.'[6] In this way, Contarini held, 'any man may easily understand, that the Duke of Venice is deprived of all meanes, whereby he might abuse his authoritie, or become a tyrant.'[7] According to the dominant understanding of Venetian self-fashioning, tyrannical rule was an abuse of authority and constituted the antithesis of republican ideals, which placed public welfare, stability and the freedom of the republic at the centre of political behaviour.

Paolo Paruta, nominated *storiografo pubblico* in February 1580, elaborated this political metaphor even further. In his treatise *Della perfezzione della vita politica* ('On the perfection of political life') he not only transferred the Venetian principle of mixed government to the household, but also elaborated the specific role that women played within this idealised government. Paruta emphasised that the monarchic government of the household ruler was – like that of the doge – ideally limited by transferring the principle of mixed government to family life. With the co-operation of the wife in running the household, autocratic rule was modified into a government of the few, while the services of the brothers, oriented towards the public welfare of the household members, symbolised the democratic element.[8] The much-praised republican ideal of the Venetian mixed constitution thus paralleled the ideal government of the household. As in political rule, tyranny and abuse of authority were prevented through a system of control in which gender played an important role.

This ideal of reasonable, sound and moderate rule was expressed not only in treatises for patrician households or in political theory. As will be shown, 'tyranny' was an effective image used by women in litigation. When gender conflicts and spousal or parental disputes reached the Venetian courts, litigants elaborated a moral framework that condemned violent, 'unbound' and, thus, 'tyrannical' rule by husbands and parents alike. Even post-Tridentine marriage doctrine (see Chapter 3) emphasised that wives need not tolerate atrocities without reason and that children should consent to marry rather than be forced. When

---

[6] Contarini, 1599, p. 40. On *Venezia stato misto* see Gaeta, 1961, pp. 58–75 and Gilmore, 1973, pp. 431–44.

[7] Contarini, 1599, p. 42.

[8] Paruta, 1579, p. 632.

children claimed that their marriage had taken place under coercion, the legal allegations were elaborated in order to evoke the powerful image of tyrannical rule – a type of governance that ran counter to the myth of Venice as a free and righteous republic.[9] During the seventeenth century, when anonymous publications increasingly criticised the Venetian political system for being an oligarchy, allegations brought by female litigants in particular might have affected Venetian sensibilities.[10] Since misrule threatened household order, husbands and fathers who abused their authority over women weakened rather than affirmed the social order.

The ideal of household government that emerges in contemporary litigants' statements, I shall argue, was therefore one of a balanced use of the resources that patriarchy had bestowed on men. Witness depositions are crucial in assessing moral values in early modern communities, since their intervention and perception reveal attitudes towards and limits of male authority. The public evaluation of domestic disputes was, however, never unanimous; male and female neighbours had their own opinions about a husband disciplining his wilful wife or about a father marrying off his disobedient daughter. The moral and social values underlying household dramas could be contested, and a wife's or daughter's punishment could be perceived as either mistreatment or as justified 'moderate correction'. These opinions differed not so much between men and women but depended more generally on the circumstances in which women were chastised. Although moral judgements were to a certain degree individual, female and male neighbours demanded the enforcement of patriarchy when wives clearly neglected their household tasks and children disobeyed their superiors. But their legal depositions also demonstrate the general belief that government had to be wise, and thus witnesses shared the ideals of the moderate use of domestic authority and power. Only in disputes between children and parents did the majority emphasise as a first reaction to disobedience that daughters had to bow to the wishes of their parents. When parental authority deteriorated into misrule, by contrast, parents and legal guardians were equally perceived as having misused their authority.

In order to maintain household stability, parental and patriarchal authority and power thus had to be used wisely, modestly and rationally. Excessiveness was abusive and the abuse of authority endangered the fundamental principles of order and obedience within households. In this respect social and household order were perceived as working from

---

9 On this argument see Hacke, 2001a, pp. 216–17.
10 On the arguments of the 'anti-myth' during this century cf. Zanetto 1991.

the same principles: a strict domestic patriarchy which guaranteed the stability of marriages but which, at the same time, was tempered with an understanding of judicious rule. It was the duty of the head of the household to provide order and reasonable discipline and to take care of the nutritional, material and spiritual needs of household members. A good household ruler had, moreover, to live according to Christian values. Moral integrity and a good work ethic were therefore crucial, as drunkenness and laziness exploited the household economy.

To enforce female subordination husbands and fathers had to prove their 'natural' superiority through a modest use of authority, the expression of their greater rationality. As I argue throughout this book, according to the dominant understanding in early modern Venice 'bad' government was equated with misrule in material, physical, economic and symbolic terms. In both political and legal discourse, when rule deteriorated it was easily conceived as tyranny. Arcangela Tarabotti, an eloquent 'protofeminist' nun who participated in a 'feminist' literary debate known as the 'battle of the sexes' (*Querelle des femmes*) in the seventeenth century, measured the behaviour of patrician fathers against their stated political ideals. She singled out worldly pride and the 'desire to pile up riches' as the reasons for some patrician daughters being forced into convents – a practice that enabled family wealth to be invested in the dowries of the other daughter(s).[11] Whereas Venice outwardly promoted an image of civic harmony and liberty, Tarabotti wrote with bitter sarcasm about the ruling patricians who contradicted their own stated principles, arguing that '[p]aternal tyranny is concealed under the majesty of senatorial robes, [which] has set up its seat in the Ducal Palace and now rules the entire city'.[12]

Although Arcangela Tarabotti was an educated woman well acquainted with the main tropes of the Venetian myth, the majority of the female protagonists in this book were not. It is therefore difficult to decide whether the ideal of a moderate government, as expressed in treatises on patrician household government and in political theory, reached 'women, children and servants via sermons, plays and verbal orders', as Dennis Romano has suggested.[13] Perhaps this ideal was

---

[11] Chojnacki, 1998, p. 70. On forced claustration in Venice see Sperling, 1999 and Laven, 2002.

[12] Quoted in Cox, 1995, pp. 536–7. Venetian political thought on liberty was also reflected in the writings of Venetian women such as Moderata Fonte and Lucrezia Marinella. For a discussion see Labalme, 1981, p. 108 and Hacke, 2001b, pp. 54–5.

[13] Romano, 1996, p. 4. At least the diarist Marino Sanudo, however, observed that some aspects of the Venetian myth had reached the lower stratum of the population via sermons. See Finlay, 1980, p. 30.

rooted in daily life as well, shaped by the experiences and material necessities that made men and women, children and parents rely on each other.

Marriage and litigation

The fact that marriage was crucial to social stability leads to the question of which legal institutions actually exercised control over marital litigation and deviant behaviour such as premarital and extramarital sex in Counter-Reformation Venice. Although it was a contentious issue in many European states, in the early sixteenth century the legal competencies that secular and ecclesiastical authorities held over marital litigation had been resolved. While in Protestant areas such as parts of Germany and Switzerland civic Marriage Courts were institutionalised soon after the Reformation, Catholic theologians and canonists defended their right to rule over and judge marital disputes. In Catholic Venice, unlike in France, the decrees issued by the Catholic reform movement, the Council of Trent (1545–63), were accepted and published on 17 September 1564 in the city's parishes.[14] The Venetian state intervened shortly thereafter and successfully expanded its jurisdiction over disputes related to failed marriage formation. The secular Executors against Blasphemy became one of the most powerful magistracies in Venice, overseeing the application of the Tridentine decrees in daily marital practice together with the moral well-being of its citizens, whereas lawsuits concerning divorce (that is, annulment and separation cases) remained under Church authority in the form of the Patriarchal Court.

The Patriarchal Court

The Venetian patriarchate had been established in the mid-fifteenth century when Pope Nicolò V combined the diocese of Castello and the patriarchate of Grado to form the new patriarchate of Venice following the bull *Regis aeterni* of 8 October 1451. The influence of the Venetian senate in this process remains an open question intensely debated by

---

14 The Patriarch Giovanni Trevisan, who had attended the last meeting of the Council of Trent, ordered that when the 'major part of the populace' was assembled, the Tridentine decrees had to be pronounced with a 'loud and clear voice' in order to prevent female and male parishioners claiming that they were unknown to them; cf. B.N.M., Misc. 2689.7: *Parte sostantiale delli decreti del sacro et general Concilio di Trento, che furono publicati nella sinodo Diocesana di Venetia di XVII di Settembre*, Venice 1564, fol. 1v.

scholars.[15] The church of S. Pietro di Castello henceforth became the city's cathedral until 1807, when, during the Napoleonic period, this function was transferred to St Mark's, transforming the ducal chapel into a cathedral church. Thus, the city's political and religious centre at St Mark's Square was separated from its ecclesiastical heart at S. Pietro di Castello. The cathedral also served as the parish church, whose priest and two sacristans oversaw the religious and devotional life of the parishioners.

The Patriarchs often came from the most distinguished ranks of the Venetian patrician ruling class and were elected by the senate for life (see Figure 1.3). In a bull dated 15 September 1561 Pope Paul IV reiterated the ecclesiastical privileges of the Venetian republic – among them the right to elect Patriarchs, who were then approved by the Pope. After his election the Patriarch had to swear loyalty to the doge and the government.

Although these influential men – the highest judges of the Patriarchal

1.3   The Venetian Patriarch (Grevembroch, *Gli Abiti de' Veneziani*)

---

15 Tramontin, 1991, p. 98.

Court – had often followed a secular career, they were not qualified in canon or Roman law.[16] Therefore, when the layman Francesco Vendramin was elected Patriarch, Pope Paul V demanded that Venetian Patriarchs henceforth be examined by a papal congregation before receiving the pontifical approval. These included Lorenzo Priuli (1590–1600), successor to Giovanni Trevisan who was decisive for the application of the Tridentine decrees in Venice and who had an impressive career as an ambassador at the European courts before he was elected Patriarch on 4 August 1590. His successors Matteo Zane (1600–1605), Francesco Vendramin (1605–19) and Alvise Sagredo (1678–88) were equally distinguished and long-serving diplomats at the Italian and European courts before becoming the representative of the Venetian Church. Indeed, only two of the Patriarchs in the period under consideration here began their ecclesiastical careers at St Mark's: Giovanni Tiepolo (1619–31), author of various theological writings, and Giovanni Badoer (1688–1706); Gianfrancesco Morosini (1644–78) – nephew of Cardinal Giovanni Morosini – came from a distinguished ecclesiastical family.[17]

Perhaps because they were not especially trained in canon or in Roman law, in their daily court business Patriarchs were assisted by vicars with a legal education. Their ecclesiastical jurisdiction functioned at various levels. The Patriarch presided over all but one of Venice's 71 parishes (St Mark's was under the doge's jurisdiction) as well as over the dependent suffragan dioceses. The range of cases heard in this court was wide: it was here that the clergy was tried for criminal deeds, but it was also where layperson's marital disputes were decided. The court of appeal was the Apostolic Court in Rome.

Venice during the course of Counter-Reformation confessionalism

With the intervention of the state in ecclesiastical jurisdiction, the implementation of the Council of Trent's Tridentine decrees on the reform of marital law was henceforth supervised by a secular magistracy – the aforementioned Executor's against Blasphemy – and remained under state control until the fall of the republic in 1797.[18] The state, it

---

16 Benedictine Giovanni Trevisan (1559–90), a *juris utriusque doctor*, and Frederico Corner (1631–44), the former bishop of Bergamo, are two exceptions in the period under consideration.

17 On the careers of the Patriarchs see Niero, 1961, pp. 93–127.

18 See Cozzi, 1976, pp. 169–213 and Derosas, 1980, pp. 431–528 on jurisdictional infringement and Cozzi, 1991, pp. 7–96 on this magistracy; for the legal practice during the eighteenth century cf. Gambier, 1980, pp. 529–75.

was argued, had more effective legal means to punish those men who had engaged in premarital sex and then did not marry the women they had deflowered under the pretext of marriage. Improperly solemnised marriages and extramarital sex resulted in disputes and loss of female and family honour, thus endangering the institution of marriage and weakening its stability. The implementation of Christian values was therefore increasingly enforced by the state throughout the seventeenth century and in the eighteenth century the state's interest in securing even greater influence over marital dysfunction was institutionalised successfully. In Venice it was then a combination of secular and ecclesiastical legal institutions that exercised control over marriage.

By examining actual legal practices this study thus explores the complex marital policies in post-Tridentine Venice through investigating the ways in which both the city's civil magistracies and the ecclesiastical tribunal defended the institution of marriage. What seems to be central to the historian Joanne Ferraro are cases of marital litigation brought before the ecclesiastical Patriarchal Court, yet she fails to look at the state's attempts to enforce its vision of a morally ordered society.[19] Because the state played a crucial role in punishing men who deflowered women with false promises of marriage and in disciplining adulterous wives or bigamous husbands, we need to investigate the moral policies of both the Church and the state in the confessional age in order to unravel the impact of confessional policies on the lives of women and men. It was the state that pursued more vigorously a policy that institutionalised sex within marriage and within ordered households. Whereas the ecclesiastical tribunal, in sentencing cases of marital discord, defended the sacramentality of marriage, the state was not bound to respect this theologian principle. Secular governmental authorities, I shall argue, could thus more actively pursue and enforce a moral legislation that was central to the interests of the Venetian state.[20]

In doing so, however, they relied on the co-operation of ordinary people in bringing cases to court. Because a high percentage of women filed their requests with the Venetian courts, this study throws light on their use of the law. Women were plaintiffs against men who had taken their virginity without keeping promises of marriage, and women also initiated a high percentage of lawsuits against 'cruel' husbands and parents. Women thus fought in cases of illicit sex and marital disputes that were linked closely to female gender identity – but they also attacked

---

[19] As far as I can tell, Ferraro, 2001, discusses only one case of adultery investigated by a secular magistracy.

[20] For a similar argument in relation to seventeenth-century Tuscany see Lombardi, 2001, pp. 345–7.

male gender identity when pointing to the limits of acceptable patriarchal power, particularly when it was abused.[21] Legal records therefore allow us to examine the institution of marriage from a perspective that emphasises female expectations of future husbands and marital life.

To take a broader view, although historians have only just started to address changes in social and gender relations in the course of Counter-Reformation confessionalism, more attention has been paid to assessing the impact of the Protestant Reformation on the lives of women. With the abolition of convents, the closing of brothels and the acceptance of a celibate priesthood, reformers strengthened the institution of marriage by reducing the options open to women (convent or marriage) and making marriage the only institution in which they could lead honourable Christian lives. The Reformation's effect on women, as Lyndal Roper has argued, was therefore 'deeply ambiguous', as it denied them religious experiences outside marriage and led to a 'renewed patriarchalism'.[22] Roper emphasises that the 'domestication' of the Reformation in Augsburg, Germany, therefore must be understood as a 'theology of gender' that increasingly fostered Christian households and strengthened patriarchy and gender hierarchy in order to stabilise social order.

Whereas Roper highlights the Reformation's new moral policies, Susanna Burghartz, in her study on Protestant Basel, stresses more clearly its continuity. During the fifteenth century Basel's city council promoted an ideal of morality (*Sittlichkeitsideal*) centred on the defence of marriage. The establishment of Marriage Courts in Basel created a legal institution in which the urban discourse on morality (*Sittlichkeitsdiskurs*) and the theologian discourse on purity (*Reinheitsdiskurs*) intersected markedly to create a morally 'pure' society. The Reformation, however, not only strengthened the institution of marriage and criminalised premarital and extramarital sexual activity, but also re-evaluated sex *within* marriage, enabling women in particular to claim their conjugal rights against men who had sexually enjoyed and then abandoned them. Therefore, Burghartz argues, it was not so much after the Reformation but rather during the age of the confessional that a discourse on fornication (*Unzuchtsdiskurs*), which had marginalising and devaluing tendencies, increasingly unfolded. Women in particular

---

21 I make this point to reaffirm the importance of the marital status for women; Chojnacka, 2001, pp. 58–60, has suggested that it may have been somewhat irrelevant both to the women in question and to the male and female persons who knew them.

22 See Roper's seminal study, 1993, p. 2, where she has profoundly altered Steven Ozment's vision of the Reformation as promoting the ideal of a companionate marital relationship; 1983, here especially p. 99.

were affected because it became more difficult for them to prove that they had lost their virginity 'honourably'.[23] The Marriage Court was therefore also the place where 'gender' was continually reshaped and where relationships between a man and a woman were increasingly defined in terms of hierarchy and asymmetry.[24] By contrast, in his study on Freiburg, Basel and Constance, Safley has maintained that women and the judicial authority of the Marriage Court had entered into an alliance which ensured, at least in part, protection from their husbands from the second half of the sixteenth century onwards.[25]

When it came to punishing sexual offences, however, the main targets of the 'renewed moralism' and moral discipline were single mothers, and 'lewd wenches' in particular, as Ulinka Rublack has shown in her study on southwest Germany.[26] The 'moral dimension' of sex, as Laura Gowing demonstrates in her work on the Anglican Church Court in early modern London, was especially connected to the 'weakness of women' and was 'repeatedly penalised'. Morality was gendered, and this view of a sexual 'double standard' was shared and supported by women and men both inside and outside the London Church Court. The meaning of women's and men's sexual behaviour was conceived as being 'incommensurably different', as women's adultery – which involved the breaking of vows and of the sacrament – was a weightier matter than men's fornication.[27]

While comparative studies have taught us not to overemphasise the confessional differences with regard to legal practice and marriage ideals,[28] we still have comparatively fewer works that measure the impact of the Counter-Reformation on the lives of both single and married women.[29] In Italian and Venetian historiography especially, continuing research on the history of women and gender has concentrated on the reform of convents and charitable Counter-Reformation institutions for 'fallen women'.[30] Jutta Sperling's recent

---

[23] This point is made more explicitly in her earlier work, 1992, pp. 13–40.

[24] Burghartz, 1999a, pp. 19–27. This argument was first developed by Gleixner, 1994.

[25] Safley, 1984, p. 139f. See also Schmidt, 1998, especially pp. 224–5.

[26] Rublack, 1999, pp. 7 and 147.

[27] Gowing, 1996, pp. 3–4.

[28] Safley, 1984 and Harrington, 1995.

[29] In her study on marital litigation in Venice, Joanne Ferraro does not discuss her findings within the historiographical debate outlined above. Cf. Ferraro, 2001.

[30] For a new trend in Italian historiography, see the recent publication of the important volumes edited by Silvana Seidel Menchi and Diego Quaglioni, 2000 and 2001. They present valid collections of case studies on marital disputes in Italy by various authors; these authors, however, do not discuss their findings within the historiographical debate on confessionalism.

book emphasises the strategy used by Venetian patrician fathers to maintain the 'purity' and 'integrity' of the 'body politic' by forcing daughters to take the veil in times of restricted marriage policies and rising dowries. At the cost of declining birth rates, Sperling argues, the ruling class preserved the 'integrity' and 'virginity' of the patriciate at the cost of its 'physical extinction'. Mary Laven's study of Venetian nuns explores in particular the impact that the Counter-Reformation had on their lives. By combining urban history with the demands of women's history, Laven has been able to unravel the many close contacts that nuns maintained with the outside world, despite the enforcement of stricter convent enclosure in post-Tridentine Venice.[31]

This book, then, assesses the impact that moral policies had on the lives of married and single women living in post-Tridentine Venice. The study's time frame begins in 1570, shortly after the Council of Trent's last session, but the main focus is on the seventeenth century – a period still under-represented in the social and gender history of Venice – when confessional policies were increasingly enforced. With the reform of canon marital law, the boundaries between illicit premarital sex and licit marital sexual behaviour became more rigid. As Ulrike Strasser has pointed out in her article on Counter-Reformation Munich, the Tridentine reform movement had developed a 'distinctive mark of differentiation' (*Unterscheidungsmerkmal*) which supported the state in its battle against dishonourable sexual behaviour, an argument that is equally valid for the Venetian situation.[32] Whereas in Protestant Basel the Marriage Court had a dual function, serving as an institution of appeal but also prosecuting ex officio, Venetian government authorities relied exclusively on cases brought to court by women. In Catholic Venice women were accorded legal means to claim their right to be married or be given a dowry and not to be subject to moral prosecution themselves. Thomas Kuehn, in his sensitive attempt to write a 'legal anthropology', has emphasised that the law and its institutions actually defended the rights of Florentine women.[33]

The present study also highlights the legal means that Venetian society accorded women and, to a certain extent, men; but it argues as well that opportunities to win these 'rights' were complex and ambiguous: they varied over the centuries under consideration and differed in regard to the legal institutions (secular and ecclesiastical

---

[31] Sperling, 1999 and Laven, 2002.

[32] Strasser, 1999a, p. 231.

[33] In doing so Kuehn has moderated Klapisch-Zuber's argument in her seminal study, which holds that women occupied a more irrelevant place in Florentine patrilineal society. Klapisch-Zuber, 1987 and Kuehn, 1991.

tribunals). Because the state could *force* a man to marry or to dower an honourable woman he had deflowered under the pretext of marriage, the moral legislation the state had enforced served more clearly the interests of women. In legal practice, however, it were still women, not men, who had to prove that they had consented to premarital sexual intercourse only after a marriage promise was given and that they had behaved honourably during courtship. It will be shown that women's chances of success in the courts worsened during the seventeenth century – except towards its end – as local secular authorities increasingly protected respectable men from being sued by 'lewd' and 'dishonourable' women. The state could, however, counterbalance legal severity with a highly flexible Venetian judicial system that attempted to restore moral order to households and that abstained from legal punishments when men and women, husbands and wives were reconciled. Meanwhile, the ecclesiastical tribunal was bound by the sacramental nature of marriage and its indissolubility in sentencing cases of marital dysfunction. The Patriarchal Court's responses to the needs of wives and daughters, I shall argue, were therefore more ambiguous and more complex than has been suggested hitherto.[34]

This book therefore explores the attitudes of ordinary people in early modern Venice towards domestic disorder, dysfunctional marriages and the different means employed by the state and the Church to regulate marital disputes and related sexual offences during the confessional age. The conflicts that blighted the lives of the city's husbands, wives, parents and children will be explored in detail through contemporary case studies. It is left to the reader to evaluate the much-praised 'civic harmony' of Venice within the context of marital discord and family dissent. Let us first introduce the city itself: Venice.

---

[34] Ferraro, especially 1995, pp. 492–512, and 2001, pp. 30–31, has judged the legal situation of married women attempting to obtain separations more positively.

CHAPTER TWO

The City: Principles of Early Modern Venetian Society

At the time when Elena and Alessandro's marital dispute reached the court in the 1580s, Venice was still a cosmopolitan European metropolis. The population during the late sixteenth and seventeenth centuries, although in decline, still reached up to 140 000; during the seventeenth century, it was reduced by more than a third through the horrible plague of 1630–33. Still, in 1696 the city's administrators counted almost 140 000 persons living in the capital of the Venetian republic.[1] Venice had made its fortune by being one of the most important centres within the Mediterranean economy. By the sixteenth century trade routes to southern Germany and the Netherlands were firmly established, as was trade with the East. Not restricted to luxury goods such as dyes, glassware from Murano or works of art, Venice was a commercial centre for spices, cotton and silk (due to the Venetian production industry), soap, wax and other commodities. During the seventeenth century, Dutch shipping entered the Mediterranean and took over Venice's traditional role in trade with the Levant. It was merchants from Holland, and not from Venice, who henceforth dominated trade between northern and southern Europe. However, with the Arsenal, the republic's shipyard located very near to where Alessandro and Elena lived, Venice was still a leading sea power.

Given the importance of trade for the republic, it is not surprising that Venice developed into a 'centre for economic information', especially information on the Ottoman Empire, where a Venetian colony of merchants was based in Istanbul. Merchants often wrote home from abroad and helped, together with diplomats, to disseminate information, including important political news, about foreign countries. As early as 1567, one German called Venice a 'metropolis of news'.[2] The city was, of course, a cultural centre of publishing as well. Even during the sixteenth century, when Paris overtook Venice, 15 000 to 17 500 titles were presumably printed over the course of the century by 500 publishers.[3] The spread of the Counter-Reformation stopped the

---

1 Beltrami, 1954, p. 38.
2 Burke, 2000, p. 397.
3 Ibid., p. 398.

flourishing cultural climate: books were burned on St Mark's Square and near the Rialto, the Venetian Inquisition was founded and an *Index of Prohibited Books* was produced. During the seventeenth century, however, Venice acquired its role as a 'centre of scientific information', and in the mid-seventeenth century Venetian publishers increasingly printed books on recent history. In this later period the city was extraordinarily important in providing information about itself; guides to the city, such as Sansovino's *Cose maravigliose* or his massive *Città nobilissima*, and treatises on the government of Venice, helped to spread the city's fame throughout Europe, as well as inform about its beauties, freedom, stability and perfect constitution.[4]

Social and political order

Yet it was the nature of the Venetian political system in particular which made its stability and putative civic harmony especially striking. With the closing (*serrata*) of the Great Council in 1297, the ruling class was legally defined and hereditary, with its power limited to the patrician families that had been members of the Great Council for the preceding four years (these amounted to about 4 to 4.5 per cent of the entire population from the mid-sixteenth to the beginning of the seventeenth century).[5] Unlike in German cities of the time, guilds had no political representation at all. And yet Venice witnessed very little political unrest.[6] As the patrician Gasparo Contarini himself noted with surprise, it was 'a matter surely strange and scarcely credible, that the people being so many years deprived of the publique government, did never refuse nor unwillingly support the government of the nobilitie, neyther yet did ever attempt any thing whereby the forme of the commonewealth might be altered.'[7]

Historians have tried to explain the absence of popular riots by pointing (though not exclusively) to the functions of social and economic institutions in Venice. Craftsmen, for instance, were organised in guilds (*arte*) of the same occupation. The social and economic

---

4 Ibid., pp. 406–8.

5 Aggregations of families were formed in 1381. Important differentiations on social stratification have recently made by Chojancki, 2000c, pp. 263–94 and Rösch, 2000, pp. 67–88.

6 Frederick C. Lane has argued that there were few popular outbreaks because the republic enjoyed an adequate food supply; inadequate food supplies were generally a very common source of popular riots. 'Ships and its domination in the Adriatic enabled Venice to avoid famine more effectively than did most cities and to moderate the swings in bread prices.' See Lane, 1973, p. 109.

7 Contarini, 1599, p. 138.

interests of guild members were presided over by these institutions, yet
– as Richard Mackenney has argued – they did not threaten the interests
of the ruling class. 'The absence of *furor populi* may be explained in part
by the close administrative and separate economic interests of the guilds
and the government. But, more positively, it was the interests of the
rulers of Venice to permit, even to promote, this formation of guilds.[8]
Furthermore, the accessibility of courts of appeal helped to maintain
stability and served as 'important compensations for guildsmen'.[9]
Women were allowed to work in the Venetian economy controlled by
guilds, but only if they were a daughter or wife of a master in that trade.
They usually received a lower wage for the same work and could never
become a master, unlike male journeymen. Despite these restrictions,
some women came to fame. Maria Barovier was well known during the
Renaissance, as she was a glassblower to whom the 'invention of
Chevron-beads' was attributed in the mid-fifteenth century. More
commonly, however, women were involved in the less prestigious aspects
of trade, such as renting out goods and street-peddling.[10]

Guilds had often – though not always – their own religious
confraternity (*scuola*). The members of devotional confraternities
developed close ties of religious brotherhood; annual feasts were held,
saints celebrated and support for ill or dying members provided. The
charitable functions of confraternities included the distribution of alms,
provision of burial, and banqueting. Brian Pullan has emphasised the
integrative social function of the six powerful Venetian confraternities of
S. Rocco, S. Giovanni Evangelista, S. Marco, S. Teodoro, the
Misericordia and the Carità (one for each of the six Venetian *sestieri*) –
which were entitled to 500 to 600 members. These great confraternities
had socially stabilising functions because wealth was distributed among
members of different social and economic circumstances. Of their total
income, these confraternities spent about 30 per cent and more on
dowries. The confraternity of S. Marco, for example, which could afford
to spend 50 per cent, and S. Giovanni Evangelista even 75 per cent.[11]

At a parochial level, smaller confraternities in rising numbers (from
over 100 in 1521 to more than 350 in 1732) existed throughout the city,
but these lacked the financial resources of the larger fraternities.[12] They

---

8   Mackenney, 1987, p. 29. For the continuance of guild and government collaboration
in the seventeenth century see Rapp, 1976.

9   Mackenney, 1987, p. 29.

10   Trivellato, 1998, pp. 49–51. A monograph on the second-hand market in Venice is
currently being written by Patricia Allerston.

11   Pullan, 1971, p. 183–7; how much the less powerful confraternities spent on
dowries is, however, unclear. Cf. Black, 1989, p. 181.

12   Pullan, 1971, p. 34.

had charitable and philanthropic functions and promoted neighbourhood piety. Female membership is often harder to calculate in mixed confraternities, and the role of females within the confraternities is obscure. As Christopher Black has argued, post-Tridentine control might have increased female involvement because it 'should have made the society morally safer than it might have been when dominated by autonomous laymen'.[13] Some confraternities had particular social functions, such as the *scuola* of S. Fantin, which accompanied criminals to their executions and offered spiritual consolation. As early as the fourteenth century, the confraternities founded almshouses and hospitals for the poor and sick. By participating in elaborate processions a bond between rulers and ruled might have been created, since they 'offered a means by which men of many social ranks could assemble under religious banners to express collectively the official sentiments of the Venetian government.'[14] Women were denied this collective experience and were forced to observe the processions from a safe distance.[15] During the Interdict of 1606–07, when the Venetian state was defending the right to punish criminal clergymen, to enact regulations concerning the bequests of property to ecclesiastical institutions and to tax clerics, the great confraternities helped unite the people in Venice by making the government's theories plausible to the population.[16] Furthermore, the great confraternities were places where the *cittadini* (a legally defined class below the nobility, which gradually evolved into the economic and cultural elite) could realise their political ambitions. Their involvement in the great confraternities might explain why the imbalance between their exclusion from office-holding (except the *cancelliere grande* and positions in the bureaucracy) and the considerable wealth they sometimes acquired never found radical political expression. A strict division of Venetian society into nobles and commoners was qualified by the complex and multifaceted ties patricians and *popolani* (approximately 90 per cent during the sixteenth and seventeenth centuries)[17] developed through the creation of a 'network of networks' within the many local communities, which in turn gave shape to the cultural diversity of early modern Venice.[18]

---

13 Black, 1989, pp. 105 and 36–8.

14 Pullan, 1971, p. 53. Edward Muir has presented a similar argument in his book on civic rituals: the 'important feast days became more and more the occasions for pageantry display'. See Muir, 1981, p. 301.

15 Ibid., p. 303.

16 Pullan, 1971, p. 55.

17 Beltrami, 1954, pp. 72–3.

18 Quotation in Romano, 1987, p. 10.

Parishes, the household and gender

Within these local communities, household structures and residential patterns were complex and varied considerably.[19] Because of the working and living arrangements in Venice each guild or craft had its own *ruga* (street of market stalls and workshops) at Rialto. As Dennis Romano has noted, for most trades the residential patterns were relatively more complex, as there was a tendency for Venetian artisans to favour certain parishes as their residences, 'yet in no case did all members of a trade live in those parishes'.[20] An exception was the bakers, who lived in every part of the city, because every neighbourhood had need of fresh bread. But still, some Venetian artisans lived in one part of the city and worked in another. Workplace and residence were identical only for some trades, such as in the case of the glassmakers and the tanners: the former had their occupation confined to Murano, the latter to the Giudecca for reasons of public safety. Additionally, certain parishes were especially distinct. The neighbourhood around the Arsenale (the city's shipbuilding industry), for example, has been described as having a strong worker identity and rather humble living standards.[21]

Perhaps because male trade was more generally identified with public city spaces in Venice,[22] the neighbourhood has been described as a complex network of female 'economic interdependency'.[23] Women rented out rooms to other women, exchanged services and material

---

[19] During the centuries under consideration here, the city's parishes were very heterogeneous and varied considerably in their number of inhabitants (and in the preponderance of female and male parishioners). In 1586 the most populous parish, S. Pietro di Castello, counted 9393 residents, followed by S. Geremia with 7842 and S. Marcuola with 7392 parish members. Next in size were parishes like S. Moisè and SS. Apostoli, with 3489 and 3631 parishioners respectively. Middling ones counted 1000 to 2000 residents. Very small parishes counted only 731 (S. Beneto), 864 (S. Paternian) or even 477 (S. Fantin) parish members. After the pestilence severely minimised the population in 1633, S. Pietro di Castello was reduced to only 5496 parishioners, S. Geremia to 4303 and S. Marcuola to 4573. Small parishes, such as S. Beneto, S. Paternian and S. Fantin, equally suffered from the plague, and in 1633 counted only 431, 555 and 352, respectively. See Beltrami, 1954, Appendix, Table 2.

[20] Romano, 1987, p. 79. Dennis Romano's portrait of the residential patterns concerns fifteenth-century Venice. Robert Davis has also found that in the community of the *arsenalotti* the workplace and the household were separated. See Davis, 1991, especially p. 107.

[21] Davis, 1991, pp. 84–5.

[22] Romano, 1989, pp. 339–53 and Davis, 1998, pp. 19–38; for a class-specific re-assessment see Chojnacka, 2001, chap. 5.

[23] Chojnacka, 2001, p. 76. She, however, emphasises female mobility throughout the city.

goods or worked as domestic servants for other women. These horizontal networks and social interactions were favoured to the extent that entire streets, courtyards and alleys throughout the city were dominated by women. A shared status as single women and a shared profession were the means by which women were sometimes drawn together in the same neighbourhood. As a result, streets 'full of women were streets full of female work'.[24] Privileged women who participated less actively in neighbourhood life assisted in key rituals, such as in marriages and funerals of parish members. Whereas the networks among *popolane* women were horizontal, those of patrician women were vertical because these privileged women created 'cross-class relationships' by establishing networks of 'economic patronage'.[25] This may be one reason Venetians identified themselves with their resident parish, their *contrada* or *parrochia* – terms that take their meaning 'from their ecclesiastical function, as the boundaries of a parish'[26]: it was this small community that formed the civic and religious identities of female and male Venetians.[27] The parishioners' vision of parochial life was shaped by a day-to-day sociability: neighbourhoods were not only places of female economy, but of daily interaction too. The social networks and ties of friendship that women developed sometimes even broke 'down along levels of wealth'.[28]

Not only the residential patterns but also the living arrangements in Venice varied considerably. The most common household structure from 1589 to 1607 consisted of a married couple heading its own household: of nearly 20 000 households, more than 12 000 were headed by a married couple. On marrying, the bride and groom left the household of their family of origin and formed 'their own home' – or, to put it differently, 'couples [in Venice as elsewhere] usually did not marry until they could move directly into their own place'.[29] Half of the married

---

[24] Prostitution was one of the professions that brought women together. See Chojnacka, 2001, pp. 52–5, quotation on p. 55.

[25] Chojnacka, 2001, p. 76 and Romano, 1987, p. 133.

[26] Chojnacka, 2001, p. 50.

[27] Traditionally, parishes had their own religious festivals and rituals. With the increasing number of confraternities of the cult of the Eucharist, parish and devotional life became more closely tied. In 1395 only one confraternity of the cult of the Eucharist existed, but several more were founded shortly after 1500 and, in more rapid succession, after 1540 as a consequence of Pope Paul III's intention to establish the Scuole of the Blessed Sacrament – for the reverence of the Eucharist – in every parish. These new devotional confraternities, as Richard Mackenney has argued, 'were a vital means of extending the influence of the Counter-Reformation'. See Mackenney, 1987, p. 170, and, sustaining the same argument, Black, 1989, p. 75.

[28] Chojnacka, 2001, pp. 76–9, quotation on p. 76.

[29] Ibid., p. 4 and Table 1.1 on p. 5.

couples heading their own household between 1589 and 1607 lived with their own children (6492, or 51 per cent), and only a small proportion lived alone (1714, or 14 per cent). As Monica Chojnacka has observed, about one third 'shared their homes with adult children and grandchildren, other family members, servants and boarders'.[30] These early modern Venetian households were likely to include unmarried, widowed or sometimes even married sisters and brothers.[31] Just as married women and men only very seldom lived in the household of their parents, it was also common for widows and widowers to not return to their family of origin.[32] A woman with or without children did not return or could not count on her parents to offer her shelter following the death of her husband although some widows did provide shelter for their parents. The ties that bound Venetian households together were thus not necessarily organised around natal family lines, although, as mentioned, some of the married couples took in married sisters and brothers. Thus, women not only might have contributed to the household economy, but also might have had 'a say' in the composition of the household.[33]

Just as married couples heading their own household made different residential choices in late sixteenth- and early seventeenth-century Venice, so, too, could single women choose among different options of how and with whom to live. The presence of households headed by a single woman was greater and more constant in Venetian neighbourhoods than those headed by a single man: twice as many single women headed their own household than men, and three times as many widows than widowers.[34] Some widows lived with their children – perhaps in their old dwelling – after the husband died; other widows took in relatives, servants or others. Single women, whether widowed or unmarried, and even married women who had separated informally from their husbands, sometimes came together and formed a new household – financial hardship may have been overcome more easily together, and life was more enjoyable with companionship.[35] When women lived and worked in one household they were very likely to be either domestic servants or prostitutes.[36]

---

30 Ibid., pp. 6–7.
31 Ibid., pp. 7–8, Tables 1.3 and 1.4. On the difficulty of assessing the character of Venetian households, see Romano, 1996, p. 110; see, however, pp. 99–110 for a discussion of servants in the artisan household.
32 Chojnacka, 2001, p. 12–13, and Tables 1.5 and 1.7.
33 As suggested by Chojnacka, 2001, p. 25.
34 Ibid., p. 14.
35 Ibid., p. 19.
36 Ibid., p. 21–2.

This variety in family life and living patterns was further differentiated through the overlapping functions that servants and apprentices performed in *popolani* households. As Dennis Romano has observed, in these households apprentices 'performed many of the tasks associated with servants, servants were drawn from the same status group (...) as apprentices, and through either formal or informal adoption apprentices and servants became part of the kinship circle'. The lines separating masters from servants were thus 'much less clearly demarcated than among patricians and (...) cittadini'.[37] These porous social and cultural boundaries and the flexible attitude towards service might be explained by taking into consideration that most *popolane* women and *popolani* men spent part of their lives in service, either as domestic servants or apprentices. Although Dennis Romano is convinced that servant-keeping 'extended throughout Venetian society, from the princely household to the doge to the humble homes of artisans', he has to admit that it is difficult to quantify the actual number of domestic servants in artisan households.[38] However, where we have comparable data, servant-keeping appears to have been more clearly associated with nobility and with households of some social distinction, whereas parishioners from the less distinctive sphere apparently only very rarely employed domestic servants.[39] This might also explain why the 'density of servants increased as one moved towards the centres of political and economic power, along the Grand Canal and in the zone from San Marco to Rialto'.[40]

We may conclude that the living standard of patricians and cittadini required servant-keeping as an expression of wealth and status, whereas the Venetian dwellings of the rest of the populace seemingly only rarely included live-in servants or female housekeepers. When these households collapsed or household life was overshadowed by marital and family conflict, servants, as we shall see, only played a minor role in family disputes. It was parish members, in particular, who became involved – sometimes even emotionally – when the marriage of neighbours broke down. Before we turn to the legal role that these members of the civic communities of early modern Venice played as witnesses of household disputes, we shall consider in the next chapter

---

[37] Romano, 1996, p. 104.

[38] Of course, the practices and purposes of servant-keeping varied 'with wealth and status'. Romano, 1996, p. 105. For a discussion of the actual numbers in artisan households, see pp. 106–17.

[39] Ibid., p. 115.

[40] Ibid., p. 112.

the attempts by the Church and the state to stabilise social and household order by regulating and sentencing marital disputes and related sexual offences.

PART ONE

Boundary Making: Church, State and Marital Transgressions

CHAPTER THREE

Marital Litigation and the Courts

During the sixteenth century, a period of confessionalisation and state-building, both the state and the Church enforced a policy of moral reforms. Despite fundamental political and religious transformations at the time, the main target of the legal, social and religious reforms was to morally shape marriages and households, in both Catholic and Protestant countries.[1] Although Protestant and Catholic reformers debated where and which reforms were most needed, they nonetheless did agree that the gap between marital law and marital practice had a 'detrimental effect on the holy estate of matrimony'.[2] Despite different confessional rhetoric, the 'true focus' of marriage reforms in Catholic and Protestant countries was the legal enforcement of the new sixteenth-century moral policies.[3]

In its effort to reform actual marital practice, the Catholic reform movement – the Council of Trent (1545–63) – made the establishment of the marital bond a public ritual firmly grounded in parish life. After protracted debates at various sessions of the Council of Trent, the council fathers finally issued a decree 'concerning the Reform of Marriage' in the name of *Tametsi* (1563). In this decree it was commanded that the parish priest of the would-be spouses had to announce publicly during the celebration of mass and on three subsequent Sundays between whom the bond of marriage was to be concluded. This publicity would enable parish members to intervene during the making of marriage and to reveal existing impediments, such as the man already having promised marriage to another woman. Only when no member of the civic community had intervened during these three weeks in which the banns were published should the priest bless the couple *in facie ecclesiae* (in church) in the presence of two or three witnesses – but then only after future wife and husband expressed their mutual consent to marry freely. Through this public solemnization of marriage the marital couple was legally allowed to set up a household together and to 'sacramentalise' the union through physical consummation. In its attempt to regulate the state of matrimony, the post-Tridentine marital doctrine firmly placed sex and procreation within matrimony.[4]

---

[1] For an overview see Harrington, 1995, pp. 25–47, especially p. 26.
[2] Ibid., p. 33.
[3] Ibid., p. 14.
[4] Canons and Decrees, pp. 183–5.

These formalities regarding the publicity of marriages issued by the Council of Trent had been encouraged by the Church in earlier centuries, but the Church had never gone as far as invalidating marriages that had not been completed with the required publicity. These marriages were illegitimate and clandestine but still valid. The significant feature of pre-Tridentine marriages was that the formation of marriage was a *process* to which the exchange of words (that is, a promise of future marriage) against deeds (sexual intercourse) was central. The Tridentine reforms, by contrast, developed a selective concept of marriage which was defined in a specific *moment*, namely, when the public ceremony and the necessary formalities had been observed. Only then would the marriage actually be registered in the women's parish church book together with the witnesses who had attended the ritual.[5] With the shift from privately or clandestinely exchanged words to a publicly solemnised marriage, not only were valid and invalid marriages defined more precisely, but also the border between illegitimate (premarital) and legitimate (marital) sexual activity was drawn more strictly.

The Executors against Blasphemy

In ensuring that marriage was a holy, indissoluble and consensual unit, Catholic reformers also defended the Church courts' role in legal validation. However, in its attempt to make the sexual order the foundation of a morally ordered society, the Venetian state intervened in ecclesiastical jurisdiction only 14 years after the Council of Trent had reaffirmed its jurisdiction over marriage, and after the Church had established its monopoly on the celebration of valid marriages. The state insisted that broken marriage promises were criminal offences under its jurisdiction.

The secular magistracy Executors against Blasphemy (Esecutori contro la Bestemmia) were appointed to judge special cases of premarital sex or seduction among the popular classes when the sexual contact had been preceded by a marriage promise, possibly exchanged in the presence of witnesses. A law issued on 27 August 1577 attempted to impede a common practice by decreeing to punish those 'wicked men' (*uomini scelerati*) who had taken a wife under the pretext of marriage, but without observing the formalities required by the Church and, as the law went on, 'after having violated and enjoyed them for a while, they

---

5 Ibid., p. 185.

leave them and seek the dissolution of the marriage from ecclesiastical judges, from whom they easily obtain it, since such marriages were made contrary to the decrees of the Council of Trent'.[6] Because the ecclesiastical court, as the law stated, quite willingly freed these men from their obligation to fulfil the promise, women ran the risk of losing their honour. In lawsuits over non-fulfilment of the marriage promise (including premarital sexual intercourse) the ecclesiastical judge could enforce its fulfilment only if consent had been expressed by both litigants, possibly in the presence of witnesses. This constellation gave rise to an awkward situation in the ecclesiastical courtroom: the judge could not order the fulfilment of marriage without undermining the principle of consensual marriages, because the obligation to keep a marriage promise would *force* the unwilling partner into a marriage against their own will. And there was no doubt in Catholic marriage doctrine about the principle that forced marriages were considered null and void.[7]

By relying on the post-Tridentine conception of marriage as a publicly defined act, the Venetian governmental authorities criminalised traditional courtship rituals. Here, the concerns of state, Church and society (families) deeply intersected – the aforementioned *Tametsi* decree issued by the Council of Trent was in accordance with the moral concerns of the secular authorities attempting to define the legitimacy of sexual contacts. Disorderly sexual circumstances were to be countered with a new conception of marriage in which its formation was precisely marked out. Catholic marriage became a central institution through which sexual discipline and moral behaviour were defined, and thus negotiated and maintained the sexual and social order of Venetian society as well. In other words, by criminalising premarital sexual activity the state defended a sexual order that was the foundation of a morally ordered society.

It was against this backdrop that the secular magistracy Executors against Blasphemy was entrusted to rule on disputes concerning the formation of marriage (that is, broken marriage promises) from August 1577 onwards.[8] This lay magistracy was one of early modern Venice's

---

[6] *Leggi criminali venete*, p. 63. See also ASV, *Esecutori contro la Bestemmia*, b. 54: Capitolare, fols 59r–v. On this secular intervention into ecclesiastical jurisdiction see Cozzi, 1976, especially pp. 184–7.

[7] On this argument see, moreover, Lombardi, 1994, pp. 142–56.

[8] On 15 January 1578, the law was expanded to the Venetian territory *da Terra, et da Mar.* Cf. ASV, *Compilazione delle Leggi*, b. 277 (Matrimonio), fol. 424. Like other Venetian regulations, it was published in the political and economic centre of the city, in St Mark's and at the Rialto, and in all parishes of Venice 'at a time when the most part of

most powerful, with the authority to rule on matters concerning the moral behaviour of the city's inhabitants. The Executors against Blasphemy, founded by the Council of Ten supreme judicial court in 1537, initially ruled on crimes against God such as blasphemy, but its jurisdiction was soon expanded to include a whole range of offences against moral order. In the second half of the sixteenth century the competence of the three Venetian noblemen – four during the seventeenth century – who comprised the Executors against Blasphemy encompassed offences such as blasphemy, gambling and sinful sexual activity, such as prostitution, adultery, bigamy and premarital sex (including rape). From 1553 the Executors functioned as an appeal court for verdicts that had been passed by the Ufficiali di Sanità in matters of prostitution, and in 1615 they directly assumed the authority to punish cases of prostitutes' immoral behaviour. The Council of Ten delegated some cases – such as those dealing with violence, weapons, murder and abduction – to the Executors.[9] The process of jurisdictional expansion was concluded around the 1620s. By then the Executors against Blasphemy had assumed an extremely important role within the Venetian legal system, which, according to the historian Renzo Derosas, could only be compared with the legal function of the powerful Venetian governmental institution, the Inquisitors of State (Inquisitori di Stato). Whereas the former had jurisdiction over the general populace, the latter tried, among other things, similar crimes committed by the patriciate.[10]

The Venetian Patriarch did not insist on his ecclesiastical jurisdiction in cases of broken marriage promises, and instead readily agreed to collaborate with the state. A lawsuit initiated at the Patriarchal Court in July 1577 was – immediately after enforcement of the law in August 1577 – handed over to the secular tribunal.[11] The co-operation between state and Church continued to be unproblematic, and on 26 May 1629 the Great Council reaffirmed the authority of the Executors.[12] In the second half of the seventeenth century Patriarch Gianfrancesco Morosini even expressed the need for state support. He complained

the populace is present and intelligible for everybody'. ASV, *Esecutori contro la Bestemmia*, b. 54: Capitolare, fol. 59r.

9   During the devastating plague of 1630–33, this tribunal could also investigate cases that had not been tried by the Provveditori alla Sanità and the Pressidenti de Sestieri. See ASV, *Senato Terra*, reg. 107, August 1632, fols 278r–279v.

10   Derosas, 1980, p. 453.

11   ASPV, Curia, II, Reg. 73: 29 July 1577, Paule Balduine Zancari cum Hieronimo Bono. The sentence of the Executor's is to be found in ASV, *Esecutori contro la Bestemmia*, b. 56, raspa 2, fols 138v, 161r.

12   ASV, *Esecutori contro la Bestemmia*, b. 54: Capitolare, fol. 59v and Cozzi, 1976, p. 186.

that people from various social backgrounds were still getting married without respecting the solemnities as required by the *sacri concilii* (Holy Councils). In response the senate passed a law at the end of February 1663 which enforced more detailed regulations for the stricter application of Tridentine decrees. The Avogaria di Comun, which already controlled patrician marriage practices,[13] was entitled to supervise the solemnisation of noble marriages according to the formalities required by the Church. It was charged with registering in the *Libro d'oro* (golden book) only those patrician marriages for which the parties involved could present proof of their wedding. In cases of marriages of ordinary people, as the law went on, the Executors had to ensure that 'all marriages are celebrated with the required solemnities'.[14] After 1685, moreover, witnesses who had been abusing the formalities introduced by the Council of Trent were open to prosecution.[15] About 120 years after the Council of Trent had introduced public solemnities as a condition for valid marriage, their implementation in everyday marital practice was still an issue that led to the enforcement of stricter moral legislation. Arguably, because the Patriarchs came from the highest ranks of the Venetian ruling class, in Venice the state and the Church were united in their aim of minimising the marital and sexual problems that disturbed the stability and peace of the city.[16]

With the Tridentine marriage reforms, the most decisive characteristic of the post-Tridentine Catholic marriage became its indissolubility as set down in canon law. When a marital bond had been established validly and the spouses had expressed mutual consent publicly in the presence of a priest and witnesses in church, this union was holy and thus indissoluble. Catholic marriage was a sacrament and what 'God had put together, no man could put asunder' (Matthew 19:4–6). Under canon law, however, separation was allowed on four principal grounds:

---

[13] The marriages of nobles and *cittadini* attracted the attention of the Venetian government in the early sixteenth century. From 1526 the Avogadori di Comun – three state attorneys who formed the Avogaria di Comun – were in charge of the marriage practices of the Venetian ruling class. Each patrician marriage had to be registered in the *Libro d'oro* within a month. Mismatches between patricians and non-patricians were to be prevented through this enforced state control, otherwise sons born from such marriages ran the risk of losing their hereditary political right to membership in the governing body known as the Great Council. See Chojnacki, 2000a, pp. 53–75.

[14] ASV, *Esecutori contro la Bestemmia*, b. 54: Capitolare, fols 60r–v and Cozzi, 1976, p. 187.

[15] ASV, *Esecutori contro la Bestemmia*, b. 59, Notatorio 98, fols 122–4r, especially 123r.

[16] On the similarity of patrician values and interests and that of the Patriarchs see Ferraro, 2001, p. 26.

adultery, cruelty (*saevitia*), deep hatred and contagious disease. Under no circumstances were the partners allowed to remarry during their lifetime, as this would lead to a bigamous marriage (and, moreover, to adultery). Because the marital bond persisted, the continuing obligation to remain sexually faithful was emphasised, although both partners were freed from the obligation to pay the marital debt.[17] In defending the holiness of the union, Catholic Church doctrine also allowed three exceptions to indissolubility: under certain circumstances where one party was not a Christian, when a marriage had not been consummated (and hence no marital bond had been established) or in a marriage that had been contracted notwithstanding a serious impediment such as fear and force.[18] With the reiteration of the sacramentality of Catholic marriage the spiritual and legal aspects of this institution were firmly in the hands of ecclesiastical tribunals. They did not, however, rule on the economic aspects of marriage – alimony payments and the restitution of dowries were more generally left to secular authorities.

In Venice it was not only in the formation of marriage that ecclesiastical jurisdiction was contested. From August 1374 a minor magistracy, the court of the Giudici del Procurator, could also rule on alimony payments (usually 6 per cent of the dowry) and on the restitution of dowries. This court was aimed at regulating marital conflicts pragmatically and at settling the economic matters of separated couples – even if the separation had not been effected by a formal judgement of the Patriarchal Court. However, the Giudici del Procurator gradually extended its legal competencies and started to formally dissolve marriages of so-called *donne malmaritate* ('badly married women') – women in valid marriages to husbands who mistreated and disrespected them – by decreeing separations without ecclesiastical authorisation.[19] A law promulgated on 4 November 1553 by the Great Council reaffirmed the initial economic competence of the Giudici del Procurator and listed in detail the legal procedure that had to be followed and the witnesses who had to be called to court. Only one sentence alluded to the actual practice of the Giudici in decreeing separations by referring somewhat vaguely to *altri terminazioni* (other regulations) – a fact that historian Angelo Rigo interprets as the republic's interest in leaving this jurisdictional transgression in the

---

17 Phillips, 1988, pp. 13–14. Only when both marital partners wished to dedicate their lives to the Church was a separation on the basis of mutual consent possible; cf. Esmein, 1891, II, pp. 21–9.

18 Phillips, 1988, p. 2.

19 Rigo, 1992–93, pp. 241–66 and 2000, pp. 519–36. We still, however, need a systematic assessment of the legal practice during the seventeenth century, which Ferraro does not provide: 2001, pp. 136–8.

dark.[20] That the Great Council was informed about the Giudici's practice becomes evident some years later when, on 6 August 1559, the Great Council critically addressed the court's legal practice – but not its jurisdictional transgression. The publicising of private conflicts and the separating of couples by these judges resulted, it was argued, only in the 'shame' and 'disgrace' of the families concerned. This 'dishonourable and damaging disorder', the law went on, would not arise if marital conflicts were settled privately by family members.[21]

Thus, the state was clearly interested in preserving marriages, households and families, which were the foundations of social order. It preferred marital disputes to be settled amicably, thereby promoting social order, civic harmony and social stability. From a different perspective, the attitude of the Venetian Church towards these jurisdictional transgressions is quite astonishing. Apparently, no comment was passed and no attempt at defending the ecclesiastical jurisdiction was made. However, although lawsuits concerning the formation of marriage (except annulment suits) came almost entirely under state control from 1577 onwards, most cases concerning separations were still decided before the Patriarchal Court. This situation might explain why the Patriarchs passed no comment on the activities of the Giudici del Procurator. Only the nuncio (papal ambassador) Alberto Bolognetti, in a letter to the Holy See, lamented the jurisdictional infringements of Venetian magistracies, in particular that 'a secular judge emanates sentences concerning the validity or invalidity of marriages.'[22]

It was, again, the potentially damaging effect of judicial publicity in the context of marital dysfunction that was a major concern at the beginning of the seventeenth century. The republic's Consultore in Iure (legal consultant) Paolo Sarpi claimed that separation cases should be placed under secular jurisdiction, or at least *mixti fori* – a combination of secular and ecclesiastical jurisdiction. This explicit attack on ecclesiastical jurisdiction was launched in May 1608 and must be understood in the broader context of the crisis of the Interdict (1606–07), when Pope Paul V (1605–21) excommunicated Venice, but, thanks to Sarpi, the Venetian republic stood strong. What is of direct interest here is Sarpi's claim that 'temporal' marital conflicts should be judged by secular judges rather than by the Patriarchal Court. Sarpi emphasised that marital partners sometimes separated only temporarily, because of 'some secret mistake of the wife' (that is, adultery) or other

---

[20] Rigo, 1992–93, pp. 248–9.
[21] The law is quoted in Rigo, 1992–93, p. 245.
[22] Quoted in Rigo, 2000, p. 533.

reasons. Cases at the Patriarchal Court involved a high degree of publicity; family members and other witnesses from the neighbourhood had to be summoned to give evidence. The witnesses would then have to comment in detail on intimate matters and events that some husbands and wives would prefer not be revealed in court. With the ecclesiastical court's involvement, Sarpi concluded, chances of reconciliation were minimal, since the legal procedure itself promoted divisiveness rather than marital accord.[23]

Following Paolo Sarpi's deliberations on judicial matters in 1608 the question of how to regulate marital litigation according to the interests of the Venetian republic became a concern of the Consultori in Iure, in particular from the second half of the seventeenth century. In about 1656 the legal consultant Bortoletti had even composed a lengthy scripture on the subject. But it was only during the Enlightenment in the late seventeenth and early eighteenth centuries that the state firmly readdressed the 'issue of divorces' – meaning lawsuits concerning annulments and separations – which, according to the Heads of the Council of Ten,[24] endangered the 'security of the state and the decorum of the families'.[25] In June 1782 the Council of Ten consulted the canonists of the University of Padua on this matter (and, additionally, the Consultore in Iure). They responded by pointing to the impediments that invalidated a marriage, grounds for granting separation and, finally, the procedures ecclesiastical tribunals had to follow. As a result of their enquiries, in August 1782 the Heads of the Council of Ten strengthened their control over legal practice at the Patriarchal Court. The Venetian Patriarch was to inform the Heads of the Council of Ten about requests filed in his court. Moreover, after the Council considered their cases, women petitioning for divorce were put in convents or other safe places where they had to live with the 'required modesty' until a final verdict was issued. In this way the Venetian state attempted to minimise the number of lawsuits that resulted in the dissolution of marriages – a practice, it held, which led to the collapse of family economies and disturbed 'private and public peace'.[26] Although legal practice of the Patriarchal Court was henceforth placed under stricter state surveillance, the jurisdiction that Venetian ecclesiastical judges exercised over marital litigation was not directly undermined by local government.[27]

---

23   ASV, Consultori in Iure, 1608, filza 132, fols 241v–242r.

24   The three most important and powerful members of the Council of Ten, who could act separately from the Council as a whole.

25   Quoted in Cozzi, 1981, p. 276.

26   Ibid., pp. 322–3; the detailed response of the canonists is reported on pp. 304–17.

27   De Biase, however, seems to suggest that from 1789 to 1796, shortly before the fall of the republic, the Council of Ten actually judged cases concerning the dissolution of

From a legal perspective cases involving criminal offences such as adultery and bigamy had always been complex. Venetian legislation emphasised, especially in adultery cases, that jurisdiction over this offence was not limited to either the Church or the state. By pointing to marital crimes the author of *Il diritto ecclesiastico* let no doubt arise that 'if it is not for the criminal aspect, that is, for the punishment, but for the sole separation or the divorce of the spouses, this question should be left to the cognition of the ecclesiastical judge.'[28] In earlier centuries, too, adultery and bigamy cases were '*di foro comune*', and lawsuits could thus be initiated either in ecclesiastical or in secular tribunals.[29] This would set in motion two different aims and legal procedures. The state's jurisdiction in offences like adultery was limited to questions regarding the *crime*; secular judges could not rule on the validity and the sacramental character of marriage, as in annulment and separation suits.

This emphasis on *mixti fori* had various implications for ordinary people's experience of the law and its institutions. Owing to the mixed jurisdiction husbands and wives could appear at either of the Venetian courts – the Patriarchal Court or the Avogaria di Comun and sometimes at the Executors against Blasphemy – in both bigamy and adultery cases. The two suits required different procedures and had different aims: separation or punishment in adultery trials and annulment or punishment in bigamy trials. Because the Patriarchal Court's authority over laypersons was restricted to civil matters (annulment and separation), the only punishment in these cases was excommunication. Otherwise, as Sarpi pointed out, the Patriarchal Court would judge laypersons in secular matters, which was an abuse of authority.[30] According to the court's civil procedures defendants were allowed to live either at home or with friends or parents during the course of the trial. Defendants had relatively little involvement with the trial, as procurators often presented the party in toto in court.[31] Criminal procedures, by contrast, were severe and aimed at punishing the guilty party (loss of dowry, fines, prison or exile). After evidence was assembled defendants had to defend themselves in court. Because criminal proceedings tended to be slow, defendants could spend up to several years in prison[32] before

---

marriages. See De Biase, 1981–82, p. 148. An eighteenth-century document details the jurisdictional competencies in matrimonial matters; cf. ASV, *Compilazione delle Leggi*, b. 277 (Matrimonio), fols 311v–316r.

28 Bianchini, 1786, p. 130.

29 Barbaro, 1739, p. 98.

30 ASV, Consultori in Iure, filza 132, fol. 241v.

31 See my discussion of the legal processes in chap. 4.

32 In 1532, for example, the *Quarantia Criminal* decided to release a man who had spent four years in prison and was still waiting to be tried. See Cozzi, 1973, p. 337.

their case was actually investigated and a sentence pronounced.[33]

In practice the Venetian courts were used in different ways by husbands and wives and for different charges. Wives especially filed requests for separation at the Patriarchal Court. Women rarely brought charges of adultery against their husbands. Instead, the betrayal of the marital bond was discussed more generally in the wider context of misconduct and severe cruelty. By contrast, few husbands sued their wives for separation; when they did it was for a different charge, namely, adultery. More generally they relied on secular tribunals to prosecute their adulterous wives as criminals.[34] Their aim in these cases was not separation, but rather punishment of the wife (and of the male adulterer), the restitution of the dowry and the regaining of honour. Venetian legislation actually encouraged husbands to sue at a secular court because the Patriarchal Court had no jurisdiction over property rights such as dowries. Incentives for criminal proceedings were therefore based on material, social and emotional interests. When a favourable verdict was reached, not only did husbands benefit financially, but their masculine honour was upheld in court as well. Marriage was no longer an option open to them, as remarriage was prohibited under canon law. Spouses' everyday experience of the law therefore differed immensely. In the cases I have studied it was husbands and not wives who sued their adulterous partners at criminal tribunals. Adulterous husbands were subject to civil proceedings and were not usually punished with fines, prison or exile, as was the case with adulterous wives. Thus, the use of criminal and civil law, the experiences of married couples in the courts and the aims of these parties were gender-specific in early modern Venice.

Women in the court of the Venetian Patriarch

Although the ecclesiastical tribunal was geographically isolated from the political and commercial centres of the city (a fact lamented by Patriarch Francesco Vendramin in 1612 and Patriarch Giovanni Tiepolo in 1622),[35] 'andare a Castello' (to go to court in Castello) was part of the

---

33 Scarabello, 1980a, pp. 317–76, especially p. 324. While trials held at the praetorial courts on the mainland were relatively short, cases handed over to the Council of Ten implied 'lunghissime carcerazioni preventive'. See Cozzi, 1989, p. 6. Also Cozzi, 1973, p. 323: 'The *Avogadori* were slow to take action, this resulted from their numbers which were too small in relation to the mass of work they had to despatch'. Trials held before the Council of Ten under the *rito* procedure, by contrast, were rapid.

34 For the same gender-specific prosecution pattern in early modern Rome, see Blastenbrei, 1995, p. 272.

35 Tramontin, 1992, p. 62.

Venetian vernacular. It was here that the legal process was initiated and here that the Venetian Patriarch or, more commonly, his vicar signed the citation summoning an accused husband or wife to appear in court. It was therefore Castello – rather than the patriarchal chancellery at S. Bartolomeo di Rialto, where daily court business often took place – that ordinary couples associated with ecclesiastical tribunals.

By the beginning of the seventeenth century the court of the Venetian Patriarch had become essentially a women's court: marital cases were increasingly brought by women, while male plaintiffs outnumbered female plaintiffs only in cases for the restitution of conjugal rights (see Figure 3.1). However, the Venetian ecclesiastical court is only one example of overwhelmingly female legal agencies of marital litigation during the late sixteenth and the seventeenth centuries.[36] There was a similar situation in Bologna,[37] and in some east London parishes women brought 86 per cent of the sex and marriage cases – an exceptionally high proportion even for such a metropolis.[38]

The fact that marital disputes were of public concern might have increased parishioners' knowledge about the Patriarchal Court, particularly among women, who made up the majority of plaintiffs. During the late sixteenth and the seventeenth centuries daily court business was concerned mostly with disputes that came from the Venetian parishes and not from the dependent dioceses. It was neither the very rich nor the very poor who pleaded in the majority of cases; litigants and witnesses came from the heterogeneous world of artisans, with very different standards of living. Only among litigants pleading for annulment on grounds of 'fear and force' was the percentage of female patricians higher.[39] The Court of the Venetian Patriarch was therefore widely used by the general populace to resolve their marital conflicts; daily court business was steady during the period under consideration. During the seventeenth century an average of three or

---

[36] For patricians' use of the law in the eighteenth century see De Biase, 1981–82, pp. 150 and 156–7.

[37] In Bologna women sued their partner in 60 per cent of all court cases. See Ferrante, 1994, p. 906.

[38] Gowing, 1996, p. 36.

[39] During the period 1570–1681 only one male patrician plaintiff sued his patrician wife for the annulment of marriage. Cf. Hacke, 2001a, pp. 208–10. Male patricians either resolved their family problems privately, avoided direct opposition with kin and family by contracting a secret marriage, or tried not to establish a collateral line with a claim to inheritance by simply not letting their marriages be registered by the Avogaria di Comun. On these practices see Hunecke, 1995, pp. 111, 241 and Cozzi, 1976, pp. 184ff. and 204ff.

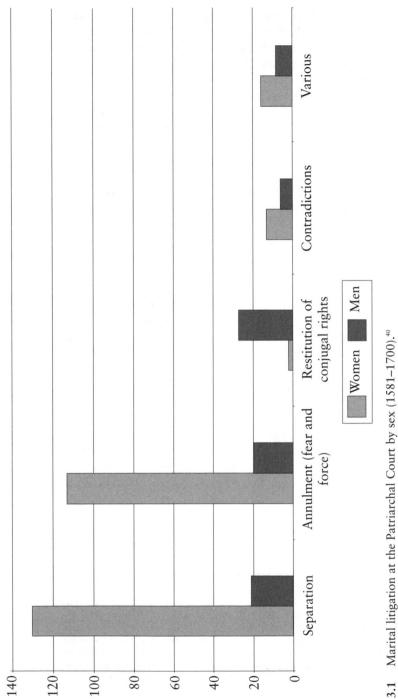

3.1   Marital litigation at the Patriarchal Court by sex (1581–1700).[40]

[40] Cases concerning the formation of marriage, that is cases concerning the fulfillment or the breaking of the marriage promise ('super legimitate', super sponsalibus', 'super diffamatoribus') and the dissolution of an engagement are included in the figure 'various grounds'. This analysis is based on the verdicts of the Patriarchal Court in order to assess how many women actually brought their marital case to an final end. See ASPV, Curia II, *Sententiarum*, Reg.: 4, 6, 8, 9, 10 (the registers 4 and 9 have considerable lacunae). Predominately female legal agency is, however, reflected at any stage of the legal process. See ASPV, Curia, II, *Actorum, Mandatorum*, Reg.: 72, 79, 80, 82, 87, 88, 100, 104, 111, 117, 124.

even four requests per month were filed with the Patriarchal Court (see Table 3.1). In the years 1621, 1643–44 and 1655, use of the Patriarchal Court was on average higher: in these years more than four requests a month were filed. Towards the end of the seventeenth century there is a slight indication of a decline in the Church courts' activity: an average of less than three appeals were made per month.[41] In the second half of the eighteenth century the total had risen to an average of five citations per month, and these only concerned the requests for annulment and separation.[42]

Table 3.1 Cases brought to the Patriarchal Court annually[43]

Year	Separations	Annulments (fear and force)	Conjugal rights	Total
Jan.–Dec. 1602	14	7	14[44]	35
Jan.–Dec. 1612	16	5	9	30
Jan.–Dec.1621	31	12	11	54
Jan.–Dec. 1637	22	4	3	29
Jan. 1643–Apr. 1644	35	24	4	63
Mar.–Dec. 1655	33	8	1	42
May–Dec. 1677	17	5	2	24
Jan. 1695–Dec. 1696	43	21	2	66

State intervention in ecclesiastical jurisdiction changed daily court practice considerably. Before 1577 matrimonial cases heard in the Patriarchal Court were concerned with premarital issues as well, such as the giving and the breaking of a marriage promise.[45] After 1577 the tribunal of the Venetian Patriarch had been transformed almost into a

---

[41] This trend corresponds with Laura Gowing's findings on the London Church courts' activity. Gowing, 1996, pp. 182–3.

[42] Between 1 January 1771 and 31 December 1775. Cozzi, 1981, pp. 275–360, especially pp. 278–9. For the later period (20 August 1777 to 20 August 1782), Cozzi counts 309 *monitori* (293 for separation and 16 for annulment), which makes an average of five requests per month.

[43] ASPV, Curia, II, Actorum, Mandatorum, Praeceptorum, Reg. 79, 80, 82, 87, 88, 100, 104, 111, 117, 124.

[44] One case appears twice in this register (and I have counted it twice) because the husband first sued his wife for the restitution of conjugal rights and the wife then filed a request for the separation of marriage.

[45] Cecilia Cristellon is currently assessing actual marital litigation from 1420 onwards in order to provide the actual numbers. Some numbers are reported by Seidel Menchi, 2000, p. 89, for Venice and by Lombardi, 2001, pp. 169–75, for Siena.

'marital court', and requests for separations and annulments henceforth dominated marital litigation.[46] Only in some cases, such as 'contradiction' suits, was the Venetian ecclesiastical court still ruling on questions concerning marriage formalities.[47] In these cases people objected to a marriage during its solemnization in the parish church. The alleged grounds for this intervention were often broken marriage promises, such as in defamation suits in which the accused – more often women – was ordered to stop spreading rumours that a certain person was engaged to her (or him).

The Patriarch's jurisdiction in separation and annulment cases made the court especially receptive to the needs of distressed wives and daughters, who may have then passed on their experience to other women. Husbands encountering marital distress seem more likely to have resolved their conflicts privately, although actual numbers are difficult to establish.[48] The verdicts reflect, however, that fewer husbands than wives pleaded for legal separation at the Patriarchal Court, and this outcome was certainly not due to the fact that they brought fewer cases to a favourable verdict (see Table 3.2).

On the one hand, women were more likely to request leave to separate from their husbands, but, on the other, they were also more likely to be ordered to fulfil the obligation of cohabitation – the sharing of 'bed and board', which, as mentioned earlier, was a conjugal duty set in stone. When spouses drifted apart or wives looked for shelter in

---

[46] In Bologna between 1544 and 1595, 50.7 per cent of cases were concerned with broken marriage promises, 22.7 per cent with separations and 18.8 per cent with annulments. See Ferrante, 1994, pp. 905 and 907. For medieval England Helmholz, 1974, has found that Church courts were primarily premarital courts concerned with the enforcement of marriage contracts. Cases concerning the dissolution of marriage, such as separation and annulment suits, rarely came to the attention of the authorities, a result which was confirmed later for early modern England as well. Cf. Houlbrooke, 1979, pp. 55–6, and Ingram, 1990, p. 171. At the Protestant court in Neuchâtel, only during the eighteenth century did cases concerning the dissolution of marriage displace contract disputes as the most common ground of marital disputes. See Watt, 1992, p. 219. According to Houlbrooke, 1979, p. 75, it may be that few suits pleading for a separation *a mensa et thoro* (from bed and board) were initiated because spouses simply abandoned each other. Separations may have been arranged privately, with friends acting as mediators between quarrelling partners. This might be one explanation why in early modern London the proportion of separation suits on grounds of severe violence declined during the seventeenth century and why it became less likely for a final sentence to be given. See Gowing, 1996, pp. 182–3.

[47] Exceptions to this rule are a handful of cases concerning broken marriage promises which, despite the state's intervention into ecclesiastical jurisdiction, were heard before the Patriarchal Court.

[48] Rigo, 2000, pp. 527–8, reports that wives relying on the Giudici del Procurator had often been abandoned by their husbands.

Table 3.2 Patriarchal Court judgements in separation and conjugal rights cases[49]

	Separation Favourable/unfavourable	Conjugal rights Favourable/unfavourable
1591–99		
Wives	10/4	–/1
Husbands	3/–	7/3
Ex-officio	–/–	–/1
1600–07		
Wives	18/6	–/–
Husbands	2/1[50]	5/4
1620–38		
Wives	36[51]/9	–/–
Husbands	5/1	4/–
1641–63[52]		
Wives	18/5	–/–
Husbands	–/–	1/2
1665–98		
Wives	19/5	–/–
Husbands	7/1[53]	–/1

convents or with their parents, the deserted partner could sue them to 'stay with them and pay them the marital debt, and to share conjugal cohabitation'. Requests for the restitution of conjugal rights (adherence cases) were, however, relatively uncommon and were 'in similar fashion to (or were superseded by) separation cases'.[54] In these cases of extreme disobedience and desertion men filed requests in the ecclesiastical

---

49 ASPV, Curia, II, *Sententiarum*, Reg. 4, 6, 8, 9, 10.

50 Separation was granted not because of adultery, but because of severe cruelty, as the wife had claimed in her counter-allegation.

51 Surprisingly, one separation was granted on grounds of impotence.

52 I have counted one verdict twice because both husband and wife wanted to be separated.

53 Separation was granted not because of adultery, but because of severe cruelty, as the wife had claimed in her counter-allegation.

54 Ingram, 1990, p. 181. This might, additionally, explain why only few of these cases reached the stage of a verdict.

tribunal which demanded their wives' return to the shared dwelling in order to live together as legitimate spouses.[55] In counter-allegations wives would allege that cruelty, general mistreatment or, occasionally, non-consensual marriage had forced them to leave. In the first two cases they would plead for separation and in the latter case for an annulment of the marriage.

The verdicts reflect not only a predominantly female legal agency; the judgements these women received in marriage cases from 1591 to 1698 also display a high percentage of favourable verdicts. On average over 75 per cent of their pleas for separation were granted. In 13 of these verdicts, however, the wife was allowed to separate only temporarily, as the husband and wife were ordered to reconcile at a later point in time while only one husband received such a verdict. It was Patriarch Gianfrancesco Morosini (1644–78) – who came from a distinguished ecclesiastical family – who issued eight of these verdicts. Although the small numbers are difficult to quantify, husbands were apparently more successful, winning about 85 per cent of their separation cases. It seems male litigants were more determined to bring their case to a favourable end.[56] Only in cases for the restitution of conjugal rights was the proportion of favourable verdicts on average lower (less than 70 per cent) and less stable over the years. The same is true for annulment suits in which the existence of a marital bond was under consideration (see Table 3.3).

Young women claiming to have been married against their will won

Table 3.3   Patriarchal Court verdicts in annulment cases based on fear and force[57]

	Favourable Wives/husbands	Unfavourable Wives/husbands
1587–97	3/–	2/–
1600–07	17/1	1/–
1620–31	43/6	7/–
1642–63	9/4	3/2
1664–98	15/2	14/5[58]

---

55 As, for example, in ASPV, Curia, II, *Sententiarum*, Reg. 8, fol. 8r.

56 Because the legal process was intentionally flexible and could be stopped at any time, it may be that women dropped their case more often, whereas men fought it through to the end.

57 ASPV, Curia, II, *Sententiarum*, Reg. 4, 6, 8, 9, 10.

58 One of these marriages was not annulled, but a separation was granted.

the majority of their cases, though from 1664 to 1698 verdicts for and against them were almost even. This was also the only period in which men lost more cases than they won. This positive trend continued until the end of the eighteenth century, when 67 per cent of annulment suits and 79 per cent of separations ended favourably.[59] The verdicts and investigated trial material reflect considerable gender bias with respect to the use of the court and the contours of litigation, that is, the charges initiated. To reiterate, wives pleaded for an end to conjugal cohabitation (separation) or to annul the marriage, and husbands more often requested the restitution of conjugal rights (or sued their wives for adultery).

Because of the indissolubility of a validly contracted marriage, separation would give partners only the permission to terminate conjugal cohabitation (*divortium a mensa et thora*). In contrast to annulments (*divortium a sacramento*), they did not touch the marital bond, and partners were still held to be husband and wife. Church courts could only dissolve marriages that were impossible to consummate (for example, because of impotence) or that had been contracted invalidly, such as with fear and force, which were impediments against the free consent of at least one of the spouses.[60] In annulment cases favourable verdicts freed the couple to (re)marry, as no matrimonial bond had been established when it had been contracted, owing to the existence of fear and force. When the union could not be consummated because of impotence, however, only the healthy partner was allowed to remarry. In separation cases unfavourable verdicts ordered couples to continue cohabiting and compelled husbands to treat their wives with more care and respect. Favourable verdicts, by contrast,

---

[59] De Biase, 1981–82, p. 155, n. 15. De Biase gives only the total number of verdicts; I have carried out the calculation independently.

[60] Canon law offered numerous serious impediments that rendered a marriage null and void unless the couple obtained special dispensations. These impediments presented considerable obstacles to marriage, as they limited the individual choice of a partner. They were, however, very rarely used in divorces. The impediment of consanguinity and affinity – the relationship by blood and marriage between spouses – was reduced by the Fourth Lateran Council (1215) from the seventh to the fourth degree and by the Council of Trent to the second degree. Affinity, however, was also produced by sexual intercourse. 'Known as the impediment of *affinitas illegitima*, this prevented a man from marrying the sister, or first, second or third cousin of any woman with whom he had had a sexual relationship.' See Phillips, 1988, p. 6. Other impediments, known as *impedimentum criminis*, were based on criminal offences (murder or adultery) carried out by couples in order to get married. Adultery could also be an *impedimentum criminis* if extramarital sex took place with the promise of marriage. Further impediments existed if one partner had taken religious vows or had already entered into a valid marriage. For an introduction to impediments see Phillips, 1988, pp. 5–9, and Schmugge et al., 1996, pp. 71–4.

allowed couples to separate from 'bed and board', albeit sometimes only temporarily. In these cases spouses were obliged to live chastely because their marital bond persisted. Thus, remarriage in Catholic countries was not an option available to dissatisfied couples.

As discussed earlier, when a valid marital bond had been established according to post-Tridentine law, the union was deemed indissoluble. How, then, does one explain the apparent leniency of the Venetian Patriarchs in quite often allowing partners to separate or declaring marriages null and void, but almost equally as often ordering wives to share the marital home, as in the cases in which husbands sued for the restitution of conjugal rights? As most studies on Church courts have argued, the principles of canon law and the desires of ordinary people were usually incompatible. Ecclesiastical judges were bound by canon law to defend the indissolubility of the marital bond, which prevented many cases from even reaching court.[61] The Venetian court was obligated to operate under the same legal principles. Stringent selection procedures by the ecclesiastical staff – only choosing to bring to court those cases which, after initial investigations, merited full legal attention – might have stalled many requests, possibly due to insufficient grounds according to canon law, although some plaintiffs sought legal advice before bringing their domestic dispute to court. Even before the citation was actually delivered ecclesiastical judges were obliged to investigate carefully the chances of mediation between the spouses, thus preventing the full legal process from being set in motion.[62]

As research across Europe has shown, reconciliation was the aim at every stage of the legal process, and Church tribunals actively supported out-of-court settlements or discouraged plaintiffs from pursuing cases to a conclusion in an attempt to force an accord.[63] This made lawsuits less

---

[61] See Ingram, 1990, p. 171, and Houlbrooke, 1979, pp. 55–6. Addressing the period after the Reformation had transferred legal authority on conjugal matters to secular officials, Safley compares the activities of the courts in Protestant Basel and Catholic Freiburg and Constance. He finds that divorce was more frequent among Protestants than Catholics, although the Basel *Ehegericht* granted divorce only in cases of 'the most extreme necessity – almost as an emergency measure – and with the clearest legal foundation'. See Safley, 1984, p. 132. Susanna Burghartz confirmed this finding for Basel: from the second half of the sixteenth century divorces were seldom granted. See Burghartz, 1999, p. 118 and Table 5 (appendix). For early modern rural Catholic Bavaria, Beck, 1992, has demonstrated that only a few female plaintiffs were awarded separation from their husbands, albeit only for one, two or three years. Amicable settlements were still preferable.

[62] Bianchini, 1786, p. 160. He emphasised the role of ecclesiastical judges as mediators between litigating parties.

[63] For medieval and early modern England see Helmholz, 1974, pp. 100–107, and Houlbrooke, 1979, pp. 43–4 and 271, although Houlbrooke notes that procedure became

expensive for litigants, and some would abandon the case following successful negotiations and attempts at reconciliation.[64] Functioning primarily as a court of mediation, the ecclesiastical court communicated to its parishioners moral and Christian values, such as the holiness of marriage, the need for conjugal cohabitation and marital conjugality.[65] The judges at the Patriarchal Court, I shall argue, therefore employed every conceivable means to convince spouses to stay together or to avoid a legal annulment of the marriage. When women claimed that the conjugal bond had been contracted invalidly, it was the task of the Venetian ecclesiastical judge to argue in favour of matrimony (*al favor matrimonii*) – the court of Siena even employed a defender of matrimony (*il defensor matrimonii*) in these lawsuits.[66] Although in dissolving marriages that had been contracted irregularly the Church court was – to a certain extent – defending marriage as a sacrament, the practice of separating marital partners more clearly interfered with the principle of marriage as holy and inseparable. When arbitrary discipline and severe cruelty had disrupted marital life, ecclesiastical examiners tried hard to convince partners to stay together, particularly if the husband, after having confessed to abusing his authority, promised to moderate his behaviour.[67] The *gentildonna* Claudia Grimani, for example, had abandoned her husband Francesco Bono because, as she alleged, she had lived in mortal danger with him. When he sued her for the restitution of conjugal rights at the Patriarchal Court in 1584, the judges tried to make the couple reach an amicable settlement and reinforce marital concord:

---

more formal in the mid-sixteenth century. Martin Ingram explained the shift from a more flexible approach of the Church courts in medieval England towards a more formal and rigorous attitude in later times as a consequence of the growing insistence on the sanctity of marriage. See Ingram, 1990, p. 185. As Safley has shown, the *Ehegericht* in Basel also ordered negotiations and reconciliation of distressed partners, and the judges 'employed every conceivable means to avoid the dissolution of marriage'; separation was approved only for a short period. Safely, 1984, pp. 131–2. In Protestant Neuchâtel it seems that fewer cases were abandoned, and a greater number of favourable verdicts with regard to all divorce cases were handed down. Divorce lawsuits on the grounds of cruelty were, however, extremely rare (two cases in the period 1547 to 1706), although after marriage contract cases, divorces were the most common grounds for marital litigation. See Watt, 1992, p. 123.

[64] Ingram, 1990, p. 50.

[65] Very recently, the role of the Patriarchal Court as a tribunal that attempted to mediate between couples has been confirmed for an earlier period (1420–1532). See Cristellon, 2003, pp. 851–98.

[66] Ibid., p. 859; for Siena see Lombardi, 2001, pp. 175–6.

[67] It is in this role that the function of the ecclesiastical judge as an inquisitor and confessor becomes apparent. Cristellon, 2003, pp. 851–98, here p. 856.

> ... even if this has been true, now the said Francesco wants you to
> return to him ... and offers you to be a good companion; and you
> [Francesco] should also assure [your wife] that you will never
> offend her, but convince her to forget the old stories and to come
> back to her husband as God commands.[68]

Marital discord and violence were not necessarily grounds on which separation was granted. Conflicts might be temporary, partners might be reconciled and married life – as the ecclesiastical judges hoped – might return to normal. Mediating between disputing couples, ecclesiastical authorities emphasised the good and the bad times partners had to manage, side by side. They discouraged distressed couples from pursuing legal actions further and, in recalling biblical words, stressed the indissolubility of the marital bond, for 'the holy scripture says, that those who were joined by God, no man could put asunder'.[69] Only if the woman's life was in danger and there was no hope for reconciliation and accord was a long-term separation granted. Other couples were only granted temporary separation until the husband's behaviour improved, in particular his attitude towards violence.

Did legal proceedings therefore have the inherent potential to promote reconciliation and avoid confrontation because both partners were forced to reflect on their behaviour and to remember their duty to live as Christians? If proceedings were set in motion the possibility of reconciliation was arguably highest at an early stage, as the longer it took to prove a husband's 'bad' government or a wife's disobedience, the more detailed the reproaches became and the more witnesses were heard. Some husbands stressed bluntly that their wives' desertion had caused them 'great dishonour'. It is therefore very likely that the legal process aroused, as has been argued, 'hostility and divisiveness' between litigant couples.[70] Because the publicising of private conflicts affected male honour in particular, we are left to imagine how these dishonoured men treated their wives after being forced by the court to resume conjugal cohabitation.

The ambivalent nature of ecclesiastical legal practice might explain why only a very small proportion of the many requests filed with the Venetian Patriarchal Court was actually investigated and delivered a final conclusion (see Table 3.4).

---

68 ASPV, Curia, II, C.M., Reg. 78: 26 April 1584, Francisci Bono cum Claudia eius uxore, 8 July 1584. See, aditionally, ASPV, Curia, II, C.M., Reg. 75: Clare Gritti cum Paolo Priolo, not foliated. Although the patrician woman claimed to have suffered heavily during marriage and wished to be legally separated from her husband, he was only reminded to treat her with greater care.

69 ASCP, C.M., Reg. 78: 24 October 1583, Justine q.m Baptiste de Morsariy cum Aloysio Inchiostro, fol. 7r.

70 Gowing, 1996, p. 137. This was, too, the argument of Paolo Sarpi, as expressed in 1608, see pp. 37–8 in this volume.

Table 3.4 Cases brought to and sentenced by the Patriarchal Court annually[71]

	Separation	Annulment (fear and force)	Conjugal rights
	Requests/Verdicts	Requests/Verdicts	Requests/Verdicts
1621	31/13	12/8	11/–
1637	22/0	4/1	3/–
1643/44	35/2	24/4	4/–
1655	33/1	8/0	1/–
1677	17/–	5/–	2/–
1695/96	43/1	21/5	2/–

Even if we take into account that the archival evidence is fragmentary and that verdicts might have been lost, an important tendency of Church court business emerges: many more requests were filed with the Patriarchal Court for all different types of marital litigation, but only a small percentage actually reached the final legal stage, that is, received a verdict.[72] This tendency continued well into the eighteenth century, a fact lamented by one of the republic's Consultore in Iure.[73] Only 31 of 349 requests for separation and annulment were fought to the end from January 1771 to December 1775, and only 28 of 309 in the period from August 1777 to August 1782.[74] Hence, only 8.8 per cent of all plaintiffs in the earlier period, and 9 per cent in the later period, received a final verdict. Even if one takes into consideration that some of the daughters and wives claiming that their marriages were concluded under conditions of fear and force or were overshadowed by violence might have willingly withdrawn their lawsuits, the gap between women who attempted to change their marital situation by turning to the Patriarchal Court and those whose marital cases were actually sentenced, is considerable. As I have argued, this reluctance to actually touch the sacramental bond qualified the nature of the Patriarchal Court, which conceived of itself as a court of mediation. Initially, wives in particular approached this legal institution in order to win freedom from the company of their husbands, whereas men appealing to the court wished

---

[71] ASPV, Curia, II, *Actorum, Mandatorum, Praeceptorum*, Reg. 87, 88, 100, 104, 111, 117, 124 and ASPV, Curia, II, *Sententiarum*, Reg. 8 and 10.

[72] That none of the conjugal rights lawsuits received a final verdict is less astonishing, as these lawsuits were often superseded by separation cases. Since only three of the surviving registers of verdicts allow a systematical analysis, I have based my comparison of requests and verdicts on these years only.

[73] Quoted in Cozzi, 1981, p. 311.

[74] Ibid., pp. 278–9.

to have their wives ordered to return to the conjugal dwelling. As the figures in Table 3.4 strongly suggest, the interests of plaintiffs and the court's approach to marital disputes were not necessarily compatible. The role the Patriarchal Court played in resolving marital problems was thus more ambiguous than has been stated hitherto.[75]

It is difficult to assess what impact the court's reluctance to grant separations and annulments had on the lives of distressed wives, as historians are unable to follow their plight beyond the court case and thus to assess whether or not they managed to live amicably with their husbands. Unsuccessful plaintiffs may have turned to a higher court, hoping for a new investigation of their case and a more favourable verdict.[76] Other women may have lived apart from their spouses without legal permission, or tried to convince their husbands to treat them with respect and care. A presumably high 'dark figure' of couples resolved their marital problems privately without even approaching the Patriarchal Court. Separations may also have been arranged privately, with friends and relatives mediating between partners or with spouses simply abandoning each other.[77]

Women at the magistracy of the Executors against Blasphemy

The Executors against Blasphemy had a comparably wide scope in passing verdicts against men who had taken a woman's virginity under the pretext of marriage. No precise punishment was required by the aforementioned law of August 1577, leaving it up to the authority and power of this tribunal to investigate, judge and punish each case individually. The penalties stipulated comprised the galleys, imprisonment, exile and fines, but the harshness of any punishment was left entirely to the Executors.[78] They assessed the length of imprisonment and the level of fine from case to case, always offering defendants present at trial the alternative to marry or to dower the woman concerned. Only those tried in absentia were usually exiled from Venice and its surrounding territories, as happened in 147 out of

---

[75] Ferraro does not consider the high percentage of requests but bases her interpretation on the verdicts alone. Because a high percentage of women brought their cases to a favourable end, she concludes that the Patriarchal Court was receptive to the needs of women. Ferraro, 2001, pp. 30–31. In her earlier work, however, she paid attention to the considerable gap between requests filed and verdicts received but still concludes that the Patriarchal Court showed 'sympathy for the plight of women'. Ferraro, 1995, pp. 496–8, quotation on p. 498.

[76] This argument is from the Consultori in Iure. See Cozzi, 1981, p. 311 and on female petitioners in the Papal penitentiary see Schmugge, 2000, pp. 685–705.

[77] Casey, 1983, pp. 189–217. Helmholz and Houlbrooke (among others) have emphasised the relatively high 'dark figure' in these instances.

[78] *Leggi criminali venete*, p. 63.

466 cases.[79] Cases of non-appearance increased steadily during the second half of the seventeenth century. Because this magistracy followed a policy of re-establishing female honour, if exiled criminals finally appeared or petitioned for their case to be reheard, exile was commonly commuted to something like the marrying or dowering of the woman; short prison sentences were also occasionally inflicted. However, non-appearance before the magistracy was initially punished. Bearing this in mind, it is not surprising that in the period under consideration about 74 per cent (345) of all male defendants were judged guilty: 198 while present in court and 147 while absent.

By contrast, men who obeyed state orders and were tried before the Executors against Blasphemy had a comparably good chance of being acquitted (110, or about 36 per cent; see Table 3.5). This number includes cases in which both parties were reconciled during the trial or

Table 3.5 Verdicts against male defendants present in court[80]

	Guilty	Not guilty	Total
1577–1600	25	3	28
1601–20	62	20	82
1621–40	35	16	51
1641–60	43	54	97
1661–80	28	16	44
1681–1700	5	1	6

the suing party was said to be content; in very few cases (9) the woman simply withdrew the suit without explanation. When female honour was re-established, the state had no incentive to continue prosecution.

But who were these women who relied on the Executors against Blasphemy to regain honour? They came, overwhelmingly, from artisan families – as did the men facing charges – and only in cases that had been delegated by the Council of Ten were patricians involved.[81] In about a

---

[79] Only in one case was a man not present for prosecution pronounced not guilty.

[80] The prosecutions are for breaking marriage promises and premarital sexual relations. The reliability of the registers of verdicts varies considerably. Particularly for the periods 1577 to 1600 and 1681 to 1700 there are most likely considerable gaps. These figures must, therefore, be understood as an indication of tendencies.

[81] To give an idea of the variety of professions in the families of female plaintiffs, I have come across retail spice dealer (*specier*), cloth retailer (*drappier*), broker (*sanser*), gondolier or boatman (*barcarol*), painter (*disenador*), glazier (*fenester*), woolworker (*laner*), goldsmith and jeweller (*orese*), metalworker (*fabbri*), mosaic worker in St Mark's church (*mosaico nella Chiesa di S. Marco*), ropemaker (*cordarol*), masons (*mureri*), butcher (*lughaner*) and, finally, carpenters (*marangoni*) working in the Venetian arsenal.

quarter of all cases the women were fatherless and had therefore been without male protection during their failed marriage formation which included negotiations about the future marriage, such as the nuptial contract. The high percentage of suits, however, demonstrates that they relied quite frequently on the Executors against Blasphemy and claimed to be married or dowered. Widows, by contrast, very seldom sued on their own behalf, although they did sometimes start a lawsuit on behalf of a deflowered daughter after a marriage promise had been broken and premarital sex had followed. Their legal situation was ambiguous, for the law of 1577 expressly protected honourable women who had been deflowered by violence or fraud, without mentioning widows at all. A woman who had already exchanged her virginity for an honourable marriage was thus in an unclear legal situation.

Similarly, female domestic servants claiming that they had been abandoned after having had sexual intercourse with men who had promised to marry them also rarely relied on the Executors. In August 1541 the Council of Ten had transferred authority over domestic servants from the *Capi di sestieri* to the office of the censors (*censori*), which quickly released a flood of new regulations.[82] In sixteenth-century legislation servants appear as deceitful and insolent, and the censors exercised their power to discipline and punish them. Penalties included whipping, branding and sometimes draconian punishments such as blinding and even death. These new regulations, as Dennis Romano has argued, represented 'a major shift in the attitudes and concerns of the servant-keeping classes.' They express upper-class fears and anxieties about unruly servants and boatmen, and were aimed at protecting masters from servants. They focused in particular on the moral behaviour of male servants (insults, gatherings, brawls, blocking quays and moonlighting) and also regulated the relationship between masters and servants.[83]

Men's chances of being released as innocent varied considerably over time. The highest proportion of 'not guilty' verdicts (about 55 per cent, see Table 3.5) was passed in the period 1641–60, at the peak of the Executors' activity (see Table 3.6).

---

[82]   Romano, 1996, pp. 43–74.

[83]   Ibid., p. 57. The regulations stipulated that male servants should not use violence against female servants (or intimidate other male servants) or induce female servants to steal or to engage in sexual relations with them. Servants should not bring prostitutes to their master's house, and the master's consent was necessary if male servants married or promised to marry a female servant. Between 1569 and 1600, 85 nobles sued servants because of sex crimes, whereas only 31 commoners and 19 others approached the censors for the same offence. These suits were aimed at protecting the honour of the master's household.

Table 3.6 Total number of verdicts against male defendants[84]

Year	Total
1577–1600	31
1601–20	86
1621–40	57
1641–60	133
1661–80	100
1681–1700	59

This was also the period when the Venetian republic was unsuccessful in defending its maritime possessions against the Turks, surrendering Crete to the Turks in 1669 after a siege lasting 21 years. This failed military experience might have been why the Executors were unwilling to inflict severe punishment and instead sentenced men – the potential military force – with more leniency. Moreover, these figures reflect a moral policy that had a negative impact on women in particular as, during the confessional age, it was more difficult for them to argue convincingly that they had lost their virginity 'honourably' and consented to premarital sex only after a marriage promise had been exchanged.[85] By contrast, from 1577 to 1600, shortly after enforcement of the law, only 12 per cent of the accused men were found not guilty, though this percentage increased steadily until the second half of the seventeenth century. From the 1670s and 1680s onwards defendants were again convicted at greater rates: from 1681 to 1700 only 17 per cent of defendants present at trial were found not guilty – although these figures are hard to measure due to gaps in the sources. This was also the time, as will be discussed later, when the Executors emphasised the problems men encountered in paying dowries, thus preventing women from receiving a dowry.

Male defendants who were convicted while present in court were usually imprisoned, but, as an alternative, they could choose to marry or to dower the deflowered woman by paying a fine. This policy of the Executors followed the aim of re-establishing female honour. Male defendants usually were held in prison during their trial. If ordered to dower or to marry the woman, they normally were released from prison only after consenting. The fines imposed were around 100–200 ducats (dowry payments over 300 ducats were less common, as were those of

---

[84] These figures do not include cases of sexual violence against women (without mention of a promise of marriage) or the defloration or rape of minors.

[85] For the conflicting legal narratives of women and men in these cases, see chap. 8.

50 ducats or less). Occasionally they reached 400 or even 500 ducats, and on rare occasions a fine of 1000 ducats was imposed.[86] As 50 ducats was equivalent to about five months' wages for a skilled worker of the time,[87] paying the fine could be problematic, especially for poor men. Indeed, the unfortunate Girolamo Falvo spent 21 years in prison because he was unable to pay a fine of 200 ducats. Because of his extreme poverty the deflowered woman Isabella Gorgo (called Moresina) pleaded in March 1640 for his release, and even renounced all 200 ducats because she wanted neither to marry nor to become a nun.[88] In another case a certain Steffano della Villa d'Ales appealed to the Council of Ten for mercy because his extreme poverty made it impossible to pay a fine of 150 ducats as the alternative to five years' imprisonment (reduced to six months). He thus pleaded for the option to marry the deflowered woman, who had already consented to take him as her husband.[89] By contrast Giovanni Maria da Venetia, a boat official, remained in prison because he could not afford the costs for his trial. In 1622 his wife begged the Executors for his release, stressing his extreme poverty.[90] These cases were not exceptional. As Giovanni Scarabello has noted, Venetian prisons were crowded with prisoners who were unable to pay the compensation or simply the costs of the trial.[91]

Punishment could be mitigated: alternatives to dowry payment could be allowed, and fines could be reduced with the approval of the woman concerned or if guarantors vouched for prisoners. The approach to mercy requests was quite flexible: each case was judged individually, but with the interest of the deflowered woman always kept in mind. Battista, for example, was exiled on 23 September 1594 for 10 years, with the condition that he could only be released from exile after paying 200 ducats to Maria Furlana. In the event that he would live with and care for their son, the sum would be reduced to 100 ducats. However,

---

[86] Fines of 50 ducats were among the most frequent in the category of 100 ducats and under (followed by 40 ducats), but were slightly less common than fines of 200 ducats. In addition, the costs for the arrest had to be paid by the defendant, and these varied from 20 ducats for the *capo delle prigioni* in 1599, 10 ducats in 1605, 4 ducats in 1607 and 20 ducats in 1632, not including the costs for the trial. See ASV, *Esecutori contro la Bestemmia*, b. 61, Notatorio 1, fols 43r, 103v, 130r and ASV, *Esecutori contro la Bestemmia*, b. 68, raspa 1, fols 36v–37r.

[87] Rapp, 1976, p. 135. In addition, Brian Pullan has investigated the wages of masters and *lavoranti* working in the *Scuola di S. Rocco*, which were recorded daily from 1550 to 1630. Pullan, 1968, p. 158.

[88] ASV, *Esecutori contro la Bestemmia*, b. 58, Notatorio 95, fol. 255v.

[89] Ibid., Notatorio 96, fol. 57v.

[90] Ibid., Notatorio 95, fol. 135v.

[91] Scarabello, 1980a, pp. 324–5.

because the child had died in the interim he pleaded in December 1595 to be excused from paying the additional 100 ducats for reasons of extreme poverty.[92] Others could be provisionally released from prison with the help of guarantors – who would vouch for the payment of the fine in the presence of the Executors – or by paying a bail.[93] The relationship between guarantors and the people they vouched for is hard to assess because hardly any known evidence exists. In the few cases where information is available we find that one guarantor was the accused's mother, one his brother and a third shared the same profession.[94] Arguably these guarantors had close and trusting relationships as they were held responsible for payment of the money. People without close ties in the community were therefore less likely to be supported financially. Sometimes there was more than one guarantor, or they were mentioned in alimony payments, as in the case of the widow Antonia.[95] In one case the guarantee involved an immediate dowry payment of 50 ducats and another 50 ducats within three months.[96] Although the practice of guarantors made the payment of fines more flexible, it was still difficult sometimes to raise the amount needed. The guarantor of the convicted shoemaker Alessandro, for example, had difficulties paying the fine of 30 ducats. Because the deflowered woman Felicità had died in the meantime, he was allowed to pay five ducats per month.[97] In most of the cases, however, we do not know if and when the fines were paid, and therefore how long the men actually stayed in prison. Sometimes a deposit was paid within a month or so of the verdict.[98] And those convicted might have had financial support from relatives or received credits and alms.[99]

The Executors against Blasphemy watched carefully over the money deposited as a dowry for a future marriage. Usually the fine was paid into the magistracy's cash point (*cassa*) and not directly to the deflowered woman, unless a marriage certificate or proof of entering a convent was presented.[100] In addition to the deposit, the accumulated

---

[92] ASV, *Esecutori contro la Bestemmia*, b. 57, Notatorio 3, fols 270v–271r.

[93] Scarabello, 1980a, p. 320.

[94] ASV, *Esecutori contro la Bestemmia*, b. 58, Notatorio 95, fols 40v–41r, 67v and 70r.

[95] Ibid., fols 52v and 76r.

[96] Ibid., Notatorio 96, fol. 34v.

[97] Ibid., Notatorio 95, fol. 67v.

[98] Cesare paid a fine of 200 ducats approximately three weeks after the verdict was passed. ASV, *Esecutori contro la Bestemmia*, b. 63, raspa 11, fol. 19v. See also b. 68, raspa 2, fol. 132r.

[99] ASV, *Esecutori contro la Bestemmia*, b. 57, Notatorio 3, fols 270v–271r.

[100] In 1578, however, there is evidence that the money was administered by the 'banco

interest was handed over to the woman in order to cover inflation.[101] A strict time limit by which she should have married or entered a convent was commonly specified in the verdict.[102] These conditions sometimes created problems, as women who had neither married nor become nuns within the stipulated time ran the risk of losing their dowries. Some women married the men who had deflowered them, whereas others found different husbands. These cases were not rare and show that it was possible for deflowered women to find husbands after successfully defending their honour in court. Female honour could be regained, although it is difficult to say exactly how often, and women still had the chance of honourable, married lives.

Although the fines paid by convicted men generally were not at the disposal of the women concerned, petitions submitted by women show that the Executors made exceptions in individual cases. As a result of Giustina's petition in 1697 she was allowed, in an act of benevolence, to dispose freely of the money deposited by Giovanni Battista Viani, although she had neither married nor entered a convent.[103] Laura's petition was treated with equal benevolence. Because she was too poor to pay the costs of her medication, she was granted 10 ducats from the deposit of 100, after a physician's certificate was presented.[104] Sometimes the fine deposited was never paid out because the woman had neither married nor entered a convent; when she died, family members sometimes felt that the money legally belonged to them. Thus, a widow filed a petition in January 1599 to use a 70-ducat deposit intended for her deceased daughter Caterina as a dowry for her remaining two daughters Marietta and Betta. Because of her poverty she was allowed to dower each child with 35 ducats.[105] Although the deposit could not be used for other relatives, cases could – as we have seen – be decided in favour of the petitioner. In another case the father of Elena – who had been deflowered by Oratio Conti – filed a plea after her death for the transfer of the 200-ducat deposit to Olivio, the illegitimate son of Oratio and Elena. The Executors handed this petition over to the heads of the

---

pisani et thiepolo'. See ASV, *Esecutori contro la Bestemmia*, b. 56, Notatorio 2, fols 143v and 149r. More usually it was paid into the *zecca* (state mint), but in December 1633 deposit payments proved difficult because of a lack of state funds: Ibid., b. 58, Notatorio 95, fol. 201v. What had happened? Costs from the plague had used up a great deal of money, which may have been taken from the *zecca*. ASV, *Senato Terra*, Reg. 107, August 1632, fols 278r–v.

[101] ASV, *Esecutori contro la Bestemmia*, b. 58, Notatorio 95, fols 92r–v.
[102] Ibid., b. 59, Notatorio 98, fol. 92r.
[103] Ibid., fol. 213r.
[104] Ibid., b. 58, Notatorio 95, fols 130r–v.
[105] Ibid., b. 57, Notatorio 4, fols 30v–31r.

Council of Ten, who followed the Executors' suggestion and paid the deposit to Olivio.[106]

As an alternative to paying a fine 'for marriage or monachisation', the convicted man could marry the woman he had deflowered, but this did not always result in his immediate release from prison. Venturin, for example, was sentenced to 10 years' imprisonment, with the alternative of marrying his victim. In this case the sentence was reduced to one year.[107] Scipione Judicibus Somador, by contrast, spent comparably less time in prison. He married the woman he had deflowered almost three months after the verdict was released on 16 September 1596. He was given the alternative of marrying Ancilla or staying in prison until he had paid 200 ducats for her dowry. He most likely spent three months or so in prison, including the duration of the trial; in addition he had to pay the costs of the trial.[108]

The evidence has shown so far that the Venetian justice system was flexible and that alternatives were allowed in cases of imprisonment or exile. Moreover, payment conditions were frequently altered to fit the financial situation not only of the convicted men, but also of the female plaintiffs or sometimes even their families. In everyday legal practice the interests of the deflowered women were kept very much in mind, especially when dealing with ex gratia requests, as the express aim of the Executors was to protect women from sin and to make dowry payments possible. Men were certainly severely punished when exiled or imprisoned, but women were not reimbursed for their lost honour (unless the man was present for prosecution). In 1670 the Executors directly addressed the problem with regard to of the poverty of delinquents:

> ... considering that especially when in alternative verdicts 100 ducats are inflicted [as punishment], this [sum] will soon be more than 200 [ducats] adding the money which additionally has to be paid [the *aggionti*], so that this burden is unbearable for delinquents and being unable to embrace the alternative because of their poverty, they will be exiled; and in this way women who have lost their virginity cannot profit from this beneficial money, nor can the magistracy in consequence profit from those of the additional payment.[109]

The alternative punishment to imprisonment or exile aimed at

---

[106] Ibid., b. 58, Notatorio 95, fols 223v–224r and *Consiglio dei Dieci*, Parti Comuni, filza 448, 2 September 1636.

[107] ASV, *Esecutori contro la Bestemmia*, b. 59, Notatorio 97, fol. 67v.

[108] Ibid., b. 61, Notatorio 1, fol. 22r.

[109] Ibid., b. 59, Notatorio 97, fol. 145v. I am not, however, entirely sure how payment of the *aggionti* functioned in practice.

guaranteeing the compensation (dowry) of the deflowered women, but in practice poverty could threaten this policy, which was aimed at re-establishing female honour.[110] Compassion moved some deflowered women to plead for mitigation, to accept reduced payments or, as we have seen earlier in the case of Isabella Gorgo, to forego payment altogether. Marietta pleaded for Francesco Buranello's release from prison, giving him the opportunity to marry whomever he wished.[111] Exiled men were also released from banishment if they were willing to fulfil the alternative, but could not be released if the woman refused to marry the man who had deflowered her.[112] Fiorini Rossi, by contrast, was already married to one Antonio Boron when she petitioned for the release from exile of Antonio Mian – the man who had deflowered her.[113]

Different social realities were at stake when men who had already been banished petitioned to have the verdict reversed. Giovanni Battista Zapella, who had been exiled for 10 years on 23 May 1655 for deflowering Polonia and breaking his marriage promise, pleaded on 5 July 1656 for permission to marry Polonia, although he had already been caught violating the ban.[114] In another case the deflowered woman presented the supplication. Antonio de Giovanni Moron had been exiled because his father had hindered him from fulfilling the alternative and marrying the woman he had deflowered. His victim now pleaded to allow his return to the *patria* so that he could marry her.[115] Sometimes exiled defendants were unable to present themselves within the strict time limits, but their non-appearance was only seen as a sign of guilt after 16 months of absence. Defendants offered a variety of excuses and mitigating circumstances for their lateness or non-appearance at court. Heavy rains that flooded the streets could prevent the accused from appearing in time, as happened to Girolamo Serena in 1675.[116] Andrea Piloto, by contrast, claimed to have been exiled without his knowledge

---

110 A case in point is that of the soldier Andrea, who was exiled on 6 February 1650 after having been found guilty of abducting a certain Caterina from her father's house and deflowering her. As stressed in the verdict he could only regain his freedom after paying 100 ducats and performing community service in Dalmatia. On 16 June 1655 Andrea begged the Executors to release him from the *aggionti* of another 100 ducats because he had already paid 100 ducats and served in Dalmatia; ASV, *Esecutori contro la Bestemmia*, b. 59, Notatorio 97, fol. 9v.

111 ASV, *Esecutori contro la Bestemmia*, b. 59, Notatorio 97, fol. 95r; see also Notatorio 98, fol. 108r, where the defendant pleaded for release from prison because the offended party was content.

112 ASV, *Esecutori contro la Bestemmia*, b. 58, Notatorio 95, fol. 178v.

113 Ibid., b. 59, Notatorio 98, fol. 82r; cf. also fol. 96v.

114 Ibid., Notatorio 97, fol. 23r.

115 Ibid., fol. 12v.

116 Ibid., Notatorio 98, fol. 32v.

because he was in Bologna at the time.[117] And Antonio Mezzaroli could not appear in court because of his illness.[118] In legal practice the accused could plead for a more flexible handling of strict time limits. Augustin Borizzo, for example, presented his petition in August 1680, willing to fulfil the conditions of his sentence. He had been exiled the year before for seven years, with the alternative of paying a fine of 400 ducats within two months, returning items he had received from Giovanna Gaia and caring for the child he had fathered with her. Because he exceeded the specified time limit the Executors handed his petition to the Heads of the Council of Ten in 'an act of pure mercy'.[119] Exile, however, had no measurable impact on men's willingness to embrace the alternatives and to marry or dower their female victims. According to the records of the Executors against Blasphemy, 74 out of 147 men convicted while absent and 73 out of 198 convicted while present were 'cancelled from the raspa' (*dipenato di raspa*).[120] Taken altogether, this means that about 42 per cent of the convicted men married or dowered their victims. In the period 1641–60 alone, 33 per cent of these men married the deflowered women as a result of their conviction, and thus were released from prison. This figure was, however, generally much lower (around 10 per cent or even less).

The discussion so far has shown that initial punishment was harsh (imprisonment, fines or exile), but that severe verdicts could be mitigated, demonstrating to a certain extent the flexibility of the Venetian judicial system. An aspect not yet discussed concerns the strategies that women might choose when approaching the court. In one extraordinarily fascinating case on 26 August 1654 Giustina, wife of Bernardo Portelli, related to the Executors against Blasphemy the circumstances under which her husband had been exiled. Bernardo Portelli was absent from Venice when one day a mandate from the Executors was brought to his house. He was asked to defend himself against the accusation of having deflowered a certain Andrianella, daughter of the widowed Anetta, four years or so earlier. According to Giustina, the moment to submit the accusation had been chosen carefully. She accused mother and daughter of having

> ... artificially delayed the process of releasing a mandate ... [and that they have only sued him] after he had left [Venice] many days

---

[117] Ibid., Notatorio 97, fols 156r–v; see also Notatorio 98, fol. 9v. For another case see b. 57, Notatorio 4, fol. 145r.

[118] ASV, *Esecutori contro la Bestemmia*, b. 58, Notatorio 96, fol. 121r.

[119] Ibid., b. 59, Notatorio 98, fols 79r–v; see also fol. 81v.

[120] The raspa is the volume in which the verdicts were collated. In the margin it was noted when a man had actually paid the dowry or married the woman concerned.

ago ... and this only with the intention [in mind] that he will be banished, since they could be sure that it would be impossible for him to be informed [about the criminal proceedings initiated against him] so that – although innocent – he was unable to appear [before the tribunal].[121]

Giustina suggested a tantalising, tactical use or exploitation of the Venetian legal system: by delaying the start of the lawsuit, exile was unavoidable. But the Executors' response shows that the charge was presented two days before Bernardo Portelli left Venice; it seems that Giustina herself had made up this argument.[122] However tactical Giustina's assertion might have been, it introduces the possibility that plaintiffs might have willingly delayed the start of a lawsuit until the defendant had left Venice, thereby circumventing the difficult assessment of female honour during the trial.[123]

Out-of-court settlements

Sometimes a lawsuit was terminated because the defendant had married the deflowered woman after the trial had begun[124] or because the woman claimed to be content. Public notaries may have been consulted during trials when attempts at reconciliation had been successful. In legal mediation the level of the dowry payment was fixed and payment terms settled. The party who had initiated the trial at the Executors against Blasphemy then promised to withdraw the charge. With this legal document all claims were held to be satisfied, now and in the future.[125] This out-of-court settlement was advantageous for both parties: the defendant eluded further prosecution and punishment, the plaintiff received a dowry. Sometimes public notaries were consulted without a case going to court, as in the case of Angela from the parish S. Martin on Murano who in 1702 reached a settlement with the man who had deflowered her. In mediation in front of witnesses and the notary she accepted the payment of 25 ducats in return for her promise 'neither to pretend, nor to claim anything in future'.[126] Andriana, daughter of the deceased carpenter Giovanni de Gioppo, had made a statement of

---

121 ASV, *Esecutori contro la Bestemmia*, b. 59, Notatorio 97, fol. 1v.

122 Ibid.

123 See my wider discussion in chap. 8.

124 See, for example, ASV, *Esecutori contro la Bestemmia*, b. 62, raspa 4, fols 21v, 38r, 151v; and b. 62, raspa 5, fol. 27r.

125 ASV, *Notarile Atti*, 5511, Emo Giorgio, Protocollo 1656–57, fols 267v–268r.

126 Ibid., 6121, Marco et Antonio Fratina, Protocollo, fols 79v–80r. For another case see Ibid., 692, Francesco Beaziano e Andrea Bronzini, fol. 3r.

mediation on 27 December 1639 with a notary because Giovanni Batta Bovis had promised, in turn, to dower her with 200 ducats.[127] Caterina used a different method, submitting a written withdrawal to the public notary on 23 July, most likely in 1665.[128]

These legal mediations give interesting and unique insights into the way ordinary people resolved their conflicts out of court with the help of their families, yet in the presence of notaries and witnesses. The Venetian notarial material is extraordinarily rich and awaits further investigation, as the relationship between notaries and the court, for example, is not entirely clear. Some evidence suggests that parties simply withdrew their complaints and that the Executors against Blasphemy ended the lawsuit when the plaintiff was content. But in 1688 the Executors expressed their anger about this habit:

> It must be considered that the abuse is not to be tolerated which has been introduced by many young women who present an document at this most excellent magistracy describing the pain [*scrittura d'indolenza*] the loss of their virginity under the pretext of marriage had caused them; and later they reach a settlement with the accused party and appear in some acts of public notaries and reconcile, withdrawing every claim. And then they present this document [at this magistracy] asking the justice to stop criminal proceedings. Various inconveniences might be caused by this habit and they might be violated, deceived or others.[129]

Therefore, as the text went on, this magistracy should not simply accept the withdrawal of a lawsuit; the parties concerned had to appear in person. At the end of the seventeenth century the Executors against Blasphemy attempted to exercise stricter control when settlements were reached out of court. Although this magistracy could also prosecute ex officio, the state nevertheless relied on the co-operation of women in bringing their cases to its knowledge.[130] In order to enforce their moral policies the Executors had to be informed about legal steps that circumvented the complex apparatus of Venetian justice.

As we have seen, female honour not only could be lost: the intervention of various mediators and the involvement of the family in legal mediation in particular demonstrate that female (and family)

---

[127] ASV, *Esecutori contro la Bestemmia*, b. 58, Notatorio 96, fol. 35r.

[128] Ibid., b. 62, raspa 6, fol. 146v. For a different use of notaries in baroque Rome see Nussdorfer, 1993, pp. 103–18.

[129] ASV, *Esecutori contro la Bestemmia*, b. 59, Notatorio 98, fol. 159v.

[130] The possibility of prosecuting ex officio is mentioned in the law dated 27 August 1577; see *Leggi criminali venete*, p. 63 and also ASV, *Esecutori contro la Bestemmia*, b. 54: Capitolare, fols 59r–v. In legal practice, however, the majority of cases were initiated on the grounds of a private accusation.

honour could be regained – an argument continually emphasised during attempts at reconciliation. As Chapter 8 will reveal, the settling of marital conflicts out of court was an established practice in early modern communities which involved the members of the families concerned, the neighbourhood and, usually, a priest. All these people were likely to be acquainted with the tropes of disputed marriages and had heard endless stories about broken marriage promises and lost (female) honour. Secular courts were therefore the last hope, and only approached when people could not resolve their conflicts privately. The differing circumstances, however, made each story individual. The courts essentially adopted a flexible approach, treating each case on its own merits. Dowry fines were imposed at the discretion of the courts according to individual circumstances, and decisions could be swayed in mitigating circumstances, such as compassionate motives.

CHAPTER FOUR

Narratives in Court

When complaints about broken marriage promises, disrupted marriages and household disputes reached the courts, a series of legal actions were set in motion. The courts depended largely on ordinary people to instigate lawsuits, gather evidence or identify suspects. According to legal procedure, private offences, on which this study is based, could be prosecuted only on the strength of accusations made by the offended party. In adultery cases, for example, the state had to rely on the co-operation of betrayed husbands or other family members who were willing to report sexual misconduct. Plaintiffs could appear in person in court to denounce an offence or submit a written accusation. It is very likely that lawyers and procurators (or scribes) assisted in writing legal documents and helped in building up the arguments of the charge (even where they are not mentioned), especially if the case was presented point by point. Witnesses to support the charge were usually called by the plaintiff at the end of the accusation. They were crucial to criminal and civil proceedings and were questioned in court in order to evaluate the accusation. Witness statements were shaped to a certain degree by the accusation, but more so by personal involvement in the events under investigation. Because neighbours often had the most detailed insights into the life and moral conduct of fellow parishioners, men and women from the same parish (or sharing the same household or profession) were responsible for most witness statements.

A charge could be strengthened through evidence, such as private letters, which could serve different legal purposes. For example, in adultery trials love letters received by an allegedly unfaithful wife were considered concrete proof of sexual misconduct and therefore strong evidence for the prosecution. In lawsuits over broken marriage promises love letters were submitted by female plaintiffs to prove an emotional relationship between the deflowered woman and her alleged seducer. Handwriting tests were occasionally carried out to identify the writer. Any present given to the deflowered woman (such as a ring) was considered particularly incriminating, even when the defendant and the plaintiff debated its emotional meaning during the proceedings.

After all the evidence for the prosecution had been gathered, the proceedings passed to the next stage. Only if the judge upheld the accusation as reasonable were the defendants summoned to defend themselves before the judges.[1] In order to arrest criminals the Avogadori di Comun required the authorisation of the *Quarantia Criminal* (Criminal Council of Forty), except in urgent cases.[2] If the location of the accused was unknown (or if they could not be found at home), the judge immediately passed to the proclamation of serious crimes. According to Marc'Antonio Tirabosco, Secretary of the Executors of Blasphemy at the beginning of the seventeenth century, a proclamation 'is nothing else but the substance of the process, by which the accusation is made known to the accused person; he is thus asked to appear in order to defend himself against the accusations.'[3] The proclamation was published in Venice at the Rialto, in St Mark's Square and in similar public places on the mainland. It was a concise summary of the 'facts' assembled in the interrogations and depositions of plaintiffs and witnesses. In practice suspects usually had eight to ten days to appear and to present themselves at prison; in exceptional cases only three days were given, and another eight to ten days could also be granted. If the proclaimed person did not appear, they usually were exiled in absentia for their contumacy (*bando ad inquirendum*). As the Venetian senate had decreed in 1504, the non-appearance of exiled persons was interpreted as a confession of guilt only after 16 months, and it was rather the refusal to follow the state's orders promptly that was punished with exile.[4] This severe punishment was inflicted on both male and female defendants; only if the person concerned was granted a retrial could a defence be submitted. In these cases a *salvocondotto* was ordered and the person concerned was escorted to the relevant court.[5]

The interrogation of the defendant (*constituto de plano*) followed soon after imprisonment. A written defence was submitted within a certain time limit established in court. Single points (*capitoli*) could be rejected if they were contradictory or insulting. Plaintiffs and defendants were entitled to a copy of the statements. Additional *capitoli* could be submitted by each party, and more witnesses could be named in their favour. Defendants were commonly supported by lawyers, though this was not the case in trials conducted with the *rito*, the most severe procedure of the Venetian republic, invented in the Middle Ages under

---

1   An exception was made for sexual offenders caught in flagrante delicto. Paolo della Chiave, tried at the Praetorial court in Vicenza in 1691, was arrested and imprisoned when caught in the adulterous act. ASV, A.d.C., Misc. pen. 239.5: Paolo della Chiave, Domenica Zampa, adulterio.

2   Cozzi, 1973, p. 309.

3   Tirabosco, 1636, p. 34.

4   Povolo, 1997, pp. 120–23; Tirabosco, 1636, p. 39.

5   A case in point is ASV, A.d.C., Misc. pen. 158. 6: Giovanni Verci, Cleves Caterina moglie di Bolzoni, adulterio, fols 42v–43v.

the influence of inquisitorial procedures. It was applied by the Council of Ten (and, in a similar but less strict form, by the Executors against Blasphemy) and involved secrecy at every step: the defendant was not entitled to know even the name of the plaintiff and witnesses, was prosecuted in camera with no lawyer, and did not even receive a copy of the trial. As Gaetano Cozzi noted, the defendant had to rely exclusively on his memory, as the accusation was only read aloud. Only public documents were allowed under the *rito*, and the defendant was entirely at the mercy of the court.[6]

In practice, however, the *rito* was handled less severely. In the tribunal of the Executors against Blasphemy, for example, limitations placed on the defence had already been abolished by the end of the seventeenth century. Defendants could openly consult their lawyers, and during the eighteenth century lawyers (rather than defendants) were usually the ones conducting the defence case. In practice the rights of defendants increasingly were taken into account as a result of a 'new sensibility'.[7] They were sometimes reflected in the eighteenth-century debate on the reform of criminal law. However, as Cozzi has argued, the improvements regarding defendants' rights in trials conducted by the *rito* were at the same time accompanied by the intent to suppress them in the name of summary and speedy justice.[8]

During the criminal proceedings under examination here poor prisoners could rely on the help of the *avvocati de' preggioneri*, prison lawyers from an office reserved for patricians.[9] If the Avogadori di Comun was in charge of the investigations, the defendant's interrogation was carried out by an *avogadore* in the presence of a committee of five other people (see Figure 4.1). The interrogations were minuted and handed over to the defendant's lawyer.[10] At the magistracy of the Executors against Blasphemy the notary usually conducted the interrogations. Their legal practice was controlled in part by the Council of Ten, who passed regulations in 1558 concerning the examination of witnesses and the necessary daily presence of the Executors in order to guarantee speedy proceedings. The system of rotation posed serious

---

6 See Povolo, 1980, pp. 165–6 and Cozzi, 1989, pp. 1–28. However, as Cozzi notes, 'we must differentiate among trials conducted with the *rito* held at the Council of Ten and those conducted with the *rito* before tribunals that were dependent on the Council of Ten, such as the Executors against Blasphemy ... . The Council of Ten applied the *rito* "con solemnintà", that is, fully ... in other tribunals, however, these formalities were, in the end, hardly or not at all applied'. The quotation is on pp. 19–20.

7 Cozzi, 1989, p. 27.

8 Ibid., pp. 28–33.

9 Ibid., especially p. 28. See also Lazzarini, 1910–11, pp. 1471–1507.

10 Cozzi, 1973, p. 309.

4.1   Avogadore (Grevembroch, *Gli Abiti de' Veneziani*)

problems in daily court practice (every six months two new Executors were elected by the Council of Ten; after 1628 they were elected by the senate). Whereas the Executors against Blasphemy were not judicial specialists and served only for short periods, the staff who held office for life had accumulated technical knowledge and wide experience through daily legal practice. The notaries' power in particular in conducting trials was quite limitless: they issued summonses, interrogated witnesses and defendants and took down their testimonies.[11]

Interrogations often started with questions about the accused's detention. The opening question of the interrogation, 'Have you been informed about the reason for your arrest?',[12] offered considerable scope for the arrested person to answer: one could decide to admit guilt immediately (if one was guilty) or could tactically answer 'no'. Because the evidence against every person who was arrested was usually strong,

---

[11] See Derosas, 1980, here p. 478; for the eighteenth century see Cozzi, 1955, pp. 931–52.

[12] Tirabosco, 1636, p. 45.

the defendant's guilt must have seemed likely for the prosecuting court members. Defendants were constantly interrupted by the examiners, and their credibility contested by the evidence of witnesses. Because answers had to be clear and focused, cross-examiners were persistent, repeating the same question several times and exerting pressure on defendants unwilling to confess. Faced with undeniable proof from credible witnesses, defendants hardly had any defence strategy that would work: denial was taken as proof of their 'bad' character and made them appear obdurate rather than reasonable and remorseful.

At the beginning of the seventeenth century Lorenzo Priori, the late sixteenth-century 'criminologist' renowned for his work *Prattica Criminale* (1622), and the aforementioned Marc'Antonio Tirabosco advised examiners to observe suspects' reactions with care, as facial expression, firmness of the voice and general behaviour were indicators that could help to reveal the 'truth'.[13] Although these particular details usually were not documented,[14] examiners' judgements were not based on the 'facts' alone. They presumably also considered the defendants' behaviour – the way they responded to questioning and the willingness with which answers were given. Obstreperous defendants were admonished to give up obstinacy and impenitence. Because a confession was, however, not pertinent to the passing of a verdict, torture was used only in a few, particularly serious cases.[15] It was therefore the oral testimony of the witnesses which carried fundamental weight in Venetian criminal trials.[16]

If torture was occasionally exercised it was aimed not to compel the defendant to confess but, as Tirabosco explained, to 'make him [or her] answer the interrogation dutifully.' Children under 14 years, elderly or injured people and pregnant women were excluded from torture.[17] In these extremely rare cases the defendant was first guided into a chamber where the interrogation continued under the threat of impending torture. If the accused continued to deny the charge, they were then

---

[13] Priori, 1622, p. 29 and Tirabosco, 1636, p. 44.

[14] In one exceptional case the emotional reaction in a deposition was recorded. When a mother was interrogated about the rape of her mentally insane daughter she replied, 'o Jesus Maria … maybe my daughter has lost her honour, *and here she sighed and cried* [my italics] … oh my God what had happened to my daughter. I feel my heart breaking.' See ASV, A.d.C., Misc. pen. 128.14 and 282.13: Polazzo Pellegrini, stupro, 1690, fol. 68v.

[15] The Council of Ten, by contrast, may have used torture more frequently. See Cozzi, 1955, pp. 931–52, especially p. 945. Guido Ruggiero, 1980, p. 24, reports that for the Middle Ages torture was relatively rare in interrogations carried out by the Avogaria di Comun.

[16] Buganza, 1991, pp. 124–38.

[17] Tirabosco, 1636, pp. 45 and 50.

[18] ASV, A.d.C., Misc. pen. 238.3: Giovanni Colle, seduzione di Fasello, Diamante,

bound with a rope and was asked to reconsider. If the accused replied, 'I do not want to confess something I have not done',[18] they were then hoisted up. While the suspect was hanging in the air, the judges exerted further pressure by listing the evidence brought forward in court. The tortured would be let down after a period if they remained resolute in denying the accusation, but might be pulled up again later. Contemporaries were, however, conscious that physical force made interrogations less reliable, and the tortured themselves addressed the extreme conditions of their confessions.[19]

During the trial defendants were held in prison, but could be released on bail (*piezaria*) when members of the community vouched for them.[20] Guarantors had a very close and trusting relationship with the persons they vouched for, because they were held responsible for the payment of the money. Persons without close ties in the community were less likely to be supported by a guarantor. Women could plead for release from prison in cases of pregnancy, being placed instead under house arrest. Because women gave birth to future citizens they could insist that generosity should temper severe criminal procedures.[21] And as the defendant's life was threatened in cases of illness, imprisonment during trial could be circumvented by presenting a supporting reference from a medical practitioner. Towards the end of the trial, when all the evidence had been assembled and the witnesses interrogated, the defendant usually was asked if they had anything else to add. No verdict was passed until both parties had brought all material details and evidence to light – a sign that the secular courts were endeavouring to guarantee fairness and justice. Both parties usually were granted a fair hearing, and defendants were punished only in cases of conclusive evidence.

When all evidence had been assembled and all witnesses heard, the case was handed over to the *Quarantia Criminal* (Criminal Council of Forty) because the Avogaria di Comun – in contrast to the Executors against Blasphemy – had no authority to pass verdicts, although it could suggest the punishment. Proceedings before the Criminal Council of Forty were public and, according to the patrician Marco Barbaro, based on arguments between the Avogador di Comun (who assumed the role of a public prosecutor) and the defence lawyer.[22] The Venetian diarist

---

1638, 6 January 1639.

19 Ibid.

20 Scarabello, 1980a, especially p. 320.

21 For example, Margherita Muti stressed in her petition that she was a mother and asked to replace confinement in prison with imprisonment at home, for the sake of the unborn child: ASV, A.d.C., Misc. pen. 268. 21, Romani-Muti, Margarita, adulterio 1670, fols 41r and 43r.

22 Povolo, 1980, p. 200.

Marino Sanudo, a fervent admirer of the Avogaria, described its role as arguing 'as advocates for the commune, whence comes their title "avogadori" ... and they argue in support of their suspensions ... and act as guardians of the law'.[23] This procedure was admired by foreigners for the 'liveliness of the debate it produced, and especially for the protection it offered the defendant'.[24] No more evidence could be assembled at this stage of the trial, and the Criminal Council of Forty, who had not followed the earlier stages of the trial, sentenced the defendant on the basis of the debate and the summary provided to them.[25] In crimes related to sexual offences, fines and imprisonment (or exile in cases of absence) were common punishments; shaming punishments, such as corporal mutilation or even execution, were not. The judicial system in Venice functioned flexibly, and if partners were reconciled, for example in adultery cases, the state had no incentive to prosecute.

The legal process in civil cases, such as the annulment and separation suits under examination here, was intentionally flexible. As discussed in Chapter 3, church courts had been places of mediation since the Middle Ages, and this intent to actually make partners stay together favoured the termination of lawsuits at any stage. Thus in comparison with secular courts, the majority of cases were not fought through until a final sentence was passed. When disputes concerning the acceptable use of violence against disobedient children (annulment suits)[26] or wives (separation cases) or, less commonly, cases concerning female obedience (adultery and restitution of conjugal rights) reached the court, the first step was the release of a *monitorio* or *citazione* (summons) by the Patriarch. The *monitorio* comprised the accusation and was an ecclesiastical order for the defendant to appear and comment on it. Before a citation was released, however, the ecclesiastical judge would 'examine ... whether the matter could be settled amicably without legal dispute and to restore concord among the parties.'[27] The summons was delivered by a *ministro publico* (member of the court) to the home of the accused. If they were not present, domestic servants were informed about their master's or mistress's duty to appear in court. Defendants

---

23 Quoted in Cozzi, 1973, p. 303. As Cozzi stressed, 'it was, then, a mixed proceeding in which there were elements of the old accusatorial process and of the inquisitorial process of medieval origin'. Ibid., p. 309.

24 Ibid.

25 In trials held at praetorial courts on the Venetian mainland and within the maritime possessions, the judge passed the verdict and sent a copy of the trial to the Avogaria di Comun. In this way (and by appointing Venetian patricians as rectors in the praetorial courts) the Venetian republic watched over the legal practice on the mainland. See Povolo, 1980, especially pp. 156–60 and, additionally, Tedoldi, 1999.

26 That is, those children who were forced into a marriage against their will.

27 Bianchini, 1786, p. 159.

who failed in this duty ultimately faced the penalty of excommunication. The summons also could be displayed in a public place,[28] the parish church for instance, especially if the defendant's address was unknown or if they were away. Only rarely did priests deliver it personally.[29]

The citation was followed by the presentation of the libel or petition (*positiones*) in which the plaintiff argued the charge point by point.[30] Plaintiffs and defendants, when presenting counter-allegations, relied on legal advisors, namely, procurators (*procuratore*) to prepare the documentation, although their competencies often overlapped with those of the ecclesiastical lawyers (*avocato ecclesiastico*) trained in canon law.[31] The procurators' task was to represent the parties as *dominis litis* in court and to submit the list of witnesses to be summoned to the vicar, who, in the majority of cases, supervised the litigation process.[32] Legal advisors could be family members, but usually were members of the Patriarchal Court. This court employed procurators over several years, who specialised in either prosecution or defence.[33] In marital disputes then, regardless of the social position, wealth or power of the litigants, their interests were represented by the same procurator – a fact that made the process of litigation egalitarian.[34]

The presentation of the *positiones* was followed by the contesting of the suit, with the defendant answering the presented case point by point, generally under oath. Usually the defendant denied all or most of the alleged facts. Sometimes the answers were very short ('That's right' or 'That's not right') and noted directly on the statement. It was up to the plaintiffs to prove their case, but defendants and plaintiffs alike could

---

28 Ibid.

29 A case in point is ASPV, Curia, II, C.M., Reg. 94: 14 September 1680, Hieronimi Cornelio cum Delphina Theupolo, not foliated.

30 For the libel (*libello*) see Ferro, 1845, vol. 2, p. 186.

31 The role of the ecclesiastical lawyers is not entirely clear, as they are not always mentioned (like the procurators). That they played a role during the legal proceedings only sometimes becomes apparent when they are mentioned in notary acts and in legal invoices (*spese*).

32 For the different tasks of lawyers and procurators see, however, Ferraro, 2001, pp. 22–3.

33 In the 1620s and 1630s, for example, the procurator Giovanni de Rubeis (Ioannes de Rubeis) was often mentioned as supporting the plaintiff, while Marco Caraffonus represented the defendant; in the late 1630s Bernardo Rota and Matteo de Matteis represented the plaintiff and the defendant, respectively.

34 The rights and duties of these legal advisors (lawyers and procurators alike) were formally fixed in a notary act and embraced all sorts of legal actions: defending the parties' interests, challenging opposing libels, producing testimonies and contesting opposing statements, listening to the verdict and appealing against unfavourable verdicts. See ASPV, Curia, II, C.M., Reg. 94: 9 July 1697, Processus pro asserto matrimonio contracto inter N.V. Joem Bapta Cellini, et Josepham Madonnis Contra Plebana S. Joannis in Oleo.

express their points of view more fully during interrogation. In lawsuits that investigated the means by which a woman had been married (that is, in annulment suits), these interrogations, as emphasised in canon law, were to be carried out by the ecclesiastical judge in the presence of a notary or *cancelliere* in a safe place, thereby giving the woman the liberty to express herself freely and away from the influence of her parents, who might exercise moral threat and pressure. This legal norm was consistently applied in legal practice, but only in the case of the 'weaker' sex (namely, women); young men, even when they had married under similar conditions, were denied this particular legal protection.[35]

When plaintiff and defendant (when presenting counter-allegations) had submitted all information to strengthen their case, the next stage was the interrogation of witnesses.[36] Although two supporting witnesses were deemed sufficient when depositions were not contradictory, in practice usually more were summoned and examined under oath.[37] Their testimonies were given at S. Bartolomeo di Rialto, in the patriarchal chancellery, but also could be recorded in a nunnery or at some other private place, such as the witness's home or the vicar's residence. Each point was read to them, and their answers were recorded by a scribe in the Venetian dialect (the questions, when preserved, are in Latin and Italian). Interrogations regarding the allegations in the libel (*interrogatorio speciale*) were commonly preceded by questions about the moral integrity of the witnesses and their relationship with the relevant party (*interrogatorio generale*). Usually these were basic questions about name, parish, age, profession and, in the case of women, marital status, but occasionally they could be more specialised. Sometimes witnesses were questioned on their religious practice and on whether they had confessed their sins. Witnesses had to be impartial in order to guarantee justice; financial dependence on the party for which they testified weakened their credibility because it could imply bribery for false testimonies. If single points (*articoli*) of a libel remained unproven or contested, special witnesses were called who might be able to clarify them. Opposing procurators could cross-examine witnesses to contest their credibility.

After witness interrogations the depositions were read aloud in open court, and each party was entitled to a copy. Until the final verdict was

---

35 See Cristellon, 2003, pp. 853–4.

36 However, witnesses were only interrogated when the defendant had contradicted the *positiones* of the plaintiff. Ibid., p. 852.

37 From 8 June 1310 witnesses who gave false statements in marital disputes at the bishop's court could be prosecuted by the Signori di Notte and the Avogadori di Comun. See Guzzetti, 1998, p. 155.

passed (during the trial an interim verdict might have been issued) both parties could supply additional articles or documentary evidence to strengthen their case (new witnesses also might be summoned). Large numbers of various *dilazioni* (terms assigned by the judge to prepare the next legal step) could lengthen a trial. The Council of Trent had decreed therefore that a suit should be completed within two years (and that *dilazioni* should not be used to delay a final verdict), otherwise litigants could bring the case to a superior court.[38] In practice, however, the Venetian Patriarchal Court worked quickly and effectively, and the average trial lasted less than a year.[39] Marital disputes sometimes were resolved very speedily, with a verdict being passed after two months. Only rarely did trials last up to five or even eight years. Thus, proceedings in the Venetian ecclesiastical court were not, unlike in English Church courts, 'scandalously slow and vexatious'.[40] Although efficiency could vary considerably depending on the complexity of each case, the proceedings generally were quite straightforward because procurators represented their clients in toto in court. The ecclesiastical judge had considerable impact on the length of a trial because he fixed the terms under which witnesses could be produced and contested, and because he could question the importance of further *dilazioni*. Eventually he assigned the terms to conclude, after which time no further evidence could be assembled. If the proceedings reached this last stage, the final verdict was given.

Witness status, credibility and public opinion

When a husband accused his wife of infidelity or a woman claimed that male cruelty made marital life unbearable (or resulted in a forced marriage), these serious allegations had to be proven by credible and reliable witnesses. Early modern legal theorists therefore emphasised that witnesses were one of the most important means in the judicial search for truth.[41] Plaintiffs and defendants had considerable scope to pursue their aims, and by nominating witnesses they contributed tactically to the gathering of proof and hence to the reaching of a final verdict. They could call their own witnesses and challenge those of the

---

[38] Bianchini, 1786, p. 163.

[39] These results are based on a sample of 28 cases in which both the trial and the verdict has come down to us.

[40] Quoted in Ingram, 1990, p. 49. Historian Martin Ingram opposes this view and argues for the efficiency of English Church courts. Ingram, 1990, pp. 49–50.

[41] See Tirabosco, 1636, pp. 28ff. and Ferro, vol. 2, p. 796.

opposing party. The success of a lawsuit, I shall argue, thus depended in part on the tactical naming of witnesses: the more plausible, credible and powerful their testimonies were, the more likely the party was to bring the case to a favourable end.[42]

Witnesses were required to remember specific circumstances of the case: spousal or parental violence, the sexual reputation of wives accused of adultery and the degree of intimacy and familiarity between litigants. Witnesses thus endeavoured to remember even the smallest details, like the bitter tears a daughter had shed when forced into a marriage or other particulars of quarrels between litigants. Because they had differently detailed insights, witnesses could be used selectively to provide evidence or to confirm allegations. In an adultery case from 1614, for example, the defendant Giovanni Verci nominated 16 witnesses and indicated precisely the points on which they should be heard. Some were questioned only about a single argument, which demonstrates that naming witnesses was tactical and to some degree circumstantial.[43] However, only when witness depositions created a uniform picture of conjugal discord or of the sexual misconduct of a woman, for example, could the plaintiff bring the case to a favourable conclusion.

The credibility of witnesses was then measured by comparing other testimonies made during the proceedings. Deviations from other depositions rendered witnesses suspect, and did not help to prove the facts of their testimonies. Contradictory statements thus diminished the chance of success. In Venetian criminal proceedings the reaching of a final verdict largely depended on witness interrogations because a confession by the accused was not required and torture was, as noted earlier, uncommon in legal practice. It was the word of the witnesses, as argued earlier, that was accorded fundamental weight on the judicial scale of Venetian criminal and civil proceedings.[44]

Although witnesses were central in early modern legal culture, their reliability and credibility could vary considerably, with the statements of different witnesses carrying different weight on the scales of justice. In order to determine the substance of witness testimonies, early modern legal scholars looked to separate the wheat from the chaff. Legal theorists warned the court not to put too much weight on female interrogations, for women, construed as the weaker sex, were thought to be less reliable than men because they were more easily seduced.

---

42 For a similar argument see Gowing, 1996, pp. 42–3.

43 ASV, A.d.C., Misc. pen. 158.6: Verci, Giovanni, Cleves Caterina, adulterio, 1614, fols 26r–v.

44 Buganza, 1991, pp. 124–38.

Because their words had less credit 'nobody should be sentenced on the grounds of two depositions made by women.'[45] For Venetian court practice, however, it is hard to assess whether women's depositions were viewed and treated as more precarious (occasionally, even a prostitute was summoned to testify to the sexual reputation of a wife accused of adultery).[46] Female witnesses never were asked whether they understood the meaning of oaths, and they were addressed with the same respect during their interrogations as men were.[47] Witnesses' credibility and reliability was measured individually in each case and varied more from witness to witness than from woman to man. The Secretary of the Executors of Blasphemy, Marc'Antonio Tirabosco, thus advocated distinguishing between *de visu* witnesses who had actually seen the crime and *de scientia* and *de auditu* witnesses who had only heard about a misdeed – a suggestion that usually was followed in legal practice.

In the early eighteenth century Francesco Teobaldo, author of a treatise on legal criminal procedure, held that 'witnesses who deposit according to public opinion [*fama*] should be interrogated how and from whom they have heard what they are deposing and on what fundament hearsay is based, whether it is universal or not.'[48] During the sixteenth and seventeenth centuries secular and ecclesiastical authorities were already well aware of the possibility that litigants had created a 'public opinion' in their favour. Hearsay or gossip was, to a certain degree, manipulable and, naturally, what witnesses had seen with their own eyes was considered more reliable than information they had received from the litigants or heard in the neighbourhood. Thus, only witnesses who testified *de visu* were apparently completely reliable.

Nevertheless, public opinion played a central role in the courtroom. Adulteresses were seldom caught in flagrante delicto – incontestable proof according to Tirabosco, and few witnesses were present when a man and a woman exchanged promises of marriage. Rings or even love letters that could clarify the degree of intimacy or even prove that binding steps towards matrimony had been taken were rarely submitted in lawsuits on the non-fulfilment of a betrothal. Without such material evidence it was one word against another. Moreover, when married

---

45   Ferro, 1845, vol. 2, p. 793.

46   ASV, A.d.C., Misc. pen. 416.13: Brun, Angela, rapita moglie di Nicolò, 1675, not foliated, witness Caterina Padovana.

47   It was the practice in London courtrooms to ask women whether they understood the oath. See Gowing, 1996, p. 50.

48   Teobaldo, 1736, p. 8.

couples were not sharing a home with siblings or other people,[49] women were less likely to be able to call witnesses in their favour who actually had been present when the husband allegedly abused his authority. Therefore, it was relatively more usual to have a greater number of *de auditu* witnesses in these lawsuits, and public opinion was formed in the long term. When these gender and household disputes reached the Venetian courts it was thus the accused woman's sexual reputation and moral conduct or the husband's reputation as head of the household – together with other details neighbours may have observed – that was relevant in civil and criminal proceedings.

When disputes came to court, both male and female plaintiffs thus used public opinion to support their charges. The *fama* – as we learn from a notary interrogating a seventeenth-century defendant accused of breaking a promise of marriage – constituted the 'voice of the populace'.[50] Although it could not prove a crime, as Tirabosco insisted, the *fama* could reveal what men and women in densely populated early modern Venice were saying about moral or criminal misdeeds. The *fama* referred to both the urban neighbourhood assessments and the moral judgements of the community on partners whether married or not. As a product of cultural practice, public opinion conveyed what neighbours thought of each other – it either testified to or contested the honour and reputation of members of Venetian society. Thus, when witnesses referred to the *fama pubblica*, they were expressing not so much their own moral judgement but the urban community's assessment of, for example, a husband's moral integrity or a wife's sexual conduct. During legal proceedings they were encouraged to do so, as the last point in defendants' and plaintiffs' statements was generally to underline that all complaints listed were known publicly (*publica et notoria voce*). The patrician wife Cornelia Zane, for example, argued in her statement that 'it was generally held impossible by neighbours and acquaintances that she could suffer any longer' from the cruelty of her husband.[51] Emphasis on the publicity was aimed at making allegations believable and at pointing to the public evaluation of domestic disputes. Because women and men in the neighbourhood exchanged greetings or stopped to chat about family life, witnesses living in the neighbourhood where a crime was committed or where domestic violence endangered domestic harmony were thought to have the most detailed insights into events –

---

[49] For the exact figures see Chojnacka, 2001, pp. 6–8. Some insights into Venetian household structure are also given in chap. 2 of this volume.

[50] Derosas, 1980, pp. 564–5.

[51] ASPV, C.M., Reg. 92: 29 January 1641, Cornelie Zane cum Joe Battista Salomano, February 1641.

after family members, work colleagues and domestic servants. However, because the latter were seldom part of artisan households, they played only a minor role in the process of gathering witness depositions.[52]

Because they were noticed and commented on by neighbours, friends and relatives outside the physical walls of the house, domestic disputes were not private conflicts. Witnesses would hear a woman screaming or occasionally observe paternal violence through keyholes, and neighbours would intervene in slanderous marital disputes. This social knowledge, together with assumptions, about the moral conduct of women and men easily spread. In court, witnesses referred to the moral judgement of the community through expressions like 'I have heard people mutter about her', 'According to what I have heard ... from the neighbours' and 'People were always ... speaking unkindly about her', which show the extent to which intimate matters were of public concern.[53] Some events were part of the community's collective memory, when large numbers of witnesses might testify. In other instances witnesses remembered their own involvement in the event more precisely. It was thus the witnesses' interrogations that placed allegations of arbitrary domestic violence, female sexual misconduct or failed marriage formation in a wider context by drawing attention to the circumstances of household discord. Because of their involvement, acquaintance or even just physical proximity, neighbours made obvious witnesses in the majority of cases. Their perception of household disputes could influence a hearing and, to a certain degree, the sentence passed.

As depositions reveal, the neighbourhood could even be involved before disputes reached the court. Neighbours were among the first who were informed, whether directly by 'women in crisis', or by the *fama* spread in the neighbourhood. Parishioners intervened directly in marital disputes or rescued wives and daughters from mortal danger. An abusive husband therefore did his best to prevent physical attack being noticed from outside his own walls. Wives alleged in court that their husbands had gagged them and had threatened to murder them if they cried out – thus reducing the number of possible witnesses as far as possible. These measures could conceal single outbursts of temper, but not a marital

---

[52] The actual number of servants in artisan households is, however, difficult to measure. See my discussion in chap. 2, Romano, 1996, pp. 106–17 and Chojnacka, 2001, pp. 17–19.

[53] ASPV, Curia, II, C.M., Reg. 90: 29 July 1630, Matthei de Armatis cum Angela Valery Simolini, witness Joannes q. Petri Garbellator; ASV, A.d.C., Misc. pen. 276, 24: Filarete Lucia, adulterio, 1609, witness Paula q. Giacomo Parisotto; ASV, A.d.C., Misc. pen. 45.4: Ventura, Margarita per adulterio e procurato aborto e Donati Prete Giovanni, adulterio, fol. 3r.

crisis in the long run. Sometimes the litigating family members themselves informed neighbours about the particulars of their disagreements. When domestic harmony was at risk, confidants (parish and family members) were asked to mediate and to negotiate; later, in court, if their attempts at restoring household peace and harmony had failed, they made strong and reliable witnesses.

Neighbourly witnesses were not only a source of support for women – in these face-to-face societies parish members also exerted social control and expressed moral judgements against women (and against men, as we have already seen) on a day-to-day basis. The neighbourhood, as the place for male and female interaction, inevitably also increased residents' social knowledge about neighbours and their moral integrity in the densely populated Venetian parishes.[54] Thus, if a man and a woman were attracted to each other, parishioners observed growing intimacy during courtship rituals[55] and whether the courted woman was faithful to only one man. Before prospective grooms were introduced into the households of their future brides, the women occasionally stood on the balcony while the men courted them from the street – a practice that transformed the courting ritual into a public act. The balcony thus allowed women to make contacts with the outside world while remaining within the household. This particular 'private' space carried an ambivalent meaning. It not only allowed the neighbourhood to participate and observe more directly the life of female parishioners; it also enabled men to address women. In S. Fosca, for example, a married woman had been observed daily 'standing on the balcony ... laughing with everybody publicly and casually' – actions a witness judged to be inappropriate for a 'good and honourable woman'.[56]

The movements, behaviour and gestures that married women exchanged with other men did, too, not go unnoticed and were interpreted with care. Because contacts were usually made in the parish, neighbours could easily observe a married woman's contacts with other men. Witnesses testified to the interest generated among neighbours by the development of physical familiarity and, eventually, intimacy. Venetian urban structure favoured this level of social control. In the city's narrow streets balconies and windows offered direct views into

---

[54] In my opinion the neighbourhood as a place of daily interaction and (female) support has been overstressed in Venetian historiography at the expense of daily conflicts, and in particular social discipline, which was also excercised in these communities. See Chojnacka, 2001, pp. 62–4 and 138–9 where she emphasises the networks of support.

[55] A case in point is ASPV, Curia, II, Reg. 93: 8 July 1652, Ottavio Garbarotto cum Sebastiana Buffetto, fols 11r–13r.

[56] ASV, A.d.C., Misc. pen. 268. 21: Romani-Muti, Margarita, adulterio 1670, fol. 8r.

neighbouring homes, sometimes even into bedrooms. In 1640 the washerwoman Marietta Lavandara testified to the adultery of one Laura, who had run away from her husband. She had actually witnessed the adulterous act; as she revealed in court, she had 'seen [the servant Paolo] in bed with her on the occasion of being at my altana'.[57] Other witnesses had observed suspicious conversations or secret meetings, which served as strong evidence of sexual misconduct.

Even the general exchange of words between men and women came under scrutiny. Angela, the wife of Matteo de Armatis, had been seen 'near the bridge di Mori in the parish of S. Marcilian ... talking with a young man who is the son of Gerolamo ... a linen seller.'[58] Even if residents emphasised that nobody came to visit a suspected wife (thus testifying to her innocence), it is nevertheless revealed how closely the neighbourhood observed dubious conversations, nightly meetings and suspicious contacts. By memorising the details of parish life, in court it later became apparent who had been an attentive observer of neighbourhood life and who, moreover, was regarded as a good member of the moral Christian community.

Because the community had, to different degrees, been informed about neighbourhood conflicts and had mediated in marital disputes or admonished cruel husbands and unfaithful wives before matters reached the courts, their witness depositions were never 'neutral' but were shaped by individual involvement and personal concern. Called to court, they had to reflect again on events; to testify thus required a certain amount of self-consciousness and critical self-reflection. Witnesses therefore had to develop their own position with regard to the conflicting narratives in marital litigation. Had they not done so earlier, during the legal proceedings witnesses also had to decide whom they were more likely to believe: for example, the woman claiming that she had consented to premarital sex only after receiving a promise of marriage, or the man denying that he had ever proposed. Witnesses thus had to decide which litigant to support in the legal battle.[59] They then had to recall the precise circumstances, the exact words that were spoken and the actions that followed in order to make their story plausible: testimonies are full of (apparently) authentic details. Thus, testifying in court occasionally had its own dynamic, and witnesses responded individually, however precise the questions. Despite careful

57 ASPV, Curia, II, C.M., Reg. 92: 13 February 1640, Michaelis Barbaro cum Laura Fabrity, witness Marietta Lavandara.

58 Ibid., Reg. 90: 29 July 1630, Matthei de Armatis cum Angela Valery Simolini, witness Petro q. Bergomensis.

59 On this argument see Gowing, 1996, p. 233.

attempts to limit personal interest in court, witnesses clearly favoured one party over the other. They were directly asked in court who had 'right' in the lawsuit and willingly expressed their prejudices, hidden assumptions and moral judgements. But still they had to argue coherently if they wished to be supportive. In all likelihood witnesses were conscious that the more coherently they presented their arguments in court, the more likely judges would be to believe their version of events. Although the legal process shaped the way stories were told and evidence was assembled, it left considerable scope for the actors in court. The power of narratives in courts, it has been argued, depended in part on their structure: the better a story was told, the more likely it was to be believed.[60]

From the spoken to the written word

The discussion so far has shown that early modern legal culture was complex, with highly developed processes, and that plaintiffs and defendants relied on 'prejudicial' public opinion that had been formed before marital disputes reached the courts. This section is concerned with legal texts and suggests ways in which these 'biased' sources may enrich our understanding of the codes of marriage culture in early modern Venice.

When plaintiffs and defendants were interrogated in court, or when witnesses spoke in detail about marital disputes and people's reputations, their words were recorded. Because we depend entirely on court transcripts of speeches delivered before and in the courtroom, attention should be paid to the process of transforming spoken words into written text. In recording the words delivered by plaintiffs, defendants and witnesses in the judicial forum, the scribe might have 'Italianised' depositions made in the Venetian dialect. Some trial documents have been copied, and many of the original features of depositions may have been lost in this process. Still, they do preserve some characteristics of the verbal testimonies, which were incorporated into legal texts in order to provide conclusive evidence and to make them appear authentic. Sentences are extremely long and punctuated only by casual commas. Interrogations and depositions were normally written in the first person, whereas direct speech was converted into the third person if the witness being questioned remembered the precise words exchanged. Judges themselves were concerned that interrogations

---

[60] Ibid., pp. 56 and 232–62.

and witness depositions were accurate and complete. The defendant Biasio Savelli, for instance, was asked 'to recount what he wants, everything will be recorded.'[61] Thus, many depositions are remarkably individual and consist (at least in part) of a verbatim report. Accuracy in transcription was essential because a copy was given to the other party at a certain stage of the trial.

Depositions made by witnesses thus formed part of a predominantly oral culture. They were never neutral, even when witnesses endeavoured to remember the precise circumstances of events. When neighbours advised a father to use his power with moderation, or if they witnessed extreme violence against a disobedient daughter, they remembered and memorised such details according to the expectations of contemporary culture; retold in court, the recollections were reshaped yet again.[62] Although it is generally assumed that witnesses relied on lawyers who suggested the right words to them, I agree with Miranda Chaytor that legal narratives carried emotional weight for witnesses,[63] especially when they themselves had been involved in the domestic dramas.

While witness testimonies had been shaped by legal knowledge only to a small degree,[64] litigants were more likely to be advised on how to behave during their interrogations. This is not to argue that legal advisors prompted every line that plaintiffs and defendants delivered; but they might have suggested a general tone of argumentation and given advice on which details of the conflict were best concealed in oral hearings. Although this legal influence is hard to measure in the interrogations and testimonies, it is highly visible in the written statements. These legal documents were usually well composed and could, in criminal cases, also include rhetorical expressions like 'We are informed about the crime, now we need to find the criminal.'[65] Latin quotations were sometimes inserted – proof that in criminal proceedings lawyers, and not the accused parties themselves, had formulated the text. The selective process underlying the written statements of both litigants was therefore considerable in two ways. Both parties had time to reflect on events outside the courtroom (as had the many witnesses called to court), a form of self-reflection that shaped the legal statements. When they retold their version of events in court – to a

---

61 ASV, A.d.C., Misc. pen. 310.15: Savelli, Biasio, deflorazione, 1644, fols 55r–v.
62 On this argument see Gowing, 1996, pp. 54–5 and Chaytor, 1995, pp 378–9.
63 Chaytor, 1995, p. 380.
64 For a different assessment see Ferraro, 2001, p. 25.
65 ASV, A.d.C., Misc. pen. 141.16: Bertocco, Domenico, deflorazione, 1639, first page of defendant's statement.

lawyer or procurator or, later, in their interrogations – their narratives were influenced by personal 'strategic and unconscious reshapings' of the events. They were subject to selective recollection and represented the narrator's own interpretation.[66] Moreover, with the involvement of legal advisors, these narratives were rearranged in the statements. In building up the written statement it was most probably procurators (or lawyers, in criminal proceedings) who suggested how best to present the case. Thus, the narratives were shared products of litigant and legal advisor: the plaintiff and the defendant told their versions of the conflict, and these versions were then formulated, organised and arranged.

Because of a highly developed legal process and because litigants had to fulfil the requirements of criminal and canon law if they wished to win their case, these statements were often standardised. The argumentation was not always gender-specific, as annulment cases in particular demonstrate. Although female plaintiffs clearly outnumbered male plaintiffs at the Patriarchal Court, both sexes arranged their statements exclusively around the impediment of fear and force in order to prove that a marriage had been contracted invalidly. With the help of their lawyers, children in court composed dramatic and well-constructed accusations in which the undesired marriage was presented as the result of fear and force. Although offspring expressly referred to their own will, their accusations nevertheless evoke the image of their powerlessness in the face of parents' tyranny: successful resistance was virtually impossible. In this way canon law shaped the way family disputes could be addressed in court.

Although the written statements are well-constructed legal artefacts, they do have considerable gaps, however coherent they might appear to be. The reshaping of events meant that additional, legally relevant information might have been suppressed, whereas other significant facts, such as the excessive use of force against wives and children, for example, were emphasised. Through their legal expertise, advisors were well aware of the arguments that were most likely to convince the judges and, arguably, also selected the evidence to be given. These legally relevant facts were listed point by point without reference to the actual context in which the violence against a wife or daughter, for example, had taken place. Legal documents highlight deeds at the expense of social or emotional context, providing us with an extraordinarily fragmented version of domestic and emotional conflicts. Only interrogations and depositions by litigants and witnesses tend to

---

[66] Narratives in early modern London courts, as Laura Gowing has argued, were shaped by set models and literary tropes from outside the courtroom: Gowing, 1996, pp. 54–8, quotation on pp. 54–5.

counter-balance these gaps; oral hearings offered the possibility to develop more fully the wider context of filial, marital and parental behaviour. Because allegations often produced counter-statements (and thus more witness depositions), these legal documents are multivocal: they provide us with conflicting narratives of household dramas that disturbed marital and parental harmony, tested conjugality and endangered neighbourhood peace.

Legal documents (written statements in particular) were composed, as I have argued, according to the requirements of canon and criminal law. Still, in building up their case, litigants (with the help of lawyers or procurators) and witnesses not only were arguing within early modern legal culture, but also were expressing their sentiments, understandings and moral judgements of proper gender behaviour and marital conjugality in so far as they defined their ideas of proper filial, paternal or spousal behaviour. Incorporated into legal texts, these moral judgements shaped the legal narratives of litigants and witnesses, making contemporary categories of gendered norms the basis of legal discourse.[67]

Recent research has explored the ways in which this institutional framework, the courtroom, shaped the way in which gender conflicts were represented. Female plaintiffs, as has been argued, relied on stereotypes of womanhood when using the judicial public forum: conflicts with the opposite sex were thus addressed in terms of female weakness and male aggression. In this sense the courtroom was a place where women could try to achieve their aims.[68] Such strategic negotiating only worked within the realms of a system of moral values and norms that were shared by the judicial authority, thus shaping the way conflicts were represented in court. To talk about sexual violence against women, for example, was only possible by stressing the male will as responsible for the 'realised sexual act' and by underlying the honourable behaviour of the woman at the same time. Thus, the legal conventions of the court not only shaped the way in which conflicts were addressed but also influenced the details that had to be suppressed, in this case the 'lust' of women.[69] This dialectic of power led men and women in court to reconstruct their experiences differently.[70]

Whereas judges, in sentencing these cases, had to decide who had 'right', historians are not bound to make these decisions. Because

---

[67] On this argument see in particular Gleixner, 1994, pp. 211–19 and Burghartz, 1999b, pp. 25–7.

[68] Habermas, 1992, especially pp. 110–11.

[69] Burghartz, 1999b, pp. 41–56.

[70] Roper, 1994, pp. 53–78.

depositions were always made within a cultural frame of interpretation, they convey, despite their individuality and diversity, dominant understandings of gendered morality and, moreover, collective marital expectations through their description of the opposite: an archetype of what sexual behaviour and family and marital life are not expected to be.[71] Thus, historians can unravel the buried moral values and hidden assumptions that stood behind domestic dramas and slanderous disputes. In this perspective legal narratives can be an extremely rich resource that also reflect the dynamics of parish life and social relations.[72]

Depositions also demonstrate the appropriation of dominant Christian values and norms as well as social attitudes towards sexual misconduct, marriage and its disputes. Contemporary marriage culture, such as a couple's conjugality and a wife's loyalty to her husband, was intrinsically linked with the stories told in court. In these cases the Christian model of marriage, with its stress on indissolubility, was shared by the populace. It motivated many attempts at reconciliation in order to ensure (unsuccessfully, as it turned out) that future legal steps would not have to be taken. Only in the most extreme situations, for example when a woman's life was in danger, or sometimes when female sexual misconduct endangered marital conjugality, was the neighbourhood split over its perception of the woman and the future steps to take.

Despite the 'biased' character of legal documents, they still provide us with multivocal accounts of the lives of ordinary parents, children, husbands and wives in moments of conflict and exceptional crises. They take us back to the world and thoughts of illiterate women and men, to their perceptions and knowledge of moral norms and values propagated by the Church and the state and, finally, to their understanding of a marriage culture in early modern Venice which historians would otherwise be unable to recapture.

---

[71] Farge and Foucault, 1989, p. 27.

[72] Rublack, 1999, p. 255 and Muir and Ruggiero, 1994, pp. 226–36, who equally stress the many possibilities of legal sources.

PART TWO

Couples in Court: The Church and Marital Disputes

CHAPTER FIVE

Children and Parents: Consensual Marriage and Parental Authority

In early modern societies, the 'proper' making of the conjugal bond involved a 'precarious balance' between the canonical model of consensual marriage and parental authority.[1] From the twelfth century onwards, the doctrine of consensualism was firmly established in canon law, which made the freely exchanged consent of spouses the essential condition for the establishment of marriage.[2] Without any formalities or the parents' consent, a couple could freely declare to be husband and wife, though there were many local restrictions.[3] With the Catholic reform movement this ecclesiastical conception of a consensual marriage, which posed a considerable challenge to the secular ideology of household hierarchy and, in particular, the principle of patriarchal rule and obedience, was readdressed in legal discourse. Catholic reformers at various sessions of the Council of Trent hotly debated the influence of parents on their children's choice of spouse. Whereas advocates of consensual marriage insisted on the free will of the couple, opponents defended the interests of parents and demanded that 'clandestine marriages' be declared invalid. Discussions were complicated further by the double meaning of the term 'clandestine marriage', for it referred to marriages contracted without the knowledge of parents and to those contracted informally.[4] The Council of Trent's *Tametsi* decree of 1563 finally reaffirmed the sacramental nature of Catholic marriage and held the consent of the couple to be fundamental to the validity of the union.[5] Chapter 1 of the session on the

---

[1] Harrington, 1995, p. 169.

[2] The canonist Peter Lombard (c. 1100–60) had even argued that the word of present consent alone made a valid marriage, in contrast to Gratian (died 1159?), who maintained that consent expressed by two persons had to be followed by the physical consummation; both canonists, however, agreed that, as a sacrament, marriage was 'dependent only on the consent of the participants for its efficacy'. See Harrington, 1995, pp. 55–6.

[3] Which defined 'the licity of a marriage with various formalities and possible civil and ecclesiastical punishments', ibid., p. 57.

[4] On clandestine marriages see the seminal article by Gottlieb, 1980, pp. 49–83. On the abolition of clandestine marriages at the Council of Trent see Zarri, 1996, pp. 437–84.

[5] The Tridentine decrees were not accepted by the French crown, which insisted on parental consent as a condition for the validity of a marriage.

'Reformation of Matrimony' emphasised the right to marry without parental consent. The free consent of sons and daughters was essential for a valid marriage and became central to canon law after the promulgation of the Council's decrees.[6] Even though children were expected to ask respectfully for their parents' agreement, parental consent was not necessary to validate a marriage.

Although this view of marriage as an undertaking based on individual consent was already well established in Catholic tradition, the Council of Trent not only reiterated its importance: it went a step further in 'defining the exercise of free will'. Canon 9 of the Council's session on marriage explicitly restricted the measures that civil authorities could take in these cases – namely, that they should neither impose penalties nor use threats to force a couple to marry.[7] While the Church deprived parents and local government authorities of their control over marriage conventions, in Venice local government authorities reinforced the positions of parents and thus secular control. In order to prevent ill-considered marriages contracted without parental knowledge from endangering the social, economic and political interests of Venetian families, civil law accorded parents the right to disinherit their children. In placing the will of parents above the mutual consent of children, the state attempted to undermine the consensualist doctrine of the Church. This parental right granted by civil law constituted a considerable challenge to canon law and to children who were not obeying their elders. According to Volker Hunecke it practically devalued the Tridentine principle of free choice concerning marital partner.[8] But although Venetian parents enjoyed effective legal means to exert pressure during the making of marriage, the cases that reached the Patriarchal Court nevertheless demonstrated that canon law offered important corrective measures against strict parental rule. The authority of parents, legal guardians and relatives could be undermined by the legal agency that canon law had accorded to children facing forced marriages. In theory, as John Bossy noted:

> The Council of Trent ... enacted a matrimonial code which ran counter to the collectivist and contractual traditions of kinship morality by invalidating marriages not performed in public before the parish priest, insisting on individual liberty in the choice of the partners, and affirming that marriages contracted by minors without parental consent were valid, though not lawful.[9]

---

6 Canons and Decrees, p. 123. For the earlier period, cf. Donahue, 1983, pp. 144–58.
7 Seed, 1988, pp. 33–4 and Dean, 1998, pp. 89–94, for the laws requiring parental consent in pre-Tridentine Italy.
8 Hunecke, 1995, p. 141.
9 Bossy, 1970, pp. 56–7.

The structural tensions outlined so far become explicit in the actual making of marriage. When daughters and sons were to marry in late sixteenth- and seventeenth-century Venice, conflicting concepts about the establishment of marriage had to be overcome and negotiated; but it was when children opposed or even contradicted their parental and familial marital plans that the precise implications of those conflicting conceptions of marriage emerged most clearly. However, the family disagreements that could arise between the individual wishes of children and the obedience these children had to pay to their superiors had not been resolved through the Tridentine decree. As Patricia Seed has argued, the Council had not clarified sufficiently the extent to which 'parents could exert control over marriage'.[10] Parents were not to force their offspring into marriage, but were children then allowed to put personal preference and even emotional fulfilment before the marital plans of their families? Leading Italian Church jurists of the late sixteenth century argued in favour of parental authority, although they did not go as far as Protestant reformers, who had placed parental authority over the individual wishes of children. Prospero Fabani and Roberto Bellarminio, for example (the latter had studied theology in Padua), held that 'children had to bow to their parents' wishes', and only when children were 'ordered to marry unjustly' could they reject the marriage. Moreover, in selecting the future groom, it was the parents who were accorded greater authority.[11]

Apart from differing contemporary legal discourses, forced marriages further led to questions concerning the role of the parish priests. Following the Tridentine decrees Venetian parish priests began to assume a key role in the solemnisation of marriages through the enforcement of the principle of marriage as a public act. Although the priests were obliged to ask the bride and groom about their mutual consent (as the decrees demanded),[12] the cases that reached the Patriarchal Court show that it was not always expressed freely and willingly by couples about to marry. Young Venetian daughters, and occasionally sons,[13] would respond only reluctantly to the question and

---

10 Seed, 1988, p. 35.

11 An exception to that rule is the Spanish canonist Tomás Sánchez, who placed children's wishes first. Only in exceptional cases, when the establishment of peace or reasons of state were a concern in royal families, did parents have the right to reject a child's choice. Cf. Seed, 1988, p. 36; on Italian jurists see Chojnacki, 2000a, pp. 11–12 and 175–6; for this debate among pre-Tridentine lawyers and jurists see Dean, 1998, pp. 93–4.

12 Canons and Decrees, p. 123.

13 For the years 1571–1697 only a handful of cases are preserved in the sample Causarum Matrimoniorum in which a man claimed to have been forced into a marriage against his will.

were depicted by witnesses as crying, melancholic, pale or confused. Some freshly wed brides (see Figure 5.1) were said to have left the church 'trembling as if they had fever'.[14] Yet the apparent existence of impediments such as fear and force did not prevent the priests from celebrating the marriage. In the cases debated at the ecclesiastical tribunal, few priests had expressed their astonishment or had refused to solemnise forced marriages.[15] Lawsuits seeking the annulment of marriages therefore enhance our understanding not only of the conflicting meanings of the establishment of the conjugal bond, but also of the application of the Tridentine decrees.

Crucial to the application of the Tridentine decrees was the professional training of the clergy. Traditionally this was based on parochial schools supplemented early on by the much better organised

5.1   Young bride (Grevembroch, *Gli Abiti de' Veneziani*)

---

14 ASPV, Curia, II, F.C., Reg. 34: 9 August 1618, Felicite filie Anastasy de Venetiy cum Matheo Fada, witness Lucrezia q. Bernardin Cocco, 22 February 1620, fol. 11r.

15 A case in point is ASPV, Curia, II, C.M., Reg. 90: 4 May 1628, Joanette q.m Valentini Hortulani cum Francisco Fabrilignario Arsenatus, fol. 31v.

schools of the *sestieri*. Following the decrees new institutions, notably the so-called seminary, were established in Venice, albeit slowly.[16] This might explain in part why priests were ill-informed about impediments to marriage under canon law, and why they were – especially shortly after the implementation of the new ordinances – so ignorant of correct procedures that they were unsure about the number of witnesses necessary for the solemnisation of a marriage or about the place where a marriage should be celebrated, resulting in sacerdotal blessings being given at homes and not in *facie ecclesiae*, as the Council of Trent had commanded. Even in mid-seventeenth-century Venice a priest was occasionally unsure about whether he had presided over an engagement or a marriage.[17] At the end of the sixteenth and the beginning of the seventeenth centuries in particular, parish clerics apparently were not a reliable source for distressed children who could not place their trust in the public ritual of marriage, and this situation first changed only after the newly available professional training bore fruit. Despite these uncertainties in the establishment of marriages and despite the secular legislative efforts to regain control over the formation of marriage, by according spouses the legal means to make their unhappy marital circumstances a legal case, the Church sided with children against the marital wishes of their elders. By analysing failed marriage formation, this chapter also highlights the legal means that canon law offered children to reinforce a consensual marriage (by invalidating those which had been contracted forcibly); it contextualises the theory of consensualism within a popular marital culture and emphasises the complex household dynamics during forced marriage formation. In Catholic Venice, the sacramental nature of marriage (and hence the free will to marry) could be defended at a higher level if children brought a lawsuit to the attention of the Patriarchal Court.

Household order, unwanted marriages and the neighbourhood

When it came to the making of marriages, the greatest enemy of children was, thus, the patriarchal authority that civil legal culture had bestowed on parents. Male and female children stood under the *patria potestas* of the household's ruler, a power used to educate and to correct his

---

16 See Prodi, 1973, pp. 420–21 and Tramontin, 1965, pp. 363–77.

17 ASPV, Curia, II, C.M., Reg. 93: 12 November 1654, Jacobi Maccarini cum Lucretia Bianchi, testimony of Hieronimis Cappareus. Moreover, in the first half of the seventeenth century priests who were not from the resident parish of the couple (as the Council of Trent required) were still performing the marital ritual. See Canons and Decrees, p. 184.

offspring.[18] Legally, the *patria potestas* was not limited to the children alone but also included their goods, as the father was the usufructuary of the presents and bequests that his unemancipated sons and unmarried daughters received. Only upon the death of the head of the household did the *patria potestas* end,[19] unless a public emancipation of the sons, through which they acquired their full judicial capacity, had been made beforehand.[20] Daughters were not inevitably emancipated through marriage, as the passive power of the father coexisted with the more active power of the husband.[21] Even though the patriarchal power (*patria potestas*) limited the autonomy of children, it nevertheless entailed paternal responsibilities and duties. As the head of the household, the father had to take care of the material and spiritual well-being of his children, which demanded different methods of education according to their age, sex and social class.[22] According to the eighteenth-century legal historian Marco Ferro, the *patria potestas* was intended both to protect children during their childhood and to guide them during their adolescence; it was to be based on mutual respect and affection after their marriage.[23]

These principles of parental rule and household order were firmly grounded in everyday life; they were reflected in Venetian popular marital culture precisely when children had circumvented the influence of their elders in making marital choices. Their importance is illustrated through the reaction of the elderly Bartolomeo Cottini, who had a supportive and caring relationship with his adolescent daughter Bona. When he discovered that Bona had married a carpenter without his knowledge or consent, advice or involvement, not only had a relationship based on mutual trust been destroyed, but Cottini's authority had been undermined.[24] In such situations it was,

---

18 Tamassia, 1971, p. 248.

19 Kuehn, 1982, p. 10. According to medieval and Roman law, the *patria potestas* covered all legitimate descendants of the male line. 'Thus, a grandfather (*avus*) who remained *paterfamilias* to his sons was also *paterfamilias* to his grandsons, the children of his sons; and the *paterfamilias* retained his *patria potestas* over them, no matter what their age'. Ibid., p. 11.

20 Tamassia, 1971, p. 203. According to Ferro, 1845, vol. 1, p. 672, emancipation in Venice was not a public act. For the actual practice of emancipation in Venice during the late seventeenth and eighteenth centuries, see Hunecke, 1995, pp. 271ff.

21 Kuehn, 1991, pp. 197–211.

22 For a detailed description of the education of a patrician son, see Frigo, 1985, pp. 116–22.

23 Unfortunately, Ferro gives no concrete age when referring to the different life stages. Ferro, 1845, vol. 2, pp. 453–6.

24 ASPV, Curia, II, C.M., Reg. 86: 19 April 1619, Bona fia Bartolomeo Cottini cum Francesco di Theoldi.

unsurprisingly, children and not parents who were believed to be the cause of disharmony. These daughters were perceived as putting personal preferences above the marital plans of their parents and the social and economic well-being of their family.[25] Their behaviour implied an assertiveness wholly inappropriate to their age, their social position and their sex and, as we will see, endangered the peace of the household and of the neighbourhood.

Advice to respect parental will was thus usually the first reaction to disobedience by offspring. By highlighting their duty to be modest and to respect parental authority, neighbours reminded young women of the limitations on freedom of choice, for inexperienced girls needed advice in choosing their marital partners. This was akin to the duty and the right of responsible parents to choose marital partners sensibly and carefully. Parents had to ensure that children overwhelmed by passion and improper motivations were prevented from entering unsuitable marriages. In some early modern cities, such as Augsburg, 'ill-considered youthful marriages' were even made 'responsible for the city's economic and social misery'.[26] In an act of balancing controversies, the Council of Trent had decreed that children should seek the advice of their parents, although parental consent did not affect the validity of the marriage.

What many female plaintiffs lamented when pleading at the Patriarchal Court was, however, the abruptness with which parents or guardians had proposed a spouse and immediately demanded their consent without allowing them time for due reflection. Daughters complained about parents who had made wedding plans for them without their knowledge and without giving them the right to decide when (or whether) they wanted to marry. As we shall see, gradual familiarity and intimacy between a man and a woman were central to early modern Venetian courtship rituals and culture.[27] The young women who pleaded at the Patriarchal Court claimed that they had been denied these important experiences. Coerced marriages then allegedly took place unexpectedly (during the night for example), without the bride's prior knowledge and sometimes without the bride even having met the groom. Children who were denied the chance of participating in their own marriage arrangements would accuse their parents of not respecting their wishes and of not fulfilling their roles as caring guardians.[28]

---

25 A different perspective on parent–child relations is provided by lawsuits over broken engagements, when parents and children would be united in court against a man who had abandoned a daughter without honouring his promise of marriage (see chap. 8).

26 Roper, 1993, p. 163.

27 For a wider discussion of courtship rituals see chap. 8.

28 Judicious parents, by contrast, were sensitive and involved their children in the

Not only when parental influence was simply circumvented, but even more so when daughters were in open disagreement with their parents' choice of groom, did the neighbourhood criticise the behaviour of these young women. In particular when the prospective groom was thought to be acceptable, resistance by offspring to marrying was perceived as exceeding the established family roles and structures within ordered households. It was not the consensuality of marriage that was highlighted at this early stage of marriage formation but rather parental authority and juvenile deference and submission. Members of the civic community thus advised children to comply with the wishes of their parents and not put the ruling principle of Venetian society at risk. Men and women alike would admonish an obstreperous daughter to marry the man that her parents had proposed – even when she threatened to harm herself.[29] Disobedient children were an open challenge to their superiors' ability to rule, as their behaviour implied that parents or guardians had not chosen the future groom carefully. Male and female neighbours, relatives, friends or others would admonish wilful daughters for their disobedience and support parental authority, even when the marriage broke down shortly after its solemnisation. Blanca, the widow of a Venetian glassmaker, for example, still firmly supported a father's decision even after the couple had been separated informally for some 15 years. Despite the fact that the marriage had collapsed long ago, the witness Blanca emphasised that the father had been right in forcing his adolescent daughter to marry because the groom was, after all, an 'honourable young man'.[30]

When parents and children were in open conflict, the will of the children and parental authority constituted forceful opponents, disrupting domestic and neighbourhood life. Neighbours, friends or relatives often expressed their disregard for disobedient daughters or even intervened in domestic disputes – and, indeed, were asked for help by the litigant families themselves. Parents hoped that a third party might break the resistance of a disobedient child more readily, whereas a desperate

---

marriage formalities, as demonstrated in one case. Around 1608 Joanetta Hortolani fell in love with Giovanni Calafaro, the son of a mariner. Although Joanetta's father Valentin had approved her choice of groom without hesitation, he was concerned because Joanetta was only 13. Valentin begged the future groom to postpone the marriage until she was 15. See ASPV, Curia, II, C.M., Reg. 90: 4 May 1628, Joanette q.m Valentini Hortulani cum Francisco Fabrilignario Arsenatus, fols 32r–34r.

[29] ASPV, Curia, II, C.M., Reg. 74: 10 January 1579, Morosine filie Leonardi Pectinary cum Joanne Maria Pectinario, fol. 24v. According to the witness Margherita, Morosina had threatened to drown herself.

[30] ASPV, Curia, II, C.M., Reg. 90: 20 April 1629, Pauline filie Joannis Sutoris cum Laurentio Comelli, fols 3r–v.

daughter would plead with trusted acquaintances to persuade her authoritarian parents to desist from their marital plans and to moderate their use of physical coercion. These go-betweens advised and mediated between children and their parents and expressed moral judgements on the use of force, for example, or on the behaviour of wilful adolescent girls. In court their depositions would dwell on the means of physical and mental coercion and filial resistance. In commenting on disobedient children and authoritarian parents, they revealed their understanding of household hierarchy and their ignorance or disregard of the required consensuality of children. Thus, witness statements allow one to get a sense of contemporary notions of patriarchal authority and the adoption and appropriation of theologian values such as consensuality.

A case in point is that of Morosina, the young daughter of Leonardo Pectinary, from the parish of S. Giminian. In 1579 Morosina sued her husband Gianmaria at the Patriarchal Court; he was the son of Battista Trevisani and a journeyman in her father's workshop. She pleaded for an annulment of their marriage, which, she alleged, had been contracted by force. One Guglielmo, a witness on her behalf, affirmed that Morosina had rejected her father's plan for her to marry Gianmaria while they were all dining together. Although testifying that Morosina had clearly expressed her unwillingness to marry, Guglielmo had not interfered – apparently he sided with the father and his right to rule. In court, Guglielmo recalled how, approximately two years earlier, he had exhorted and admonished the disobedient child to bow to her father's wishes as somebody 'who had raised her'.[31] Rumours quickly spread both about a child's unwillingness to accept new marital circumstances and about violent parents. A 40-year-old married woman by the name of Camilla testified that she had reproached Morosina after the marriage for her ongoing repugnance towards her 'husband'. During the night the entire neighbourhood could hear her calling for the devil when the husband attempted to consummate the marriage. Camilla reported in court how she had visited Morosina one morning and had berated the young woman with the words, 'Are you not ashamed of your behaviour? The entire neighbourhood can hear you yelling.' Yet her visit was not made to show compassion, but rather to exert moral pressure on Morosina to accept her new domestic circumstances.[32] This young woman was perceived as having been not only disrespectful towards her parents, but also disobedient towards her husband.

Female wilfulness and assertiveness could, then, endanger domestic

---

[31] ASPV, Curia, II, C.M., Reg. 74: 10 January 1579, Morosine filie Leonardi Pectinary cum Joanne Maria Pectinario, fol. 4r.
[32] Ibid., fol. 23r.

hierarchy in the long term. Fathers, as head of the household and prime agents in the formation of marriages, were also vulnerable in their authority. When marriages were arranged they first vouched for its effectuation with their word. A daughter's resistance could therefore threaten her father's reputation as head of the household if he was unable to enforce his authority. Fathers were aware of the delicate nature of domestic disputes and would forcefully try to regain power. In these situations they would loudly demand obedience from obstreperous daughters, using exclamations like 'I want you to marry him',[33] 'I want you to do what I command'[34] and 'I'm the boss',[35] which vividly express the will to exercise power. Contemporary moralists depicted the *ordered* household, but these cases highlight the domestic *disorders* that arose when children (particularly daughters) behaved disrespectfully. When tensions over the choice of groom threatened the 'natural' hierarchy of household life, parents or guardians ordered deference from their offspring. They had to demand obedience in order to avoid domestic discord.

Parental authority was therefore not always immediate; it had to be restored and exercised. The obedience demanded by parents was an expression of their authority; its biggest obstacle was the free will that the Church accorded to the couple entering into marriage. It not only endangered their authority but was also a threat to male honour (which was based on successful rule over women). The above-mentioned Leonardo Pectinary, for example, had, according to his daughter, threatened her with the devil 'if you cause me this dishonour' by not agreeing to the marriage.[36]

Whereas Leonardo Pectinary finally regained authority over his child, the wealthy silk merchant Raimondo Vidali from S. Maria Formosa was less fortunate and more clearly experienced the limits of his authority. In 1606 he had attempted to arrange the marriage of his daughter Virginia to Giovanni Battista Cigala. This business (*negotio*) promised to be lucrative: although the dowry was despite dowry restrictions enormously high (10 000 ducats), Virginia's brother Alessandro would receive the conspicuous sum of 14 000 ducats by simultaneously marrying Isabella, most likely Cigala's sister. Vidali considered the

---

[33] ASPV, Curia, II, C.M., Reg. 74: 4 November 1579, Francisci de Vulgaris cum Ursetta de Coltis, not foliated, 27 November 1579.

[34] ASPV, Curia, II, C.M., Reg. 90: 1 July 1628, Victorie Cesana cum Joe Baptista Barbaro, fol. 21v. I have changed the quotation slightly.

[35] ASPV, Curia, II, C.M., Reg. 88: 20 September 1625, Magdalene de Franciscis cum Alysio Bonamico, fol. 4v.

[36] ASPV, Curia, II, C.M., Reg. 74: 10 January 1579, Morosine filie Leonardi Pectinary cum Joanne Maria Pectinario, fol. 9r.

marriage to be an excellent match. Cigala was a rich young merchant and had, additionally, promised to pay 2000 ducats as a counter-dowry. In Vidali's deposition, made at his house in S. Maria Formosa in January 1611, he admitted that Virginia had refused to consent to marry Cigala from the beginning. With tears in her eyes, Vidali recalled, she had told him 'that she did not want [Cigala] and that she would never have a good life'. Her resistance continued and Vidali had to admit his loss of power, since he 'did not know what to do'. He begged Virginia earnestly to consent to the marriage, otherwise it 'would be the cause of [his] ruin'.[37] Pietro Michieli, a merchant from the same parish who was involved in this family disagreement, emphasised that a failed marriage would be the 'cause for the dishonour and the ruin of both families'.[38] Here Vidali's reputation was also at stake: his credibility was fundamental to his profession because business between merchants was often preceded by a verbal agreement before being fixed in a written contract. The same was true for a marriage. His loss of control over his child therefore had wide-ranging consequences for his professional credibility and his honour.

As Virginia alleged in court, Vidali had used this concept of honour to put moral pressure on her, saying that 'he had already given his word and in case the marriage would not be contracted, he would not dare to go to the piazza or to meet other merchants and this would be his ruin and his death alike.'[39] If marriage between high-ranking Venetian families was seen above all as a business deal, its success was evidence of the shrewdness and credibility of the instigator. In the same way, its failure meant a loss of credibility and honour which threatened his livelihood.

Spousal and maternal influence and power

Vidali's desperation was increased by the fact that he could not count on his wife. The informal power that wives had within the household and in the relationship with their husbands is not to be underestimated. Although household hierarchies were structured in terms of power and obedience, individuals (husbands, wives and children) nevertheless could fulfil their roles individually. Wives could advise their husbands, and marital plans could be discussed between them. Sometimes they had quite resolute attitudes towards corporal punishment; sometimes they

---

37 ASPV, Curia, II, C.M., Reg. 84: 10 November 1610, Virgine de Vitalibus cum Joanne Baptista Cigala, not foliated, 27 January 1611 and 15 November 1616.

38 Ibid., 27 February 1611.

39 Ibid., 15 November 1610.

played the role of mediator. They could also, as in Vidali's case, criticise the husband's decision. As Stanley Chojnacki has argued, in patrician marriages wealth could strengthen a wife's role, as patrician wives could collaborate in family strategies and have a positive impact on the future of their daughters.[40]

In artisan households craftsmen had to rely on their wives to govern the household and to face the complexities of everyday life. Work responsibilities were gendered but shared, and women were important for managing the household income, childcare and, in the absence or death of the husband, for maintaining domestic order and arranging marriages for any daughters. The resolute attitude of widows towards violence could be taken as an indication of the pressure they experienced when forced to arrange honourable marriages for their daughters alone. Although it is difficult to quantify, wives sometimes supported the household economy by washing, sewing or helping out in the workshop. When tensions overshadowed household life, each family member was obliged to take sides: a mother, especially, would be forced to behave unambiguously in support of either her husband or her daughter. If she refused to remain loyal to her husband the conflict could then turn into a battle of the sexes. Although fathers usually arranged the marriage, mothers were particularly influential in imposing the paternal decision on a disobedient daughter. Women enjoyed a longer and more intimate contact with their children and usually spent more time with them at home.[41] In infancy they also were responsible for the children's education. Leon Battista Alberti, the 'Renaissance man' par excellence, sums up well how a mother's moral qualities might be passed on to her children: 'The child's moral education in infancy continues under the mother's guidance, until a pious, dutiful, and self-restrained young person is prepared for intellectual training under his father's direction.'[42]

Because of their importance as a moral authority, mothers were also accorded an important function in restoring the domestic hierarchy, as shown in the case of Pasquetta, the mother in the Perron family. About 1614 her husband Giovanni Perron, a tailor with a workshop in the parish of S. Felice, proposed Lorenzo Comelli, son of a cloth merchant, as the prospective groom for his 16-year-old daughter Paolina. She opposed the marriage – perhaps, as was speculated during the trial, because she was in love with another man. Both parents, however, persistently attempted to realise the union. In 1629 Pasquetta explained

---

40 Chojnacki, 2000a, pp. 127–31 and 142–3.
41 Herlihy, 1972, p. 149.
42 Quoted in Ruggiero, 1993b, pp. 12–13.

her role and position within the household to the ecclesiastical examiner. Paolina, she told them,

> ... was living under the obedience of both my husband and me, and it is true that she feared us and was very scared of us, but more of me than of my husband, because as a woman I was always at home ... and I governed my daughter with great fear – and I was also more fierce [rabbioso] in governing her than my husband ... We threatened her because we knew the girl was timid and feared us, and that she would do what we said.[43]

As this case demonstrates, Venetian spouses not only were united in the aim of marrying their daughters; a mother could also use her domestic and maternal authority to break a child's resistance. Although the mother had been through the 'marriage-making' experience herself, this did not inevitably lead her to try to spare her daughter the distress of an unwanted marriage. Indeed, in some cases, mothers have been found to be the perpetrators of violence against their daughters and the instigators of forced marriages. Moreover, as witness depositions have already revealed, it seems that women in general were not especially sympathetic to filial suffering. When Isabella Floriani's father forced her at the age of 14 or 15 to marry the teacher Ambrosio Mazzoni – he had arranged the marriage when she was only seven years old[44] – Isabella alleged in court that her mother and aunt had exercised moral pressure to try to break her resistance. She would be the 'reason of his death', they had reproached when she refused to obey her father's wishes – words confirmed by Mazzoni himself.[45] Lack of support among women can be connected to early modern household hierarchy and ideals of obedience: when daughters behaved disrespectfully, mothers did not hesitate to use the authority they possessed over daughters in order to command obedience.

In court parents made reliable witnesses because when they referred to their use of authority and force they produced conclusive evidence as to why a coerced marriage had finally been solemnised against the expressed will of the daughter. In reporting the details of physical coercion, they thereby strengthened the legal case of their children. Because the marriage into which they had once forced their children apparently had failed, they might have regretted not having respected their children's wishes.

---

[43] ASPV, Curia, II, C.M., Reg. 90: 20 April 1629, Pauline filie Joannis Sutoris cum Laurentio Comelli.

[44] Perhaps because Mazzoni had accepted her with a small dowry, or even nothing.

[45] ASPV, Curia, II, C.M., Reg. 81: 5 August 1588, Isabelle Floriani cum Ambrosio Mazzoni, 8 March 1589.

Because parents were supposed to govern children strictly, when asked they never denied the enforcement of authority. When Magdalena Pectinary gave evidence in the case that her aforementioned stepdaughter Morosina had initiated at the Patriarchal Court in 1579, she responded without hesitation. She reported how she had firmly supported her husband's decision to marry the young girl to the journeyman Gianmaria, insisting that she had to comply with her father's wishes.[46] Gianmaria's reputation, however, was not faultless. Although he was known to be good and hard-working, it was also said that he spent all his income on drink and sexual amusements – in marriage formation male sexual conduct mattered in terms of a man's reputation.[47] In fact, Morosina alleged that Gianmaria had a venereal disease that forced him to sleep in trousers. She also referred to the social disparity between them: she was well off and he was a poor apprentice in her father's workshop. That her father Leonardo Pectinary attempted to marry her, despite this social inequality, might be explained by hardship: Pectinary may have wished to bind Gianmaria (who was working for more than one master) to his workshop, as the plague had decimated the population and thus the Venetian workforce.[48] Even after this marriage had failed, Magdalena Pectinary justified her husband's decision by referring to his moral integrity: he had worked hard all his life to earn his family a living. He was a good and reliable ruler who fulfilled his family duties with exemplarity.

The resistance of the child to marrying Gianmaria was probably perceived as a lack of gratitude towards these efforts: as others pointed out clearly in similar circumstances, 'it was not her business to choose [a husband]'.[49] Behind this sentiment lay the notion that children had to be content and accept the decisions of the family members, and not place personal wishes before family interests – especially not in times of hardship and distress. Many parents may have believed that with time a child's resistance would transform into respect and love for her husband.[50]

However, occasionally parents would be forced to reflect on their

---

[46] ASPV, Curia, II, C.M., Reg. 74: 10 January 1579, Morosine filie Leonardi Pectinary cum Joanne Maria Pectinario, fol. 30v.

[47] Ibid., fols 7v–8r.

[48] For the exact figures see Beltrami, 1954, p. 38; on the shortage of skilled labourers after the plague see Pullan, 1968, pp. 146–74, especially 159–60.

[49] ASPV, Curia, II, C.M., Reg. 82: 21 April 1590, Hersilie Pegorini cum Bernardio Struppiolo, Interrogatorio Hersilia, 16 June 1593.

[50] A case in point can be found in ASPV, Curia, II, C.M., Reg. 90: 1 July 1628, Victorie Cesana cum Joe Baptista Barbaro, testimony of Vir Nobilis Theodorus Minicio, fol. 17r.

behaviour and admit that they had made a mistake. During subsequent legal proceedings parents then had a second chance to reflect on their use (or misuse) of authority, as in the following case. While her sailor father Anastasio Bigarelli was away, Felicità's mother Lucietta – a woman with a fierce disposition – had forced Felicità to marry Matteo Fada, a merchant from S. Zulian. A widow by the name Lucrezia testified to how she had persuaded Felicità to consent to the marriage although the girl had confessed to her that she had 'not given him her heart'. Lucrezia had insisted that she obey her mother, even when Felicità had started to cry. As Faustina, Felicità's sister, revealed, in her desperation the girl had even warned her mother that at the public ceremony in church she would respond to the priest's question with a simple 'no'.[51] Shortly before the public blessing was to be given in church, mother and daughter were still in open disagreement. The marriage was solemnised despite all this (Felicità apparently had not carried out her threat), but only about a year later Felicità attempted to change her marital circumstances, petitioning in 1619 at the Patriarchal Court to be freed from Fada. Her mother Lucietta (who now acted as a legal witness on behalf of her daughter) confirmed that Felicità immediately had expressed her dislike of the spouse, and she then detailed her own response:

> And the first time I yelled at her and told her expressively that I wanted her at all cost to take him and she could not tell me why she refused to marry him, since I was not listening and only using my authority as a mother and furiously I … threatened her that she would get this husband or no one.[52]

Although Matteo Fada was in his mid-30s and Felicità was around 18 years old, Lucietta had not chosen a husband who was excessively older than her daughter. Nor did he have a reputation for being a drunkard or a womaniser. In short, Matteo Fada was a prosperous man without vices, whom Lucietta could confidently claim was a good match. As became apparent only after the marriage was solemnised, Matteo suffered so seriously from gonorrhoea that Felicità had left her husband only after 35 days. Her parents had consulted four physicians, who, however, could not recommend any medical treatment, as Matteo's illness was at an advanced stage.[53] The tone of self-critique audible in

---

51 ASPV, Curia, II, F.C., Reg. 34: 9 August 1618: Felicite filie Anastasy de Venetiy cum Matheo Fada, witness Faustina, daughter of Anastasio Bigarelli, fol. 4v.

52 Ibid., witness (pro parte Felicità) Lucietta, wife of Anastasio Bigarelli, fol. 2r. The trial starts in ASPV, Curia, II, C.M., Reg. 86: 9 April 1619.

53 ASPV, Curia, II, F.C., Reg. 34, fols 1v–2r.

Lucietta's deposition ('I was not listening') might be attributed to this late disclosure of the disease, which had prevented the marriage from being consummated. As this case graphically demonstrates, parental choice of spouse had not been so wise after all.

As a result, marriage formation often became a battlefield for children and parents. When different or even opposing interests had to be negotiated, marriage formation, as we have seen, carried a potential for household conflict: patrician parents, in particular, had property transactions, social and political networks and social status in mind when marrying their children.[54] As has been suggested recently, the emotional wishes of children and marital strategies of parents could go hand in hand without risking domestic harmony.[55] Yet, where fathers forged advantageous marriage alliances, family interests clearly overruled the emotional wishes of the offspring. Marriages were socially important among craftsmen as well, for they united two nuclear families and created a 'support network' for both. In the working classes abilities and work contacts played a major role in the formation of new marriages and households. But, because husbands and wives had to rely on each other constantly – in facing everyday problems, managing the patrimony and bringing up children – conjugal households were, unsurprisingly, more stable when grounded on mutual respect and care than on deep aversion.[56] In forging marriages, wise and sound parents therefore had to negotiate different expectations and, ideally, reconcile their own interests with the emotional wishes of their children.

Malicious and unjust actions: violence against children

Daughters who petitioned for an annulment of their marriage were faced with a difficult task. To obtain an annulment they had to prove

---

54 Patrician women in Venice were in a relatively better social and economic position, because they could actually bequeath their dowries, something which Florentine women were not allowed to do. See Chojnacki, 2000a, p. 13. For Florence see the seminal work of Klapisch-Zuber, 1987. She has emphasised that physically and symbolically women were 'passing guests' in Florentine households, as they were only considered in relation to men, such as fathers, brothers or husbands. Even a widow's destiny depended on the marital strategies of her family of origin. Rosenthal's view is more moderate and describes the position of women in Renaissance Florence as neither autonomous nor subservient: cf. Rosenthal, 1988, pp. 369–81. Kuehn, 1991, has moderated Klapisch-Zuber's view. He has emphasised the importance of conflicts between family members, which demonstrate the fragility of family continuity.

55 Chojnacki, 2000a, pp. 11–12 and 175–6.

56 Romano, 1987, pp. 60–61; see also Davis, 1991, especially pp. 89ff., for the importance of the neighbourhood in selecting the future spouse.

that the marriage had been contracted despite serious impediments such as grave 'fear and force' (*vim et metum*). In court the amount of violence inflicted was decisive because female plaintiffs had to explain convincingly why they had consented to a marriage that they later would claim had been contracted without the necessary consent. Only when the union had been completed through the excessive use of authority could the Patriarchal Court declare that it had been contracted invalidly.[57] The fear resulting from the respect and deference that children normally paid their 'natural' superiors was not sufficient to nullify a marriage. Only when physical coercion, threats of disinheritance or grave psychological pressure were exerted did the majority of early modern theorists consider the marriage worthy of invalidation.[58] Initial resistance to a proposed groom which changed over the course of time into acceptance did not necessarily constitute a nullifying impediment. Once solemnised in church, a marriage could only be annulled if it had been solemnised notwithstanding the existence of an impediment, like the excessive use of force or violence (and continuous resistance to the marriage) and non-consummation. Because of the ecclesiastical jurisdiction in sacramental matters, the decisions made by this court could not be contested by secular authorities. The Patriarchal Court based its verdicts on the criteria of canon law alone, without reference to worldly concerns such as socially promising marital alliances. In making their decisions the ecclesiastical tribunal defended the principle of consensuality as well as that of the holiness of marriage.

Female plaintiffs therefore had to provide concrete examples of coercion: slaps or blows (with hands or even with sticks) certainly would not do, as these chastisements were culturally accepted as 'moderate corrections' and a parental right to discipline disobedient offspring.[59] Their legal cases had to prove convincingly the physical and moral coercion that had made filial resistance impossible in the long term. The motives for their resistance were secondary (and only rarely mentioned); lack of mutual consent alone had to be proven during legal proceedings. Because the litigants in annulment suits were husband and wife, not parents or legal guardians, the presentation of the family conflict comes almost exclusively from the children's version of events. Only in rare cases in which Venetian parents were called as witnesses in court did

---

57 This 'diriment' impediment was a serious barrier to a marriage and was sufficient to nullify it. 'Impedient' or obstructive impediments, by contrast, did not prevent a marriage from being valid: Phillips, 1988, p. 5. Transgressions were punished with a fine or spiritual penalty.

58 See the discussion in Sommerville, 1995, pp. 174–82.

59 See Tamassia, 1971, p. 258, on the advice to punish with moderation.

they reveal their understanding of power relations and social order in early modern households.

Although the allegations usually had to convey malicious and unjust actions, the libels that children (with the help of legal advisors) presented in court do reveal something of the internal dynamic of early modern households. Talks, persuasion and insistent pleas mentioned in various disputes show that parental authority was not immediately equated with corporal punishment. Occasionally insults are alleged to have followed verbal insistence – Antonia's mother was accused of having insulted her child as being a 'swine' and a *poltrona* when she had refused to marry Andrea Lampez.[60] Because no physical means were exercised during these first attempts at persuasion, such ways of exerting influence were not in direct conflict with the theory of consent, although the moderate Spanish canonist Tomás Sánchez even rejected excessive pleas and psychological pressure as morally wrong.[61] Only when these verbal means of achieving agreement within the family were succeeded by physical violence did they run counter to the theory of consent.

Children thus had to demonstrate how their right to consent had been violated. They did so by pointing to the escalation of family disputes that resulted in the abuse of parental authority. The single points of the lawsuits are tactically arranged in order to reflect the growing tension and, finally, the cruelty with which parents opposed the disobedience of wilful daughters. As one Arcangela alleged in 1620, she had first expressed her unwillingness to marry the groom whom her mother Donna Antonia (who reared her alone) had proposed when she was 14 years of age; her mother first had verbally insisted that she marry him. With the girl's growing resistance the parent's behaviour also become more resolute. Arcangela alleged that Antonia had threatened to beat her and had warned her that she would even throw her out of the house and abandon her entirely if she did not comply with her wishes. Because Arcangela continued in her resistance, on Fat Thursday (*Giovedi Grasso*) – the day she was to marry – her mother had intimidated her by saying she would murder her and treat her as her 'capital enemy' if she did not consent. The marriage, Arcangela argued in court, was the result of increasing moral pressure, threats and violence, and had not been solemnised in accordance with her free will.[62]

---

[60] Literally *poltrona* means 'lazybones', but the way in which this insult is used against disobedient daughters and adulterous wives in early modern Venice makes it very likely that it was more generally applied to indicate misbehaviour. See ASPV, Curia, II, C.M., Reg. 91: 7 January 1632, Antonie Zuchetta cum Andrea Lampez, fol. 14r.

[61] Seed, 1988, p. 41.

[62] ASPV, Curia, II, C.M., Reg. 86: 9 July 1620, Archangele Cerajone cum Bernardino Gubè, written statement of Arcangela.

Some children stated that the threat of violence alone had been sufficient to break their resistance, but more often threats and physical coercion went hand in hand. In about 1612 Magdalena, daughter of the deceased Giovanni Battista de Franciscus, had been forced to marry the merchant Alvise Bonamico; she pleaded for an annulment some 13 years later. Her widowed mother supported her daughter during the legal proceedings by stating that Magdalena, a timid child, had feared her father and that he had battered her frequently.[63]

Children, however, did not only build cases on allegations of simple corporal punishment; they had to prove convincingly that their superiors had intimidated them to such a degree that resistance was impossible and that, on occasion, their life had been in danger. Witnesses were crucial in this respect. In order to test their reliability they were interrogated about how they had come to know about the family disputes of others, whether they had actually heard children screaming and about where they had been when the domestic disputes had escalated. Depositions from neighbours or relatives who had intervened in the domestic battle and rescued offspring from mortal danger carried special legal weight. These credible witnesses were of crucial importance in civil legal proceedings. A witness who could testify to the abuse of parental authority provided conclusive evidence in favour of the child.

A case in point is Benedetta, the daughter of Gregorio Aguzin, who worked in a special prison near St Mark's Square. Her mother Isabella, the driving force in this domestic battle, had married Benedetta to the much older Giacomo de Fusta when the child was only 14 years of age. Despite Giacomo's advanced age and the fact that he was lame, the witness Donna Margherita, a nurse at the hospital for criminals in S. Antonio, approved the mother's choice of groom because he shared Gregorio's profession. When this case came to the attention of the Patriarchal Court in 1661 Benedetta provided 16 witnesses in her favour. Among them was Donna Caterina, who was informally separated from her husband because he had squandered the dowry and treated her badly. She bore witness to Isabella's unruly government over her daughter and reported some of the violent means by which the child had been coerced. The mother had beaten Benedetta in the face with a bunch of keys so that she bled, had given her a black eye and had thrown a bottle of wine after her. Marietta and Pietro Tacca, neighbours of the Aguzins, testified to the ongoing quarrels between daughter and mother. Initially, it seems, Pietro had admonished Benedetta to bow to

---

63 ASPV, Curia, II, C.M., Reg. 88: 20 September 1625, Magdalene de Franciscis cum Alysio Bonamico, fols 10r–v.

her mother's wishes. But then the couple had spoken openly with the mother and advised her to be patient with the girl – a tactic that had brought Marietta Tacca herself good results. Bendetta, Pietro Tacca stated, had lived in great fear of her mother, who frequently had battered her 'for little or nothing'. Marietta Tacca was even more explicit, reporting in court how she had criticised the cruel means by which Isabella had tried to enforce her will on the child, threatening and battering her severely, and with no attempt to persuade her with kindness (con le buone).[64] In another dispute one Laura Contarini intervened when the domestic conflict between a widowed mother Chiara and her daughter Orsetta was about to escalate. With words that strongly recalled the theory of consent, Laura had reproached the mother by stressing that one was not allowed to force children into marriages to which they did not consent.[65]

The emphasis on free will was presented as an argument precisely at the moment when conflicts were about to escalate and a child's life was put in danger. In court witnesses provided evidence of unrestrained paternal discipline through physical violence and coercion. Their comments and feelings of compassion or resentment denote a critique of the 'unbound' and unreasonable employment of authority by parents or guardians. They point to the limits of parental authority and an understanding of household government oriented towards balanced rule and the moderate and sound use of that authority. That parents were supposed to chastise disobedient children was never in question; but parental authority was to be used wisely, and corporal punishment was not to exceed certain limits. Witnesses testifying that parents struck their children with their hands come si suole referred to a social norm. 'Moderate corrections' aimed at maintaining social order and civil peace were the accepted practice in early modern Venice; severe and cruel violence was not. Physical coercion was perceived as excessive and equated with tyrannical rule rather than with righteous, prudent and wise government.

The limits of parental authority become explicit in a case involving the Vancastra household in about 1618. In this exceptional case both partners allegedly were forced into marriage. The driving force in this parent–child drama was Isabella Vancastra, mother of Magdalena. Five years earlier – while Isabella still lived with her family in the sestier of Cannaregio – a man named Vancastri had dragged Isabella away from

---

64 ASPV, Curia, II, C.M., Reg. 93: 30 March 1661, Jacobi de Fusta cum Benedicta Gregory Marinary, fols 29r, 21r and 9v–10r, respectively.

65 ASPV, Curia, II, C.M., Reg. 74: 4 November 1579, Francisci de Vulgaris cum Ursetta de Coltis, not foliated, 27 November 1579.

her father. From then on she had called herself Vancastra without being properly married. The relationship eventually broke down, but Isabella's circumstances changed for the better when she met the nobleman Giuseppe Suriano. Isabella became his concubine and he supported her, providing food and paying her rent. Isabella Vancastra was well aware that her relationship with Suriano was sinful and kept her daughter outside the household. Her hopes for an honourable marital life for Magdalena seemed to be unrealistic when neighbourhood gossip began about the relationship between Magdalena and a certain Angelo Faniente, a sailmaker. The suspicion increased and they were said to have had sex together. A marriage promise was never mentioned. Giuseppe Suriano, however, offered to provide the dowry. With a marriage it seemed that everything could go back to normal and honour could be restored.[66]

However, both children were unwilling to marry. Angelo's sister Lucrezia deposed how Suriano had exhorted considerable pressure on Angelo when threatening to kill him; other witnesses revealed during the legal proceedings that Suriano also had threatened Angelo's family until they had finally agreed to the marriage. Giovanni Mora, a butcher from the parish of S. Geremia and a friend of Isabella Vancastra, stated that the mother had given Magdalena several slaps and had beaten her on the shoulder when the child refused her marital plans. When Isabella was heard at the Patriarchal Chancellery in 1619, she admitted that one day she had lost control; overwhelmed by anger and fury, she had grabbed her daughter by the throat and had almost strangled her. As the widowed washerwoman Giacoba testified in 1618, she and one Zavonetto Becher had arrived just in time to prevent the mother from murdering her child. Although Giacoba supported the mother's view that a daughter should respect and obey her superiors, she strongly disapproved of the violent and life-threatening means that the mother had employed to enforce her will.[67]

Physical coercion, as this case suggests, was not always an expression of superior authority. Strangely enough, unbound cruelty and arbitrary discipline might be read as an indication of the powerlessness of single mothers in particular, who reached their limits before they could implement their will. The helplessness of parents can be detected in their outrage, fury and irrational behaviour (such as murder attempts) in the face of wilful daughters. When parents were governed by emotions, and not by rationality, they endangered household and social order, as

---

[66] ASPV, Curia, II, C.M., Reg. 86: 13 August 1618, Magdalene Filosi cum Angelo Faniente. This narrative follows Isabella Vancastra's statement.

[67] Ibid., depositions of Lucrezia, Giovanni Mora, fols 62r–v and Giacoba, fols 37r–v.

irrationality was the inverse of sound and stable household government. Family disputes thus demonstrate that young women could exert counter-pressure on their parents and that they could, at least for a time, upset the social order in early modern households. By refusing to consent to marriages arranged for them, they behaved disrespectfully towards their parents or, in the case of orphaned children, towards their legal guardians. The expressed will of women, not taken into consideration in other trials,[68] emerges in annulment suits as part of their resistance to superiors.

Parents or legal guardians had, however, more staying power and more powerful resources. Physical coercion, although central to the complaints brought by daughters, was not the only argument that children advanced to explain why their resistance finally had been broken. Threats of disinheritance and psychological means of exerting moral pressure also figure in their lawsuits; they constituted a common element of domestic dramas and demonstrate that these battles were fought between unequal contenders. Children were dependent on their parents or guardians in a way that their superiors were not. Threats of expulsion from the parental household and threats to retreat from the caring role or the supervision of the estate were powerful moral weapons employed in conflicts between children and parents. But daughters could also exert moral pressure in response to parents' marital plans. Whereas parents' menaces were directed against others – namely, their children – daughters' distress manifested itself through threats of self-harm, suicide (a grave sin) or claustration.

As we have seen, allegations against cruel and heartless parents dwelt upon the dependence and helplessness of offspring. By emphasising children's obedience and timidity and their later exceptional resistance to coerced marriages (that is, in other circumstances these children paid the required respect to their parents or guardians), these lawsuits explain the giving of consent as a result of singular cruelty endured over an extended period. Although children expressly referred to their own will, the allegations and witness depositions nevertheless evoke the image of their powerlessness in the face of parents' tyranny: successful resistance was virtually impossible. The dependence of children due to their young age reinforced this impression. A high proportion of the 'women' were aged between 14 and 16, the rest were between 12 and 19, and in one exceptional case the girl was only 11 years old – and therefore below the minimum age for marriage established by canon law. Descriptions of the characters involved in the litigation also reinforced this impression:

---

68   See Roper, 1994, pp. 53–78 and Burghartz, 1999b, pp. 41–56.

plaintiffs and witnesses portrayed parents as cruel, vindictive and frightening, and as ruling over shy, intimidated and frightened children. Hersilia was 'shy and shamefaced', Angelica was 'timid ... modest and obedient' and Giacomo had 'a very shy nature'. The latter lived under the supervision of the *maestro* Fernandino Ferrari, whom he followed promptly in respect and obedience.[69] Accusations, then, were built up not only by addressing juridical arguments (that is, 'grave fear') but also by evoking images of helplessness in the face of tyrannical rule – a type of governance that ran counter to the myth of Venice as a free and righteous republic.

Unsound marital arrangements

When household government had deteriorated into tyrannical rule, parents and legal guardians had clearly misused their authority. The precise implications and the meaning of parental misrule not only become apparent when superiors abused their physical authority over children: parental misrule extended to unsound wedding arrangements and, more precisely, to the disputable choice of a groom. In these instances, when the choice of spouse demonstrated that the parents had made an unsound decision (and nevertheless forced the child to obey), people responded with astonishment, wonder or occasionally even disregard for parents' marital plans. As marital litigation cases suggest, contemporaries held that the age gap between spouses should not greatly exceed the average, otherwise it would be difficult to achieve conjugality. Advanced age also was associated with corporal frailty and with ugliness. Illness (both physical and mental) was an impediment to marriage, and in contemporary Venetian marriage culture physical deficiencies were perceived as convincing reasons to oppose a marriage. Judicious parents should avoid marrying their child to someone with physical defects, as these unions carried the danger that the marriage could not be consummated, especially if insanity was involved. Therefore, a considerable age gap, social disparity, physical infirmity or – as in one exceptional case – mental insanity transgressed the limits of the acceptable.

In one example of a case of social disparity, Vittoria Cesana described at the Patriarchal Court in 1628 the violent means by which she had

---

69 ASPV, Curia, II, C.M., Reg. 82: 21 April 1590, Hersilie Pegorini cum Bernardio Struppiolo, 30 April 1593, not foliated; Reg. 92: 12 May 1648, Angelice Pellizzoli cum Scipione Albano, fols 13r–v; Reg. 93: 12 November 1654, Jacobi Maccarini cum Lucretia Bianchi, fol. 5r.

been forced to marry the nobleman Giovanni Battista Barbaro. The support she had received during the time of this coercion had come primarily from two cousins, Theodoro Minio and Antonio Baldù, noblemen living in S. Vidal. They were well acquainted with the family (Minio was Antonio Cesana's godfather) and were persons of confidence; at Vittoria's request Minio had approached her father twice in vain attempts to dissuade him from his marital plans. This plea had fallen on deaf ears, as the father had placed the prospect of an attractive marriage to a member of the Venetian patriciate over his daughter's emotional fulfilment. Minio recalled how Antonio Cesana had, referring to his authority as a father, retorted that 'he did not intend to lose this good match' when Minio had mentioned Vittoria's aversion to her future groom. The girl was said to be attracted to another man, with whom she already had exchanged a promise of marriage (itself an additional impediment to her marrying Barbaro). Minio also repeated a moral judgement in court which the lover of Vittoria had expressed about his astonishment at a father forcing his child into a match with someone who was not of the same social standing and, presumably not of the same economic standing either. In Minio's opinion the significant social disparity was not a solid basis for a good working marital relationship. He was thus certain that the couple would encounter troubles in the future.[70]

Not only age and social disparity were obstacles to a successful marriage – mental disabilities also were a challenge to forming the conjugal bond. No case shows a priest behaving more incomprehensibly than that in which a cleric blessed the marriage between the mentally insane *gentiluomo* Giovanni Badoer and the *gentildonna* Helena Corner. Their marriage had been performed publicly in 1585 in the church of S. Cristoforo; some 11 years later, after the death of her mother Augusta (who had contrived the union), Helena went to the Patriarchal Court to annul the marriage. Helena alleged that it was great fear of her mother that had prevented her from seeking an annulment during Augusta's lifetime. Her case was not built solely upon the means of coercion by which her mother had forced her into the marriage. Helena provided many witnesses who could testify to Badoer's insanity, and thus to a marriage that had been contracted despite at least two major

---

[70] ASPV, Curia, II, C.M., Reg. 90: 1 July 1628, Victorie Cesana cum Joe Baptisa Barbaro, witness Theodoro Minio; part of the trial is found in ASPV, Curia, II, F.C., Reg. 42, Cesana, 1628. An excellent example of the potential risks of excessive age disparity is the fascinating case of adultery involving Margherita Romani-Muti and her husband Giovanni, discussed in chap. 9. Although Margherita's precise age is not known, she was presumably in her 20s or 30s, while her husband was 75.

impediments (fear and force *and* insanity).[71] Badoer's domestic servant Menega, who gave the fullest testimony, reported that his master's illness had started 26 years earlier, when Badoer had lived on the mainland in Padua. At this time he would dress in *maneghe a comeo* (wide sleeves that only patricians and *cittadini* were allowed to wear) and perform his political duties in the council. Suddenly he had begun to utter weird, incoherent and disjointed phrases during the night, which, according to Menega, was when his madness started. Badoer's mother was informed about these alarming signs. She moved her son to the Venetian parish of S. Martino, where his condition initially improved, only to deteriorate more rapidly. One day he plunged himself from a balcony into the canal. From that day on his madness continued. He talked bizarrely and incoherently and addressed everybody by the wrong name; when he started to read a book, all of a sudden he would tear it to pieces. His condition was alarming, as he was 'out of his senses' (*non sta in cervello*). For safety he was locked in his room with grilles on the window and was looked after by his servant 'like a little dog'.[72] This was his condition when Augusta Corner had decided to marry off her daughter to him. She had been admonished by her brother Battista Boldù for her marital plans. Menega recalled that Augusta had retorted that Badoer was 'a good match, and very rich and not at all mad, but had a very lucid brain'.[73] Economic prospects, it seems, were the driving force for Augusta Corner when she arranged the marriage, disregarding the advice of many and the express will of her daughter.

There were other obstacles to negotiate in forming this union. As a noble, Giovanni Badoer had to inform the Avogaria di Comun about his marriage and swear an oath in front of them. Another servant named Bertolo rehearsed the procedure again and again with his master, who was then supposed to repeat the scenes he had memorised – such as how to place his hand on the scripture. Badoer acted like a puppet, and this significant social and political act was meaningless to him.[74] Despite the rehearsals, when before the priest Bertolo still needed to prompt his master to say his lines. In this way, according to a witness, one spoke with a parrot and not with an intelligent human being.[75] In spite of all this the marriage was solemnised but the wedding night passed without incident,

---

[71] The impediment of consanguinity might also have existed, but evidence is unclear in the sources.

[72] For the most powerful description of his madness see the testimony of the servant Menega, in ASPV, Curia, II, C.M., Reg. 82: 10 June 1596, Helena figlia Corner cum Giovanni Baduaria, fols 74r–77r.

[73] Ibid., fol. 64r.

[74] Ibid., fols 62v–63r.

[75] Ibid., fol. 17v.

for the sleeping Giovanni Badoer did not even touch his 'wife', thus sparing her the sexual violence that other young brides had to endure.

'Ho detto di si con la bocca ma non col cuore': sexual violence and unstable marriages

Litigants' narratives and complaints about extreme violence, physical coercion and unsound marital plans did not end here. Women who pleaded for the annulment of their marriages at the Patriarchal Court alleged to have endured violence over a long period and from different sources. They argued of unjust and malicious physical coercion and threats of disinheritance from parents and guardians before and during the solemnisation ceremony, and of sexual violence from their husbands after the marriage, in demanding its consummation. Since the public exchange of vows alone was not binding, the marriage only came into being after sexual intercourse had taken place. Sexual relations then 'embodied consent to marriage'.[76] When a woman was successful in her resistance to sexual intercourse, this behaviour denoted not only her persistent, lasting and resolute opposition to the marriage, but also her repugnance towards a man whom she had never desired as a husband. The position of these women in court was arguably stronger because no binding and indissoluble marital bond had been established.

Sexual violence was a woman's complaint, and husbands – when they were heard in the lawsuit – usually did not deny the use of force and sexual violence. They had, after all, a right to consummate the marriage and to demand sexual obedience. In March 1613 Girolamo Mazzola confirmed without hesitation the legal statement at the Patriarchal Chancellery of his 'wife' Barbara Meretti, who had reported that for twenty long nights he had attempted to deflower her, while she had cried, yelled and fled the marital bed.[77]

In 1629 the aforementioned Paolina Perron reported in detail how her father Giovanni had dragged her into the bedroom and how she had fled several times. She had spent her wedding night crying while still wearing her maiden dress and lying with her undressed groom Lorenzo Comelli in the matrimonial bed. On the second night, however, she was forced to undress and Comelli had violently consummated the marriage. Lorenzo Comelli did not deny this when interrogated about his and Paolina's parents' use of force. He, additionally, reported that Paolina's

---

76 Sommerville, 1995, p. 185.

77 ASPV, Curia, II, C.M., Reg. 20: January 1613, Barbare Meretti cum Hieronimo Mazzola, 6 March 1613.

mother had been playing an active role in violently forcing her daughter into bed with him. After the marriage had been consummated Paolina had continued her resistance and her firm conviction that she was not his wife because she had accepted him against her will. For three months they had lived in 'war day and night' until Paolina finally returned to her parents, who by now regretted their decision.[78]

This mother was – like others – not a reliable ally of a daughter who refused to have sexual intercourse and to make her marriage union indissoluble. Mothers, or female relatives more generally, seem not to have been moved immediately by shared experiences, not even when it came to sparing young women the distress of sexual violence. Their behaviour could, however, change during the course of attempts to make a young woman consent to sexual intercourse; eventually, they could become a source of help and redress. An example is provided by the case of Paolina Businella, a 'timid' woman aged 15 who in the 1590s lived under the supervision of her legal guardian Alessandro Businelli, whom she paid 'extreme reverence'. Alessandro's wife Laura and his sister Camilla both played a part in attempts to force the young bride into bed with Girolamo Cernotta, the man Paolina held not to be her husband because she had never consented to marry him. However, both women had arranged a compromise. The husband was asked not to touch his 'wife' while they were lying in the wedding bed – a proposal that they thought would make Paolina slowly, and with time, accept her new living circumstances, and at the same time would not prevent the marriage from being consummated in the long run. Only after Paolina had been firm in her resistance and Girolamo had employed every conceivable means to consummate the marriage, including sexual violence and domestic confinement, did Camilla Businelli finally accompany the young woman to the Jesuits.[79] They studied her case and advised her to take refuge in the Casa del Soccorso, a charitable institution that sheltered mistreated wives and 'fallen women' (but that equally functioned as a means by which husbands could confine 'lewd women').[80]

Sexual violence thus makes up part of the experiences of young women forced into a marriage and part of their legal narrative. Only very few couples, such as Angelo Faniente and Magdalena Vancastra, did not become involved in the battles around the marital bed and

---

[78] See Ferraro, 2001, pp. 48–9 for Lorenzo's statement.

[79] Jesuits seem to have acted as legal advisors, as they were very well acquainted with canon law.

[80] ASPV, Curia, II, C.M., Reg. 84: 19 December 1607: Hieronimi Cernota cum Paulina Businella, 26 May 1608 and 14 January 1609.

simply turned their back on each other during the night.[81] Because
neither had agreed to marriage they refused to exchange signs of
affection, such as kisses and caresses. If the marital bed was a symbol for
the corporal union of the spouses and for the consummation of the
marriage, it could also symbolise, inversely, the deep division between
partners.

The sexual violence inflicted on Flaminia, daughter of the deceased
boatman Francesco Veneto, took place under different circumstances.
The child had been raised by the *gentildonna* Caterina Mocenigo, who
had taken her from the Pietà.[82] Flaminia was said to be extremely
beautiful, but also simple-minded. In 1623 she was married to
Cristoforo Callegaro, son of the deceased Alessio. She was then only 11
years old and had not yet reached the canonical minimum age for
marriage (12 for girls and 14 for boys).[83] The widow Margherita,
Flaminia's mother-in-law, recalled how she had agreed to Caterina
Mocenigo's proposal to not let the little child share the matrimonial bed
until she was 12 years old and regarded as suitable for consummating
the marriage. This arrangement created a rather unusual situation, with
the potential for conflict in the Callegaro household. After the
solemnisation of the marriage Margherita slept with Flaminia in one
bed, while Cristoforo spent his nights alone. A close neighbour,
Benvenuta Vasalli, reported in November 1624 how she had observed
the couple from her balcony, which offered a direct view into Madonna
Margherita's house. Madonna Flaminia, she recalled, 'was always
playing with dolls ... and made the gestures of a little girl who is without
a brain'. When Cristoforo attempted to exchange signs of marital
affection such as kisses or other gestures, the little girl started to cry and
fled. The Callegaros' world was turned upside down, for no *patrona*
(mistress of the house), but a child who needed supervision by her
mother-in-law, had entered their household. Even Madonna Margherita
had lamented this choice of bride. The widow Maria Spadari testified in
private about how Margherita had complained to many people that she

---

81 ASPV, Curia, II, C.M., Reg. 86: 13 August 1618, Magdalene Filosi cum Angelo
Faniente, testimony Giovanni Mora, fol. 31v.

82 ASPV, Curia, II, C.M., Reg. 88: 28 October 1624, Flaminie q. m Francisci de
Venetis cum Christoforo q.m Alexy. The Pietà was an institution for foundlings, children
who had been abandoned by their parents (or a parent) out of poverty or shame.

83 Occasionally marriage could be arranged years in advance of these ages, especially
when there were problems such as a lack of dowry. Marital arrangements were dependent
on prosperity, and in practice the average age for marriage was high among artisans – at
least 23 for brides and 26 for grooms. Data are lacking for Venice, so this refers to
European marriage patterns; see Hajnal, 1965, pp. 101–43, and some data provided by
Chojnacka, 2001, p. 5.

not only had to govern her daughter-in-law but also had to look after her and to protect her from Cristoforo. Flaminia was reluctant to have any form of physical contact with Cristoforo, let alone sexual intercourse. Madonna Margherita reported how Cristoforo had ignored her pleas and warnings to preserve Flaminia's virginity until she was old enough to consummate the marriage. He had violently dragged Flaminia out of his mother's bed, slapped and beaten her and forcibly put her to bed. After 15 long days he finally succeeded in forcing her to consent to intercourse. The violence had left marks on her young body, a fact observed by the midwife Madonna Marietta, who stated in 1624 that Flaminia was marked with the physical abuse of her husband 'in various parts of her body'.[84]

The age impediment to marriage, as this exceptional case demonstrates, was no mere formality to contemporary marriage culture; a certain amount of maturity was required to comprehend the transition from virginity to wifehood, with all its implied duties and rights. This perception was firmly grounded in daily household life. In contemporary culture the degree of maturity was more flexible than canon law foresaw. As other cases show, young women aged 13 or so could still be perceived as too immature to run their own households. Immaturity, then, endangered domestic hierarchy: when a woman had to protect her young daughter-in-law against her own son the world was turned upside down. In this perspective a favourable verdict from the Patriarchal Court reiterated not only household order but also the order upon which society was built.

In the end the 'fear and force' through which parents and guardians attempted to realise their marital plans often backfired. Cases involving coerced marriages which reached the ecclesiastical tribunal had been unstable and broke down shortly after the wedding (although a legal annulment was sometimes attempted only after years). Some couples stayed together for months, but others separated after only a couple of days; very few spent years together. Because the women were determined in their decision, they frequently escaped from their new homes, often to be returned several times. Husbands sometimes left their wives without any intention of reconciliation or were occasionally resigned to their situation by the time the case reached the attention of the court. When children 'had said yes only with their mouth but not with their heart', as a common formula ran, the victory parents had gained was short-lived.

Repugnance and aversion were therefore obviously not stable grounds for establishing a household and for managing its day-to-day

---

84 ASPV, Curia, II. C.M., Reg. 88: 28 October 1624, Flaminie q. m Francisci de Venetis cum Christoforo q. m Alexy, fols 29v and 16v.

complexities. If spouses were to rule side by side over their children and husbands were to rule over wives, then mutual consent was important to make a marriage work. Coercion, by contrast, made it difficult for a woman to afford her husband the necessary obedience and respect as her 'natural' superior. Even without physical coercion and moral pressure, conjugality was not an easy state to achieve, and marital life embodied a powerful potential for domestic discord.

CHAPTER SIX

Husbands and Wives: Marital Discord

Contemporary early modern marriage culture communicated conflicting ideals.[1] On the one hand household rule was based on domestic patriarchy; but on the other, marriage was increasingly perceived in terms of a compassionate ideal, especially by Protestant reformers.[2] Contemporary Italian humanists, too – such as the sixteenth-century writer Ludovico Dolce – although emphasising the patriarchal structure of early modern households, conceived of marriage as a partnership.[3] These household structural tensions were embedded in early modern marriages and implied a strong potential for disputes. When the head of the household abused his authority or when household patriarchy was contested, the situation could become the source for domestic tensions, putting conjugal and household harmony at risk. Typical battles between husbands and wives centred on the 'proper' management of household and property, the necessary respect to be shown a partner, the noncompliance of patriarchal prescriptions or the tyranny of physical violence. They focused in particular on the abuse of patriarchal power by husbands and the disobedience and sexual conduct of wives – a product of unsuccessful rule. Hence, marital disharmony was linked intrinsically to the disobedience of wives and to 'bad' government by the head of the household, whereas marital order, like social order, was the result of the husband's sound and well-balanced rule.

Failure to realise conjugal and household ideals was evident when dysfunctional marriages reached the courts. When shared households collapsed and domestic litigation made marital life unbearable, litigants in court spoke at length about the grounds for marital breakdown, relating their stories according to the tropes of canon law. Women accused their husbands of severe cruelty, arbitrary discipline and moral misconduct; husbands complained about disobedient and adulterous

---

[1] Overviews are provided by Kelso, 1956, Jordan, 1990, pp. 248–53 and Romano, 1996, pp. 3–42.

[2] Ozment, 1983, pp. 50–72. See, however, Roper's critique, 1993, pp. 1–2.

[3] Dolce, 1545, p. 5 and Fortini Brown, 2002, p. 314: 'The model of good marriage that comes through in these treatises, while it may well be patriarchal, is one of a partnership.' (Here she refers to Piccolomini.)

wives. Whereas a woman's reproach thus focused on extreme cruelty, a man's accusation centred on female disobedience or female unchastity – sexual misconduct alone was sufficient to free him from her company. Only few husbands in early modern Venice, however, sought a legal separation on the grounds of adultery. Behind this general pattern of accusation we get insights into contemporary moral culture, especially into expectations about the marital state. The charges describe in detail the disappointed marital expectations, thereby revealing a model against which actual marital relationships were measured. They demonstrate the gendered roles of spouses in the highly ordered household and refer to an accepted social norm. Moreover, they show how much pressure lay on both partners to fulfil their duties and to live according to the Christian marriage ideal. The right to patriarchal authority not only expressed asymmetrical power relations, but also referred to gender-specific expectations that men had to fulfil and to negotiate.

Ideals of obedience and authority

It is in the sources pertaining to marital breakdown that the highly idealised nature of the ordered household and the Christian marriage ideal of conjugality become most evident. Court records address marital life from a completely different perspective, emphasizing problems rather than principles. They demonstrate that in early modern societies gender roles and duties were not 'naturally' given – their implementation was a process that had to be learned, appropriated and internalised, sometimes over years. Admonishments and criticism by neighbours and family members helped to shape and redefine gendered behaviour and conduct. In the cases that reached the Patriarchal Court, however, these strategies had not been helpful: domestic harmony had turned into domestic conflict. A man did not 'naturally' become a good household ruler, just as a woman's obedience did not come overnight – 'natural patriarchal authority' and the responses to it were complex.[4]

Although sons and daughters alike were subordinate to their parents, 'the distinctly female form of subjection' was that of wives, for in consenting to marry a woman consented to subjection.[5] She therefore had to submit to and obey her husband regardless of the fact that she stood together with him at the head of the domestic hierarchy. When leaving the household, for example, an obedient wife had to ask her husband for permission, as reported by the wife Hersilia in the 1590s.

---

4 Roper, 1993, p. 165.
5 Sommerville, 1995, p. 174.

Every time she desired to attend a service or to visit friends or family members, she respectfully asked her husband Bernardino Struppiolo – a man she portrayed as caring and prudent – whether she had his allowance to do so: 'Normally I asked Maestro Bernardino modestly for permission, which he gave me, and I begged an honourable woman from the neighbourhood to accompany me'.[6]

Thus, an obedient wife lived according to these principles and accepted the power structures within the marriage, whereas a stubborn and strong-minded wife challenged the husband's authority and thereby ran the risk of being punished 'in moderation'. As the Italian author Cristoforo Bronzini ironically phrased it, a husband would rather live in a desert than with an unruly wife.[7] There was no doubt that wives should not argue with their husbands, as this could be interpreted as an attack on or criticism of his ruling capacities. It was a husband's duty to decide and a wife's to obey.

Physical corrections undoubtedly comprised part of household rule, yet they are mentioned only rarely in treatises on household government. These works focused more generally on marital complementarity, emphasizing ideals, not problems.[8] This omission is remarkable, as patriarchy was based on the husband's right to reprove and, when necessary, to punish disobedient household members. In the rare instances in which Italian humanists mentioned marital conflicts, the emphasis was placed on the husband's *right* and *duty* to punish errant behaviour. Physical discipline was ascribed a positive meaning: it was an expression of male authority as well as a fulfilment of his responsibility to educate the household members. However, these 'moderate corrections' were not to exceed certain limits. The Italian author Giuseppe Passi, well-known for his misogynist treatise on *The Defects of Women* (*I Donneschi Difetti*, first published 1599), wisely advised husbands in his later work entitled *On the Marital State* (*Dello stato maritale*) to rule with patience and prudence over their wives.[9] Domestic discipline had to be stern, but just.

The abuse of patriarchy is another topic that is rarely mentioned by Italian humanists in their treatises on household government.[10] Female

---

6 ASCP, C.M., Reg. 82: 21 April 1593, Hersilie Pegorini cum Bernardino Struppiolo, not foliated, interrogation on 16 June 1593.

7 Bronzini, 1622, p. 83.

8 Jordan, 1990, p. 41.

9 Passi, 1602, p. 144.

10 An exception is Henricus Cornelius Agrippa, who in his *De nobilitate et praecellentia foeminei sexus* (1529) condemned the general 'tyranny' men exerted over women. The few writers who adopted the tyranny argument tended, however, as Virgina Cox has argued, 'to hold back from pursuing their argument to any socially subversive conclusion'. See Cox, 1995, pp. 516–18. For a legal discussion see Quaglioni, 2000, pp. 111–16.

writers, however, discussed this issue, sometimes at length. They described a cultural model that could be defined as the 'unruly and violent husband'. 'Then there are those husbands', Moderata Fonte emphasised in 1600, 'who spend all their time shouting at their wives and who, if they don't find everything done just as they like it, abuse the poor creatures or even beat them over the most trivial matters, and who are always picking fault with the way in which the household is run, as though their wives were completely useless.'[11] In these situations, when the husband became furious and angry the wife was to 'conquer' the household ruler by imitating a physician's cure: 'The remedy or the best way to conquer strange and choleric husbands', Cristoforo Bronzini held, 'is the wife's imitation of physicians, that is, to cure the husband's faults with contrary medicine; so when he is cruel and imperious the wife should overcome him with humiliation; when he is furious, she should be silent, since the answer of wise women is silence'.[12] Male violence and misrule were to be countered with female obedience, humiliation and silence. Transgressions of idealised gendered conduct had, therefore, very different meanings for men and women: whereas unruly wives should be punished with 'moderate corrections', unruly husbands who had disturbed the household order through their ill-tempered behaviour should be handled with leniency. At the most, as the aforementioned Cristoforo Bronzini conceded, a prudent wife could carefully choose the right moment and talk openly with her husband, though she should avoid having any servants present.[13] Apparently, Bronzini sensed that there was potential for conflict even in this situation: the woman might go too far and contradict her husband, thereby challenging his authority 'in public'.[14]

Thus, when the household ruler had abused his authority, it was the female's responsibility at the end of the sixteenth and at the beginning of the seventeenth centuries to restore household harmony and to avoid domestic litigation. This fundamental contradiction implies a strong potential for domestic tension, especially when domestic patriarchy was contested. Whereas a wife's obedience, respect and love for her husband was tested by male abuse and misrule, a husband had to negotiate between conflicting ideals, for the right to beat his wife tested marital conjugality, as did female stubbornness and wilfulness. For a husband, a woman's loose tongue was a threat to household order, questioning the principle of conjugality in marriage. Such wilful wives put domestic

---

[11] See the English edition ed. by Cox, 1997, pp. 70–71.
[12] Bronzini, 1622, p. 82.
[13] Ibid.
[14] Ibid., p. 83.

hierarchy and, as a consequence, domestic harmony, at risk. The following is a strong case in point.

In 1636 Benedetta Spinelli sought separation at the Patriarchal Court from her blacksmith husband Pietro Franchini on grounds of cruelty.[15] However, according to one witness, Giovanni Sartory, Benedetta's lack of moderation had clearly endangered the marital union. In court Sartory expressed his disregard for the quarrelsome and assertive wife:

> Several times I heard her quarrelling with Messer Pietro and, when he was about to say one word, she would respond with ten. More than once she confessed to my wife and to me in my house that she did not want to live like this anymore and that she was used to living in a more civilised fashion. We asked her what exactly she was lacking and she retorted 'nothing', but that she did not want to remain with her husband. We begged her to stay, saying that it was a great sin and shame in this world to separate from the husband, to which she replied that she didn't care and that she wanted what she wanted.[16]

In March 1638 a married woman, Donna Natalina, outlined in court how Pietro had called her to his workshop, where he was quarrelling with his wife under the gaze of the neighbouring artisans. When he asked Donna Natalina to take his wife home, Benedetta called him a 'swine', adding that he was 'not worthy of having received her in his hands'. Donna Natalina had later admonished Benedetta for having uttered these dishonest words – to which Benedetta had responded with further insults.[17]

The wife's wilfulness ran counter to contemporary notions of gender roles. Stubbornness was perceived as a form of female self-determination and assertiveness that, according to the aforementioned witness Satory, threatened the sanctity of marriage. Although this parishioner had internalised Christian marriage doctrine well, the indissolubility of the marital union was no argument to appease Benedetta's restlessness. (She had deserted her husband once before, but had been ordered back by the Avogaria di Comun.) In his defence Pietro Franchini alleged in court that his wife was a 'bad' woman: arrogant, terrible and disobedient. She had stolen money from his workshop and failed to show respect and submission, having dared to speak to him in the familiar form of address.[18] Her loose tongue not only had

---

15 ASPV, Curia, II, C.M., Reg. 92: 22 September 1637, Benedicte Spinelli cum Petro Franchino.

16 Ibid., 13 March 1638.

17 Ibid., 20 March 1638.

18 Ibid., point seven of his legal statement. The latter was revealed by the witness Giovanni Sartory, 13 March 1638.

undermined his authority; she also had committed the criminal offence of blasphemy when insulting the name of God and of the Holy Virgin Mary.

Benedetta Spinelli was perceived in the neighbourhood as unruly and her behaviour described as 'wild' and 'threatening'. The way she lived and behaved was the antithesis to the rules laid down for married women. Franchini and his witnesses agreed that Benedetta's behaviour not only was putting holy matrimony at risk, but also was destroying neighbourly peace. Because many witnesses were heard who despised Benedetta's marital conduct, her lawsuit was unsuccessful and she and her husband were ordered to reconcile and to fulfil their matrimonial obligations. When Franchini finally reasserted his patriarchal authority over his wife, the neighbourhood strongly approved of his behaviour:

> I heard Madonna Benedetta insulting her husband from the balcony by calling him a swine, a wimp and a cuckold [*cornuto*], whereupon Messer Pietro turned around and said, 'Are you calling me a cuckold?' – and gave her some slaps. And the people in the street below were saying, 'Blessed are those hands', meaning that he had done well to beat her.[19]

Words were the sharpest weapon women possessed in the early modern period, because speech had the power to dishonour and thus to damage reputations. It was verbal violence that Benedetta Spinelli had unjustly inflicted on her male superior. When insulting her husband by labelling him a cuckold – and thus a man who had lost his sexual ownership – Benedetta had, strangely enough, used a slander that referred to her own sexual conduct. By insulting her husband publicly Benedetta had subverted male authority and was punished by being cuffed. The approval voiced by the neighbours illustrates the importance of reinforcing the household hierarchy when wives behaved disrespectfully; when male authority was challenged it had to be restored immediately.

Benedetta's loose tongue, as we have seen, was perceived as a subversion of male authority. From a broader perspective stubbornness and wilfulness incorporated the threat of female domination in the household in general. As an infringement it endangered social and political order in both real and symbolic terms. In the aforementioned treatise on *The Defects of Women* (1599) Giuseppe Passi had compared a woman 'who intrudes herself into the affairs of men with a tyrant who usurps power not rightfully his'. Such a woman was like a tyrant 'who obtains power in a republic illegally'.[20] Sometimes these fears were expressed directly in the Venetian community. In a marital dispute

---

[19] Ibid., witness Donna Natalina, 20 March 1638.
[20] Quoted in Jordan, 1990, p. 250.

debated at the ecclesiastical tribunal in 1610, the wife was described as 'an obstinate woman who has her own head and who wants to govern alone, not only her household but also that of her children-in-law'.[21] Female government, it seems, was perceived of being in danger to deteriorate into misrule and tyranny, as illustrated by the case of Magdalena Vincentine. In 1616 she had been sued at the Signori di Notte al Criminal by her husband Gasparo, a worker on a goods ship: he had accused his wife of theft during his absence from Venice. After the witnesses were heard and both litigants questioned, the case was handed over to the ecclesiastical authorities of the Patriarchal Court.[22] Magdalena alleged general mistreatment, but Gasparo accused her of adultery and cruelty, both verbal and physical, claiming that she had insulted and slapped him and had refused to render the marital debt – a duty that both husband and wife had to pay.[23] Gasparo admittedly had lost authority and control over his own wife, and her behaviour shows that this unleashed uncontrolled emotions and power. Clearly, the world and the symbolic order of the household were turned upside down.[24]

Violence and obedience: fundaments of Venetian households

Disobedience and violence were thus among the most important issues negotiated in the courtroom in cases of marital disputes, and litigants and witnesses alike argued at length the meaning of corporal punishment and the limits of patriarchal authority. When some Italian humanists mentioned 'moderate corrections' as legitimate means to punish unruly wives, they were in perfect harmony with canon law. Tomás Sánchez (1550–1610), the Spanish canonist reputed for his mild judgements, had devoted a section in his work on matrimony to corporal punishment and the question of whether wife-beating was a sufficient cause to endorse separation. He argued against severe beating, advising that the husband's rule should be limited to 'mild and moderate corrections' when a wife went astray, and that corrections should never include 'atrocities' against the wife. The husband's misbehaviour, however, was no guarantee that a legal separation might be granted. For example, if the husband was behaving unjustly and punishing his wife

---

21 ASPV, Curia, II, C.M., Reg. 84: 10 November 1610, Virgine de Vitalibus cum Joanne Baptista Cigala, not foliated, point 17 of his legal statement.

22 ASPV, Curia, II, C.M., Reg. 85: 3 June 1616, Magdalene Vincente cum Gaspare eius marito.

23 For a discussion of marital problems connected to the marital debt, see chap. 7.

24 ASPV, Curia, II, C.M., Reg. 85: 3 June 1616, Magdalene Vincente cum Gaspare eius marito.

without reason, *but only mildly*, then this was not necessarily grounds on which a separation might be endorsed. Only when punishment was both severe and unjust should a wife be allowed to separate from her husband.[25]

Although canon law was quite explicit, in legal practice the interpretation of corporal punishment was variable. When pleas to be freed from the company of violent husbands reached the court, the vicar (who administered justice *in spiritualibus*) and the Venetian Patriarch had great discretionary powers at their disposal in sentencing these cases. When ecclesiastical examiners sought the reasons for unjust and cruel government, they sometimes interrogated women as to the 'serious reason' (*causa grave*) that had motivated the husband to mistreat his wife. Deep hatred (*odio grave*) constituted one of the four grounds on which a separation might be granted, but not if it had been caused by female disobedience.[26] A woman thus had to convince the ecclesiastical judges that she had served her husband diligently – she would even attempt to do the impossible and provide her husband with the 'milk of a chicken', as one woman claimed in her deposition. She explained her husband's insensitive behaviour as a symptom of his 'bad character', emphasising the arbitrariness and excessiveness of his use of force over both her and the household. It was his hatred rather than her behaviour, she argued, which was the reason for marital discord.[27] It was, then, the listening to depositions from litigants and witnesses by which the meaning of wife-beating had to be assessed in the courtroom – had it exceeded the limits of the acceptable or had it been applied 'justly' and 'with reason'? Whereas husbands' complaints about adulterous wives concentrated on single acts of infidelity or immoral behaviour, women's complaints about domestic violence had to prove that patriarchal authority had been continuously abused, sometimes over years. Conjugal violence, as Laura Gowing has demonstrated, was a 'complex and subjectively determined affair' that was harder 'to measure and to sentence' than adultery.[28] Because the assessment depended on both the circumstances and the extent, allegations brought by women had to argue convincingly that husbands had used their authority excessively and 'without any foundation'. It was wives,

---

[25] My emphasis. For the legal discussion see Quaglioni, 2000, p. 111ff. and Sánchez, 1607, Book X, Disputatio 18, liber 10, p. 884, para. 46. For a humanist view see Passi, 1602, p. 144.

[26] Quaglioni, 2000, p. 114.

[27] ASPV, Curia, II, C.M., Reg. 78: 26 April 1584, Francisci Bono cum Claudia eius uxore, not foliated, interrogation of Claudia Grimani, 8 July 1584.

[28] Gowing, 1996, p. 207.

not husbands, who had to prove that their behaviour was both honourable and deferential. Only then could women plausibly allege that marital dysfunction and breakdown were caused by male misrule and abuse of authority.

But, as we have seen, women were easily open to attack because of the husband's right to punish and correct his wife. Because the meaning and the extent of corporal punishment, and therefore the nature of patriarchal authority itself, was debated in court, wives always had to be prepared for counter-allegations defending male household rule. Ecclesiastical judges were thus forced to listen to endless legal battles between women and men who could never agree on either the level of domestic violence or the circumstances.

A case which forcefully demonstrates the contested meaning of domestic violence and patriarchal authority, is that which Pasquetta Peregrini initiated at the Patriarchal Court in April 1584. The plaintiff Pasquetta Peregrini complained to the notary (who recorded her deposition while she was staying in the convent of Sant'Andrea) that during her four-year marriage to Romano Cavatia, a Venetian manuscript illuminator (*Venetus miniator*), she had suffered continuously and had not experienced 'four good hours'. Because of poor nutrition and the violence inflicted on her she had black eyes from having been beaten so severely.[29] Pasquetta alleged that her husband had locked her in a room and gagged her with a handkerchief in order to prevent their neighbours in the parish of S. Moisè from witnessing his abuse. Domestic confinement such as this was a drastic measure, but it served to reduce the possibility of credible witnesses who might later testify that they had heard the woman screaming. Only two days after their wedding Pasquetta and her husband had argued, seemingly over a trivial issue. Pasquetta stated that she had wished to colour her hair blonde, a Venetian fashion that men generally seem to have disliked and criticised at the end of the sixteenth century (see Figure 6.1).[30] Years later Pasquetta recalled in her statement how her husband had 'come up' (most probably to an *altana* where women commonly bleached their hair) 'in a fury and had dragged me down with force ... and gave me five or six slaps'.

Although this behaviour could still be regarded as 'moderate correction', the intervention of her brother Vincenzo when Cavatia attacked her with a dagger demonstrates that she had been in serious

---

[29] ASPV, Curia, II, C.M., Reg. 78: 26 April 1584, Pasquette cum Romano Cavatia, fols 20r–v.

[30] According to Moderata Fonte. See Cox, 1997, p. 234.

6.1   Woman bleaching her hair (Grevembroch, *Gli Abiti de' Veneziani*)

danger. Indeed, Vincenzo himself had lost a finger in the struggle.[31] Beatings resulting in the spilling of blood seem to have crossed contemporary sensibilities. When Romano Cavatia was interrogated as to whether he had 'ever battered his wife until she was bleeding and had given her black eyes, especially during the holy week', he firmly denied the accusations.[32] Whereas Pasquetta argued that she had been treated unjustly and beaten severely without reason, Romano attacked her sexual honour by portraying her mother as a female pimp. He also argued that Pasquetta had not been forced to abandon the conjugal household because she lived in mortal danger (as she had claimed), but that she had left willingly and had gone to live with her mother and her sister, whom he portrayed as women with a bad reputation – and there

---

[31] ASPV, Curia, II, C.M., Reg. 78: 26 April 1584, Pasquette cum Romano Cavatia, fols 20r–v.

[32] Ibid., fol. 24v. For different sensibilities in Florence, see Di Simplicio, 1990, pp. 33–50, especially 46.

was no doubt that he implied that their immoral behaviour reflected hers as well.[33]

In transforming domestic and marital disputes into legal battles, the escalation of household disputes was commonly interpreted as the husband's loss of temper and good sense. Wife-beating husbands are portrayed as furious and as having given up prudence and wisdom, overpowered by their emotions. Just as they would deny the use of excessive violence, husbands would also reject allegations of abuse of patriarchal authority which reinforced the image of misrule, or even of tyranny. Rule and misrule were two different expressions of patriarchal authority: one was equated with sound government whereas the other was perceived as abusive. Because cruelty and severe domestic violence could easily be associated with tyrannical rule, husbands rejected accusations of atrocities and cruelty against their wives. When husbands occasionally admitted to corporal punishment, they simply referred to the essential goods that patriarchy had bestowed on them, namely, the right to correct female disobedience moderately.

As in annulment suits, complaints of violence that reached the Patriarchal Court had to allege the extreme. Because chastisement was a right that the husband could exercise over his wife, women had to emphasise that they had been continuously the victim of unjustified physical violence, to the extent that their life had been endangered. Unrestrained domestic violence was central to the charges of marital cruelty, and a threat of mortal danger often was alleged. Suffering caused by casual battering and severe household government did not guarantee an end to marital conjugality; canon marital law permitted a separation only when the life of the woman was endangered.[34] In making their unhappy or even dangerous marital circumstances a legal case, women therefore had to emphasise the life-threatening violence and heavy injuries that they had suffered. The impression of life-threatening physical punishment increased, as we have seen, when husbands were accused of having used weapons such as knives or daggers either to threaten or to actually attack their wives. Allegations of cruelty and violence were, additionally, strengthened when it could be proven that a husband had forced his wife to write her will and bequeath everything to him immediately after solemnisation of the marriage. When property concerns were an issue, wives claimed that husbands even attempted murder.[35]

---

[33] ASPV, Curia, II, C.M., Reg. 78: 26 April 1584, fol. 24v.

[34] Quaglioni, 2000, p. 115.

[35] A case in point is ASPV, Curia, II, C.M., Reg. 91, 12 May 1634, Ursete Targhetta cum Annibale Ricamatore, fols 12r–v, 14r–v, 16v and 18r. On this case see Ferraro, 2000, pp. 141–90.

Not just the domestic violence itself but also its circumstances were in dispute. Neighbours and physicians who had seen black and swollen eyes, bodily wounds and other traces of physical mistreatment on a woman were powerful witnesses. Yet still the spouses quarrelled over the causes and the meaning of injuries, serious or otherwise. Whereas women cited them as evidence of cruelty and atrocities, men could interpret wounds as the result of an accident during an argument. As one shoemaker argued in court, while he and his wife were having a dispute he had shoved her and she had fallen on to a chest and injured her head seriously enough to require treatment by the physician Zaccaria in S. Felice.[36]

Violent attacks during pregnancy – a time when a husband was supposed to support his wife and treat her with great care[37] – were sometimes given as additional evidence for severe cruelty. Careless behaviour (such as failing to call a doctor when necessary) or arbitrary violence endangered the life of both mother and child, and in early modern Venice physical mistreatment of pregnant wives was perceived as especially unjustified, as it carried the danger of a miscarriage. In one case Paolina Portello emphasised in court that her husband Francesco de Fullatorio had never cared about the fact that she was pregnant. Although she was in the sixth month or so, as she specified in her legal statement, he 'had punched and slapped her and had battered her with a stick and with a whip all over her body so that it had become black from head to toe, without any regard for the creature she was carrying.'[38] She even accused him of being responsible for her miscarriage, for he had subsequently kicked her down the stairs. In cases such as these midwives became powerful witnesses who had to assess whether a miscarriage or premature birth was due to violence inflicted on the mother or some other cause.

Household government and moral integrity

Although canon law restricted the right to grant separations on grounds of cruelty and deep hatred, women's allegations did not end here, for a husband's moral integrity was an essential aspect of good household

---

36 ASPV, Curia, II, C.M., Reg. 82: 5 July 1593, Alexandri Calegary cum Cecilia q. Stephani Muschiary, not foliated; deposition of Cecilia and responses by Alessandro on 12 July 1593.

37 On this argument see Rublack, 1996, pp. 84–110.

38 ASPV, Curia, II, C.M., Reg. 75: 13 May 1580, Francisci de Fulatoribus cum Pauline filia q.m Antony Portello, fols 9v–10r and 42r–v.

government. These ideals were measured by focusing on their opposite: immoral behaviour such as drinking, whoring, gambling and the dissipation of household resources. These allegations illustrate the pressure to rule with wisdom and care, demonstrate the head of the household's responsibility for his wife, children and servants, and reveal the disappointed marital expectations of wives. 'Bad' government, understood in both economic and moral terms, was a particularly common accusation. Lucrezia Nardi, whose husband had a spice shop, alleged in court that soon after their marriage 'the misrule of Messer Pietro began, when he let everything go and cared neither for his wife, nor his house'.[39] Had her husband ruled sensibly and taken care of his wife, it was implied, she would not have been forced to seek a legal separation at the Patriarchal Court.

When spouses drifted apart, this not only threatened the marital union but also affected the entire household. As in disputes between children and parents, in those between husband and wife every household member had to adopt a position. Children were forced to behave unambiguously when domestic disputes escalated. They had to decide whether to side with their father or their mother. If they supported the mother, they behaved disrespectfully towards the father. These moral dilemmas were dispelled, however, when the life of the mother was in danger. In these situations children (and other family members) reported in court how they had intervened in order to prevent physical violence from becoming life-threatening. The following is an exteme case in point.

The wife Angela Barbara who sought a legal separation at the ecclesiastical tribunal in July 1585, was married to Natalino, a man without a profession (*facci arte nessuna*).[40] As Angela's adoptive daughter Paolina emphasised in court, he had the reputation of being a lazy drunkard.[41] In about 1578 he had moved into her household in S. Giacomo dall'Orio. According to Paolina, initially all was well, but then early in the seven-year marriage Natalino's work ethos as a painter began to deteriorate. He had started drinking in the morning and was usually so drunk that it was 'impossible to live with him'. As Paolina remarked in court: '[Natalino] never wanted to work, and bought, instead, ready-made goods ... and when he came home he would bring barrels of white wine with him, which he would often take as breakfast

---

[39] ASPV, Curia, II, C.M., Reg. 87: 23 August 1623, Lucretie Nardi cum Petro Grattarolo, fol. 7v.

[40] ASPV, Curia, II, C.M., Reg. 80: 12 July 1585, Angele Barbare cum Natalino, witness deposition of Angela's female servant, 14 July 1585.

[41] Ibid., deposition of Paolina, 13 July 1585, not foliated.

... so that he would get drunk.'[42] When he came home drunk he was especially likely to quarrel and to beat his wife. Paolina recalled one day when Natalino's behaviour was especially menacing and he had threatened Angela with a sword, whereupon all members of the household started shrieking. On another occasion he had asked Angela to come to bed (presumably to pay the marital debt); when she had not followed immediately, he had flown into an enormous fury. Paolina went on to describe in detail 'how Natalino had pulled out half of Angela's hair, and had punched and strangled her.' He had then threatened her with a knife, at which point Paolina, her uncle Andrea Zurcato and another child had intervened and were punched and thrown to the ground. In Paolina's legal narrative, Natalino's government was equated with misrule and metaphorically reinforced the image of tyranny. The way he used his male authority was not a stabilising factor in maintaining the gendered order of family and household life. The arbitrariness of Natalino's cruelty was emphasised when Paolina alleged that anybody interfering in this household drama had become the victim of violence and aggression. Indeed, when Paolina's grandmother intervened to help her, the infuriated Natalino tried to push the old woman into a canal. If Angela Barbara, who had deserted her husband, was to return to him, it was argued that she would encounter mortal danger.[43]

Together with physical violence and other atrocities, economic misery of the household and its members were the subject of dispute in a number of cases which reached the Patriarchal Court. The privations wives alleged were caused exclusively by the cruel and immoral behaviour of their heartless husbands, and not by any economic or material crisis. Cecilia Bartolomeo Bressan Garzotti, for example, had deserted her husband Oratio Cerdono several times. When in January 1580 he sued her for the restitution of conjugal rights, she alleged financial deprivation and life-threatening violence during pregnancy. His excessive violence had caused her miscarriage, as one Lucrezia from the parish of S. Vidal reported. In March 1580 Constantino was summoned as a witness. He made a connection between the physical mistreatment and the dissipation of household resources. Cecilia's sufferings, he found, were caused by Oratio, a man 'who does not know how to lead a civilised life and who spends much more than he is earning; and when he is without money, he quarrels with his wife and beats her.' He therefore had reproached Oratio various times, shouting at him and asking the reason for such harsh government and arbitrary discipline

---

42 Ibid.
43 Ibid.

over his wife. Unsurprisingly, Oratio had portrayed his behaviour as his right as a husband to inflict 'moderate corrections' on his disobedient wife.[44]

Industriousness, working abilities and discipline were crucial to the contemporary understanding of a moral Christian life and were a measure of civic values. In the Venetian communities, female and male witnesses alike expressed their disapproval of lazy husbands and their compassion for mistreated wives. The witness Matteo, who had been a neighbour of Barbara de Grandi and Pietro Nini when they were living in the parish of S. Giacomo dall'Orio, had noticed Barbara because she was often crying. He had inquired into the reasons for her tears, and she had told him about her unhappy marriage, accusing her husband of going with prostitutes, deflowering a virgin and cohabiting with a married woman. Through Pietro Nini's *poltroneria* (as Barbara de Grandi described his misconduct) he had squandered the dowry, beaten her unjustly and generally caused misery to the family. According to Barbara, Nini's laziness went so far as to convince her to make up the economic shortfall by selling her body to other men, yet her husband was reluctant to earn money as a painter.[45] By associating Pietro Nini's dishonourable lifestyle first of all with his lack of endeavour, in his deposition Matteo made a connection between labour and moral values in early modern communities. He then confirmed Barbara's allegation of adultery.[46] Here, male infidelity received legal weight because it was perceived as an argument for Pietro Nini's general immoral behaviour. In the perception of parish members, laziness and immoral behaviour clearly endangered the economic union of marriage and marital conjugality as such, resulting, ultimately, in the collapse of household order.

The failure to care for and to support the household members might even turn the household order upside down. Camilla Bellotto – daughter of a respectable tailor – had been married to Angelo de Bossi for some 25 years. In this time they had shared a conjugal home for only about six months. In 1617 she pleaded for a separation from him on the grounds of severe cruelty. Her husband's laziness, she alleged, had gone as far as forcing her to do the shopping and to run the household – tasks that were part of the husband's household duties.[47] When he had made

---

[44] ASPV, Curia, II, Reg. 75: 8 January 1580, Oraty q.m Battiste Cerdonis cum Cecilia Bartholamei Bressan Garzotti, 15 March 1580.

[45] ASPV, C.M., Reg. 94: 11 August 1685, Barbare filie Nicolai de Grandis cum Petro Nini, deposition of Barbara de Grandi, 5 September 1685.

[46] Ibid., witness Matteo.

[47] Striking in this context is the amount of control that husbands had over food and

use of her 'honest beauty', as she alleged, and had made money by selling her 'flesh' to other men, she had abandoned him. Angelo, however, denied the allegations and stressed that Camilla was a 'whore' leading a sinful life – while he dutifully received the sacraments.[48]

Mothers in particular were furious when their daughters' misery was caused by the idleness of their sons-in-law. Orsetta, daughter of the deceased Venetian wool merchant Giacomo Targhetta, had brought her case to court only six or seven months after she had married Annibale Basso, a tailor. In 1634 Orsetta alleged the extreme: attempted murder by poisoning. Before this couple came before the ecclesiastical judges they had not lived in harmony: soon after their wedding Annibale had committed adultery, an allegation he denied. He had insulted his wife, calling her a 'mad woman' and a 'beast', and had sold her wedding ring and earrings. According to Orsetta, her widowed mother Bortola had quarrelled with Annibale, reminding him to lead a better life and to care for his family and household.[49]

Disputes over possessions: household goods and dowries

While the causing of the general misery of the household, as we have seen, was a complaint wives brought forward together with physical violence and other atrocities, more specifically, household goods were another subject of dispute, and complaints focusing on insufficient clothes and other textiles for the household were brought forward by women suing for separation. Inventories from the late sixteenth century onwards give insights into the material culture of early modern households that was under dispute. These inventories display the wealth and the surprising quantities of household possessions of Venetian artisans and shopkeepers. Workers from the arsenal lived and died, as Robert Davis has remarked, in the 'midst of personal worlds filled with material goods'.[50] Apparently, some sort of adornment was not unusual

---

other household goods that could be seen as female responsibilities. Thomas Coryat was equally struck by seeing a *gentiluomo* shopping at the Rialto – a job, he notes, which should be carried out by servants and not by the master himself. See Coryat, 1611, vol. 2, pp. 31–2. It would seem that the husband had control over the money and provided the necessary goods for the household, such as bread, wine, oil and wood. A woman's duty consisted in utilising them. Evidence for this division of labour and responsibilities is given in Chapter 9.

48 ASPV, Curia, II, C.M., Reg. 85: Camille Bellotti cum Angelo de Bossis, fol. 11r.

49 Ibid., Reg. 91: 12 May 1634, Ursette Targhetta cum Annibale Ricamatore, fols 12v–13r On the social disparity of this couple see Ferraro, 2000, pp. 143–4.

50 Davis, 1991, p. 100. The making of marriages was also a financial transfer of

in better-off *popolani* families, for pearls or rings are also often mentioned when artisan women abandoned their husbands and took movable goods with them.[51] Also the previously mentioned household of Benedetta Spinelli and Pietro Franchini seems to have been blessed with material goods. Because the use and the ownership of these goods was contested, in January 1638 a witness was questioned about whether he had pawned rings, earrings, a silver salt cellar, the wedding ring, bracelets and other possessions of Donna Benedetta. He answered that he had given her five *scudi d'argento* for the salt cellar, the wedding ring and another ring, and that after selling the ring he had given her the rest of the money, which she needed for living costs and for buying extra clothes because the winter was so exceptionally cold.[52] Because within marriage these material goods – including the woman's clothes – were considered to be the husband's possessions, even though the wife had the right to use and wear them, this issue had been brought up in court.

During legal proceedings at the Patriarchal Court clothes and other material goods were, therefore, discussed in the wider context of a husband's duty to care and provide for his wife. In the early modern period, clothes had a distinctive social function. These items played an increasingly important role as indicators of status in the context of urban societies.[53] They were important for the fostering of individual identities – not only of the patrician elite – and might have functioned as a means of collective identification as well.[54] When the head of the household wasted the dowry he put at risk the resources designated for his wife's clothes and other items. Poor clothing and a lack of household goods as a consequence of financial mismanagement could then be seen as a variation of male misrule. A case in point is that of Laura, who demanded that her husband Filippo Sansary 'should be obliged to provide food and clothes for me'. He had received 400 ducats as a dowry, enough to clothe her as demanded by her social position as a

---

goods. The dowry, for example, in the marriage between Nicolosa (daughter of a fustian dealer) and Marco (son of Francesco, a *traghetto* gondolier at the Rialto) included 20 blouses, 19 handkerchiefs, 24 tablecloths, 13 pairs of socks (including one silk pair), 12 pairs of shoes (plus one pair of high heels), 12 silver nails and assorted kitchen utensils. Because Marco also gave Nicolosa 133 ducats as a counter-dowry, this couple had 800 ducats at their disposal when they married in 1633. See ASV, *Atti Notarili*, 10902: Paganuzzi, Gerolamo, fol. 14v, 4 March 1657.

[51] See, for example, ASPV, Curia, II, C.M., Reg. 85: 3 June 1616: Magdalene Vincentine cum Gaspare eius marito. Interrogation of Magdalena.

[52] ASPV, Curia, II, C.M., Reg. 92: 22 September 1637, Benedicte Spinelli cum Petro Franchino, witness Hilarius, 28 January 1638.

[53] On artisans and clothes during the sixteenth century, see Schmidt, 1990, p. 39.

[54] Allerston, 2000, p. 381.

goldsmith's daughter. She had been forced to leave him, she claimed, because he had squandered the household resources through gambling.[55]

The lack of material goods also figures prominently in allegations by affluent citizens. Because the dowry[56] – although the wife's property – could not be invested without the husband's consent,[57] when marital peace was contested the economic autonomy of a patrician woman was seemingly weakened. Nobles Christine Priuli and Giovanni Semiteculo had married in 1631 and were living in Dorsoduro, in the parish of S. Gregorio. Part of the wife's accusations referred to the constant quarrels with her husband over property issues. These disputes had escalated approximately one year before, since the time her husband had refused to eat or drink with her or to speak to her. He had also failed to provide her with clothes and other household goods such as sheets, tablecloths or napkins.[58] In patrician marriages disputes over material goods extended to the whole living standard, which was of great concern to wives in the higher ranks of society. This can be illustrated by the troubled marriage of Elisabetta Bembo and Francesco Priuli. In 1623 Elisabetta had pleaded for a separation on grounds of her husband's severe cruelty, mental torment and infidelity. Priuli tried his best to counter the allegations of starvation and life-threatening violence, insisting that he had taken care to provide his wife with all the essentials for life as an honourable *gentildonna*. He paid her the necessary respect, as she was waited on by servants and had everything that a noble wife could wish for. He further emphasised that he had spent a considerable amount of money to provide clothes, pearls, earrings and rings for her.[59] Jewellery and luxury items were a visible and distinctive sign of patrician wives and were required in order to honour the family and to render the

---

55 ASPV, Curia, II, C.M., Reg. 74: 9 September 1579, Philippi q.m Antony Sansary cum Laura filia Sebastiani Aureficis, not foliated.

56 During the fourteenth century patrician women received a *corredo*, a sort of trousseau consisting of both 'personal goods for the bride and cash'. The importance of the *corredo* was that, in contrast to the dowry, it was given to the bride for her own use and was intended to array her 'in clothing and jewellery'. By the early fifteenth century, however, the *corredo* had evolved into a gift to the husband. However, some patrician husbands gave their wives 'some of the profits they made investing their dowries', although this practice does not seem to have been prescribed in Venetian statutes. Chojnacki, 2000a, pp. 76–94 and 123ff.

57 Chojnacki, 2000a, pp. 76–94. Chojnacki reports that patrician women owned outright possessions from legacies and non-dowry property as well. Their most important economic resource, however, remained the dowry. Ibid., p. 123ff.

58 ASPV, Curia, II, C.M., Reg. 91: 3 December 1634, Christine Priuli cum Joanne Semiteculo, January 1634.

59 He did so in his written statement, see ASPV, Curia, II, C.M., Reg. 87: 19 May 1623, Elisabeth Bembo cum Francisco Priuli, Francesco Priuli, 24 January 1624.

women beautiful.[60] In separation suits involving the patriciate (but also in artisan marriages), to put material goods at the wife's disposal was not only a measure that allowed conclusions about a husband's household rule and sense of matrimonial conjugality, but was an issue over which feelings like respect or disrespect were negotiated.

In order to secure female possessions, the amount of the dowry and the conditions of payment in terms of movable goods (*mobili*) and fixed property (*stabili*) were sometimes set in the marital contract, which paid special attention to the conservation of the dowry while it was administered by the husband. These conditions also could be fixed during the marriage, arguably when financial mismanagement was an issue, as in the following case in which a notarial act was only set up in the presence of two witnesses some 27 years after the couple had married. The husband, Francesco Capella, had received 400 ducats upon marrying Laura. In December 1657 Francesco was held 'to preserve and to protect [the dowry] as expected from a good husband and to return it to his wife in the case that a restitution of the dowry is demanded'.[61] Patrician husbands even had to put their estate 'under obligation toward repayment of his wife's dowry', and in case of his death this responsibility fell to his father, even when the son had already been emancipated. When a husband died his heirs' first task was to ensure that the widow received her dowry back.[62] However, dowry contracts could specify that part of the dowry was destined for the wife's use – for her clothes and so forth. Domenico Licini, for example, assigned 50 ducats of his daughter's dowry for her own use when she married in 1657.[63]

Because financial mismanagement brought social misery to the household and endangered its stability, in early modern Venice the protection of female property was institutionalised. To promote the stability of society it thus was in the government's interests to prevent the financial collapse of Venetian households by safeguarding dowries against dissipation by husbands. Various civil magistracies – for example the Giudici del Proprio – had jurisdiction over dowry matters.[64] The Giudici del Procurator, as mentioned in Chapter 3, had authority over the economic aspects of marital conflicts, such as alimony payments in

---

60 Labalme, 1981, pp. 81–109.

61 ASV, *Atti Notarili*, Protocollo 5511: Giorgio Emo, 1656–57, fol. 505r.

62 See Chojnacki, 2000a, p. 124, where he mentions other dowry safeguards as well.

63 ASV, *Atti Notarili*, Protocollo 5511: Giorgio Emo, 1656–57, fol. 484v. Another example is ibid., fols 504v–505r.

64 On these magistracies see Chojnacki, 2000a, chap. 4. On the Florentine case see Kirshner, 1985, pp. 256–303.

separation cases and, more generally, dowry prote
1561 this magistracy was widely used by the so-call
and was – according to Angelo Rigo – an instituti
economic aspects of marital conflicts in favour of
Women could plead legal separation at the Pa
simultaneously use the civil magistracy to settle th
their marital breakdown. An example is the af
Pasquetta Peregrini, who sued her husband
separation at the ecclesiastical tribunal while bringi
for dissipating the dowry at the Giudici del Procura
family.[66] Since she came from a wealthy artisan fami
only patrician women who took steps to protect t
their property, as cases held before the Giudici
initiated by women of all social ranks. In lower-clas
focused on the extreme misery and constraints of t
a result of their husbands' misrule, general cruel
Franceschina, who had protected her dowry,
Patriarchal Court about the material impact her h
had on her life: '... after [he had] abandoned wife
belongings he left this city and did not return
months ... [and] he never once supported or helpe

Wives thus exercised foresight and made fi
future, especially when the economic situation of
decline due to debts run up by the husba
mismanagement was an issue women had strong
and in their fathers in particular.[70] Daughters an
seen, were bound by the *patria potestas*, that is, t
father possessed over his daughter even after s

---

[65] See Rigo, 1992–93, pp. 256–8 and 2000, p. 531. Ferr
be more sceptical.

[66] ASPV, Curia, II, C.M., Reg. 78: 26 April 1584, Pasq
fol. 40v. Another case in which dowry protection is mentioned
Reg. 83: 11 January 1596, Joannis fily Pauli à Papa cum
Ausulani, fol. 20r. However, further investigation is needed
simultaneous use of ecclesiastical and civil tribunals was.

[67] On the legal practice of this magistracy see Rigo, 199
pp. 519–36.

[68] ASPV, Curia, II, C.M., Reg. 83: 11 January 1596, Jo
Franceschina filia Gratiosi Ausulani, fol. 17r.

[69] Rigo, 1992–93, p. 252.

[70] Insofar, the Venetian situation seems to have differed fr
fifteenth-century Florence, Christine Klapisch-Zuber has ar
were only 'passing guests' in the male-headed houses, with
families. Klapisch-Zuber, 1987, pp. 117–18.

government. These ideals were measured by focusing on their opposite: immoral behaviour such as drinking, whoring, gambling and the dissipation of household resources. These allegations illustrate the pressure to rule with wisdom and care, demonstrate the head of the household's responsibility for his wife, children and servants, and reveal the disappointed marital expectations of wives. 'Bad' government, understood in both economic and moral terms, was a particularly common accusation. Lucrezia Nardi, whose husband had a spice shop, alleged in court that soon after their marriage 'the misrule of Messer Pietro began, when he let everything go and cared neither for his wife, nor his house'.[39] Had her husband ruled sensibly and taken care of his wife, it was implied, she would not have been forced to seek a legal separation at the Patriarchal Court.

When spouses drifted apart, this not only threatened the marital union but also affected the entire household. As in disputes between children and parents, in those between husband and wife every household member had to adopt a position. Children were forced to behave unambiguously when domestic disputes escalated. They had to decide whether to side with their father or their mother. If they supported the mother, they behaved disrespectfully towards the father. These moral dilemmas were dispelled, however, when the life of the mother was in danger. In these situations children (and other family members) reported in court how they had intervened in order to prevent physical violence from becoming life-threatening. The following is an exteme case in point.

The wife Angela Barbara who sought a legal separation at the ecclesiastical tribunal in July 1585, was married to Natalino, a man without a profession (*facci arte nessuna*).[40] As Angela's adoptive daughter Paolina emphasised in court, he had the reputation of being a lazy drunkard.[41] In about 1578 he had moved into her household in S. Giacomo dall'Orio. According to Paolina, initially all was well, but then early in the seven-year marriage Natalino's work ethos as a painter began to deteriorate. He had started drinking in the morning and was usually so drunk that it was 'impossible to live with him'. As Paolina remarked in court: '[Natalino] never wanted to work, and bought, instead, ready-made goods ... and when he came home he would bring barrels of white wine with him, which he would often take as breakfast

---

[39] ASPV, Curia, II, C.M., Reg. 87: 23 August 1623, Lucretie Nardi cum Petro Grattarolo, fol. 7v.

[40] ASPV, Curia, II, C.M., Reg. 80: 12 July 1585, Angele Barbare cum Natalino, witness deposition of Angela's female servant, 14 July 1585.

[41] Ibid., deposition of Paolina, 13 July 1585, not foliated.

... so that he would get drunk.'[42] When he came home drunk he was especially likely to quarrel and to beat his wife. Paolina recalled one day when Natalino's behaviour was especially menacing and he had threatened Angela with a sword, whereupon all members of the household started shrieking. On another occasion he had asked Angela to come to bed (presumably to pay the marital debt); when she had not followed immediately, he had flown into an enormous fury. Paolina went on to describe in detail 'how Natalino had pulled out half of Angela's hair, and had punched and strangled her.' He had then threatened her with a knife, at which point Paolina, her uncle Andrea Zurcato and another child had intervened and were punched and thrown to the ground. In Paolina's legal narrative, Natalino's government was equated with misrule and metaphorically reinforced the image of tyranny. The way he used his male authority was not a stabilising factor in maintaining the gendered order of family and household life. The arbitrariness of Natalino's cruelty was emphasised when Paolina alleged that anybody interfering in this household drama had become the victim of violence and aggression. Indeed, when Paolina's grandmother intervened to help her, the infuriated Natalino tried to push the old woman into a canal. If Angela Barbara, who had deserted her husband, was to return to him, it was argued that she would encounter mortal danger.[43]

Together with physical violence and other atrocities, economic misery of the household and its members were the subject of dispute in a number of cases which reached the Patriarchal Court. The privations wives alleged were caused exclusively by the cruel and immoral behaviour of their heartless husbands, and not by any economic or material crisis. Cecilia Bartolomeo Bressan Garzotti, for example, had deserted her husband Oratio Cerdono several times. When in January 1580 he sued her for the restitution of conjugal rights, she alleged financial deprivation and life-threatening violence during pregnancy. His excessive violence had caused her miscarriage, as one Lucrezia from the parish of S. Vidal reported. In March 1580 Constantino was summoned as a witness. He made a connection between the physical mistreatment and the dissipation of household resources. Cecilia's sufferings, he found, were caused by Oratio, a man 'who does not know how to lead a civilised life and who spends much more than he is earning; and when he is without money, he quarrels with his wife and beats her.' He therefore had reproached Oratio various times, shouting at him and asking the reason for such harsh government and arbitrary discipline

---

[42] Ibid.
[43] Ibid.

over his wife. Unsurprisingly, Oratio had portrayed his behaviour as his right as a husband to inflict 'moderate corrections' on his disobedient wife.[44]

Industriousness, working abilities and discipline were crucial to the contemporary understanding of a moral Christian life and were a measure of civic values. In the Venetian communities, female and male witnesses alike expressed their disapproval of lazy husbands and their compassion for mistreated wives. The witness Matteo, who had been a neighbour of Barbara de Grandi and Pietro Nini when they were living in the parish of S. Giacomo dall'Orio, had noticed Barbara because she was often crying. He had inquired into the reasons for her tears, and she had told him about her unhappy marriage, accusing her husband of going with prostitutes, deflowering a virgin and cohabiting with a married woman. Through Pietro Nini's *poltroneria* (as Barbara de Grandi described his misconduct) he had squandered the dowry, beaten her unjustly and generally caused misery to the family. According to Barbara, Nini's laziness went so far as to convince her to make up the economic shortfall by selling her body to other men, yet her husband was reluctant to earn money as a painter.[45] By associating Pietro Nini's dishonourable lifestyle first of all with his lack of endeavour, in his deposition Matteo made a connection between labour and moral values in early modern communities. He then confirmed Barbara's allegation of adultery.[46] Here, male infidelity received legal weight because it was perceived as an argument for Pietro Nini's general immoral behaviour. In the perception of parish members, laziness and immoral behaviour clearly endangered the economic union of marriage and marital conjugality as such, resulting, ultimately, in the collapse of household order.

The failure to care for and to support the household members might even turn the household order upside down. Camilla Bellotto – daughter of a respectable tailor – had been married to Angelo de Bossi for some 25 years. In this time they had shared a conjugal home for only about six months. In 1617 she pleaded for a separation from him on the grounds of severe cruelty. Her husband's laziness, she alleged, had gone as far as forcing her to do the shopping and to run the household – tasks that were part of the husband's household duties.[47] When he had made

44 ASPV, Curia, II, Reg. 75: 8 January 1580, Oraty q.m Battiste Cerdonis cum Cecilia Bartholamei Bressan Garzotti, 15 March 1580.

45 ASPV, C.M., Reg. 94: 11 August 1685, Barbare filie Nicolai de Grandis cum Petro Nini, deposition of Barbara de Grandi, 5 September 1685.

46 Ibid., witness Matteo.

47 Striking in this context is the amount of control that husbands had over food and

use of her 'honest beauty', as she alleged, and had made money by selling her 'flesh' to other men, she had abandoned him. Angelo, however, denied the allegations and stressed that Camilla was a 'whore' leading a sinful life – while he dutifully received the sacraments.[48]

Mothers in particular were furious when their daughters' misery was caused by the idleness of their sons-in-law. Orsetta, daughter of the deceased Venetian wool merchant Giacomo Targhetta, had brought her case to court only six or seven months after she had married Annibale Basso, a tailor. In 1634 Orsetta alleged the extreme: attempted murder by poisoning. Before this couple came before the ecclesiastical judges they had not lived in harmony: soon after their wedding Annibale had committed adultery, an allegation he denied. He had insulted his wife, calling her a 'mad woman' and a 'beast', and had sold her wedding ring and earrings. According to Orsetta, her widowed mother Bortola had quarrelled with Annibale, reminding him to lead a better life and to care for his family and household.[49]

Disputes over possessions: household goods and dowries

While the causing of the general misery of the household, as we have seen, was a complaint wives brought forward together with physical violence and other atrocities, more specifically, household goods were another subject of dispute, and complaints focusing on insufficient clothes and other textiles for the household were brought forward by women suing for separation. Inventories from the late sixteenth century onwards give insights into the material culture of early modern households that was under dispute. These inventories display the wealth and the surprising quantities of household possessions of Venetian artisans and shopkeepers. Workers from the arsenal lived and died, as Robert Davis has remarked, in the 'midst of personal worlds filled with material goods'.[50] Apparently, some sort of adornment was not unusual

---

other household goods that could be seen as female responsibilities. Thomas Coryat was equally struck by seeing a *gentiluomo* shopping at the Rialto – a job, he notes, which should be carried out by servants and not by the master himself. See Coryat, 1611, vol. 2, pp. 31–2. It would seem that the husband had control over the money and provided the necessary goods for the household, such as bread, wine, oil and wood. A woman's duty consisted in utilising them. Evidence for this division of labour and responsibilities is given in Chapter 9.

[48] ASPV, Curia, II, C.M., Reg. 85: Camille Bellotti cum Angelo de Bossis, fol. 11r.

[49] Ibid., Reg. 91: 12 May 1634, Ursette Targhetta cum Annibale Ricamatore, fols 12v–13r On the social disparity of this couple see Ferraro, 2000, pp. 143–4.

[50] Davis, 1991, p. 100. The making of marriages was also a financial transfer of

in better-off *popolani* families, for pearls or rings are also often mentioned when artisan women abandoned their husbands and took movable goods with them.[51] Also the previously mentioned household of Benedetta Spinelli and Pietro Franchini seems to have been blessed with material goods. Because the use and the ownership of these goods was contested, in January 1638 a witness was questioned about whether he had pawned rings, earrings, a silver salt cellar, the wedding ring, bracelets and other possessions of Donna Benedetta. He answered that he had given her five *scudi d'argento* for the salt cellar, the wedding ring and another ring, and that after selling the ring he had given her the rest of the money, which she needed for living costs and for buying extra clothes because the winter was so exceptionally cold.[52] Because within marriage these material goods – including the woman's clothes – were considered to be the husband's possessions, even though the wife had the right to use and wear them, this issue had been brought up in court.

During legal proceedings at the Patriarchal Court clothes and other material goods were, therefore, discussed in the wider context of a husband's duty to care and provide for his wife. In the early modern period, clothes had a distinctive social function. These items played an increasingly important role as indicators of status in the context of urban societies.[53] They were important for the fostering of individual identities – not only of the patrician elite – and might have functioned as a means of collective identification as well.[54] When the head of the household wasted the dowry he put at risk the resources designated for his wife's clothes and other items. Poor clothing and a lack of household goods as a consequence of financial mismanagement could then be seen as a variation of male misrule. A case in point is that of Laura, who demanded that her husband Filippo Sansary 'should be obliged to provide food and clothes for me'. He had received 400 ducats as a dowry, enough to clothe her as demanded by her social position as a

---

goods. The dowry, for example, in the marriage between Nicolosa (daughter of a fustian dealer) and Marco (son of Francesco, a *traghetto* gondolier at the Rialto) included 20 blouses, 19 handkerchiefs, 24 tablecloths, 13 pairs of socks (including one silk pair), 12 pairs of shoes (plus one pair of high heels), 12 silver nails and assorted kitchen utensils. Because Marco also gave Nicolosa 133 ducats as a counter-dowry, this couple had 800 ducats at their disposal when they married in 1633. See ASV, *Atti Notarili*, 10902: Paganuzzi, Gerolamo, fol. 14v, 4 March 1657.

[51] See, for example, ASPV, Curia, II, C.M., Reg. 85: 3 June 1616: Magdalene Vincentine cum Gaspare eius marito. Interrogation of Magdalena.

[52] ASPV, Curia, II, C.M., Reg. 92: 22 September 1637, Benedicte Spinelli cum Petro Franchino, witness Hilarius, 28 January 1638.

[53] On artisans and clothes during the sixteenth century, see Schmidt, 1990, p. 39.

[54] Allerston, 2000, p. 381.

goldsmith's daughter. She had been forced to leave him, she claimed, because he had squandered the household resources through gambling.[55]

The lack of material goods also figures prominently in allegations by affluent citizens. Because the dowry[56] – although the wife's property – could not be invested without the husband's consent,[57] when marital peace was contested the economic autonomy of a patrician woman was seemingly weakened. Nobles Christine Priuli and Giovanni Semiteculo had married in 1631 and were living in Dorsoduro, in the parish of S. Gregorio. Part of the wife's accusations referred to the constant quarrels with her husband over property issues. These disputes had escalated approximately one year before, since the time her husband had refused to eat or drink with her or to speak to her. He had also failed to provide her with clothes and other household goods such as sheets, tablecloths or napkins.[58] In patrician marriages disputes over material goods extended to the whole living standard, which was of great concern to wives in the higher ranks of society. This can be illustrated by the troubled marriage of Elisabetta Bembo and Francesco Priuli. In 1623 Elisabetta had pleaded for a separation on grounds of her husband's severe cruelty, mental torment and infidelity. Priuli tried his best to counter the allegations of starvation and life-threatening violence, insisting that he had taken care to provide his wife with all the essentials for life as an honourable *gentildonna*. He paid her the necessary respect, as she was waited on by servants and had everything that a noble wife could wish for. He further emphasised that he had spent a considerable amount of money to provide clothes, pearls, earrings and rings for her.[59] Jewellery and luxury items were a visible and distinctive sign of patrician wives and were required in order to honour the family and to render the

---

[55] ASPV, Curia, II, C.M., Reg. 74: 9 September 1579, Philippi q.m Antony Sansary cum Laura filia Sebastiani Aureficis, not foliated.

[56] During the fourteenth century patrician women received a *corredo*, a sort of trousseau consisting of both 'personal goods for the bride and cash'. The importance of the *corredo* was that, in contrast to the dowry, it was given to the bride for her own use and was intended to array her 'in clothing and jewellery'. By the early fifteenth century, however, the *corredo* had evolved into a gift to the husband. However, some patrician husbands gave their wives 'some of the profits they made investing their dowries', although this practice does not seem to have been prescribed in Venetian statutes. Chojnacki, 2000a, pp. 76–94 and 123ff.

[57] Chojnacki, 2000a, pp. 76–94. Chojnacki reports that patrician women owned outright possessions from legacies and non-dowry property as well. Their most important economic resource, however, remained the dowry. Ibid., p. 123ff.

[58] ASPV, Curia, II, C.M., Reg. 91: 3 December 1634, Christine Priuli cum Joanne Semiteculo, January 1634.

[59] He did so in his written statement, see ASPV, Curia, II, C.M., Reg. 87: 19 May 1623, Elisabeth Bembo cum Francisco Priuli, Francesco Priuli, 24 January 1624.

women beautiful.[60] In separation suits involving the patriciate (but also in artisan marriages), to put material goods at the wife's disposal was not only a measure that allowed conclusions about a husband's household rule and sense of matrimonial conjugality, but was an issue over which feelings like respect or disrespect were negotiated.

In order to secure female possessions, the amount of the dowry and the conditions of payment in terms of movable goods (*mobili*) and fixed property (*stabili*) were sometimes set in the marital contract, which paid special attention to the conservation of the dowry while it was administered by the husband. These conditions also could be fixed during the marriage, arguably when financial mismanagement was an issue, as in the following case in which a notarial act was only set up in the presence of two witnesses some 27 years after the couple had married. The husband, Francesco Capella, had received 400 ducats upon marrying Laura. In December 1657 Francesco was held 'to preserve and to protect [the dowry] as expected from a good husband and to return it to his wife in the case that a restitution of the dowry is demanded'.[61] Patrician husbands even had to put their estate 'under obligation toward repayment of his wife's dowry', and in case of his death this responsibility fell to his father, even when the son had already been emancipated. When a husband died his heirs' first task was to ensure that the widow received her dowry back.[62] However, dowry contracts could specify that part of the dowry was destined for the wife's use – for her clothes and so forth. Domenico Licini, for example, assigned 50 ducats of his daughter's dowry for her own use when she married in 1657.[63]

Because financial mismanagement brought social misery to the household and endangered its stability, in early modern Venice the protection of female property was institutionalised. To promote the stability of society it thus was in the government's interests to prevent the financial collapse of Venetian households by safeguarding dowries against dissipation by husbands. Various civil magistracies – for example the Giudici del Proprio – had jurisdiction over dowry matters.[64] The Giudici del Procurator, as mentioned in Chapter 3, had authority over the economic aspects of marital conflicts, such as alimony payments in

---

60 Labalme, 1981, pp. 81–109.

61 ASV, *Atti Notarili*, Protocollo 5511: Giorgio Emo, 1656–57, fol. 505r.

62 See Chojnacki, 2000a, p. 124, where he mentions other dowry safeguards as well.

63 ASV, *Atti Notarili*, Protocollo 5511: Giorgio Emo, 1656–57, fol. 484v. Another example is ibid., fols 504v–505r.

64 On these magistracies see Chojnacki, 2000a, chap. 4. On the Florentine case see Kirshner, 1985, pp. 256–303.

separation cases and, more generally, dowry protection. From 1552 to 1561 this magistracy was widely used by the so-called *donne malmaritate* and was – according to Angelo Rigo – an institution that regulated the economic aspects of marital conflicts in favour of the female plaintiffs.[65] Women could plead legal separation at the Patriarchal Court and simultaneously use the civil magistracy to settle the financial aspects of their marital breakdown. An example is the aforementioned case of Pasquetta Peregrini, who sued her husband Romano Cavatia for separation at the ecclesiastical tribunal while bringing charges against him for dissipating the dowry at the Giudici del Procurator with the help of her family.[66] Since she came from a wealthy artisan family, it was therefore not only patrician women who took steps to protect their dowry and secure their property, as cases held before the Giudici del Procurator were initiated by women of all social ranks. In lower-class marriages these cases focused on the extreme misery and constraints of the female plaintiffs as a result of their husbands' misrule, general cruelty or even desertion.[67] Franceschina, who had protected her dowry, complained in the Patriarchal Court about the material impact her husband's desertion had had on her life: '... after [he had] abandoned wife and son and sold our belongings he left this city and did not return for approximately 14 months ... [and] he never once supported or helped his wife or his son'.[68]

Wives thus exercised foresight and made financial plans for the future, especially when the economic situation of the household was in decline due to debts run up by the husband.[69] When financial mismanagement was an issue women had strong allies in their families, and in their fathers in particular.[70] Daughters and fathers, as we have seen, were bound by the *patria potestas*, that is, the paternal authority a father possessed over his daughter even after she had been married.

---

65 See Rigo, 1992–93, pp. 256–8 and 2000, p. 531. Ferraro, 2001, p. 137, seems to be more sceptical.

66 ASPV, Curia, II, C.M., Reg. 78: 26 April 1584, Pasquette cum Romano Cavatia, fol. 40v. Another case in which dowry protection is mentioned is in ASPV, Curia, II, C.M., Reg. 83: 11 January 1596, Joannis fily Pauli à Papa cum Francischina filia Gratiosi Ausulani, fol. 20r. However, further investigation is needed to assess how common the simultaneous use of ecclesiastical and civil tribunals was.

67 On the legal practice of this magistracy see Rigo, 1992–93, pp. 251–3 and 2000, pp. 519–36.

68 ASPV, Curia, II, C.M., Reg. 83: 11 January 1596, Joannis fily Pauli à Papa cum Franceschina filia Gratiosi Ausulani, fol. 17r.

69 Rigo, 1992–93, p. 252.

70 Insofar, the Venetian situation seems to have differed from Florence. In her study of fifteenth-century Florence, Christine Klapisch-Zuber has argued that patrician women were only 'passing guests' in the male-headed houses, without close ties to their natal families. Klapisch-Zuber, 1987, pp. 117–18.

During marriage, it co-existed with the (more active) *patria potestas* that the husband had acquired over his wife.[71] The dissipation of the dowry concerned both families; bequests of patrician women, for example, reveal 'a nearly equal regard for their natal kinsmen, and thus for two distinct families'. Apart from emotional involvement, it was thus in the interests of fathers, mothers and brothers to remain loyal to their daughters and sisters, because 'they were to benefit from the loyalty that the women reciprocated'.[72]

Private matters: a public concern

In early modern Venice the household was not yet a private and intimate sphere and marital discord was the object of public evaluation. The breakdown of households was a public concern, and neighbours, particularly if they had become friends, were inclined to exchange details from private life and to lament about a cruel husband, for example, or a lascivious and disobedient wife. When households were in danger of collapse, relatives (both natal and those related through marriage), friends, neighbours and acquaintances were actively involved and, in expressing their disregard, also exercised moral and social control. The community's assessment of marital life was, however, never unanimous, and sometimes contradictory. Long before cases of marital discord reached court they would form their own opinions about who was in the right and thus decide which party to support: the wife accusing her husband of the disspipation of household resources and cruelty or the husband explaining that he had only punished his wife's disobedience 'moderately'. Their moral judgement was harsh when the marital crisis resulted from immoral behaviour, as in the case of Natalino mentioned earlier, who was held responsible for the breakdown of his marriage.

Because marital behaviour and the accusations between spouses were measured in relation to personal virtue and moral integrity, neighbours were especially supportive and compassionate towards the wife when the husband had a 'bad' reputation. To restrict such sources of support, husbands tried to limit their wives' contacts with the outside world. As Margaret Hunt has argued, husbands 'were perfectly aware that a woman's connection to her relatives and to the world beyond the conjugal household represented her main source of power'.[73] Domestic

---

71 With reference to the Florentine case see Kuehn, 1991, pp. 197–211.

72 With reference to patrician families cf. Chojnacki, 2000a, pp. 123, 144 and 175. On the ties to the family of origin through the *patria potestas*, see Kuehn, 1991, pp. 197–211.

73 Hunt, 1992, pp. 10–33.

confinement could thus be understood as an abuse of patriarchal power and as a strategic method to restore the husband's authority and power in marital disputes. In the cases that came to court, however, husbands only rarely succeeded in their aim. Although they tried their best to prevent having their marital problems noticed by the outside world, domestic disputes were very much a public concern in Venetian neighbourhoods of the time. Because outside observers played a crucial role in the assessment of domestic violence, the more unhappy wives relied on their neighbours, the more insightful or even compassionate witnesses they were able to call on later in court.

As we have seen, when the disobedience of children provoked violence against them, witnesses – at least initially – criticised the childs misconduct. Wives who had become victims of male aggression were, however, more readily supported by fellow parishioners, because, in contrast to children, wives possessed some degree of authority in their duty as co-governors of the household. Thus, misrule by a husband considered or known in his neighbourhood to be a bad Christian legitimised any resistance by his wife, as the following cases demonstrate. In the lawsuit that Paola Furlan initiated in 1610 against her husband Giacomo in the parish of S. Barnaba, Paola referred to the verbal abuse she had been suffering. Her allegation stressed that her husband had continuously insulted her and 'had never addressed her by her real name, but by shameful words as if she had been a prostitute'.[74] His reputation in the neighbourhood was contested. Girolamo de Arborio, a neighbour summoned on behalf of Paola, stated:

> Donna Fiorenza, mother of the said Paola, complained in my house ... that her son-in-law was governing his wife badly and that he was beating her frequently and even attacking her with weapons. Whereupon my wife, moved by compassion, talked to me about the situation and we made Paola come into our house and she looked after my wife, who was pregnant ... And two or three times her husband came to my house in search of his wife and demanded that I send her back. But because he was a shattered man and since I doubted that scandals might arise, I retorted that she wasn't in my house and that she was fine and that he should not bother us any more.[75]

---

[74] ASPV, Curia, II, C.M., Reg. 84: 21 June 1610, Paule cum Jacobo Furlano, point 5. Little is known about slander between spouses, although sexual slanders and defamation suits are well researched, at least for some parts of Europe. For insults and sexual slander in early modern London see Gowing, 1996, especially chaps. 3 and 4.

[75] ASPV, Curia, II, C.M., Reg. 84: 21 June 1610, Paule cum Jacobo Furlano, fols 4r–5r. Another witness, Donna Giacoba, recalled that Paola's mother had given her money and bread for her daughter; she was asked to pass it on to Paola in order to prevent the woman from starving while she was still living with her husband.

Couples who shared a house with different parties – even if only temporarily – gained especially revealing insights into marital relationships and disputes, and because of this knowlegde they themselves took sides and became emotionally involved. They were nearby and, thus, were reliable witnesses of domestic discord and expressed moral judgements if the limits of acceptable violence and general cruelty were exceeded. While testifying on behalf of Paola Furlan, Magdalena, who lived in the parish of S. Margherita, clearly expressed a moral judgement that was critical of the husband:

> Since my husband rented one room of our house to Giacomo I had the opportunity to witness ... that he often came home at night completely drunk and battered his wife without any reason. Several times my husband yelled at him that he should not treat his wife in this way, and even if he shut her in a room when he was battering her we still heard the noise of the blows and Paola's screams. And once he battered her so severely that she almost lost consciousness and he hit her so hard that she lost a tooth'.[76]

The protection and support that Paola received illustrates the direct involvement, both physical and emotional, of non-family household members in domestic disputes. Because Paola was known to be a good wife, compassion moved this friendly couple to protect her against her husband. While women in the neighbourhood sheltered wives of unruly husbands, male neighbours often reproached these men for their unchristian behaviour and the arbitrary discipline with which they ruled both household and wife. Physicians who were called in to give medical assistance to abused wives sometimes advised husbands to moderate their behaviour and urged them to treat their wives 'with greater care and to become a good companion'.[77] In stressing the conjugality and companionship required of a good marriage, the requisite qualities of the husband as a prudent ruler were investigated in court.

Statements made in court by male and female litigants, furthermore, show the importance of gendered duties on self-perception as a good partner. Hence, a husband who rejected his wife's allegations would emphasise his own qualities as a wise and prudent household ruler who had cared for the well-being of his wife and children and had treated them with respect. A woman, meanwhile, usually underlined her necessary obedience towards her husband and her performance of household tasks. Cecilia, the wife of the shoemaker Alessandro, is a case in point. In court she and her lawyer argued that

---

[76] Ibid., fols 11r–v.
[77] ASPV, Curia, II, C.M., Reg. 91: 12 May 1634, Ursete Targhetta cum Annibale Ricamatore, fol. 17r.

Madonna Cecilia for the last 10 years while living together with her husband has always governed the household with care and has been patient with her husband's children and with her own children, especially when they were ill in bed. She has never given him any reason to complain about her, since she worked and did everything that was required in the household.[78]

The same moral values were at work when witnesses expressed their opinion about litigating spouses. Angela, wife of the craftsman Matteo de Armatis, had the reputation of leading a sinful life, of being a lazy, useless and slovenly woman (*donna sfacciata*). In the face of Matteo's reputation as a good and hard-working husband, Angela's marital conduct was perceived by the neighbourhood and by Matteo's fellow workers as especially unjust. It was not hatred that he felt for this woman, as one of the witnesses clarified, but it was her 'bad deeds' which he despised – her general 'bad government' (*mal governo*), as he emphasised, was well known in the parish of S. Marcuola.[79] In the case of Benedetta Spinelli and Pietro Franchini already discussed, the witness Giovanni Sartory was equally sceptical about Benedetta's efforts in fulfilling her part of the marital agreement. Sartory believed her to be rather lazy and unwilling to carry out female duties such as cooking. He remarked that her husband Pietro had often complained about her household mismanagement; even though Benedetta received help from a woman to fulfil her household tasks, he had only seen her sewing on the balcony.[80]

Early modern marriage was thus conceptualised around gendered roles and duties that were crucial to the moral integrity of husband and wife and the fulfilment of Christian values. Although a household ruler could always justify physical violence as an expression of his greater authority and, moreover, his duty to correct his wife, excessive use of force against a modest and obedient wife was perceived as unjust and caused feelings of compassion for the mistreated wife. When the wife then abandoned the conjugal household, his unreasonable rule was thought to be the reason for the collapse of the marriage: it therefore weakened rather than affirmed social order and gender hierarchy.

Husbands and wives had, thus, to work at matrimony and the ideal of companionship. Although the gulf between marriage ideals and marital life was remarkable, the prescriptions for the ordered household

---

[78] ASPV, Curia, II, C.M., Reg. 82: 5 July 1590, Alexandri Calegary cum Cecilia q. Stephani Muschiary, not foliated.

[79] ASPV, Curia, II, C.M., Reg. 90: 29 July 1630, Matthei de Armatis cum Angela Valery Simolini, witness Pietro Jacalinus.

[80] ASPV, Curia, II, C.M., Reg. 92: 22 September 1637, Benedicte Spinelli cum Petro Franchino, witness Giovanni Sartory, 9 March 1638.

and the Christian moral conduct of husband and wife remained powerful. In admonishing unruly and lazy husbands or wilful wives, parishioners and household members participated in making the ideal of marital conjugality a daily achievement: the appropriation of Christian and civil virtues was held to be a process, and had to be repeatedly internalised. The sanctity of matrimony by which a man and a woman were bound together in the face of God had a concrete meaning for the ruling of patriarchal households in everyday life: it had to be grounded on a moderate use of patriarchal authority that made female obedience, and thus marital conjugality, possible. A husband, as members of the small parishes in Venice found, should punish his disobedient wife sternly but justly, thereby restoring order. Tyrannical rule or financial mismanagement of household resources, by contrast, endangered the stability of the family and could provoke the household's collapse. Cruel government made female obedience – so central to the patriarchal order of society, household rule and male self-perception – hard to realise. Tyrannical rule was therefore a threat to household order and neighbourhood peace and questioned the 'natural' superiority of men.

CHAPTER SEVEN

Sexuality, Impotence and Unstable Masculinities

In early modern societies sexuality and marriage were intrinsically connected. Because the formation of marriage was a two-stage process of which the public exchange of vows was only the first, these words alone were not binding: until sexual intercourse had taken place, no marriage existed. Sex without the prior exchange of consent was deemed deviant; and where no physical union followed solemnisation in church, no permanently binding marriage existed. Only sexual intercourse turned a union into a sacrament and made it indissoluble. In other words the marital act had a sacramental purpose: it created the obligation between spouses to render the marital debt upon demand, an obligation that did not exist after the exchange of consent.[1]

Because successful sexual intercourse alone made a marriage indissoluble, impotence or frigidity – both terms were used almost interchangeably[2] – threatened the ratification of the union. Canon marital law allowed couples to separate when impotence (*impotentia coeundi*) was both natural and permanent. The healthy party was then free to remarry because no sacramental union had been established. In cases where the sexual problems were more difficult to assess, the couple were obliged to attempt consummation for at least three years before an annulment suit could be brought to court. If the realisation of 'one flesh' still proved to be problematic the court could formally declare that the marriage had never been consummated. Impotence was thus a serious accusation and one of the few grounds offered by canon law to declare a marriage null and void.[3] Only if a woman had knowingly married an impotent partner was she prevented from bringing a suit to court.

To formally end unconsummated marriages women turned to the Patriarchal Court, which ruled on cases of impotence. The pursuit of these claims required detailed descriptions of the intimate and emotional life of the couple. These descriptions open a window onto the sexual

---

[1] Brundage, 1993, pp. 407ff. and, for the later period, Jerouschek, 1991, pp. 281–305.

[2] Brundage, 1982, p. 135 and Martin de Azpilcueta, better known as Navarro, author of an influential sixteenth-century manual for confessors, pp. 477–8. A case in point is ASPV, Curia, II, C.M., Reg. 90: 24 November 1628, Clare Capello cum Julio Molino.

[3] Darmon, 1985, p. 15; Phillips, 1988, p. 8.

culture of the late Italian Renaissance and, furthermore, allow us to get a sense of the fragility of manhood. As these law cases demonstrate, manhood was not a stable category but rather one that had to be proven on a day-to-day basis. Although the male sex dominated as the strong, rational and active one, a man still had to display his virility and prove his potency. If he failed, his patriarchal rule and male authority came under threat. Male sexuality was thus more problematic than has been suspected up to now.[4] Impotence trials suggest that in early modern Venice male sexuality was a source of insecurity, anxiety and even ridicule, and could become the reason for men's turbulence with their masculine identity. Manhood was just as much a biological as a cultural construct, and, as we shall see, sexual prowess and sexual ownership were matters that carried judicial, social, cultural and emotional weight.

Impotence and the Church court

Let us begin with a case study. In late November 1590 Camilla Benzoni, daughter of the citizen Giorgio Benzoni, brought a suit against her husband Gasparo Centani at the Patriarchal Court. For more than 40 months Camilla had lived with Gasparo (the son of Lorenzo, who was one of the governors at the hospital of the *Incurabili*), who made a modest living by purchasing grain. Initially everything had been quite promising: the marriage had been solemnised according to Tridentine decrees, and both Camilla and Gasparo had taken the marriage vows freely. Almost from the beginning they had shared a bed, but only when the moment came to consummate the marriage had the first problems arisen. According to Camilla's deposition Gasparo had tried to 'have sexual intercourse with me and to do what husbands do with their wives – but he combined nothing'.[5] She added with more precision that he was capable of having an erection, but that he was not able to maintain it. When asked whether their inability to consummate the marriage and, in consequence, their marital problems were due to the fact that 'the male member was not erect', she confirmed this.[6] She concluded in court, that Gasparo was undoubtedly impotent, and because of this she was not at all sure whether or not he was her husband.

Because impotence was defined as the 'inability to ejaculate semen into the vagina or the inability to receive ejaculated semen', early

---

[4] See, however, Fletcher, 1995, pp. 83–98 and Roper, 1994, pp. 117–18.

[5] ASPV, Curia, II, CM., Reg. 82: 28 November 1590, Camille Benzoni cum Gaspare Centani, fols 14v–15r.

[6] Ibid., fol. 15r.

modern definitions also included the possibility of physical incapacity that might render a woman unsuitable for sexual intercourse.[7] Vaginal tightness, for example, could hinder penetration. Equally, if the woman was unable to receive or hold the seed because, for instance, her vagina was too large, she could be judged incapable of carnal copulation. These cases were, however, extremely rare, and more commonly it was men who had to face allegations of impotence.[8]

In the courtroom allegations of impotence still had to be proven. Despite the clarity of the legal framework, in practice the assessment of the marital act was naturally a tricky and delicate matter, and physical inspections – when contradictory – often did not settle matters. Impotence cases therefore involved a high degree of ambivalence: when after years of marriage no child had been born, this did not inevitably constitute proof of the impotence of one of the partners – sterility might have been the reason. Impotence was clearly distinguished from sterility because, although both of these physical deficiencies made procreation impossible, only impotence rendered a marriage invalid. Sterile spouses had the physical capacity for carnal copulation, whereas the impotent did not.[9] In practice, however, childlessness was used in court to sustain allegations of impotence.[10]

In addition, problems in fulfilling the marital act might be only temporary. Certain injuries of the genitals or diseased organs could prevent sexual intercourse for a specific period, but did not make consummation impossible in the long term, especially when the disease was curable.[11] Disease, injury or mutilation could occur after the marriage had been consummated, and, when no child had been borne, it could be difficult to prove that a true marriage existed. Illness might have weakened the male body, temporarily mixing up bodily humours so that the man lacked the necessary heat for penetration. Medical treatments that could cure problems were well known to physicians and were no secret in the courtroom.[12] As canonists wisely acknowledged in

---

7 Noonan, 1986, p. 290.

8 Of 13 impotence cases, only one case of female impotence is found in the sample Causarum Matrimoniorum (1570–1700).

9 Noonan, 1986, p. 290.

10 ASPV, Curia, II, C.M., Reg. 78: 5 March 1584, Lucretie Ballatine cum Francisco Revisare panorum, and ASPV, Curia, II, F.C., Reg. 16, where part of the trial is to be found.

11 A case in point is ASPV, Curia, II, C.M., Reg. 86: 9 April 1619, Felicite filie Anastasy de Venetiy cum Matheo Fada. Witness depositions (pro parte Felicita) are to be found in ASPV, Curia, II, F.C., Reg. 34.

12 ASPV, Curia, II, C.M., Reg. 90: 24 November 1628: Clare Capello cum Julio Molino.

these cases, temporary impotence could also be the result of witchcraft and sorcery. In early modern societies women were thought to have the power to bind the male member and to hinder a man from having sexual intercourse with a specific woman. Because these 'impotent' men were able to perform sexually with other women it was agreed that they should be allowed to separate and remarry.[13]

In order to assess a couple's sexual problems detailed descriptions of their lives were necessary, and ecclesiastical examiners interrogated both plaintiff and defendant directly and straightforwardly as to what had happened in the marital bed. The elliptical formulation 'to consummate the marriage' was a starting point, but questions and answers soon went further. The examiners treated this question in a very technical manner and descriptions of early modern conjugal life were almost entirely without allusions to sexual pleasure. Theologians and canonists had laced concupiscence in the corset of the marital debt, although in the late sixteenth and early seventeenth centuries attitudes towards sexual delight seem to have changed slightly.[14] By making the rendering of the marital debt the purpose of intercourse, the conjugal duty was closely linked to the three 'goods of marriage': procreation, fidelity and sacrament.[15] Sexual and marital morality worked to impede sinful desires, to guarantee procreation and to be a means against fornication. The *debitum conjugale*, a concept that goes back to St Paul, perceived the sexual performance of the spouses as a mutual right that the man and the woman possessed over each other's body and that could be abrogated only by mutual consent. In requesting and rendering the conjugal debt husband and wife were equal, notwithstanding the contemporary gender asymmetry.

In court the ecclesiastical examiners were especially careful to clarify whether both partners had rendered the conjugal debt when requested. It was not the problem of how to express desire that was discussed in court, but rather the woman's sense of obedience. The male staff of the Patriarchal Court were willing initially to allow doubts about proper female behaviour. Women accused of being resistant to sexual intercourse, such as Camilla Benzoni in the case discussed above, would reject the reproach by highlighting their modesty and obedience. Camilla's husband Gasparo had claimed that from the first night onwards his wife had hindered him from fulfilling his duty: she had

---

13 Brundage, 1982, p. 136. For impotence through the workings of witchcraft in Augsburg, see Roper, 1994, pp. 125–44; for Venice, see Martin, 1989 and, for one interesting example, Ruggiero, 1993, p. 120.

14 Davidson, 1994, p. 79.

15 Noonan, 1986, pp. 126–31; Harrington, 1995, p. 50.

pushed him away and tried to strangle him so that he had to give in.[16] Thus, resistance to returning the debt could convincingly explain why a marriage had not been consummated. In 1584 the weaver Francesco Revedin also brought forward the argument of female disobedience, accusing his 22-year-old wife Lucrezia of resisting intercourse. He claimed that exactly when he was about to penetrate her, she had pulled back, so that his seed had been wasted on the sheets. Although, by referring to their wives' lack of obedience, both men had to admit that they had lost control of their spouses, they at least could still keep the question of their potency open and negotiable.

Emphasising their sense of obedience and reverence, women sometimes indicated that they would rather have ended their unhappy marriages. Angela de Fais, for example, mentioned in her written statement the distress and desperation that continuous attempts at consummating her marriage had caused her. Angela was almost 30 years younger than her partner, Bartolomeo de Albertis, a wine-carrier, and alleged that she had been married against her will by her father and her uncle, the organist at St Mark's.[17] With regard to the marital debt, she stressed that Bartolomeo had become angry when she had refused to be 'strained on', to be 'stuffed' and to be 'anguished' any longer by him. After six months she begged her parents that she might be allowed to separate informally from her husband. But they had persuaded her to stay with him, and so she had endured cohabitation.[18]

Sexual problems and the clergy

It was not only family but also father confessors who became involved before these conflicts reached the court. In post-Tridentine Venice clerics played a fundamental role in the surveillance of the populace's piety and marital attitudes, and father confessors often were involved in cases of matrimonial sexual conflict before they reached the court.[19] The Fourth Lateran Council had already made the annual confession compulsory, so that parishioners could confess their sins at least once a year. The father confessor was the embodiment of the administrator of divine justice and

---

[16] ASPV, Curia, II, C.M., Reg. 82: 28 November 1590, Camille Benzoni cum Gaspare Centani, fols 25v–26r.

[17] ASPV, Curia, II, C.M., Reg. 80: 3 February 1586, Angele q.m Petri Tessari cum Bartholomei de Albertis.

[18] ASPV, Curia, II, C.M., Reg. 74: 2 September 1579, Bartholomei de Albertis cum Angela Petri Textoris, fol. 45r.

[19] As various scholars have shown, the late sixteenth century was a period of change in the history of the confession; cf. Bossy, 1970; Prosperi, 1996; and Romeo, 1998.

the severe judge, but could equally be perceived as a spiritual father whose balanced and sound advice could soothe grief and pain.[20] It is this latter function of clerics which is mentioned in impotence trials: when sexual problems overshadowed daily life, confessors could prove helpful and offer advice – particularly to wives.[21] Already during the Middle Ages, Cherubino da Siena had actively encouraged laypersons, and women especially, to ask confessors for counsel.[22] When marriages had not been consummated, sometimes even after years, women in the confessional expressed their doubts about the nature of the relationship. Practising sex without a valid marriage to sacramentalise the physical activity made them fear, as they stated in court, that they lived in sin. These fears were reinforced by father confessors, who made them scrupulous and urged them to end sinful sexual relationships.[23] The ambivalent nature of unsuccessful sexual practices is explicit in the deposition of a Dominican friar who, as the father confessor of Angela de Fais, was summoned to court by Patriarch Giovanni Trevisan (1559–90). On 9 June 1580 he stated that

> ... every day he [Bartolomeo] stimulated her [Angela] in order to fulfil the marital debt, and he tried hard and without interruption for more than one hour; every time he made her work very hard, made her sweat, but they couldn't achieve what marriage is for, and they started to wonder, but never did they witness any effect of matrimony, although she got married in order to have children; and she realised that her husband was completely impotent and could not consummate the marriage and make children.[24]

The friar therefore earnestly advised Angela to end her invalid marriage, emphasising that the Church would have it annulled without difficulty.[25] Here it becomes apparent how this father confessor used his ecclesiastical authority to defend the principles of Catholic marriage doctrine and, thus,

---

[20] Prosperi, 1996, p. 219.

[21] On close contacts between priests and women in Counter-Reformation Venice see Martin, 1985, pp. 25–6. Romeo, 1998, pp. 184–5, has argued that in post-Tridentine Italy the confessional was a medium through which sexual norms were communicated and the sexual behaviour of laypersons controlled, in particular the behaviour of women.

[22] Bell, 1999, p. 33.

[23] Especially revealing: ASPV, Curia, II, C.M., Reg. 93: 6 July 1657, Anne Lazaroni cum Joanne Baptista Vidali. The case continues in ASPV, Curia, II, F.C., Reg. 59. See also ASPV, Curia, II, C.M., Reg. 82: 28 November 1590, Camille Benzoni cum Gaspare Centani, fol. 22r.

[24] ASPV, Curia, II, C.M., Reg. 74: 2 September 1579, Bartholomei de Albertis cum Angela Petri Textoris, fol. 9r. Some years later the case was brought again to the attention of the Patriarchal Court: see ASPV, Curia, II, C.M., Reg. 80: 3 February 1586, Angele q.m Petri Tessari cum Bartholomei de Albertis, and ASPV, Curia, II, F.C., Reg. 15.

[25] ASPV, Curia, II, C.M., Reg. 74: 2 September 1579, Bartholomei de Albertis cum Angela Petri Textoris, fols 8v–9r.

to guarantee procreation and impede sinful sexual activities. Clergymen played an important role in communicating post-Tridentine marital values to the Venetian populace, and they actually made the Tridentine decrees on marriage known in each parish. During the Counter-Reformation battle against heresy, they were important for the surveillance of religious practices and thoughts. After 1565 lay denunciations to the Holy Office increased dramatically in response, as John Martin has argued, to the 'pressures that confession brought to bear on the faithful'.[26] The role of priests in Venetian parish life was therefore ambivalent: they gave counsel and advice to distressed women but also defended the interests of the local ecclesiastical authorities. Because impotence trials made up only a very small percentage of marital litigation at the Patriarchal Court, priests' involvement in the sexual matters of married couples in Counter-Reformation Venice seemingly had only a marginal influence on their willingness to bring a lawsuit to court.[27]

Apart from the possibility of suing for annulment, spouses in Venice were advised by their father confessors to live like *fratello et sorella*[28] – that is, not to practise sex at all. This was an important alternative in cases of impotence if the partners wanted to stay together. According to the Spanish Jesuit Tomás Sánchez, the ecclesiastical judges should allow the partners to live together if that was their express will.[29] But in the private conflicts that reached the court this option was never discussed, nor was the advice to live like 'brother and sister' followed. Rather, the legal proceedings convey the impression of an obsessive sexual life that overshadowed relationships. Female plaintiffs and male defendants often testified to the frequency of their sexual activity, although with different legal intentions. Women argued that, despite persistent sexual endeavours, they still were not carnally known. Men demonstrated a greater variety in their argumentation, but often claimed that they enjoyed an active sex life with their wives, thereby implying that they had fulfilled the conjugal duty. Some couples even had intercourse during menstruation – a time in which the Catholic Church prescribed abstinence.[30] In other circumstances, modesty rather than sexual excess

---

[26] Martin, 1993, p. 186.

[27] It would be interesting to compare the role that father confessors played in late medieval Venice in order to be able to assess historical change more precisely.

[28] ASPV, Curia, II, C.M., Reg. 82: 28 November 1590, Camille Benzoni cum Gaspare Centani, fol. 23r.

[29] See Sánchez, book VII, disputatio 97, p. 386.

[30] ASPV, Curia, II, C.M., Reg. 82: 28 November 1590, Camille Benzoni cum Gaspare Centani, fol. 24v. For sexual abstinence during menstruation, see Rudolph M. Bell, 1990, pp. 121–2. See, however, Makowski, 1977, p. 109: 'Despite these regulations, the overriding sentiment was that in such cases as well, the duty to render the debt, even if unjustly demanded, was still binding.'

was the rule for Christian life. The above-mentioned Cherubino da Siena explicitly warned couples against frequent sexual activity, as intercourse drained natural male vigour and could even lead to early death.[31]

Sexual conventions

Because in the courtroom an emphasis was placed on a couple's sexual life, the repertoire of sexual practices that defendants and plaintiffs revealed was astonishingly varied. Court records reveal how couples practised intercourse lying on their sides or in a development of the missionary position, with the woman's legs on the man's shoulders.[32] Because theologians and canonists suspected that posture and sexual pleasure might be related, they emphasised that only one position was natural and beneficial for reproduction, that is, with the man on top of the woman. Other postures even contradicted the gender dichotomy, according to which the man had to play the active and the woman the passive role. Tomás Sánchez had argued in exactly this way when he declared that the missionary position was the only 'natural' position. When the woman comes to sit on top of the man, by contrast, 'one sees only the woman acting, while the man is in an inferior position'.[33] According to the contemporary medical theory the missionary position was also held to be best for conception, as the male seed could flow unhindered. Although medical theories attributed a force of attraction to the uterus, it was feared that when the couple was standing the sperm could fall downwards or not be deposited close enough to the mouth of the uterus, especially if the man entered the woman from behind.[34]

Sometimes the rules made by theologians and physicians were hard to realise in practice because of differing degrees of sexual experience. An interesting constellation could arise when the woman was widowed and had sexual experience during her first marriage and the man was sexually inexperienced. The woman might then be the active partner during sexual intercourse and govern her husband, thereby turning the dominant gender roles upside down. A case in point is Francesco Revedin, who openly admitted in court that he was sexually inexperienced when he married Lucrezia Ballatini in about 1577. It was his wife, he revealed, who had shown him how the conjugal debt might

---

31   See Bell, 1990, p. 122.
32   ASPV, Curia, II, C.M., Reg. 78: 5 March 1584, Lucretie Ballatine cum Francisco Revisare panorum, fol. 12r.
33   Quoted in Flandrin, 1984, p. 153.
34   See Cadden, 1993, p. 245.

be paid 'in various ways'.[35] Not only when men were inexperienced, but also when sexual problems arose, women lent a hand to relieve potency problems by stimulating the penis outside the vagina.[36] Whereas the medieval moral canonists and theologians had regarded the touching and kissing of private parts as sinful, the judges of the early modern period were granted far greater discretionary powers. Stimulating sexual activities were tolerated as measures that fostered marriage if they were practised in order to remove potency problems and thus as a preparation for sexual intercourse. Only when stimulation was used to increase sexual desire was it deemed sinful.[37] This concept might also explain why, in impotence trials, descriptions of 'unnatural' sexual activity were not concealed. In court they counted as proof of incurable impotence, which long-lasting, extensive and highly imaginative sexual practices had failed to alleviate.

Impotence and the body

The control men possessed over their own bodies was to a certain degree 'measurable'. Because couples well knew that successful defloration should leave tangible traces (blood) on the sheets, virility was 'visible' in the sense that it produced material signs, but only if the man was in physical control. The physical ability and sexual performance of the male partner were therefore mercilessly under scrutiny in court. The visible sign of potency was the erect penis – described by plaintiffs and defendants as *membro virile* or, more technically, as *verga* – which had the ability to penetrate easily. The most obvious explanation for an unconsummated marriage lay in the incapacity to become erect – which was among the first questions posed by ecclesiastical examiners. Angela, the daughter of Piero de Fais from S. Geremia, stated in 1579 that her partner Bartolomeo was unable to penetrate her because his penis had been never 'hard'. She also claimed that his attempts at sustaining his male member with his hand had proved unsuccessful.[38] Similarly, Lucrezia Ballatini emphasised in court that her husband Francesco Revedin was not able to penetrate her because when he had touched her 'immediately his penis had turned limp'.[39]

---

35 ASPV, Curia, II, C.M., Reg. 78: 5 March 1584, Lucretie Ballatine cum Francisco Revisare panorum, fols 11v–12r.

36 ASPV, Curia, II, C.M., Reg. 93: 6 July 1657, Anne Lazaroni cum Joanne Baptista Vidali, 5 September 1657, fol. 7v.

37 Jerouschek, 1991, p. 288.

38 ASPV, Curia, II, C.M., Reg. 74: 2 September 1579, Bartholomei de Albertis cum Angela Petri Textoris, fol. 9r.

39 ASPV, Curia, II, C.M., Reg. 78: 5 March 1584, Lucretie Ballatine cum Francisco Revisare panorum, fols 20r–v.

It was therefore not the inability to achieve an erection which was preventing sexual intercourse but rather the inability to maintain it. Despite this Francesco Revedin confidently claimed in court that he *had* consummated his marriage and had had sex with his wife almost every night for seven years. In another case Giacomo de Badilis, who was accused of impotence by his wife Marietta, could produce a witness in his defence: his former lover Letitia. She revealed in court that she had been perfectly satisfied as his sexual partner and testified, somewhat confusingly and contradictorily, to his potent sexuality: 'He has sex with women and he makes it like other men, but he can't have an erection and his penis fails to remain hard ... [still] he satisfied me seven times during one night but I don't think that he is able to deflower a woman'.[40] Even though evidence that he had satisfied a woman could be produced, Giacomo's sexual prowess was still in question.

Defloration was thus an act that required a certain amount of strength, physical control and endurance on the part of the man. The failure to destroy the hymen was connected with the lack of *forza* (strength, vigour or even violence), as the following case reveals. The nobleman Giulio Molino was sexually experienced when he married the noblewoman Clara Capello. After one year of cohabitation she left him and sought shelter in a convent. In 1628 she made their private conflict a matter of ecclesiastical concern. As Molino himself admitted in his deposition, his wife had left him because they had been unable to consummate the marriage. Although he had had sexual intercourse with various women before his marriage, he claimed that they had all been deflowered by other men. Clara, by contrast, who had led a chaste life, had entered the marriage as a virgin. Molino therefore emphasised that it was his spouse's virginity that had made it impossible for him to fulfil his conjugal duty. In court he explained that he had no 'strength' when he attempted 'to destroy the hymen'.[41] Sometimes women (for example, Camilla Benzoni) used the same argument about the lack of *forza* to describe the failed act of consummation in order to claim that, despite persistent sexual activity, they had not been carnally known and were therefore still virgins.

When men such as Camilla's husband Gasparo rejected accusations of impotence, they would stress that they had penetrated the woman so deeply that they had in fact deflowered her.[42] It was only lack of sexual

40 ASPV, Curia II, C.M., Reg. 73: 2 May 1575, Mariette Riccio de Castro Anoali cum Jacobo de Badillis, not foliated.

41 ASPV, Curia, II, C.M., Reg. 90: 24 November 1628, Clare Capello cum Julio Molino, 20 December 1628, not foliated.

42 ASPV, Curia II, C.M., Reg. 82: 28 November 1590, Camille Benzoni cum Gaspare Centani, fol. 55v.

experience that made it difficult for men to judge what they had actually achieved. The situation was generally difficult to assess in the early modern period as the only signs men and women could hope for were bloodstains as the result of defloration (or, months later, a pregnancy). When partners were arguing about the significance of their nightly endeavours, ecclesiastical examiners thus asked whether blood had been noticed on the sheets. But even blood could not always be interpreted clearly as the visible and material sign of male potency, for it might simply be an indication of vaginal injury due to unsuccessful penetration, as claimed by examiners in the case of Camilla Benzoni.[43] In this context physical sensations were brought forward as an argument. Camilla revealed in court that she had heard from other women that the act of deflowering was painful. Because she had felt no pain at all, she consequently deduced that she must still be a virgin.[44] Angela de Fais argued in the same way. Although her partner Bartolomeo had claimed that women did not feel anything at all during sexual intercourse, she had retorted, and repeated in court, that her mother had told her differently. Bartolomeo then claimed that her vagina was very 'large', thus explaining her lack of physical sensation. Angela had finally given in, hoping that Bartolomeo would leave her in peace.[45]

As ecclesiastical examiners and judges well knew, impotence could simply be a temporary problem, and in court they tried to find out whether a case of impotence was only occasional. If so, it was likely that the marriage could be consummated in future, thus making the grounds for an annulment of the marriage weak. Giulio Molino, for example, testified that although his body had 'shown no signs' of impotence he had nevertheless lacked the necessary strength to destroy his wife Clara Capello's hymen. He was asked whether he had tried any remedies, and he had. Despite freely admitting that his frigidity might pass with time and that he might be able to render the marital debt in future, he preferred not to live with her.[46] In another case, Matteo Fada, a merchant who lived in S. Zulian, countered his wife Felicità's annulment suit. In contrast to Giulio Molino he wished to continue his marriage and therefore claimed that his physical deficiency was only temporary. He suffered, as his wife had discovered only after the marriage, from gonorrhoea, a disease that she attributed to his drinking *vini grandi* while he was in the fleet of S. Marco.[47] His incontinent body

---

43 Ibid., fols 27v–28r.

44 Ibid., fol. 16r.

45 ASPV, Curia, II, C.M., Reg. 74: 2 September 1579, Bartholomei de Albertis cum Angela Petri Textoris, fols 21v–22r.

46 Ibid., Reg. 90: 24 November 1628, Clare Capello cum Julio Molino.

47 ASPV, Curia, II, C.M., Reg. 86: 9 April 1619, Felicite filie Anastasy de Venetiy cum

caused her disgust; she couldn't stand the smell of him.[48] Matteo, however, never denied having suffered from physical disorders. But, in contrast to his wife, he emphasised in court that his physical defect not only was temporary but already had been healed by the French physician Carlo Suios.[49]

In conflicting statements medical inspections were of fundamental importance. Midwives called to carry out the examination had to provide medical evidence for defloration, or for physical defects that would prevent sexual intercourse. If penetration was difficult men could and did claim that 'it is she who has a closed vagina' – a defect that impeded the possibility of fulfilling the marital act.[50] Female deficiencies discussed in court were thus linked to the constitution of her 'vessel' (*vaso*) or 'nature' (*natura*).

Midwives, sex and morality

Whereas in impotence trials in France in the ancien régime it was surgeons and physicians who carried out the medical examinations, in sixteenth- and seventeenth-century Venice physicians seldom 'saw, much less examined, female genitalia. A physician's "honesty" ... did not allow for direct examination of the organs.'[51] Instead, it was almost exclusively midwives who examined the women in question and were summoned to give medical evidence on their constitution. Midwives were mature women; usually they were married or widowed and had given birth to children. They were public figures in the neighbourhood, walking along the streets to the houses of women in labour. The birthing chair, the sign of her trade, made the midwife easily recognisable (see Figure 7.1). She was thus well known by the parishioners. Midwives not only delivered

---

Matheo Fada, point 1 of her legal statement; this was an impression her mother shared, cf. ASPV, Curia, II, F.C., Reg. 34: 9 August 1618, witness Lucietta, wife of Anastasio Bigarelli, fol. 1r. His wife, additionally, claimed that she had been married against her will, as demonstrated in chap. 5.

48 ASPV, Curia, II, C.M., Reg. 86: 9 April 1619, Felicite filie Anastasy de Venety cum Matheo Fada, point 5 of her legal statement. Another case in point is ASPV, Curia, II, C.M., Reg. 81: 7 September 1588, Ursete Blasy Marangoni cum Luciano Stin. Orsetta, too, complained that his incontinent body – most probably he also suffered from gonorrhoea – stank intolerably.

49 ASPV, Curia, II, C.M., Reg. 86: 9 April 1619, Felicite filie Anastasy de Venety cum Matheo Fada, fol. 26v.

50 ASPV, Curia, II, C.M., Reg. 82: 28 November 1590, Camille Benzoni cum Gaspare Centani, fol. 28v.

51 Bell, 1999, p. 97. An exception is Lucietta Paduani, who was examined by the physician Paulo Litigato, although he did not touch her private parts and only inspected her visually. His witness testimony is found in ASPV, Curia, II, F.C., Reg. 16, 27 February 1586.

7.1   Midwife with a servant carrying the birthing chair (Grevembroch, *Gli Abiti de' Veneziani*)

children but also assisted women in all sorts of questions related to the female body, such as 'irregular menstrual cycles, breastfeeding, sterility, rape or venereal disease'.[52] The midwife's reputation and skill were closely linked to experience based on 'traditional wisdom and lore' and on 'empirical practice'.[53] These skills were passed on to younger women during their many years of apprenticeship.

Because of their importance in parish life and their close contacts with women, midwives in post-Tridentine Venice were given an increased role in the surveillance of parochial sexual morality. The Venetian Patriarch Giovanni Trevisan ordered in a decree of 12 October 1560 that midwives had to confirm the birth of every child they delivered within one day to the parish priest or sacristan. Failure to do so would result in severe and shaming punishment.[54] In order to ensure

---

[52] Filippini, 1993, pp. 152–75, here p. 155.
[53] Ibid., p. 154.
[54] The midwife had to stand for two hours between the columns of St Mark's, wearing

baptism and registration, parochial clerics were also ordered by decree – under the threat of excommunication – to remind their parish members monthly to notify them about the birth of children within eight days. Both decrees were repeated in February 1564 and forced parish clerics and midwives to co-operate in order to further the Christianization of society.[55] In 1614 Pope Paul V released the *Rituale Romanorum*, an injunction that placed midwives under the educational surveillance of parish priests. Because midwives could administer the sacrament of baptism in cases of emergency, ecclesiastical and secular control became crucial. In 1624 the Provveditori alla Sanità set up a committee ordering all women who wanted to get the official licence and be listed on the register of midwives to present a testimonial from a parish priest in which their capacity to administer the sacrament was confirmed. Moreover, they had to present a reference from a midwife who had supervised their apprenticeship of at least two years. Transgression was punished with fines.[56] In 1689 this civic magistracy tightened control. To obtain the official licence midwives now had to be able to read Girolamo Scipion Mercurio's *La Commare o Riccoglitrice* (Venice, 1595), a manual for midwives which was first replaced in the eighteenth century. Together with attempts to raise educational levels, the Provveditori alla Sanità also made two years' attendance at anatomy lessons obligatory and demanded that an examination be carried out in the presence of two midwives and the priors of the association (*Collegio*) of physicians.[57] These examinations were, however, only pro forma, and none of the midwives was failed (even if she lacked qualifications on paper). As Nadia Maria Filippini has argued, the civic authorities tended to delegate the 'responsibility for approving midwives to the parish priests with a clear recognition that this was his role'.[58]

Precisely because midwives assisted the state and the Church in the enforcement of moral legislation, their role in court was ambivalent. Midwives were summoned in trials on abortion, infanticide, premarital sex and rape. They played an important part in investigations by testifying to whether or not sexual intercourse had taken place (as in

---

a shaming crown, and was then banished from Venice for one year. See ASPV, Curia, II, *Liber Actorum et Mandatorum*, Reg. 66 (1560–64), fol. 41v.

55 ASPV, Curia, II, *Liber Actorum et Mandatorum*, Reg. 66 (1560–64), fols 29r–v (Latin), and 41v–r (vernacular).

56 Filippini, 1993, p. 162; Pillon, 1981–82, pp. 67–68, mentions examinations that had to be carried out in front of the Provveditori alla Sanità following the decree from February 1624. On 'emergency baptism' see Wiesner, 1993, pp. 85ff.

57 Pillon, 1981–82, pp. 68–9. According to Filippini, 1993, p.162 anatomy lessons became obligatory only in 1719.

58 Filippini, 1993, p. 162.

cases of rape and premarital sex). They also had to testify as to whether a woman had given birth (in cases of infanticide) or had used herbs, for example, to terminate a pregnancy. A midwife could thus be called by (female) plaintiffs, (male) defendants or the court. During impotence trials they could even be required to give testimony on behalf of both litigants. In contrast to the common practice in the neighbourhood, where women consulted their own parish midwife, in court midwives from different parishes were summoned to carry out inspections. Some cases produced five or even more obstetrical depositions.[59] A physical examination was sometimes undertaken simultaneously by two midwives: for example, Thomasina and Bona inspected Angela Tessaria at the patriarchal vicar's house while he was visiting the convent of S. Geremia.[60] Midwives were required to testify to the woman's physical suitability for sexual intercourse. Additionally, their judgement carried weight in assessing whether sexual intercourse had taken place. If the woman was found to be a virgin still, important evidence against consummation of the marriage was provided. Clearly, this was a deposition in favour of the woman if she had accused her husband of impotence.[61]

The examination of private parts might be carried out at the house of a midwife involved in the investigation, at the place where the woman was staying during the trial, at the lawyer's house or even at the vicar's house in his absence. Only anatomical reasons for non-suitability for carnal copulation were given by midwives. One case in point is the trial of Lucietta Paduani, a midwife's daughter. Her husband Giovanni Francesco, a carpenter from the arsenal, petitioned on 24 October 1583 for an annulment, claiming that Lucietta was unable to have sexual intercourse. Because he had successfully deflowered his deceased first wife, Francesco had a strong argument in favour of his virility. The several physical inspections made in order to test Lucietta's suitability for intercourse were, however, not conclusive. One midwife named Caterina confirmed that the young woman was very 'narrow' (*stretta*), but compared with her physical state six months earlier, when the midwife almost could not stick her finger into Lucietta's vagina, she noticed a considerable difference. Now, as she stated, she arrived at the 'second joint'. Caterina therefore was not entirely sure whether Lucietta

---

[59] ASPV, Curia, II, C.M., Reg. 78: 24 November 1583, Joannis Marangoni cum Lucieta q.m Baptiste Paduani. Part of the case is found in ASPV, Curia, II, F.C., Reg. 16.

[60] ASPV, Curia, II, C.M., Reg. 74: 2 September 1579, Bartholomei de Albertis cum Angela Petri Textoris, fol. 39v.

[61] It could, equally, serve the interests of the husband if he desired to get out of the marriage.

was a virgin or whether she was capable of having sex.[62] The midwife Marietta, by contrast, was unambiguous in her judgement. She stated on 27 April 1584 that Lucietta was a woman 'incapable of having sexual relations with a man because her nature is so closed (*serrata*) that when I attempted to penetrate her with my small finger, I could only enter her with great effort, and almost did not.'[63] In this context 'closed' could mean that the woman was still a virgin,[64] but it could also indicate anatomical defects, as in Lucietta's case. Physical deficiencies were connected with the narrowness of the female genitalia, a common explanation for unsuccessful penetration. Inversely, the vagina could also be too wide, so that the woman was unable to retain the male seed.[65]

During physical inspections midwives generally worked without instruments.[66] Visual observation of the genitalia was followed by careful examination with the hands and fingers, with midwives groping for signs of sexual intercourse and of whether the hymen had been broken. The woman could assist the midwife by keeping her vagina open with her hands.[67] The midwife then attempted to penetrate the woman with her finger as deeply as possible, which could cause pain and make the woman cry. A midwife's breadth of experience and developed sense of touch led to her final opinion. Let us again take an example from the trial against Lucietta Paduani. The married midwife Magdalena Scuda testified on 29 May 1584:

> I have seen the child ... in a room ... and I asked her to lay down on the bed and I looked into her nature and never before did I see a vagina similar to this. She has a hole like other women but hers is full of flesh and I don't even know how she can urinate.[68]

Emphasis was placed on Magdalena's experience, wisdom and

---

62 ASPV, Curia, II, C.M., Reg. 78: 24 November 1583, Joannis Marangoni cum Lucieta q.m Baptiste Paduani Lucietta, fol. 49r. The physician Paolo Litigato, however, had judged her able to conjoin with a man, but he held that she would suffer considerably in childbirth because of her depressed pubic bone; see ASPV, Curia, II, F.C., Reg. 16, 27 February 1586.

63 ASPV, Curia, II, C.M., Reg. 78: 24 November 1583, Joannis Marangoni cum Lucieta q.m Baptiste Paduani, fol. 13v.

64 ASPV, Curia, II, C.M., Reg. 74: 2 September 1579, Bartholomei de Albertis cum Angela Petri Textoris, fols 39v–40r.

65 Ibid., fol. 21v. Cf. Cadden, 1993, p. 242.

66 Only in the second half of the eighteenth century were midwives advised to replace hands and fingers with instruments; see Filippini, 1993, p. 163.

67 ASPV, Curia, II, C.M., Reg. 74: 2 September 1579, Bartholomei de Albertis cum Angela Petri Textoris, fol. 39v.

68 ASPV, Curia, II, C.M., Reg. 78: 24 November 1583, Joannis Marangoni cum Lucieta q.m Baptiste Paduan, fols 25v–26r.

knowledge about the female body acquired through empirical practice. Magdalena stressed the woman's extraordinary physical constitution. Lucietta was unable to consummate the marriage, most probably because of what we would nowadays call proud flesh in the vagina. In Magdalena's second deposition a link was also drawn with a depressed pubic bone (*chel'osso è basso*).[69] Even though the first midwife Caterina was unsure in her statement, overwhelming forensic evidence was produced to support Giovanni Francesco's allegation.

Even before cases were heard in court husbands and wives would carry out their own physical examinations. A case in point is the lawsuit that Anna Lazzaroni brought in 1657 against her husband Giovanni Battista Vidali, a cheesemaker who had his workplace at the Rialto. Anna had been urged by her father confessor to sue for an annulment of her marriage because of her partner's impotence. The husband had tested her suitability for sexual intercourse. As Anna emphasised in court, her husband had simply 'stuck a finger in her nature and when he realised that it entered he admitted that it must be his defect'.[70] The same casual touching and penetrating of women is exemplified by Anna's mother and aunt, both of whom had examined her vagina with their fingers.[71] This method was used frequently by midwives and also was applied by couples dealing with everyday problems of impotence. The close contacts that women had with midwives in early modern Venice might be worth considering in this respect. One might surmise that midwives advised women on how to examine their own bodies and helped women develop a good knowledge of their bodies more generally.

When men encountered problems in fulfilling the marital duty, one possible way to test their virility was to contact other women. Anna Lazzaroni's husband Giovanni Battista Vidali, for example, was not the only one who had done so. In January 1659 he stated in court that he had believed himself to be potent when he had married Anna about five years earlier. His friend and witness Giacomo Colombo recalled in court how Giovanni had shown him Anna in the church of S. Cassiano, telling him that he liked her very much and that she was his lover (*morosa*). Potency problems were never mentioned.[72] However, consummation of the marriage was problematic because of Giovanni's external physical deficiencies. It was difficult for him, as he explained in court, to

[69] Ibid., fol. 46r. See also the assessment of the physician Paolo Litigato in ASPV, Curia, II, F.C., Reg. 16, 27 February 1586.

[70] ASPV, Curia, II, C.M., Reg. 93: 6 July 1657, Anne Lazaroni cum Joanne Baptista Vidali, fol. 5r.

[71] Ibid., fol. 7r.

[72] ASPV, Curia, II, F. C., Reg. 59, 24 January 1658.

maintain an erection. Three times he had attempted to have sexual intercourse with other women living in S. Pietro di Castello and in S. Aponal, but again he had failed. Therefore, he did not oppose his wife's petition for annulment. Astonishingly, the ecclesiastical examiner did not reproach him for engaging in shameful extramarital sex, as clearly he had attempted fornication with a 'good' intention in mind.[73]

Other men had consulted physicians. Gasparo Centani, for example, sought medical advice from two physicians at the request of Alessandro Businello, his wife's step-brother. Both doctors confirmed that his member was without defect and that he was thus able to render the marital debt. In court Gasparo could confidently claim that his penis was well proportioned, referring to its length and thickness.[74] Nonetheless Gasparo had lacked strength when he tried to deflower his wife, a fact that made him wonder whether love-magic was involved. He therefore approached the *eccellente* Benetto Flangini, a famous Venetian physician whose expertise would be praised some years later in a contemporary Venetian dialogue by the author Moderata Fonte.[75] According to Gasparo's statement in court, Flangini had supported his opinion and assured him that he might have been bewitched. The measures he took against this evil are not, however, mentioned in this trial. His wife referred to some ablutions the physicians had prescribed for him – but they surely were not a remedy against supernatural magic.[76]

As Gasparo's case makes clear, physicians considered anatomical defects to be the most likely reason for impotence. Additional concrete evidence is given in the trial of the carpenter Giovanni Francesco. The vicar of the Patriarchal Court ordered that he be inspected. On 15 January 1584 the *medico di ordine* Belisario Gadaldino testified about Giovanni's suitability for sexual intercourse. He had inspected Giovanni two days earlier in the house of a certain *messer* Angelo Brogomino, a herb seller. 'I say,' Gadaldino stated in court, 'that from what is discernible from the form and the proportions of the male member and from the testicles, I judge him able and potent to have sex with women.'[77] This deposition was confirmed by the physician Paulo Litigato. Giovanni's wife Lucietta and her procurator, however, opposed this assessment.

[73] ASPV, Curia, II, C.M., Reg. 93: 6 July 1657, Anne Lazaroni cum Joanne Baptista Vidali, fols 20r–v.

[74] ASPV, Curia, II, C.M., Reg. 82: 28 November 1590, Camille Benzoni cum Gaspare Centani, fol. 29v.

[75] I am referring here to *The Worth of Women* (Venice, 1600). See Cox, 1997, p. 183.

[76] ASPV, Curia, II, C.M., Reg. 82: 28 November 1590, Camille Benzoni cum Gaspare Centani, fols 20v, 30r–31r.

[77] ASPV, Curia, II, C.M., Reg. 78: 24 November 1583, Joannis Marangoni cum Lucieta q.m Baptiste Paduani, fol. 64r.

In the trial between Francesco Revedin and Lucrezia Ballatini, heard at the Patriarchal Court in 1584, the physical inspection did not entirely clarify matters. Francesco and Lucrezia had been married for seven years and had practised sex in the first three years of their marriage; still they were childless and Lucrezia now wished to be freed from her husband's company. The physician Hermolao di Hermolai, who was summoned on behalf of the plaintiff Lucrezia, gave an intriguing statement. He had examined Francesco Revedin in the monastery of S. Salvador in the presence of the physician Francesco Battagia. Hermolai stated in court:

> I have examined a certain limping Revedin who is of small stature and I have observed his genitals, which seem to be normal. I doubt only his ability to maintain an erection, which can even happen to men with more robust bodies, that is, that they have an erection but that it does not last, which is necessary for coitus. Only a test can give clarity.[78]

A public 'test', however, was not part of legal practice in Counter-Reformation Venice in cases of impotence. Francesco Revedin was thus freed from the humiliating obligation to demonstrate his virility in public.[79]

The case of Giulio Molino, the nobleman who was sued by his wife, introduces another aspect related to bodily perceptions. In contrast to other men accused of impotence, he freely admitted in court that he had problems fulfilling his marital duty. As he explained to the ecclesiastical examiner, he suffered from a discontinuous erection (*instabilità*), which was due to a lack of 'heat' in his body. In accordance with the contemporary theory of humours or temperaments – men were associated with hot and dry humours, women with cold and moist – the correct balance of heat was considered vital for conception. An excess of heat would lead to premature ejaculation, whereas insufficient heat would prevent the emission of semen. Giulio Molino integrated medical knowledge about his body into his deposition in court and stated that 'physicians believe that it derives from frigidity and lack of heat'.[80]

Heat had long been associated with reproductive qualities. With regard to the existence and the quality of female 'seed' – an issue that had been debated for centuries – Aristotle stressed that women were not able to produce semen because of a lack of heat. Heat was necessary to transform blood into semen, but women could not do this and produced

---

78 ASPV, Curia, II, C.M., Reg. 78: 5 March 1584, Lucretie Ballatine cum Francisco Revisare panorum, fol. 30r.

79 In France the man had to prove in front of a committee that he was able to get an erection, see Darmon, 1985.

80 ASPV, Curia, II, C.M., Reg. 90: 24 November 1628, Clare Capello cum Julio Molino, 20 December 1628.

milk instead.[81] Galen, in contrast, argued in favour of the existence of female semen and stressed the importance of simultaneous ejaculation for conception.[82] Giovanni Marinello, one of the renowned physicians of the early modern period, reproduced the opinion that female 'seed' was not important for the act of reproduction.[83] Because he copied quite freely from the famous fourteenth-century doctor Michele Savonarola, he confidently reproduced his opinion (and that of Aristotle) on the subject.[84] Marinello, however, seems to have been an exception. During the sixteenth century most physicians had adopted Galen's opinion, and the female body was assigned a greater role in the medical debates about reproduction.[85] In early modern manuals female orgasm, by which female seed would be released, was thus regarded as necessary for conception to occur.[86] Still, it was thinner, colder and feebler, whereas male semen was hot, white and thick.[87] Although interpretations of male and female orgasms differed, the 'violent pleasure' that both sexes experienced and that was intrinsically connected with successful procreation was not in dispute.[88] But what did ordinary people think about how the body worked in matters of reproduction? And was ejaculation and the female seed of any interest to them? The following case provides some indications.

Anna Lazzaroni and Battista Vidali were an especially loving and caring couple, but, despite attempts for approximately two and a half years, their marriage had not been consummated. In order to help Vidali overcome his potency problems, Anna stimulated his penis until *si corrompeva* outside the vagina.[89] The verb *corrompersi* in early modern Venice was used to describe ejaculation, as the physician Giovanni Marinello pointed out.[90] According to Gianna Pomata *corrompimento* was a term that ordinary people used to describe the material character of male semen. This seventeenth-century notion of semen as 'matter' stood in sharp contrast to medical theories.[91] In this case, both partners tested the husband's ability to emit semen through masturbation.

---

81 Pomata, 1995, pp. 61–6.
82 Ibid., pp. 66–70.
83 Marinello, 1992 (orig. 1563), pp. 50–51.
84 See Bell, 1999, p. 25.
85 Simon, 1993, pp. 95–6.
86 Bell, 1999, p. 26.
87 Simon, 1993, p. 98; Laqueur, 1992, p. 100.
88 Lacquer, 1992, p. 46. Joan Cadden, however, has found that, according to some, men's pleasure was greater than women's. See Cadden, 1993, pp. 141–62.
89 ASPV, Curia, II, C.M., Reg. 93: 6 July 1657, Anne Lazaroni cum Joanne Baptista Vidali, fol. 7r.
90 Marinello, 1992, p. 50; on Marinello, see Bell, 1999, pp. 25ff.
91 Pomata, 1995, pp. 59–85.

However, after proving his ability to emit semen, Vidali's attempts to penetrate his wife would again end in failure.[92] This approach to the problem suggests that ordinary husbands and wives were aware that the capacity for ejaculation and semen was somehow connected with successful sexual intercourse, and perhaps even with reproduction. In this sense, Francesco Revedin explained proudly to the ecclesiastical examiner that he had emitted his sperm into his wife's 'nature' and that she had 'emitted her sperm on my member while I was penetrating her'. Interestingly, he also emphasised that they had experienced simultaneous emissions in the last seven years or so of their marriage.[93] It seems, then, that ordinary people may have considered simultaneous orgasms and the release of male and female seed to be necessary for conception to take place. The thirteenth-century physician William (Guglielmo) of Saliceto had recommended that the man save 'his ejaculation until he knows that the woman has fulfilled her desire. Only at this point should he push violently with his genitals and emit his sperm'.[94]

The threat to manhood

The problem with fulfilling female desire, however, was related to the perception of the woman as the more desirous of the two sexes. Desirous women could test and exhaust male virility, as they were believed to have sexual needs that tended to be both stronger and more lasting than men's.[95] When exposed to female expectations, the humiliation of impotence, erectile dysfunction or premature ejaculation became all the more great because it was the man's duty to keep his wife happy and satisfied. Female orgasm then became 'part of the test of male potency'.[96] Demands not just to perform but to perform well increased the emotional pressure that men had to negotiate. When, therefore, in about 1580 a woman provoked her Venetian lover with the words, 'You have not the courage to have sex with me, you are not a man', her words centred precisely on a man's anxiety that he might fail in his sexual performance.[97]

---

92 ASPV, Curia, II, C.M., Reg. 93: 6 July 1657, Anne Lazaroni cum Joanne Baptista Vidali, fol. 4r.

93 ASPV, Curia, II, C.M., Reg. 78: 5 March 1584, Lucretie Ballatine cum Francisco Revisare panorum, fols 11v–12r.

94 Brundage, 1982, p. 203.

95 Rublack, 1999, p. 13 and, on strong female desire, Stolberg, 2000, p. 11.

96 Fletcher, 1995, p. 11; Bullough, 1994, pp. 41, 43.

97 ASPV, Curia, II, C.M., Reg. 75: 15 October 1580, Lucie filie Sylvestri Stephanucci cum Zermano de Manezza, fol. 5r.

The reverse of such anxieties, however, was a 'contemptuous fantasy' that men could control women 'by giving them what they most wanted'.[98] Successful rule over women was connected to male sexual mastery. If the man, by contrast, lost control over his body and his sexual performance, he also jeopardised his authority over his wife. Unable to satisfy the sexual desires of his wife, her adultery was manifest proof of his loss of authority. He might awake one day, as happened to Nicolò Brun in 1675 in Venice, to find that a *cartello infamante* had been fixed over his door in the shadow of the night.[99] In this unwelcome message, the dishonoured Brun was insulted as a *becco contento* – a happy cuckold.[100] His control over his wife failed when a male member other than his own *sta in alto* (was erected) and challenged his masculine superiority by subjecting it to public gossip.

Although virile activities and physical exercise like the fist battles held at Venetian bridges were important in early modern Venice for the display of male 'performative excellence',[101] contemporary verbal slanders show how central potency was to manhood. Men with honour had *coglioni grossi*, whereas dishonoured men were portrayed as *manso* – tame as a lamb, or even castrated.[102] Gestures of castration point in the same direction.[103] Recent research on Italian sexual culture of the Renaissance has suggested that sexual behaviour not only was a 'basic component' of male identity (identifying male or female individuals as gendered beings) but embodied a 'transformative capacity' too. Sexual practices, as Michel Rocke has argued, could 'make men into women', a point that is best illustrated by same-sex relations. In Italy they corresponded to a hierarchical pattern that conveyed the gendered meaning of sexual roles: the adult, active and penetrating part was perceived as the male role, whereas the younger, penetrated and passive (or submissive) role was deemed feminine, regardless of the actual sex of the person. A man could thus use a boy as 'a woman' or even 'as his wife', as contemporaries referred to the passive role.[104] Sexual slanders

---

[98] See Rublack, 1999, p. 13.

[99] ASV, A.d.C., Misc. Pen. 416. 13: Brun, Angela, rapita moglie di Nicolò, 1675, not foliated. This case is analysed in detail in chap. 9.

[100] For an anthropological perspective see Blok, 1981, pp. 427–40.

[101] Under the eyes of thousands of spectators they were able to display strength, endurance and aggressiveness – characteristics that women were believed not to possess. As Robert Davis has argued, in displaying their manliness fighting men dissociated themselves from the weaker sex. See Davis, 1998, pp. 24–7; on 'performative excellence' see Gilmore, 1990, pp. 30–55.

[102] A case in point is ASPV, Curia, II, C.M., Reg. 92: Bendetta Spinella cum Pietro Franchini, not foliated, 20 March 1638; see also Roodenburg, 1998, pp. 366–87, from whom I have taken the example of '*coglioni grossi*'.

[103] Burke, 1987, pp. 96–8.

also show that the defining of gender was to a certain degree independent of the actual biological sex. Men could be perceived as behaving or being in a feminine position. The expression *te ho in culo* ('I have you where you belong to be'), written on a *cartello infamante* in Rome in 1620, plays precisely with this polarity of active/passive, male/female and dominant/submissive, only to conclude that the receiver was in the passive, that is, the female, position.[105]

Impotence, status and honour

The required physical control that men had to exercise during sexual performance was sometimes hard to achieve. Some fathers may well have foreseen their sons' difficulties and advised them on how to perform properly. Where sex manuals were not available, knowledge had to be acquired through practice. Although men were supposed to be the active partner, when they lacked sexual experience (or when the marriage was difficult to consummate) women were supposed to support men during sexual practices. The experience of shame and humiliation increased in societies in which the notions of privacy and sense of shame were different from those of today. In early modern Venice impotence was discussed in public sooner or later, in the neighbourhood and by family members and clergymen.

Impotence trials reveal the close contacts that daughters in particular maintained with their family of origin and the degree to which they confided in their mothers or father confessors about sexual problems. In a case already familiar to us, Isabetta, the widowed mother of Anna Lazzaroni, was summoned to court on 5 September 1657, where she reported that Anna had complained about her husband's inability to consummate their marriage. When she had spoken openly with her son-in-law, he admitted that their problems were due to his impotence. Soon other family members were involved.[106] Camilla Benzoni, by contrast, first revealed her intimate problems to her father confessor. Because Camilla and her husband had married only one month earlier, Padre

---

104 Rocke, 1998, pp. 150, 167–8. For a more detailed discussion see Rocke, 1996, pp. 94–7, 113–19. In Venice the passive partners seem to have been younger than in Florence. Cf. Ruggiero, 1985, pp. 118, 121–5.

105 Burke, 1987, pp. 96–8 and Rocke, 1998, p. 13. Refinement in looks and dress carried, moreover, the danger that men might be perceived as soft and womanish. Sumptuary laws in Venice therefore restricted the 'fashion excesses of men'. See Chojnacki, 2000a, p. 71, and this volume, pp. 178.

106 ASPV, Curia, II, C.M., Reg. 93: 6 July 1657, Anne Lazaroni cum Joanne Baptista Vidali, fol. 6r.

Clemente advised her to be patient, 'since it was an issue of great importance to dissolve a marriage'. Alessandro Businello, who was well acquainted with his sister's marital crisis, sought legal advice. He discovered that canon marital law ordered the partners to stay together for at least three years until a suit on grounds of impotence could be brought to court. On this specific issue Camilla consulted her father confessor a second time and he confirmed this information.[107]

When asked if she had spoken about her marital problems Lucrezia Ballatini reported that she had done so, at 'various times, with various people'. Her intention to petition for annulment three and a half years earlier had been rejected by her father Antonio. He had insisted on the continuation of the marriage and had ordered her to return to her husband. Only after her father's death did Lucrezia realise her plans and appear in court.[108] Angela de Fais, by contrast, was supported by her father and mother when she left her husband Bartolomeo. She stayed with her uncle *messer* Andrea, dutifully asking the Venetian Patriarch for permission to do so.[109]

Whereas women apparently addressed matters of turning the union into a sacrament with greater ease, men were more reluctant to talk about their sexual problems. If they spoke directly about their difficulties in consummating the marriage, men turned instead to clerics – as did Giulio Molino, who asked the father of the monastery of S. Steffano for advice[110] – or to physicians.[111] Giovanni Battista Vidali, apparently a man of some education, had written to the *Canonicus Dominus* Natalin Lera to ask for counsel.[112] Some accused husbands openly reacted with displeasure towards their intimate problems being made public. Francesco Revedin, for example, argued in court that his wife Lucrezia had immediately complained to her father, mother and others about him, by 'saying that I was not a man and [then she had] left me.'[113] To be forced to inform the court in detail about

---

[107] ASPV, Curia, II, C.M., Reg. 82: 28 November 1590, Camille Benzoni cum Gaspare Centani, fols 19v–21r.

[108] ASPV, Curia, II, C.M., Reg. 78: 5 March 1584, Lucretie Ballatine cum Francisco Bevisare panorum, fol. 9v.

[109] ASPV, Curia, II, C.M., Reg. 74: 2 September 1579, Bartholomei de Albertis cum Angela Petri Textoris, fol. 46r.

[110] ASPV, Curia, II, C.M., Reg. 90: 24 November 1628, Clare Capello cum Julio Molino, not foliated, 20 December 1628. Gaspare Centani was sent to his father confessor by his wife Camilla: ASPV, Curia, II, C.M., Reg. 82: 28 November 1590, Camille Benzoni cum Gaspare Centani, fol. 23r.

[111] ASPV, Curia, II, C.M., Reg. 82: 28 November 1590, Camille Benzoni cum Gaspare Centani, fol. 30r.

[112] ASPV, Curia, II, C.M., Reg. 93: 6 July 1657, Anne Lazaroni cum Joanne Baptista Vidali, fol. 16r.

[113] ASPV, Curia, II, C.M., Reg. 78: 5 March 1584, Lucretie Ballatine cum Francisco Revisare panorum, fol. 13v.

(failed) sexual performance was a shameful situation, and particularly humiliating because male sexual honour was directly addressed by examining sexual prowess during the legal proceedings.

Men would desperately try to avoid being stigmatised publicly as impotent. In Gasparo Centani's case he vehemently opposed his wife's accusation and insisted that if the marriage were to be annulled it should be on grounds of her physical defects and not because he had failed in the marital bed.[114] It was not so much the validity of their marriage that seems to have troubled accused husbands, but rather the stigma of impotence. Physical control and sexual mastery were, however, ephemeral, for age or illness could imperil virility, as indeed could a love-magic spell cast by a woman. Men, married or not, had to master this social anxiety (which increased with public mockery),[115] for impotence could overtake them at any point during their life.

The consequences of impotence – whether male or 'female' – were different for men and women. Although female honour was, in contrast to male honour, based on sexual integrity and chastity, 'impotent' women were denied the experience and the social role of motherhood. We can only speculate about the impact this situation had on their lives. They might have returned to their parents or found shelter in one of the many charitable institutions in post-Tridentine Venice, for marriage was no longer an option. Men who had not been able to consummate the marriage could still head a workshop, for in early modern Venice sexual maturity was not 'synchronised with social, financial, and political adulthood', as in early modern Augsburg.[116] Generally craftsmen, whether married or not, were denied political rights, and only patrician men aged 25 or older sat in the Great Council. Guilds had no political representation at all. Matrimony, and thus potency, seem to have mattered in more informal ways. Bachelors held the less important and less prestigious offices in late fifteenth-century Venice, although there was no formal requirement that connected a political career with marriage. However, in patrician and in artisan culture, fatherhood was assigned great dignity and accorded a prestigious social role, that of the household ruler.[117] Although marriage and entry into a guild were not

---

114 ASPV, Curia, II, C.M., Reg. 82: 28 November 1590, Camille Benzoni cum Gaspare Centani, fol. 57v.

115 Giovanni the carpenter had known what it was like to be mocked in the neighbourhood. As his wife Lucietta alleged in court, people were saying that 'he could even have sex with a woman for a hundred years, and he would still not achieve anything'. ASPV, Curia, II, C.M., Reg. 78: 24 November 1583, Joannis Marangoni cum Lucietta q.m Baptiste Paduani, fol. 92r.

116 Roper, 1993, pp. 135–6.

117 Of the 952 patrician men from 16 families whose entry into adulthood can be documented, 412 (43.3 per cent) apparently never married. See Chojnacki, 2000a, chap.

formally required, by the time a man had completed his full term of apprenticeship with a registered master and had paid his entry fees to the guild, he likely would have met a woman who was to become his wife. With financial help in the form of her dowry, he would then be able to set up his own workshop.[118] A 'sub-category' of masters, usually street peddlers, had no shop at all, and it would be interesting to explore whether bachelors and impotent men made up a high percentage of men engaged in the less prestigious aspects of trade.[119] Success or failure in bed still had far-reaching consequences for men, because biological and cultural manhood were closely connected in the early modern period. Only a man who had proved his potency could head a household and rule a family. His potency would ensure that his wife became pregnant and that the Christian duty of procreation would be fulfilled. Potency was, furthermore, 'financially' rewarded; only a man who was able to destroy a hymen as proof of his masculinity had a claim to the dowry. But if the woman he had married remained a virgin, then the man was forced to pay back the dowry if it was evident that this unhappy circumstance resulted from his impotence.[120]

Emotional and physical stresses

On a more intimate level, impotence was an experience that partners shared, regardless of which of them was afflicted with it. The

---

12, especially pp. 249, 253. This can be explained in part by the practice of restricted marriage in mid-sixteenth-century Venice, in attempts to prevent the patrimony from being divided among too many brothers and their families. See Davis, 1975, pp. 93–106. Bachelors were the main protagonists of the sexual debauchery and sexual subculture characteristic of Renaissance Italy. Cf. Rocke, 1998, p. 152, for early modern Florence and Ruggiero, 1985, pp. 159–62 for medieval Venice. These sexual energies were clearly socially disturbing, as they destroyed the reputation of honourable women and their families.

[118] Venetian statutes prescribed no limits on the husband's use of the dowry, though it was clearly protected from maladministration. See Chojnacki, 2000, p. 124, and pp. 137–8 in this volume.

[119] I would like to thank James Shaw for providing me with this information.

[120] Cases in point are ASPV, Curia, II, C.M., Reg. 78: 5 March 1584, Lucretie Ballatine cum Francisco Revisare panorum, fol. 10r; and ASPV, Curia, II, C.M., Reg. 74: 2 September 1579, Bartholomei de Albertis cum Angela Petri Textoris, fol. 16v. In patrician marriages, the dowry was transferred to the husband usually only after the marriage had been ratified and consummated, as Stanley Chojnacki has noted; see Chojnacki, 2000a, p. 84. This precautionary measure might have been practised in patrician marriages only because in the cases quoted above the partners had been living together for seven years and one year, respectively, and the dowry already had been given to the husband despite the fact that the marriage had not yet been consummated.

consummation of the marriage became central to the life of the couple, and success or failure was fundamental for the continuance of the relationship. The threat to manhood and to matrimony, therefore, affected the entire relationship, and we can only speculate about the extent to which these couples experienced despair, hardship and psychological pressure. Some men showed signs of emotional vulnerability in expressing the fear that their women might leave them; in other cases, persistent attempts at fulfilling the marital debt had turned some partners against each other. These problems also left their mark on the men, who would confess to not wanting to live in constant strife. Some, like Giovanni Battista Vidali and his wife Anna Lazzaroni, perceived their situation in almost tragic terms. Because he could not live with the woman he loved, Vidali decided to go 'far away from her'.[121] To ease their suffering the couple were advised to petition for the annulment of their marriage, despite their mutual love and affection.

The connection drawn between emotional relationships and the success or failure of sexual practices is striking in trials on impotence, and feelings and emotions gained in relevance in disputes between spouses. Usually the husband revealed an emotional, fragile and vulnerable 'inner side' of manhood when complaining about marital disorder. More or less explicitly, a link was drawn between the stigma of impotence and the stigma of unreciprocated affection, a connection that was typical for the discourse on impotence in court.[122] The relevance of emotions and affection between the marital partners made sense to all the people involved in the trial. But it is extremely significant that it was only at the moment in which the accused husbands symbolically stood with their backs to the wall that they admitted their vulnerability.

The discourse about emotions, introduced by accused husbands in court, was taken up by the ecclesiastical interrogators, who began encouraging both parties to inform the court about the nature of their relationship, in particular about issues of consent. Giulio Molino, for example, when asked whether his marriage to Clara Capello had been contracted with their 'free consent', had to admit that Clara had not responded positively at first. Only after the *Ballavar* had prompted her with the right answer had she finally consented to marry him. This was also a cause, as he now concluded, for her lack of affection.[123]

---

[121] ASPV, Curia, II, C.M., Reg. 93: 6 July 1657, Anne Lazaroni cum Joanne Baptista Vidali, fol. 20r.

[122] Beck, 1992, pp. 137–212 has observed the same link between affection and impotence in rural Bavaria.

[123] ASPV, Curia, II, C.M., Reg. 90: 24 November 1628, Clare Capello cum Julio Molino, not foliated.

Lack of affection made a 'companionate marriage' and a caring relationship impossible, and not only in the eyes of this frustrated husband.[124] Ecclesiastical examiners also seem to have promoted an equally caring marriage ideal based on mutual love and fidelity. They encouraged partners to testify to the affectionate aspects of their marital life, and especially to whether they kissed and caressed each other 'as wife and husband should do'.[125] The wording of this commendation strongly suggests – even though it is an extremely rare archival finding – that it refers to a social norm.[126] Tenderness and affection were understood in terms of support and comfort for the male partner and gained particular importance when the marriage was not easy to consummate. Wives were expected to help their husbands in these difficult moments. In this sense men and women had to work together, and women were urged to avoid movements that would make the act of defloration more difficult for the man.[127]

Lack of sexual experience was another reason why women were supposed to support men during the physical consummation of marriage. Thus, in cases in which the reciprocation of feelings was not an issue in court, litigants and witnesses explicitly testified to the strong emotional bond between the couple in question.[128] That the partners had been attracted to each other through flirtation was the first step towards the marriage of Anna Lazzaroni and Giovanni Battista Vidali. Anna deposed that she loved Giovanni, with whom she had enjoyed a premarital sexual relationship. Giovanni also emphasised his affection for Anna. After the marriage had been solemnised their great sympathy and affection continued.[129] In court they both spoke extremely sensitively about their marital relationship. The descriptions of their sexual practices are captivating: they were not reduced to the mere act

---

124   The companionate marriage has been associated more generally with a reformed marriage ideal, as most prominently articulated in Ozment, 1983. See, however, Fortini Brown, 2002, p. 314, on the same ideal in Catholic marriages.

125   ASPV, Curia, II, C.M., Reg. 82: 28 November 1590, Camille Benzoni cum Gaspare Centani, fol. 18r.

126   In the trial preserved in the Biblioteca del Museo Correr, a witness equally stressed that husband and wife never caressed or kissed each other 'as husband and wife should do'; cf. BMC, Codice Cicogna 3287, no. 70, 13 July 1601, Clarissima Donna Lucietta filias q. Clar.mi Joannis Geno *vs* Clarissimo Marco Dolphino filius q. Joannis, fol. 9v.

127   ASPV, Curia, II, C.M., Reg. 82: 28 November 1590, Camille Benzoni cum Gaspare Centani, fol. 26v. Gasparo explained the woman's movements as the result of her pain suffered while the man fulfilled the marital act.

128   According to Chojnacki, 2000a, p. 154, husbandly affection deepened in the fifteenth century in response to an increase in the status and power of patrician women.

129   ASPV, Curia, II, C.M., Reg. 93: 6 July 1657, Anne Lazaroni cum Joanne Baptista Vidali, fol. 2v.

of reproduction, but were integrated in a web of feelings, tenderness and affectionate words. As Anna revealed in court, even before they had contracted a valid marriage they 'made love for a year and we talked ... entire nights together ... and my affections for him continued ... and we kissed and caressed each other for hours and hours'.[130] This almost suggests a modern notion of sexuality in which communication and caressing are integral elements. Interestingly, medical discourse also focused on the importance of feelings. Warmth, caresses and affection were supposed to be necessary during foreplay to produce the necessary 'heat' in both partners. The Venetian physician Giovanni Marinello also stressed the importance of emotions – only when love was involved was conception granted, not when the partners hated each other.[131]

There is no archival evidence to suggest a link in the beliefs of married couples between emotions and heat on the one hand and conception on the other. Rather, caressing and affection were perceived and practised as part of the marital debt. The normative role that affections played in the minds of ordinary husbands and wives becomes explicit when we find that a husband, such as Gasparo Centani, complained that his wife had never been affectionate, never kissed or caressed him during their marriage, even though these things 'have to take place in matrimony'.[132] Gasparo's wife Camilla Benzoni also addressed the issue in terms of marital duty. But she had to admit that 'even though I have caressed my husband as the *decoro Matrimoniale* requires, and he caressed me, nevertheless it is true that he was more affectionate towards me than I was towards him, because I couldn't get the satisfaction I should have.'[133]

It was this reciprocity of feelings that Gasparo and other husbands demanded in vain from their wives. Instead of asserting his authority, in the Patriarchal Court Gasparo referred to his emotional dependency, thus creating a connection between feelings that were not returned and his sexual failure. In post-Tridentine Venice the ideal of a companionate marriage had most likely increased the pressure on men to perform well and to treat women with more care when it came to sexual intercourse. Not only the relationship between husband and wife but also attitudes towards sexuality had changed from the Middle Ages to the early modern period.[134] In the late sixteenth and the seventeenth centuries a

---

130 Ibid., fol. 4v.

131 Marinello, 1563, p. 54.

132 ASPV, Curia, II, C.M., Reg. 82: 28 November 1590, Camille Benzoni cum Gaspare Centani, fol. 25v.

133 Ibid., fol. 18r (my italics).

134 Guido Ruggiero has observed that in fifteenth-century Venice violence was often associated with sexuality, and that 'a fair amount of violence against women may have been typical of sexuality'. See Ruggiero, 1985, pp. 30–32, quotation on p. 31.

number of Catholic moralists had accorded sexual delight a more legitimate role 'at least as a prelude to, and an assistance for, fully reproductive intercourse'.[135]

Male vulnerability

In practice, male gentleness and patriarchal authority were not generally perceived to be opposites. Husband and wife could be in perfect harmony when the man used his authority reasonably and the wife did not question his authority. Emotions, however, introduced the potential that the 'natural' superiority of the male sex might be weakened. Men therefore had to negotiate conflicting demands: they had to perform the balancing act of reaffirming their superiority while simultaneously allowing emotional closeness. If men were to meet these social and cultural demands, they had to be aware of the seductiveness of emotions. If emotions got out of control, they ran the risk that women (and other men) might make a fool of them.

A case in point is the love affair that Oratio Fugazza had entertained with the midwife Angela Zaffo. Both were married when they first met in about 1613 and started their sexual relationship. After seven years, however, Angela had preferred a younger man as her lover and sent Oratio back to his wife, a decision he found hard to accept.[136] The witnesses heard before the Holy Office noticed that Oratio would have liked to carry on this affair.[137] Because he had continued to visit her (without her agreement), discord and insults arose. Neighbours had intervened to try to reconcile them, exhorting Oratio to fulfil his duty as a husband and to go home to his wife. But he claimed that he was bound in his feelings to Angela. In his first interrogation, on 28 May 1620, Oratio Fugazza stated that their relationship had always been a 'violent friendship'. From the first sexual contact onwards he had been 'bound' to her – an expression that refers to his loss of virility and the loss of his own will due to love-magic practices. His marriage remained childless because he was unable to perform sexually with other women. In his second interrogation he continued to insist that Angela had stolen his manhood. Another woman with whom he had engaged in extramarital sexual activity confirmed that he had not been able to have sexual intercourse with her despite repeated attempts; whether love-magic had been involved, however, she could not tell. In order to prove that it was

---

[135] Davidson, 1994, p. 79.
[136] He was even accused of having threatened to murder her.
[137] ASV, S.U., b. 74: Oratio Fugazza, May 1620, witness Orsetta, fol. 8r.

supernatural powers that had weakened his virility, Oratio described his symptoms of lovesickness: the strong, almost overpowering feelings he felt for Angela and his difficulty in breathing, which had forced him to abandon the conjugal household and his work and to visit Angela. Sometimes she had let him in, sometimes not. If she opened the door, however, it was only to humiliate him. While she was in bed with her new lover Oratio was told to carry out minor services around the house.

In degradation and humiliation, Oratio was now forced to observe Angela's sexual activities with other men. It was the way she played with his feelings which troubled him and which caused his 'immense agony' and jealousy. It was also the reason the entire neighbourhood was making fun of him, because he was allowing a woman to humiliate and make a fool of him. The early modern gender hierarchy was turned upside down when a woman ruled over a man. Clearly, Oratio was aware of what he was risking, but, as he explained in court, he could not do otherwise.

Oratio's case might be taken as a powerful example of the emotional vulnerability of men and the pressure put on the 'stronger sex' in early modern Venice to control their feelings and to behave like rational 'superiors'. Emotions were a complicated matter because men had to react clearly and decisively, never allowing feelings to overpower their reason. To behave any other way would make them appear weak like women (who were believed to be more easily ruled by emotions) and, more generally, would endanger manhood. Indeed, by losing his virility Oratio was 'socially' and 'culturally' turned into a woman. If their feelings got out of control, men ran the risk of being effeminate and thus of blurring the lines demarcating gender difference.

Passionate love and strong emotions therefore made manhood a more complicated matter than has been suggested up to now. The contemporary gender discourse of sixteenth- and seventeenth-century Venice hardly offered any argumentative strategy or sublimation to 'gentle men' who were emotionally dependent on women. The only argumentative strategy available was the concept of 'stealing manhood'.[138] It was only by accusing women of love-magic that men could deal with and negotiate their feelings of jealousy and emotional frustration. Only then could they – successfully or otherwise – sublimate their lack of sexual prowess and emotional rule over women.

---

[138] Surprisingly, this cultural image available to 'unmanly' men was referred to rather briefly in impotence trials in Venice.

PART THREE

The State and Crimes Related to Marriage

CHAPTER EIGHT

'Crimes of the Flesh': The Sinful City

On 26 March 1511 a short but violent earthquake made Venice's inhabitants tremble. The Venetian diarist Girolamo Priuli conscientiously recorded how the earth was shaking and people were crying. The whole city was in turmoil. Chimneys fell from the roofs, houses were in danger of collapsing. Many churches were damaged; five figures from the façade of St Mark's tumbled down, and mosaics inside the church were destroyed. The Campanile on the Piazza cracked, and even the two columns on the Piazzetta, where the Venetian justice system executed criminals, were now slanting. The members of the Senate, startled by the noise, opened the doors of the hall and pushed outside. Most likely, they had felt the earth trembling and had heard the bells of the many Venetian churches ringing. According to Priuli, the entire city was in an uproar. This 'natural' event was read as a divine sign for an evil yet to come.

The next day this moralising interpretation was spread by the Patriarch of Venice, Antonio Contarini, who took the event as a warning and preached against sins and sinners, condemning the 'sinful city' altogether. The sexual excesses in the Venetian convents, where young nuns were living like 'public whores', were abhorrent – an offence against God. Contarini feared that they might become the cause of Venice's downfall and thus demanded that secular punishment be enforced. He suspected that many 'crimes of the flesh' were being committed not only in cloisters but also within Venetian households. The sin of sodomy had become so common in Venice that even honourable senators practised this *vitio nefando* (detestable crime). Although Contarini, in his realism, feared that 'wolves do not eat wolves', he wished the Council of Ten would make efforts to monitor morality by enacting new legislation.[1]

Contarini's perception of the city's depravity owes much to the 'mood of self-accusation' of the Venetian patriciate shortly after the defeat of Agnadello in 1509.[2] When the Venetian republic was almost conquered

---

[1] BNM, Cod. PD 252 c: Diarii di Girolamo Priuli, vol. 6, fols 125v–130v. There is also a printed version, which unfortunately was unavailable to me. My thanks go to Christiane Neerfeld for bringing this passage from Priuli's diary to my attention.

[2] See Chambers and Pullan, 1993, p. 120.

by the League of Cambrai, this trauma set in motion a debate 'within the tradition of republican thought about what should be required of the virtuous citizen to safeguard the liberty of the republic'. The patricians who had experienced the crisis quickly identified the 'moral lassitude of their fellow citizens' as worthy of criticism.[3] They connected political success with moral behaviour, and sexuality was thought to lie at the heart of morality.

Sexual morality and social distinction

In post-Tridentine Venice this growing moralism was held to be a safeguard against divine indignation directed at the city. In 1572, in a decree on prostitution, the Council of Ten ordered the enforcement of new legislation against *li vitij della carne* (sins of the flesh) in order to secure God's protection for Venice.[4] The sixteenth century witnessed an increasing intolerance towards behaviour defined as an infringement against 'public decency' and as a disturbance of the social order.[5] Attempts to define proper moral behaviour were expressed in various regulations concerning the sexual culture of early modern Venice (discussed in detail below) and in sumptuary legislation. Because a degeneration of fashion was equated with a degeneration of moral behaviour and the blurring of gender boundaries, sumptuary laws during the early modern period quickly changed their focus. Whereas fifteenth-century legislation was concerned with the economic aspects of luxury, sixteenth-century laws increasingly regulated the moral aspects of clothing. New legislation now ordered that female fashion should be chaste and that breasts should be covered.[6] Particular clothes worn by patricians which were adorned with flowers or figures were now held to provoke 'divine indignation'. Nor did men escape the attention of the legislators. A law passed on 8 May 1512 which ordered modesty and simplicity of female dress also required restraint and decency in men's attire, as fashion excesses that made men appear soft and womanly ran the risk of inciting accusations of effeminacy. Because Venice's reputation was based on its being a well-ordered, balanced and stable republic, social and political order would be perceived as endangered if Venetian patrician youths were considered to have lost 'their distinctive maleness'.[7]

---

[3] Muir, 2000, p. 139.

[4] Davidson, 1994, p. 77.

[5] Derosas, 1980, p. 444. Sperling, 1999, pp. 97–100, noted an increasingly misogynistic moralism against prostitutes and immoral women in contemporary writings.

[6] Cozzi, 1980b, pp. 52–3.

[7] Chojnacki, 2000a, p. 71.

Distinctiveness was also a key word with respect to the social and moral order of early modern Venice. In 1360 respectable women and poor wenches were physically separated when the Great Council opened a fortified brothel known as the Castelletto, which later fell into disrepair and was replaced by a new building in 1460. During the sixteenth century, however, new ordinances more vigorously emphasised confinement at the Castelletto. This attempted confinement of prostitutes does not seem to have been entirely successful, for a catalogue printed in the mid-sixteenth century named more than 200 prostitutes working from private homes all over the city (see Figure 8.1).[8] Perhaps because of this failure to completely separate prostitutes from the rest of society, extensive sumptuary legislation in Venice sought to identify and protect respectable women by making courtesans wear a distinctive yellow scarf and by permitting them to attend mass only at

8.1 Prostitute (Grevembroch, *Gli Abiti de' Veneziani*)

---

[8] BMC, Raccolta Cicogna, Manoscritto, Miscellanea 2039, fols 505–17: *Catalogo di tutte le principal et più honorate cortigiane di Venezia.* For a modern edition see Barzaghi, 1980.

less busy times. 'Lewd wenches' were forbidden to sit next to patrician and *cittadini* women.[9] In addition, a decree from the Senate dated 21 February 1542 lamented the 'indistinctiveness' between noble and citizen women and courtesans, by which the 'good' were confused with the 'bad'. By attempting to physically separate and visually differentiate unchaste women from respectable women, these detailed regulations thus aimed to protect the latter's honour. In order to reinforce the 'difference in dress', courtesans were forbidden to wear various textiles, adornments and jewellery (even at home), which would make them look like honourable women.[10] These included silk, gold, silver and pearls.[11] However, despite these measures, as late as the early 1600s the English traveller Thomas Coryat witnessed a courtesan wearing fine garments and precious jewels. She appeared, he noted, to be 'decked like the Queene and Goddesse of love'.[12] Coryat, an attentive observer of female fashion, also reported that different coloured veils made it possible to distinguish a virgin from a married or widowed woman.[13]

The social and political order that was reflected by differences in fashion was in part undermined by social emulation. The complex practices of buying, selling, renting and making gifts of clothes and textiles, as Patricia Allerston has suggested, offered a 'bewildering variety of means by which clothing changed hands in early modern Venice'. Arguably, then, 'conspicuous consumption' embodied a certain potential for subverting social order. The complexity of consumer practices even allowed female servants in mid-sixteenth-century Venice to rent expensive clothes that resembled those of their mistresses. Second-hand markets, auctions and the practice of borrowing clothes opened up further possibilities for the popular consumption of expensive items.[14] Because the legislation apparently failed to reform social practices, it was often updated, so that during the seventeenth century more than 80 sumptuary laws were issued in Venice, compared with just five in Rome.[15]

Attempts at defining proper moral behaviour were also expressed in various regulations concerning the sexual culture of early modern

9 Hughes, 1983, p. 92.

10 Chambers and Pullan, 1993, p. 127; Lorenzi, pp. 101–9.

11 On sumptuary legislation in Venice see Barzaghi, 1980, especially p. 138; Hughes, 1983, pp. 69–99; Fortini Brown, 2000, pp. 320–22.

12 Quoted in Allerston, 2000, p. 372.

13 Coryat, 1611, pp. 35–6.

14 Allerston, 2000, especially pp. 376–9.

15 Burke, 1987, p. 144. Peter Burke takes this preponderance as an indication for the 'importance of republican opposition to conspicuous consumption in the name of civic equality and "modesty"'.

Venice. Fornication with nuns – the brides of Christ – was increasingly perceived by the Venetian authorities as the 'violation of nuns' purity' and as a danger to social order. At the beginning of the sixteenth century this preoccupation prompted new regulations against fornication and a new rhetoric against this unspeakable crime.[16] Yet these efforts to protect the purity of 'virginal bodies' and 'sacred enclosures' also point to a growing preoccupation with the aforementioned social distinctions. With the compulsory seclusion of nuns in post-Tridentine Venice, the Catholic Church sought not only to safeguard the 'fragile state of angelic perfection', but also to draw stricter boundaries between the brides of Christ and the brides of laymen.[17]

In their efforts to monitor morality, the Church and the state in Counter-Reformation Venice took up one major concern for their moral reform: the strict demarcation between illicit premarital sexual activities and licit marital sexual behaviour. The main target was clandestine marriages, which 'do no good', as the Decrees and Canons of the Council of Trent emphasised. Not only did these marriages arouse uncertainties, but 'grievous sins arise from said clandestine Marriages, [and] especially those, who having left their former Wife, with whom they had privately contracted, do marry openly and publicly another, and with her live in perpetual Adultery'.[18] These Christian values promulgated by the Church during the late sixteenth century were increasingly enforced by the secular authorities of Venice. Sins were now transformed into crimes.[19] In order to enforce this moral policy, early modern societies criminalised premarital and extramarital sexuality and homosexual practices – in this respect, the confessional differences in Protestant and Catholic countries concerning marital policies were minimal.[20] In Italy Nicholas Davidson has observed that during this period the 'list of sexual activities that secular government legislation treated as crimes was extensive'. It included 'fornication, adultery, bigamy, incest, rape, masturbation, sodomy, bestiality, homosexuality (including lesbianism), prostitution and abortion'.[21] The meaning of these crimes has shifted over the course of the sixteenth century to the present day, but the list of sexual crimes still elucidates a common

---

[16] During the sixteenth century the 'plaguelike effects' and the 'contagious nature' of such crimes was stressed; see Sperling, 1999, pp. 124–5.

[17] Sperling, 1999, here p. 124 and, more generally, chap. 3.

[18] Canons and Decrees, p. 123.

[19] Davidson, 1994, pp. 96–7.

[20] Harrington, 1995, pp. 273–8.

[21] Davidson, 1994, p. 75. On concubinage see Martini, 1986–87a, pp. 301–39; on sodomy see Martini, 1986–87b and Lablame, 1984, pp. 217–54.

tendency of early modern societies: the main target of the renewed moralism was to define and legally protect the state of matrimony by punishing non-heterosexual and extramarital sexuality and by exerting influence over the establishment of the marital bond.[22] Indeed, during the fourteenth and fifteenth centuries Venetian law had tolerated premarital sexuality 'as long as it led to a socially acceptable marriage'.[23] In the course of the sixteenth century, by contrast, legislative behaviour changed dramatically, increasingly criminalising physical encounters prior to and outside marriage. The new ordinances were aimed at the protection of the institution of marriage and at defining moral and immoral behaviour, and thus 'honourable' and 'deviant' sexuality.[24]

Although legislation on sexual crimes was extensive, it has been argued that actual behaviour towards deviant sexuality was more tolerant. Giovanni Scarabello has found evidence of a willingness to accept transgressions of moral conduct in some sectors of Venetian society.[25] And Nicholas Davidson has argued that, although legislation on deviant sexual activities was intense, 'legislative severity' was not consistently applied in legal practice.[26] Because Venetian justice was 'individualistic and personal rather than fixed upon an abstract concept of justice embodied in the law', the specific circumstances of individuals were carefully investigated when cases of premarital and extramarital sexuality were being judged in Early Renaissance Venice.[27] The Venetian state pursued a policy that was orientated to stabilise conjugal households and social order. The prime concern of the Venetian governmental authorities was not to inflict harsh punishment but to restore marriages and families when possible. When a marital couple reconciled and the remorseful and penitent adulteress was taken back into the household, Venetian justice refrained from the enforcement of

---

[22] To give some examples: for Germany see the work of Rublack, 1999; for Switzerland see Burghartz, 1999a; and for France see Farr, 1995.

[23] Cf. Ruggiero, 1985, p. 44.

[24] Guido Ruggiero, too, has identified a new 'discourse on civic morality' which emerged at the turn of the sixteenth century and which was based on marriage and the family. It institutionalised sex 'in its correct place in an ordered and disciplined Christian society: within marriage.' It made wives give birth to legitimate children who were then properly married within their own social stratum, thus 'theoretically assuring the social hierarchy and protecting it from the dangers of love, passion, and sex'. It was then that the 'moral society' was increasingly based on the 'moral family', which empowered the 'moral state'. Ruggiero, 1993b, p. 13.

[25] Scarabello, 1980b, pp. 78 and 82.

[26] Davidson, 1994, pp. 90ff.

[27] Ruggiero, 1978, p. 246. I share this assessment of Venetian legal practice on grounds of my analysis of the verdicts released by the Executors against Blasphemy. See chap. 3.

severe punishment. The adulteress, then, kept her dowry rights. Mercy acts could, additionally, mitigate the punishment and guarantee some flexibility from the Venetian judicial system.[28]

Although research on both Venetian legislation and legal practice is extensive, what is still missing is a gender-specific approach to premarital sexuality and sexual crimes. Gender, as will be shown, played a crucial role in defining the moral, 'purified', society, an issue to which we next turn.

The purification of society: premarital sex and gender

Venetian legislation combined in a very special way the penal legal tradition of Roman law (punishment) with the compensative tradition of canon law (dowry or marriage).[29] In cases of sexual violence (stupro violento) the Liber promissionis maleficii – the core of Venetian criminal law codified in the early thirteenth century – proclaimed that the woman, whether virgin or already married, should be recompensed with a dowry when forced into sexual relations by a man. The sum was determined on an individual basis in accordance with the social position of both parties and was to be paid within eight days, otherwise the seducer would lose both eyes.[30] The threat of corporal punishment loomed over the seducer in order to make him accept the milder punishment of dowry payment, which would result in the restoration of female honour. The law also covered women who had already lost their virginity but were still unmarried (femmina già corotta).

At the beginning of the sixteenth century the Venetian secular authorities increasingly attempted to protect respectable Venetian citizens against accusations made by an 'infamous' woman (femmina infame) who demanded dowry payment after having consented to premarital sexuality and after having lost her virginity. On 10 June 1520 the Great Council newly defined the circumstances under which those lawsuits should be accepted: in contrast to earlier times, emphasis was now placed on the chastity of the woman and on the marriage promise, thereby greatly limiting the right of female plaintiffs to bring a case to the Venetian courts. Pleas from women should be accepted only when they could prove convincingly – through witnesses or 'in other legitimate and appropriate ways' (per altri modi giusti e convenienti) – that they

---

[28] Cf. Ruggiero, 1978, pp. 243–56 and Romano, 1983, pp. 251–68.

[29] Alessi, 1990, p. 807.

[30] See Volumen statutorum, 1597, Cap. 28, p. 137. On this law see also Alessi, 1990, p. 807.

had been tricked or forced into sexual relations, or that they had consented only after receiving a promise of marriage that was never kept.[31] Only these cases of *stupro violento* were to be accepted by the Venetian secular authorities. Had a 'lewd' woman (*femmina infame*) consented to premarital sex (*stupro volontario*), the Avogadori di Comun, the Signori di Notte and the Capi di Sestieri should not accept the suit – it was the physical intactness of female bodies that from 1520 onwards became the primary marker along which the lines between moral and immoral behaviour were defined. Female servants under the age of 16 were excluded from this regulation because they were more likely to suffer sexual violence out of fear and obedience.[32] Compared with other Italian regulations, this new ordinance enforced within the Venetian territory was harsh; its attempt to protect men from accusations made by 'infamous' women anticipated a tendency that in other Italian states occurred only during the eighteenth-century reform movement.[33]

In the second half of the sixteenth century the state, in its attempt to make the sexual order the foundation of a morally ordered society, expanded its jurisdiction over legal validation in marriage, as shown in Chapter 3 of this volume. In expanding its secular jurisdiction over clandestine marriages (that is, marriages contracted informally and maybe also without the knowledge of parents), the local government in Venice attempted to control marriage formation more firmly.[34] Although the existence of a marriage promise had received legal weight in earlier secular regulations (namely that of 1520), now it became central to the definition of illegitimate and legitimate sexuality: by decreeing that the breaking of a marriage promise following sexual intercourse constituted a punishable crime, a new ordinance penalised courtship rituals that had ignored the formalities required by the Church. In issuing the law from 27 August 1577, secular authorities in Venice stated that they were to punish those 'wicked men' who under the pretext of marriage had 'forcibly taken and enjoyed' (*violate e godute*) women for a certain period without, however, fulfilling their promise of a future marriage. It was expressly emphasised in this new ordinance that the 'conservation

---

[31] Povolo, 1996, pp. 45–7 and 66–8; Alessi, 1989, pp. 129–42; Raffaele, 1989, pp. 143–54. In March 1563 the Council of Ten additionally entrusted the Executors against Blasphemy to judge cases of *stupro minore* – violent sexual intercourse with children under the age of 14. See Cozzi, 1991, p. 25 and Martini, 1986, pp. 793–817.

[32] The law from 10 June 1520 is reproduced in *Leggi criminali venete*, pp. 25–6. On this issue see Povolo, 1996, pp. 45–7.

[33] On eighteenth-century reforms see Alessi, 1989, pp. 129–42; Raffaele, 1989, pp. 143–54, especially p. 149; and Lombardi, 2001, pp. 406–12.

[34] Cozzi, 1991, pp. 34–5.

of the honour of these women' (*la conservazione del honor di simil donne*) was the state's prime concern in its infringement in the jurisdiction of the Church.[35] This legal situation did not change until the fall of the *Serenissima* in 1797.[36]

Although the protection of female honour was explicitly mentioned in the new regulation, during legal proceedings it was especially the woman's moral behaviour during the making of marriage which was debated in court and which qualified the conflicting male and female narratives. Although this legislation apparently served the interests of women who had been abandoned after a promise of marriage and after sexual intercourse, in court it continued to be women, not men, who had to prove their honourable behaviour during courtship. As a result, during the late sixteenth century female honour became increasingly linked to virtues such as chastity and bodily purity, and thus mainly defined as sexual honour.[37]

A woman's responsibility to preserve her virginity until marriage stood in sharp contrast to male notions of honour, as men could be sexually experienced when entering marriage. In this sense prostitutes – the inverse of female honourableness – could defend honourable women, in that male sexual energy could be discharged through the prostitutes' impure bodies. Contemporary definitions of male virtue were organised along completely different lines; in the criminal records under investigation here, men's premarital sexual experiences, though they might harm a woman's reputation, did not affect male honour at all.

In early modern societies, the sexual (mis)behaviour of women and men was perceived differently. As Laura Gowing has argued, the sexual acts of women and men 'had different contexts, meanings and results'.[38] It was the purity of the female body which increasingly became linked to notions of female virtue, repute and honourableness. Despite the fact that Venetian moral legislation penalised men, during customary courtship rituals it was women who were held responsible for keeping the new moral standards. In post-Tridentine Venice, the state, in defending the honour of respectable women, counter-balanced its legal protection of the female sex by simultaneously attempting to protect male citizens against accusations from women who did not fit the new moral standards of honourableness and good repute. I shall argue that one consequence of the late sixteenth-century reform of

---

[35] For the legislation see *Leggi criminali venete*, p. 63. See also ASV, *Esecutori contro la Bestemmia*, b. 54: Capitolare, fols 59r–v, and Povolo, 1996, p. 54.

[36] On cases tried during the eighteenth century, see Gambier, 1980, pp. 529–75.

[37] See Povolo, 1997, p. 359.

[38] Gowing, 1996, p. 3.

marital law was the disciplining of women and thus the reform of the female sex.

Reforms that concentrated on women in this period were not unique to Venice. For Counter-Reformation France, for example, the historian James Farr has identified a growing moralism during the late sixteenth and seventeenth centuries in Burgundy. He has noted that discipline 'was a byword for the renewed morality of order, and fundamentally, the passions and by association women were deemed most in need of discipline'. This 'gender distinction' and 'the pervasiveness of a moralist lexicon of discipline, hierarchy, and purity suggests a growing concern for boundary marking and boundary transgression'.[39]

The notion of a 'sexualised' female body, which emerged during the sixteenth century, had an influence not only on legal narratives, as we shall see, but also, apparently, on the use that the female populace made of the secular magistracy. Because women relying on the state were predominantly women without prior marital experiences, the concept of honourable female bodies arguably restricted female legal agency to only those women who fitted the new moral and legal framework. The state's control over female honour, virginity and reproductive ability, moreover, not only defined pure bodies more precisely but also marginalised those women whose honour was a matter of negative neighbourhood assessment and debate. Sexually experienced and remarrying women who had already lost their maidenhood thus more easily became victims of accusations of immorality and thus were in a more ambiguous legal position.[40]

Despite the efforts to reform actual marital practice, in everyday life traditional courtship rituals only marginally changed, and the marriage promise – not the publicity of marriage – was still fundamental in the making of marriages.[41] The difference between the betrothal (*sponsalia per verba de futuro*) and the wedding (*sponsalia per verba de praesenti*), which had been outlined by the canonist Peter Lombard (c. 1100–60) as early as the twelfth century, had introduced further ambiguities that in sixteenth- and seventeenth-century Venetian marital practice worked to the disadvantage of women.[42] By expressing the 'words of a future

---

[39] Farr, 1995, pp. 19–20.

[40] Perhaps as a consequence, widows seldom relied on the Executors against Blasphemy to restore their honour (see chap. 3 in this volume).

[41] See the seminal article by Gottlieb, 1980, pp. 49–83 and, for Venice, Rasi, 1941, pp. 235–81.

[42] On Lombard's conception of the validity of marriages, see Harrington, 1995, pp. 53–7, and Brundage, 1987, pp. 236–7 and 264–70.

consent' (that is, a marriage promise), the man only declared his intentions to marry the woman in future. In medieval canon law the expression of the words of present or future consent (a betrothal or a promise of marriage) resulted in a valid and indissoluble marriage when followed by its physical consummation – in legal medieval discourse these words and deeds had legal relevance.[43] Only with the post-Tridentine Catholic reform and the state's control over the establishment of the marital bond in Venice, were sexual contacts prior to the 'words of present consent' (which constituted a marriage when declared in church in the presence of two or three witnesses) deemed deviant and penalised.

The new legal definition of marriage formulated by the Church and the state during the course of the sixteenth century affected the sexes differently in actual marital practice. By consenting to premarital sex on the grounds of a promise of marriage, a woman entrusted a man with her 'material good', namely, her female honour, in exchange for a promise of marriage – essentially, the promise of an honourable social position. Female sexual resistance could be overcome with a betrothal, and a man could finally gain access to the female body. By entrusting her virginity to a man, a woman effectively empowered him alone to restore her honour by marrying or dowering her. Because women were culturally constructed as having a weak, lecherous and irrational nature, they needed constant – male – guidance. And because a woman's moral behaviour not only reflected her own honourableness but also affected the honour of her entire family, control of female sexuality was the concern of fathers, brothers and, finally, husbands.[44] By leaving her family of origin, the control and protection over a woman's sexuality and her reproductive ability – and therefore also the responsibility to protect and control female and, thus, male honour – was passed from father to husband. Female honour, as Giorgia Alessi has argued, 'is – to a certain extent – not yet her own business'.[45]

The intersections between male and female honour and individual and family honour implied that the planning of a marriage in its various stages was a process in which – ideally – the entire family should be involved. Single or widowed women without a family to support them during courtship and during the forming of a marital bond were thus

---

[43] Harrington, 1995, p. 57.

[44] *Leggi criminali venete*, pp. 25–6. As Sandra Cavallo and Simona Cerutti have shown, the reputation of an individual was also formed according to the status of his or her family. In this sense a family's reputation and social standing also determined the social position of individuals in the community. Cavallo and Cerutti, 1990, pp. 73–109.

[45] Alessi, 1990, p. 139.

particularly vulnerable to moral attacks for, without a father or brother protecting and guiding them, their honour could more easily be abused, first during customary courtship and then during legal proceedings. Thus, single women in particular had to behave chastely and virtuously until marriage. Where women were said to have spoken freely with men, or laughed indecently or even let male acquaintances into their living spaces, this behaviour was noticed and judged by neighbours. Eventually, it could promote disputes over female and family honour.

Lawsuits over broken marriage promises, then, demonstrate the potential conflict embodied in courtship rituals. Men were accused of using the marriage promise to gain access to the female body; in turn, women were suspected of using a marital strategy by claiming, after having enjoyed sexual intercourse, that a marriage promise was involved. Because marriage promises were often given in private and marriage contracts were seldom drawn up for the marriage of *popolane* women, or simply are not mentioned in the sources, the exchange on which marriage formation was still based, that is, words against deeds, proved to be disadvantageous to women. Their virginity was already lost, but they had not yet acquired the promised social position, namely, that of a wife. A woman's commitment was thus comparably greater than a man's. Were marriage promises exchanged clandestinely, as was often the practice, no concrete evidence could be produced if the case reached the courts. Before the establishment of a conjugal relationship, then, women and men came to court and fought over the interpretation of courtship rituals, the gifts exchanged, the level of intimacy reached and the words expressed, thereby revealing their understanding of the meaning of conjugality.[46]

Courtship rituals

From the outset gender played a significant role in all aspects of early modern marriage formalities, and, as we shall see, men and women placed different emphases on courtship rituals according to their own agendas.[47] Courtship could be a protracted affair, and women would

---

[46] Gowing, 1996, p. 140.

[47] Because the majority of trials heard at the magistracy of the Executors against Blasphemy have been lost, this section is based on a variety of sources. In addition to few lawsuits that have come down to us, my analysis is based on the verdicts of this magistracy. They usually include a short description of the crime committed. Moreover, information on the stage that marriage formation had reached is sometimes given: rings might have been exchanged, the banns might already have been published or, occasionally, a marriage promise might have been expressed in front of witnesses. I have also used individual

sometimes first start to speak to their lovers from the balcony or receive little notes via neighbours. Before a prospective groom was introduced into the household of his future bride, the woman occasionally stood on the balcony while he courted her from the street, a ritual that was noticed by the surrounding neighbours. With increasing familiarity would come gestures of affection in the form of kisses. Finally, when intimacy had grown and visits had become more frequent, some couples would eat and drink together. Once couples reached this level of familiarity, they were likely to have already started a sexual relationship. But here, too, the significance of these rituals and intimate contacts was debated. For women they constituted the realisation of conjugality and a manifest proof that a wedding soon would be solemnised in church, especially when a marriage promise had already been given. In fact, the sharing of *mensa et thoro* (bed and board) was a key marital concept, and after the Tridentine reforms living and eating together was often equated with matrimony itself.[48]

The practice of exchanging gifts during courtship, it would seem, was also gender-specific. In the late sixteenth and seventeenth centuries Venetian women considered handkerchiefs to be appropriate gifts for their future spouses, and they were even given as part of the dowry. Handkerchiefs were also used to clean away the blood after the first sexual contact, and so carried an extremely intimate and specific sexual meaning. They therefore were typically exchanged only after a long period of courtship and intimacy.[49] The meaning of this material exchange could be considered incontestable, denoting binding steps towards a marriage. However, conflicting legal narratives from men and women demonstrate that sexual commitment was emphasised in the arguments of women, whereas the man still debated the meaning of sexual practices and thus that of the gift. The symbolism embodied in handkerchiefs became an important factor in subsequent court cases, as will be shown later.

The material goods that women received showed greater variety and included precious gifts such as rings or strings of pearls. In an illuminating case investigated at the Patriarchal Court a woman claimed that a pair of gloves and a small golden box that she had received

---

lawsuits on broken marriage promises, which, despite the jurisdictional infringement of the state, were still heard before the Patriarchal Court. Because the legal framework in the courts of the Executors and the Patriarch was the same, the legal narratives are almost identical. In writing this section I have been inspired by Laura Gowing's discussion on courtship rituals in early modern London. Cf. Gowing, 1996, chap. 5.

[48] Rasi, 1941, pp. 248–9.

[49] See Lombardi, 2001, pp. 209–10 and Paolin, 1984, pp. 201–28.

revealed the significance of her courtship, as they had been given to her as a sign of her betrothed's love. A witness in her favour claimed that they were a 'sign of matrimony'. The man, however, rejected the notion of giving emotional and judicial weight to these material goods. The meaning he ascribed to them was purely economic: they had constituted payment for the sexual services he had received. Whereas she claimed to be his future bride, he alleged that she was simply a prostitute.[50] Although the meaning of material goods during courtship was open to interpretation, the significance of the gift of a ring was less disputable; in courtship and in legal practice it constituted manifest proof of emotional involvement and a promise of marriage. Only when a ring was given to a widow – a woman who had already lost her virginity – could the man debate the significance of the present. In 1660, Bartolomeo deposed how a certain Cristoforo Capello, the head of the *Magazen* in S. Stin, had given pearls and a ring to the widow Caterina Strazzarola. Although she insisted that these gifts constituted manifest proof of a marriage promise, Cristoforo evaluated these gifts differently. He had explained to Bartolomeo that he had wished to pay Caterina for the sexual services that he had received. He claimed that he had promised her nothing – and, he asked rhetorically, who would expect him to marry a widow with four children.[51] Because gifts could easily be misinterpreted, women had to be cautious and sensible about the nature of gifts and the circumstances in which they accepted them from men.

When the meaning and significance of the relationship and the nature of the sexual contacts were contested, the moral behaviour of the woman was assessed. Because in these cases courtship rituals and sexual contacts had lost their legal relevance and a marriage promise was particularly hard to prove, the respectability and honour of the women pursuing lawsuits were crucial. Witnesses thus were interrogated about the reputation of the woman at the magistracy of the Executors against Blasphemy (and in the Court of the Venetian Patriarch). Examiners inquired whether the honour of the woman was credible and thus the allegation of a marital promise likely. The virtuous behaviour of a woman was measured by investigating her sexual loyalty to only one man and, more generally, the way she had comported herself during courtship. Courtship rituals, as these lawsuits over the non-fulfilment of marital promises show, were gendered, and the physical familiarity that

---

[50] ASPV, Curia, II, C.M., Reg. 83: 4 March 1596, Albe Junie cum Pompeo Sprechi. Cf. the witness deposition of Caterina on 27 April 1596.

[51] ASPV, Curia, II, C.M., Reg. 93: 20 August 1660, Catharine Strazzarola cum Christoforo Capello, fols 6r–9v.

these couples achieved had a long history of its own.[52] This history was grounded in the city's neighbourhood life and eventually became part of the collective memory of urban parish members. Because courtship and marriage formation consisted of many stages, including initial contacts, private visits at home, the exchange of gifts and meetings with friends and relatives and perhaps even the parish priest, it was a process and a transaction that was made under the eyes of many parishioners. Litigants and their witnesses in court spoke at length about the meaning of the growing intimacy between man and woman.

The most important and highly controversial feature of these criminal proceedings was, accordingly, the context in which increasing physical and emotional familiarity was achieved. Together with the emotional involvement that men had expressed, women alleged that the men also had promised never to marry anybody else. These words not only stood for emotional exclusivity, but were a legally binding promise of a future marriage. In court, witnesses were therefore interrogated about the specific words that had been uttered and the exact circumstances. Because these promises were exchanged mostly in private when no family member, friend or servant was present, witnesses commonly explained that they had been informed by the suing woman alone – a fact that weakened her credibility in court. The parents of relatively wealthy couples might have drawn up a marital contract and started to negotiate the dowry – economic transitions that strengthened the woman's position in court and made her narrative more believable. More often, however, no such steps had been taken. Women then simply turned to the state's legal institutions, particularly after they realised that they were pregnant and had been abandoned after the delivery of a child. In cases in which a child was born their claim before the Executors included alimony payment. In early modern Venice fathers were held responsible for the financial upbringing of their children. If a favourable verdict was passed, the father had either to take care of his child and raise it or to pay monthly alimony until the child had reached puberty. In some cases he also had to provide the dowry for a female child.

Contested virginity

When lawsuits over the non-fulfilment of a marriage promise reached the court of the Executors against Blasphemy, the credibility and social position of the litigants were of great relevance. In measuring the

---

[52] For the Florentine diocese see Lombardi, 2001, pp. 182–4.

credibility of women, the transgression of social boundaries played an important role. Women with modest social backgrounds who accused *cittadini* or even patrician men of having deflowered them after a promise of marriage had a much smaller chance of winning their case – a tendency that continued well into the eighteenth century.[53] When women entertained contacts with men from higher social ranks they were under an even greater obligation to protect themselves from improper and immoral behaviour, otherwise their allegations went unheard. It was deemed quite unlikely that a respectable patrician would marry far below his social expectations, especially once the Venetian patriciate had become increasingly status-conscious after the late fourteenth and early fifteenth centuries.[54] When courtship rituals and the planning of marriages transgressed social boundaries, the woman had to give particularly strong evidence in court to strengthen her legal position. The following is a case in point.

In December 1688 this case of disappointed feelings and destroyed marital plans was brought to the attention of the Council of Ten, which handed it over to the Executors against Blasphemy. Regina Ramini, the young daughter of naval captain Leonardo Ramini, was pleading to have her honour restored.[55] Regina claimed that she had been courted over a long period and had been deflowered by Girolamo Paruta under the pretext of marriage. When she had become pregnant and lost the child Girolamo abandoned her. Letters and a wedding ring were submitted to strengthen her case.

Their acquaintance had started approximately three years earlier, when Regina was 21 or 22 years old. She had first met Paruta in church during the Holy Eucharist and, as it seemed, his interest in her had been aroused immediately. He had started to gather information about her birth and situation. Maria Dusin, a boatsman's wife and Regina's neighbour in S. Ternità, recalled in court how Girolamo's cousin had been inquiring after Regina's 'quality' and 'condition' by asking her whether the young woman was rich or poor. He was sent away by Maria, but returned shortly thereafter wanting to know whether it was possible to speak to Regina and to pass her a letter written by Girolamo. Apparently, the cousin had asked too much for such a short acquaintance, and Maria Dusina refused, reproaching him by pointing out that Regina was a 'civil child'.[56]

---

[53] Gambier, 1980, p. 538.

[54] On the status of consciousness of the patriciate see Romano, 1987, p. 11.

[55] ASV, *Esecutori contro la Bestemmia*, b. 1. Processo contro Paruta, Girolamo per deflorazione a danno di Regina figlia di Leonardo Ramini Capitano di Nave, 1688, not foliated. Unless stated otherwise, this narrative is based on Regina's version.

[56] Ibid., Maria q. Piero Quandeli moglie di Bassian Dusin, 23 December 1688.

With time, however, familiarity between Girolamo and Regina had grown. He had courted her, initially from the street while she was stood on the balcony. Even at this stage, Regina emphasised in court, he had assured her of his serious intentions. 'If this would not end in marriage, he should rather return on his way', she had warned him. But Girolamo had assured her that he would marry her even if his relatives were not content. His emotional investment, Regina alleged, was therefore greater than his material concerns. Girolamo introduced himself to the household. He became acquainted with Regina's brother, and both were seen together in the neighbourhood. While their father was away at sea Domenico Ramini – a physician (*barbier*) in S. Provolo – was supposed to manage the marital business of his sister. Soon other relatives got involved. Regina Ramini recalled in court how Girolamo's uncle, Giovanni Batta Cechini, had persuaded her to consider Girolamo as her future groom. In his family she had already been singled out as his spouse, not because of her birth but because of her virtuous conduct and behaviour. As a sign of the future marriage Regina received a ring from Girolamo which had belonged to his mother. When Girolamo spoke to Regina's brother about the marital plans, Domenico left no doubt about the modest dowry Regina would receive. It would never reach the sums the Parutas might be used to. After a year or so physical intimacy was reached. Girolamo had 'taken' (*mi rapi*) the 'flower of her maidenhood' one evening during summer, reaffirming the promise to take her as his wife. After the first time, Girolamo had sex with Regina whenever he wished, and when she hesitated to consent he reminded her that it was her duty to render the marital debt – as if she were already his wife. When, 18 months later, Girolamo had not complied with his promise, Regina's brother Domenico had a word with him in his workshop. Still Girolamo did not discharge his debts, and never again was he seen in the house of the Raminis.

At this point Regina decided to put pressure on Girolamo and his family. Unknown to her brother she took a gondola to the Parutas' house in S. Trovaso and knocked at the door. It was opened by Giovanni Batta Cechini, Girolamo's uncle. Regina lifted her long veil (*cendal*) to allow him to see her, but rather than welcome her, she alleged, he assaulted her. Pietro Anchia, the gondolier who had brought her to S. Trovaso and the head of the local controlling body (*Capo di Contrada*), who had heard the noise, intervened to help her. The young woman stayed there for five days, together with Girolamo's mother Chiara. A priest was sent to inform Regina's brother Domenico. Both returned, in company with the nobleman Domenico Loredan from S. Stefano, who seems to have played a key role in the subsequent attempts at reconciliation. Domenico Loredan insisted in the face of Chiara Paruta that the honour of the poor child – and consequently that of her brother – needed to be restored and that she should use her authority and command her son Girolamo to fulfil his promise. Chiara Paruta, however, responded by referring to the authority of Alvise Paruta – Girolamo's elder brother – who was the head of the household. Without having heard his advice, she stated, she did not wish to give her word to this marriage business.[57]

Girolamo Paruta had gone to the house of Girolamo Pancierutti, a priest from the parish of S. Basso near St Mark's, seeking advice. The priest had told him to discuss the matter with his brother Alvise. Girolamo's mother Chiara Paruta had then asked the priest to accompany Domenico Ramini to their house, where the priest met Regina, who showed the mother the wedding ring that she had received from Girolamo. According to Father Pancierutti, this was a clear sign of a marriage promise.[58] He thus advised Girolamo to marry Regina, the girl he himself had confessed to deflowering. If it had been up to Girolamo, the priest stated, he would have willingly fulfilled his promise, but his brother Alvise opposed the match. The priest thus had approached Alvise and his mother to obtain consent to the marriage that would re-establish Regina's honour.[59] But negotiations had failed and events had escalated. As Regina alleged, Alvise had insulted her and had thrown her out of the house during the night. Because she was ashamed of returning to her brother she went to stay with her neighbour Maria Dusin and her husband. After 10 days this couple accompanied her to the home of her godmother Margherita Papadopula in S. Severo, where she found shelter during the trial.[60]

Regina was lucky to have strong evidence, such as the letters from September 1686 and, of course, the ring. According to Marc'Antonio Tirabosco, secretary of the Executors against Blasphemy, letters were items of concrete evidence.[61] During legal proceedings the authenticity of private documents usually was tested by comparing handwriting, but because Girolamo Paruta did not appear in court this method was not applied. The Executors against Blasphemy valued Girolamo's letters as proof of his emotional investment – and we are about to see why. In a letter he wrote on 12 September 1686 while absent from Venice, he assured Regina of his feelings for her:

> My highly respected Signora. On occasion that my uncle is on his

[57] Ibid., Domenego Loredan, 23 December 1688 who reported Chiara Paruta's point of view.

[58] Ibid., Girolamo Pancierutti, 23 December 1688.

[59] Ibid.

[60] Ibid., Maria Dusin, 23 December 1688, and Regina Ramini, 22 December 1688.

[61] Tirabosco, 1636, pp. 25–6.

way to Venice I will not fail to send signs of my faithfulness to who is Queen [*Regina*] of my heart. I am writing only a little, because I am in a big hurry ... Be reassured however, that my affection is unchanged and also distance will not diminish it. I am sending you my heart with a thousand kisses and I hereby declare that I am eternally your ardent lover and servant, G.P.[62]

Because Girolamo's demonstrations of his affection for Regina had, additionally, occurred in public, neighbours produced evidence in her favour. Because of her physical proximity Regina's neighbour Maria Dusin could give reliable evidence about Regina's moral behaviour and the nature of her relationship with Girolamo. As mentioned above, she stated how she had been approached by Girolamo's cousin and how she had been reluctant to respond to his requests. After she had been assured of his good intentions, that is, matrimony, she agreed to deliver a letter to Regina. The courtship soon evolved, and gifts as a sign of his emotional commitment were exchanged. One evening from her balcony Maria Dusin had witnessed Girolamo giving Regina his portrait. This act was far more than a simple transaction of a material object: it carried a greater meaning. Symbolically he was giving himself away – the portrait thus should be received as a security that he would marry her. Soon afterwards Regina received the more conventional gift of a ring. The ring, once given to Regina as a promise of a future marriage, had now changed its meaning and become a piece of concrete evidence. Maria Dusin, when shown the ring in court, confirmed that it was the one she had seen on Regina's finger.[63] Girolamo, however, was said to have contested the meaning and to have claimed that Regina had stolen it from his hand.[64]

It is presumably due to this strong evidence (portrait, love letters, ring) that the Executors against Blasphemy decided to proceed against Girolamo Paruta, notwithstanding his high social position. On 29 December 1688 the tribunal released a mandate against him. Because he was absent he was ordered to present himself within eight days. Three times was he granted additional time to appear, but he let it pass. Finally, on 15 February 1688, he was banished from Venice and its surrounding territories for three years. Only by marrying or by dowering Regina Ramini with 80 ducats would he be freed from this sentence.

This case, then, demonstrates how gendered courtship rituals became crucial to legal narratives. Regina's deposition – as well as those of her

---

[62] ASV, *Esecutori contro la Bestemmia*, b. 1. Processo contro Paruta, Girolamo, not foliated. For the culturally accepted norms of expressing intimate feelings in a letter, see Cohen, 1993, pp. 181–201.

[63] ASV, *Esecutori contro la Bestemmia*, b. 1. Processo contro Paruta, Girolamo, witness Maria Dusin, 23 December 1688.

[64] Ibid., Girolamo Paruta, 23 December 1688.

witnesses – emphasised the passivity of her comportment, which was central to contemporary understandings of proper female behaviour. Girolamo, on the other hand, was depicted in the active role. Disputed marriage cases show the necessity for women to allege and prove their honour; they demonstrate, additionally, the fragility of female honour and the need for women to present their behaviour as following ideals of female reservation and containment, in contrast to men's actions and gestures of affection. Prescriptive norms and contemporary notions of honour thus had their effects on the representation of gender conflicts. Incorporated into legal texts they shaped the narratives, making contemporary categories of gendered norms an essential element of legal discourse.

Sex and violence

The most disturbing details in some of these legal narratives are the references to sexual violence. Legal cases brought by women which are built on growing physical, emotional and sexual familiarity quite unexpectedly present a disruptive element. Women claimed to have suffered violence from their future grooms. In their legal accounts, defloration is described as an act of female resistance and male violence, regardless of whether a marriage promise had already been given: women were brusquely taken with violence and handkerchiefs were used to prevent them from screaming. When references to violence were made, legally the situation remained the same in that it was still handled as a case of broken marriage promise and not as rape. As the *cancelliere* Lorenzo Priori explained in his *Prattica Criminale*, the concept of 'violence' was not restricted to physical force alone; it also included flattering and deceitful words by which a woman had been talked into sex under the pretext of marriage.[65] Because legislation had drawn stricter boundaries between honourable and dishonourable women, in court women had to foil every suspicion that they had behaved immorally and consented to premarital sex without a promise of marriage; otherwise they easily would be regarded as shameless and without any claim to recompense. Women who were perceived as dishonourable even lost their claim for redress when they had suffered sexual violence, because it then was held to be legally irrelevant and meaningless.[66] Hence, if a man desired a woman, the woman had to be decisive in her resistance and to defend her virginity against violent

---

65 Priori, 1622, p. 179.
66 Gambier, 1980, p. 535.

attacks. The following case study provides a detailed account of the dynamics of sexual violence and reputations in litigation on disputed marriages.

On 20 May 1613 a young and pregnant widow named Nadalice appeared in court in Treviso, a city under Venetian rule. In her accusation against a certain Cristoforo di Fabris she bluntly focused on the legally interesting facts of a failed marriage formation: 'I wish to quarrel against *messer* Cristoforo di Fabris, a man who is selling medicine in a pharmacy [*speciaro*]; ... he has taken my honour ... and he has deceived me under the pretext of marriage and I demand that justice will be done.'[67]

During the trial we learn that Nadalice was orphaned as a baby. Some days after her birth she was adopted by Alessandro de Bari and his wife and raised together with their other children. With financial help from the hospital where she had spent the first days of her life, she was subsequently married to a baker. When her husband died only four months after the wedding, Alessandro de Bari accepted her back into his household because he held her to be an 'honourable child who was well suited for the company of his daughters.' After six or seven years Alessandro's married sister and her husband Vicenzo (a baker) took Nadalice into their household as a domestic servant. Only some months later the quiet and peaceful life in the household was disrupted when Nadalice claimed to have been forced by Cristoforo to consent to premarital sex.[68]

The story, however, had begun three years earlier, when Cristoforo had started to court her, revealing his affections. The young widow Nadalice had discouraged him because she was poor and socially beneath him. But Cristoforo had continued in his attempts and Nadalice had given up her resistance. Signs of emotional commitment had grown, and she claimed that Cristoforo had stressed that she was the woman he wanted to marry. The marriage promise was kept secret at his request because Cristoforo still needed to establish his own workshop.[69]

Because financial security was needed to set up an independent

---

[67] ASV, A.d.C., Misc. pen, 240.3: Fabris, Christoforo, stupro, fol. 1r. (The document is badly damaged.)

[68] Ibid., fol. 12r. Nadalice, by contrast, stated that she already had lived with Vicenzo and his wife for three years (fol. 1v).

[69] A *lavorante* in Vicenzo's workshop stated in court that Vicenzo was Christoforo's master. In this case, '*accomodarsi in una bottega*' meant that he still needed to set up his own workshop. Ibid., fol. 38r. However, Christoforo testified that he occasionally used the baker's facilities, but was not his employee proper (fol. 64r).

household so that an artisan husband could support his wife and children, Cristoforo's delay made sense to Nadalice. An open word with master and mistress did not seem sensible at this stage of events and was avoided. Only when Vicenzo and his wife Angela started to arrange a marriage for Nadalice did she reluctantly confess that she already had accepted Cristoforo as her future groom. They stopped their endeavours when Cristoforo repeated his marriage promise in front of them, holding Nadalice's hand firmly.

It is only after this public confirmation that Nadalice confessed to having had sex with Cristoforo. One night when Angela and Vicenzo were in bed Cristoforo came to the workshop and asked her to open the door. He then seduced her with words and violence. This first time Cristoforo gagged her with a handkerchief to prevent her from screaming and the household, thus, from witnessing the assault. This sexual relationship continued. Finally Cristoforo talked to Vicenzo about his marriage plans, which were approved, and transactions of material goods which carried emotional and legal weight followed: he gave Nadalice a ring as a sign of his word; she gave him a handkerchief. Their sexual practice continued openly. Only when Nadalice became pregnant and Cristoforo was still unwilling to marry her did she sue him in court.

The court was approached only after negotiations had failed. Vicenzo, doubting the sincerity of Cristoforo's intentions, had asked a priest for advice. The mediator had taken his role seriously and had talked to Cristoforo, who confirmed his willingness to marry Nadalice but stated that he needed more time.[70] The priest then blocked further marriage arrangements, for a marriage promise was legally binding and no other marriage could be arranged. Everyone involved might have been happier if Nadalice had married the shoemaker or the fruit-seller, who had already proposed to her,[71] but events took a different path. After negotiations had failed the parties were litigating in court without agreeing about the words that had been uttered, the meaning of the material goods that had been exchanged or the significance of the premarital sex. In court Cristoforo contested the versions relating their growing intimacy and their plans for a conjugal household, as told by Nadalice and her witnesses. Interrogated on 19 December 1613 he did not relate a completely different version, but one that did diverge in legally important details. He denied making the marriage promise. He did not, however, deny having enjoyed physical and sexual intimacy with Nadalice, though he did ascribe a completely different meaning to it: sexual pleasure without any binding significance.

---

70 ASV, A.d.C., Misc. pen. 240.3: Fabris, Christoforo, stupro, fol. 18r.
71 Ibid., fol. 27r.

Women were extremely vulnerable to moral attacks, especially after the legislation of 1520 and 1577 had drawn stricter boundaries between respectable and lewd women. Denying plans of future conjugality, Cristoforo attacked Nadalice's sexual reputation. Using the cultural construction of the female as the more lecherous sex, he counter-alleged that he had been seduced and tricked. While working in Vicenzo's bakery, Nadalice had approached him, offering help 'with words full of love'. Sex quickly followed. During this time Nadalice had provided him with keys in order to facilitate further sexual contact. Only then did he realise that he had been trapped. He claimed to be the victim of a conspiracy with the aim of binding him to Nadalice by marriage.[72] He elaborated on these details in his written defence.

Nadalice's sexual integrity was the crucial point of his attack. In an attempt to destroy her credibility and sexual reputation, he claimed that Nadalice was a lewd and dishonourable woman who had frequent sex with several men.[73] By stating that Nadalice had received and accepted several gifts in return for sexual pleasure he implied that she was a whore. The word 'whore' conjured up a powerful image in the early modern period and was not yet fully associated with a profession. In 1543 the Venetian Senate had defined a prostitute (*meretrice*) as 'an unmarried woman who has sexual contact with more than one man. Prostitutes are, moreover, those women who are married but live separated from their husbands and have sexual intercourse with one or more men'.[74] Indeed, in practice the Venetian government 'made little practical distinction between concubinage, adultery and prostitution' during the sixteenth century.[75] Used as a sexual slander, the expression 'whore' expressed doubts about a woman's sexual honour, whether she was married or not. Women constantly had to defend their sexual honour, both in court and in the streets. To claim that a woman lacked virtue was thus the most powerful weapon that a man had in court. It destroyed a woman's reputation and credibility, and no judge would expect a sensible man to promise marriage to a lewd and dishonourable woman. A woman, by contrast, had no comparable weapon at her disposal. Male honour was primarily based on a man's reputation as an honourable citizen, and therefore the sexual conduct of men was of no interest in court. Cristoforo's defence thus focused on Nadalice's immorality and his own credibility by underlining his family's

---

[72] Ibid., fol. 66r.
[73] His defence starts with folio number 1. ASV, A.d.C., Misc. pen. 240.3: Fabris, Christoforo, stupro, fols 1r–2v.
[74] The law is given in Cibin, 1985, p. 81.
[75] Davidson, 1994, p. 89, note 65.

honourable status.[76] According to his version, Nadalice's claims were pretentious and mere marital strategies, as no *cittadino* would freely make a marriage promise to a dishonourable and poor woman from the working class.[77]

Although this lawsuit is an individual case of people in crisis, it exemplifies common arguments and strategies used by plaintiffs and defendants. It shows how gender differences played out in daily life, and the consequences of gendered morality for female honour. Female honour was the battleground in such suits: whereas women alleged that men had used the marriage promise to gain access to their body, men accused women of being disreputable. Marriage formation was a process in which different notions of conjugality and emotional, physical and social commitment were negotiated. However, the moral culture, the gendered morality and the cultural meaning of premarital sex for women and men made women more vulnerable during this process. Women first entrusted their sexual honour to a future groom, and eventually received a social position in return. But the period of courtship was full of obstacles; when steps towards the building of new households were suddenly interrupted, perhaps because of the intervention of parents who disapproved of the choice of bride or groom, the words spoken, the gestures expressed and the gifts exchanged came under scrutiny. In court a process of ascribing meaning was initiated, with the significance of sexual intimacy crucial to this process. In legal practice the Executors against Blasphemy had to be convinced that sexual intercourse had occurred under the pretext of marriage, or that virginity had been taken with fraud and violence. During the sixteenth century sexual restraint had become a female virtue essential during the making of marriage. It also played a central role in marital life itself, as the next chapter reveals.

---

76 ASV, A.d.C., Misc. pen, 240.3: Fabris, Christoforo, stupro, fols 3v–4r.

77 It is not entirely clear whether Christoforo's family formed part of the Trevisan *cittadini*. In point nine of his defence he claimed that his father held a very honourable office, '*che viene impiegato solamente ai Cittadini*'. See ASV, A.d.C., Misc. pen. 240.3: Fabris, Christoforo, stupro, fol. 4r.

CHAPTER NINE

Adultery: A Threat to Conjugality

Adultery was a threat to, and a drama within, the ordered household. It was the extreme sign of marital breakdown and disturbed the balance between male authority and female submission. Conduct books stressed at length the husband's duty to control lecherous female sexuality; failure in these endeavours testified to the husband's loss of power over his wife. Not only during the establishment of a marriage, but during married life as well, female virtue was intrinsically connected to chastity and modesty; illicit sex by women revealed the violation of this idealised model and questioned its realisation in daily life. It was the husband who reigned at the top of the household hierarchy, and it was the husband, too, who should lie on top of his wife.[1] Women who broke this rule were sexually assertive, and not properly submissive. They violated the holy sacrament of marriage and the 'spiritual experience of becoming one flesh' by offering their body to other men.[2] Although conjugal households collapsed when wives went astray, spouses were inescapably bound together until separated by death; in Catholic countries remarriage was not an option for distressed couples.

On the legislative level, although adultery was a crime for which both men and women could be prosecuted in early modern times, it was female infidelity that stood at the heart of early modern definitions of adultery. By contrast, until the second half of the fourteenth century 'the government's concern had focussed on the male adulterer', leaving wives to the disciplining of their husbands. As Guido Ruggiero has noted, 'the 1360s mark a significant watershed for Venetian women', as they henceforth were held responsible for their crime.[3] This shift in dealing with female adulterers was reinforced in early modern definitions of adultery. According to the Venetian *cancelliere* Lorenzo Priori, three sorts of adultery could be differentiated. The first, as stated in his *Prattica Criminale*, concerned so-called *adulterio duplicato*; in this case, both the man and the woman engaged in a sexual affair were married. In the second and third types only one of the parties was legally married. 'Real adultery', however, existed when a married woman established a

---

[1] Cadden, 1993, p. 245.
[2] Rublack, 1999 p. 216.
[3] Ruggiero, 1985, pp. 53–4.

sexual contact with an unmarried man, an act against God and the matrimonial vows and sacraments.[4]

Although adultery was a punishable crime, it could not be prosecuted ex officio because it was defined as a private offence. Government authorities relied on the co-operation of the populace in bringing a suit to court. In 1622 Lorenzo Priori emphasised that the betrayed husband or the father of an adulterous daughter could choose between bringing the case before the secular or the ecclesiastical court, depending on whether punishment or separation was the aim of the lawsuit.[5] The cases under investigation here are stories of alleged female infidelity that ended in criminal proceedings. The aim of husbands who pressed charges was not separation but rather the punishment of wives and the restitution of the dowry. Venetian legislation actually encouraged husbands to sue before a secular tribunal, as the Patriarchal Court had no jurisdiction over property rights. Hence, the early modern Venetian legal theorist Antonio Barbaro bluntly stressed that 'if the husband desires to acquire the dowry of his adulterous wife he needs to sue her at the secular court'.[6] According to the aforementioned Lorenzo Priori, a woman risked losing her dowry even 'when she kisses another man, or if she allows the man to touch her breasts, since these are the signs and manifest acts of adultery.'[7] The sexual misconduct of a woman thus centred on single acts of infidelity that made her lose her claim to be a proper wife. As discussed in Chapter 6, whereas domestic violence was sufficient grounds to endorse a separation only when the husband repeatedly had abused his patriarchal authority over time and endangered the life of his conjugal partner, wives could be prosecuted as unfit partners after they had failed only once.[8] Whereas an adulteress depended, with regard to her property (dowry), on the 'generosity of her husband to forgive her, an adulterer had at most to pay maintenance, but suffered no loss of property'.[9]

The notion of adultery as an overwhelmingly female crime was also reflected in contemporary non-legal culture, as demonstrated by a witness in a lawsuit in 1640 against the adulterous wife Laura. When asked to define this sexual offence this man bluntly responded that adultery is committed when 'a married woman has sexual intercourse with another man'.[10] Although the moral behaviour of a husband was occasionally

---

4 Priori, 1622, p. 172 and, for the eighteenth century, Barbaro, 1739, p. 180.
5 Priori, 1622, p. 173; Ferro, 1845, vol. 1, p. 51.
6 Barbaro, 1739, p. 182.
7 Priori, 1622, pp. 178–89.
8 On this argument see Gowing, 1996, p. 207.
9 Guzzetti, 1998a, p. 255.
10 ASPV, Curia, II, C.M., Reg. 92, 13 February 1640, Michaelis Barbaro cum Laura, witness Maffitti Bergomensis, May 1640.

judged by his neighbours and peers, a man's sexual conduct was far less important to his reputation as a good Christian. His betrayal of the marital bond was discussed more generally only in the wider context of misconduct and severe cruelty. Turning to the Patriarchal Court, wives did express their wish to live apart from their husbands, as we have seen, but only a few of them initiated criminal proceedings against their husbands on the grounds of adultery alone. The 'double standard' had its effect on the law and on public opinion. Husbands could be quite sure that they would only rarely be accused of adultery when having sex with women other than their wives.[11] The use of criminal and civil law, the experiences of spouses with secular and ecclesiastical courts, and the aims of the parties were highly gender-specific in early modern Venice.[12]

'Bad' women: the collapse of conjugal households

Because adultery in Venice usually took place outside the home, only rarely involving domestic servants as sexual partners, sexual infidelity and, thus, the collapse of the conjugal household were highly visible in early modern culture. Suspected women usually made their contacts in the parish, where neighbours could easily observe their conduct and subsequently bear witness in court. Venetian urban structure, which could go as far as permitting a direct view into neighbours' bedrooms, favoured this social control. Because sexual misconduct was visible, it constituted a severe infringement against social and political order. And because the household mirrored society, adultery endangered not only matrimony but social order itself. It violated 'human and divine laws', as a common legal formula ran, and placed sexual desires above the holy sacrament of matrimony and the well-being of society and that of the Venetian republic.[13]

These wide implications of female adulterous acts become explicit in Ludovico Dolce's dialogue *Dialogo della institution delle donne* (Venice, 1545). This sixteenth-century author let one speaker express his disregard for immodest women:

---

11 On this double standard see the seminal article by Thomas, 1959, pp. 195–216; on a contemporary woman's critique, that of Arcangela Tarabotti, see Zanette, 1960, pp. 226–8.

12 This conclusion is based on my analysis of about 50 adultery cases in the Miscellany of the Avogaria di Comun that cover adultery trials held both in Venice and the Venetian republic.

13 In this sense, one trouser tailor named Francesco de Giovanni Maria Veronese emphasised that the adultery committed by his wife threatened the 'well-being of this most serene republic'. ASV, A.d.C., Misc. pen. 391.16: Tagiapietra, Catterina, per ruffianerimo verso Tesser Francesco rendendosi adultera la moglie, 1592, fol. 2r.

> I certainly do not know whether those who ruin their fatherland, destroy the laws, kill their fathers, and profane sacred things commit higher crimes [than adulterous women]. And how can an immodest wife rely on God's defense and the friendship of men? The laws, the fatherland, the father, the relatives, the children, and the husband condemn her, and punish her harshly. God the just castigates her with just revenge.[14]

Adultery was judged to be a capital crime, and these 'bad' women were considered to be in need of worldly and godly punishment. Women's promiscuity, as we shall see, indirectly raised questions about male ruling capacities, as the husband apparently had failed to control his wife's lecherous behaviour. Adultery, then, reflected failed conjugality, feeble household rule and the collapse of the household economy in very direct ways; equally, it raised questions about male honour, gender hierarchy and, more broadly, social and political order.

Defending male honour

A wife's sexual misconduct was the antithesis of the behaviour required by Christian and secular rules for married life. Female adultery was understood as an attack on the household unit in physical, material and emotional terms. Although according to Christian doctrine neither spouse should engage in extramarital sexual contact, as this involved breaking vows and sacraments, wives' sexual conduct generally was more widely discussed by contemporaries because of the connection drawn between female lechery and male honour. Considered to be the weaker sex, women were believed to be in need of male moral guidance; if they still behaved immorally, this introduced doubts about male ruling capacities. In an exceptional fury, another character in Ludovico Dolce's aforementioned dialogue made this connection in particular:

> What is even worse is that this disease increases every day due to blind husbands and dumb fathers who are the cause of this reprehensible custom: and there could not be a better remedy to terminate this pestiferous germ than the execution of that just sentence pronounced exclusively against all bad women. As one has to give a bad daughter death as a dowry, worms as a garment, and the tomb as a house, so one has to dig out the eyes of an infamous wife, cut off her tongue, and hack off her hands; or even ... burn her alive.[15]

---

14 Quoted in Sperling, 1999, pp. 100–101.

15 Ibid., p. 101. As she remarks, it is not entirely clear if this speaker was talking about prostitutes or about adulterous wives and immodest daughters.

The cause of immoral habits was men, but women had to bear the consequences of sexual infidelity. Towards the end of the sixteenth century, however, this double standard was occasionally criticised. Giuseppe Passi, already familiar to us, refers in his *The Defects of Women* (1599) to the critique of 'some sophisticated people' – most probably male authors – who demanded personal responsibility in cases of sexual misconduct. Passi, however, still discussed this subject in terms of female lechery and the consequences of female sexual misconduct for male honour:

> [Adulteresses] give way to their insatiable desires, even though they cuckold [their husbands] who have to walk around on the Piazza like billy goats, mocked and derided by others ...; some sophisticated people say that just as the honour is part of a person's virtue and does not belong to anybody, so rebuke and shame should also be the punishment for people's own vices and not for those of others ... and therefore they conclude that husbands should not be dishonoured when their wives and not themselves commit adultery; additionally they held that adultery committed by a husband does not result in shame for his wife, so why should then a husband be rebuked for his adulterous wife? But this is not Aristotle's opinion and I have explained it elsewhere.[16]

Women, as contemporaries agreed, had a disorderly sexuality and were perceived as the irrational and weaker sex. They required continual guidance; otherwise they would be taken over by their lecherous sexuality.[17] Religion and a limited education were held to be extremely useful in binding women's sensuality.[18] Female sexual energy endangered the household when it resulted in sexual misconduct. Such behaviour was an offence against the honour of the betrayed husband and, in short, his reputation. A husband's adulterous act, by contrast, would not affect female honour at all. Because of this gendered morality the meaning and the result of male and female sexual behaviour were different. Wives were strictly advised to behave honourably, and chastity became one of the first virtues of married life. Only female adultery disturbed the balanced household hierarchy, threatening both the economic and symbolic union of marriage and reproduction.

Female misbehaviour was, then, measured against stated ideals. It is in the accusations that reached the criminal courts that betrayed husbands stressed the sinfulness and injustice of their wives'

---

16 Passi, 1599, pp. 74–5. For an anthropological perspective on billy goats see Blok, 1981, pp. 427–40.

17 On the perception of female sexual organs in Italian treatises see Niccoli, 1988, pp. 25–43 and 1980, pp. 402–28.

18 And it was held that men (fathers and husbands) were to educate women, see Frigo, 1983, pp. 66–9.

wrongdoings and sought punishment for their behaviour.[19] Complaints to the Avogadori di Comun generally underscored the loyalty and the misfortune of the male plaintiff as well as the wife's sensuality and lack of restraint. Many of the charges presented were well composed and probably not written by the plaintiff himself. Writers or even notaries educated in Venetian law continued to prepare judicial documents and, arguably, helped to shape the elaborate style exemplified by this piece from the case of Francesco Moretti, who was exiled from Venice after being denounced for blasphemy by his wife Giovanna Grisovann Grismondi:

> Illustrious and excellent Avogadori di Comun … I, the unlucky Francesco Moretti, your subordinate and most humble servant, turn to this esteemed tribunal beseeching you to free me from my adulterous wife … Unfortunately many are the criminal deeds of my wife Giovanna Grismondi, who has lived for already eleven years in adultery with Pietro Fastidiosi, a cobbler … I was besmirched with my misfortune … In my crying misery they have forced me to tolerate it while my same wife accused me, helped by her unleashed plans.[20]

Dishonour, shame and grief were the key words in every charge, and they reveal something of the humiliating dilemma that sexual misconduct visited upon the household ruler. Plaintiffs referred to themselves as 'I, the unlucky' or 'poor me' in order to underline the immense injustice done to them. It is feasible that a lawsuit helped husbands to come to terms with the emotional crisis and loss of honour (and property) that the adultery had caused. Criminal proceedings offered the possibility of revenge through punishment; honour could be defended publicly and possibly be regained. Francesco Moretti, for example, emphasised that his motivation to sue was to 'avenge this dishonour'.[21] The connection drawn between the punishment of the wife and the regaining of male honour is especially clear in the following accusation. The betrayed husband Giovanni Muti, who initially had taken his adulterous wife to the Casa del Soccorso – a refuge for

---

[19] However, notions of this crime popular in the Middle Ages sometimes become apparent. Unmarried men were sometimes held responsible for insulting the husband's honour by stealing from him both wife and property. The woman was like other goods 'carried away' – a helpless victim. The roles that women played in adultery cases were thus more ambiguous than literary sources have suggested: even during the sixteenth and seventeenth centuries, a husband might perceive his wife as both the seducer and the seduced.

[20] ASV, A.d.C., Misc. pen. 82.9: Grismondi Giovanna, adulterio, 1696, written accusation of Francesco Moretti.

[21] Ibid.

mistreated wives and fallen women which husbands also used as a means of enclosing 'lewd women' – pleaded in 1670 for her dismissal in order to enforce punishment:

> I beg Your Excellency that you will give order to release my wife from the Casa del Soccorso where she is accommodated, since this place should not serve to make her elude punishment for her grave and atrocious transgression, so that I – for the consolation of my soul and my honour – can see this sinful woman punished who did not care about the fear of God, her own soul [and] my and her honour. She did not appreciate that I treated her well – she knew very well how to become the prey of dishonesty ....[22]

Adultery ultimately destroyed the bond between spouses, and respect or even affection turned into hate and anger. Punishment might be an effective method of remedying the natural consequences of female sexual misconduct for the household and its ruler. The attainment of the dowry in the case of a favourable verdict might have comforted many disgraced husbands. Rocco Brunetti, for example, whose wife Isabetta was found guilty of adultery, was compensated with at least 350 ducats in 1604 by putting her *beni dimissoriali* up for auction.[23] Dowry protection (*assicurazione*) already obtained by wives at the Giudici del Procurator was sometimes legally annulled if the wife had abandoned her husband and taken valuable goods with her.[24] The woman's loss of the dowry can be understood symbolically as manifest proof of her unchastity, as the dowry initially symbolised her sexual integrity.

Much of the anxiety that lay behind adultery was concerned with the threat of pregnancy. When a wife went astray, the husband had lost control over her female reproductive abilities. By suing in court men avoided financial responsibility for a child that they had never procreated, as was Raffael de Riva's concern. In 1588 he discovered that his wife Cecilia had become pregnant during his absence from Venice. The child first was given to the *Pietà*, but then his wife, as the infuriated Raffael stated, 'now ... tries very impudently to make the world believe that this is my daughter'.[25] Illegitimate children could threaten inheritance if adulterous women did not attempt an abortion. Although

---

[22] ASV, A.d.C., Misc. pen. 268. 21: Muti-Romani, Margarita, adulterio 1670, fol. 17r.

[23] ASV, *Esecutori contro la Bestemmia*, b. 57, Notatorio 4, fol. 91r. The Executors ordered the sale of Isabetta's *beni dimissoriali*, goods that were, unlike the dowry, reserved for the wife's use during marriage. See Ferro, 1845, vol. 1, pp. 596–7.

[24] ASV, *Esecutori contro la Bestemmia*, b. 57, Notatorio 4, fol. 180r.

[25] ASV, A.d.C., Misc. pen. 186: 22: Saler da Riva, Cecilia, adulterio, 1588, not foliated.

abortion constituted a punishable crime, women sometimes relied on such drastic measures.[26]

Adultery was especially disgraceful if the neighbourhood made a mockery of betrayed husbands. In 1675 Nicolò Brun from the parish of S. Angelo had such a humiliating experience when during the night a *cartello infamante* (or *libello famoso*) was illegally attached to the entrance of his apartment. The text, written in capital letters and thus easy to decipher, praised the potency of Brun's rival and sarcastically comforted the cuckold himself (Figure 9.1).[27] In seventeenth-century Italy *becco* (goat) was a widespread slander directed at the husbands of adulterous wives, using the metaphor of an animal that allows his mate to have sex with others.[28] *Becco* could be used in Mediterranean culture with contemptuous adjectives such as *becco cornuto*, *becco fottuto* and *grandissimo becco*.[29] Insults generally were ritualised and contextualised, and the publicity formed part of the humiliating and offending communication for the receiver. Because *libelli famosi* dishonoured men and disturbed public peace, in March 1540 the Council of Ten issued a law in *Materia di Libelli, e Polizze Infamatorie* which encouraged people to denounce this criminal deed and ordered the burning of these notices.[30]

The message of the *cartello infamante*, written in a nice rhyme, centred on the husband's loss of power over his wife by praising her extramarital sexual activity. Nicolò Brun's powerlessness was thus demonstrated through tolerance of his wife Angela's adulterous liaisons. In fact, during the trial neighbours provided strong evidence of the contact that Angela enjoyed with a certain Paolo Ghirardi, who apparently lived nearby. The prostitute Caterina Padovana stated on 21

---

[26] Margarita Ventura, who was accused of having had sex with the village priest in the absence of her husband, was suspected of having aborted the illegitimate child. See ASV, A.d.C., Misc. pen. 45.4: Ventura Margarita, per adulterio e procurato aborto e Donato Prete Giovanni, adulterio, 1690. Cecilia Saler also was suspected of having an abortion: ASV, A.d.C., Misc. pen. 186: 22: Saler de Riva Cecilia, adulterio, 1588, not foliated.

[27] ASV, A.d.C., Misc. pen. 416.13: Brun, Angela, rapita moglie di Nicolò, 1675, not foliated. The *cartello infamante* is difficult to translate because of the ambiguous meanings, especially of the third and fourth strophes, and the sexual innuendoes, which presumably indicate that Brun's wife Angela could satisfy both men. However, the straightforward meaning of the text is as follows: After the wife attended nearly every party/dancing with her lover/the *paron* [husband] had reasons to stand tall [or erect]/because she had raised also his head [that is, she had betrayed him]/but don't be tormented too much/because you are not the first to be a happy cuckold. On sexual mockery and male honour in early modern England see Foyster, 1999, pp. 104–15.

[28] Blok, 1981, pp. 427–40.

[29] Burke, 1987, pp. 96–7.

[30] *Leggi criminali venete*, p. 36.

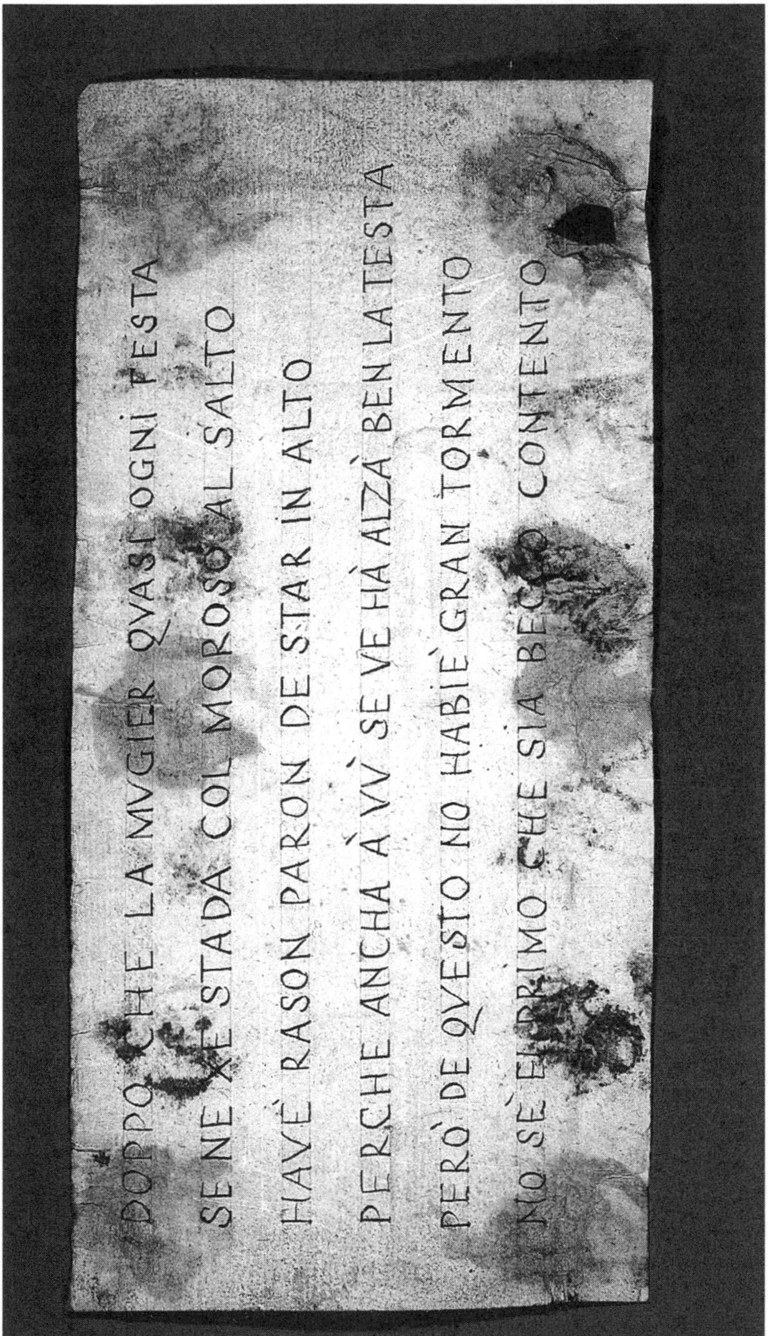

9.1 *Cartello infamante* di Nicolò Brun, 1675

January 1675 that she had observed their nightly meetings; when Angela left her home she had seen Paolo following her. Lodovica Sagia, a domestic servant of a nobleman, referred to the public opinion (*fama*) during her deposition, remarking on 24 January 1675 that it was well known in the neighbourhood that Angela was in love with Paolo. Her husband Nicolò had tried to avoid any scandal and, according to what people were saying, had even ordered Paolo to leave his wife in peace.[31] But this attempt at gaining influence was in vain. Angela and Paolo apparently fled Venice with some movable goods and never appeared before the Avogaria di Comun. The sentence stipulated permanent banishment, but on 12 January 1683 the Council of Forty released Angela from this harsh punishment, after she apparently pleaded for mercy.

Contextualising adultery

The breakdown of marriage did not come overnight, and the drastic measures that wives sometimes took had a long story of their own. In the woman's defence the adultery was placed in the wider context of the marital relationship, drawing a connection between disappointed expectations, hardship, domestic disputes and extramarital sexuality. Women accused of sexual misconduct alleged domestic violence, mistreatment and misconduct by the household ruler as their motivation, forcing them to seek a better life outside marriage. Thus, from a different perspective adultery also addresses the complaints about marital conflicts already familiar to us. It is through these acts of infidelity that the limits of female compliance and the limits of male misrule emerge most clearly. These structural elements show the need to discuss adultery as an integrated element of marriage formation and marital disputes.

The following case study is an especially detailed trial embracing different aspects of domestic disputes and their possible causes.[32] In presenting it I draw attention to perceptions of adulterous wives in their neighbourhoods, revealing the moral values that underlay those

---

31 ASV, A.d.C., Misc. pen. 416.13: Brun, Angela, rapita moglie di Nicolò, 1675, not foliated, witnesses Caterina Padovana, Lodovica Sagia and Anna, wife of Biasco Schizer Todesco, respectively.

32 ASV, A.d.C., Misc. pen. 366.5: Vegia, da Gregorio, adulterio, 1587, 6 January 1586. This trial is damaged; references to testimonies therefore will be incomplete. Antonia's interrogations were carried out in April and July of 1587.

perceptions. In 1582 Gregorio, servant of the patrician Giovanni Venier, married Antonia, daughter of the boatman Bernardo. Bernardo paid him a modest dowry of only 100 ducats, so for a good economic start to the marriage Gregorio himself paid 100 ducats as a counter-dowry. He and his bride moved into his small house in the vicinity of the hospital at S. Vido, given to him by the *Clarissimi Signori Procuratori* after his long and loyal service. Gregorio then had to accompany his master Giovanni Venier to his villa on the Venetian mainland. After a long absence he returned to Venice around December 1586 to find his house locked and his wife gone. The following January he sued her at the Avogaria di Comun, accusing her of having sex with a certain Angelo Sartor, the servant Vettor and various other men. On 3 July 1587 Gregorio informed the Avogadori di Comun of the possessions that his wife had taken to her mother's house, including (almost exclusively) female clothing and a string of pearls.[33]

Neighbourhood witnesses were summoned to court and asked about the details of the marital infidelity. Crucial to perceptions of sexual betrayal were the contacts that women enjoyed with male members of the Venetian community. Giovanni Maria Violi, for example, spoke in Gregorio's defence of how he had observed Angelo Sartor visiting Antonia in the absence of her husband, how they would have supper together and how the man would stay with her until the next morning – an allegation confirmed by Violi's wife.[34] Antonio di Putti, living in close vicinity, could produce equally damaging evidence. He had observed from his balcony a man leaving the da Vegia household early in the morning during Gregorio's absence. As eyewitnesses who were not reliant on the *fama*, or public opinion, all three provided powerful evidence against Antonia. Because the adulterous act itself was only very rarely observed, eating and sleeping under the same roof was strong evidence and testified to the familiarity that the wife had developed with another man during her husband's absence. Female honour thus could easily be attacked. The moral judgements that the witnesses expressed were not particularly gender-specific, for women and men alike condemned Antonia's dishonest conduct.

Antonia first rejected the charge of sexual misconduct, but subsequently confessed to having had extramarital sex, but only once, with the tailor Angelo. The Avogadori, however, pressed her to make further confessions. The witness depositions had been very disadvantageous for her, as the neighbours had unanimously reported on her immoral and sinful behaviour. Because adultery was a crime difficult to prove, and adulterers were almost never caught committing

---

[33] Ibid., fol. 13r.
[34] Ibid., fols 2r and 4v.

the sinful deed, the many *de visu* witnesses who had actually observed Antonia receiving other men provided strong evidence against her. The course of the investigation changed suddenly when Antonia was asked what she could produce in her defence. She then justified abandoning her husband's house because of his abuse of patriarchal power, an argument already familiar to us:

> [After the marriage] he brought me there as his guard of his belongings not as his wife ... he gave me nothing to eat and to drink and he locked me in like a dog ... and I had to stay in the dark like an animal, and he often battered me.[35]

Antonia alleged severe physical and psychological cruelty and lack of respect in her defence. Conjugality, she argued, had never come into being in the marital relationship. To prevent her from screaming, she alleged, Gregorio had put his hands over her mouth. The severe physical violence, domestic imprisonment and poor nutrition had, she claimed, forced her to seek a better life outside marriage – long before she had committed adultery, she seemed to imply. Her legal narrative thus emphasised that Gregorio had abandoned the principles of household conjugality, which in turn defend against sexual infidelity. She could not, however, produce strong evidence in her defence. The witnesses summoned had come to learn about the poor nutrition, imprisonment and cruel household management only through Antonia, her mother and her late father. They had not heard her screaming, seen the marks of physical violence on her body or actually witnessed how Gregorio had abused his authority – a fact that weakened the testimonies. Antonia herself might have influenced the neighbourhood in their perception of the domestic disorder, thereby forming a prejudicial public opinion in her favour. One witness in court, for example, reported that he had been informed only by Antonia about how Gregorio did not allow her to make friends with the neighbours. She had not, however, mentioned starvation and excessive violence, a fact that also made her defence incredible. Other witness depositions equally failed to back up her allegations and thus provide concrete evidence.

Her husband, however, was able to provide witnesses to testify to his good household rule: they affirmed that he kept her well fed and well dressed and that she had all the necessary household goods at her disposal. Only when witnesses were questioned about the compatibility of the spouses did neighbours express some sympathy for Antonia. She herself had stated that her father had chosen Gregorio only because people were saying that he was rich. The wedding had been an event

---

[35] Ibid., fol. 29r.

noticed and commented on within the neighbourhood. People had been quite astonished at her father's choice, for Gregorio was only a 'serving man' – implying social inequality of the spouses. Other parishioners mentioned the age gap between Antonia and Gregorio, which was perceived as intolerable, making conjugality hard to achieve (although this was not stated outright). The moral principles, however, were still the same. Despite the compassion and understanding that some of the neighbours might have felt for her, in their perception it did not justify Antonia's immoral conduct. She was said to be an adulteress, and one neighbour even had tried to prevent her child from having contact with her, because she had 'heard bad things about her'.[36] On a day-to-day basis male and female neighbours expressed moral judgements and made pragmatic decisions which were not necessarily gender-specific. Parishioners formed their own opinions, sometimes on the basis of neighbourhood talk and gatherings. They knew perfectly well who was 'right' in a domestic battle and who deserved compassion and support. Probably because the neighbours gave detailed and reliable evidence about Antonia's immoral conduct, she was found guilty and sentenced on 23 October 1587 by the Council of Forty to six months' imprisonment. Additionally, she lost the dowry and counter-dowry, which legally became her husband's.

Adultery, property and theft

Central to the charge of adultery is the connection drawn between adultery and theft. Property concerns were crucial to the disciplining of adulterous wives at every level of society. Inventories abound in the trial proceedings; these precisely list the number and value of items that had been taken away. Most of the items mentioned were textiles, clothes and jewellery; less frequently there are references to stolen money. They made up, most probably, part of the dowry that the husband had received as a contribution to the household economy. Legally these things belonged to the woman, but the man had the right to administer them during marriage. When couples were separating legally the Giudici del Procurator were concerned with the financial aspects, and women were very likely to win this battle during the sixteenth century, especially when they could prove that the husband had dissipated the dowry.[37] In cases of abandonment and sexual misconduct, however, the legal situation was different. Because the husband had not been released from

---

[36] Ibid., 8 July 1587.
[37] See Rigo, 1992–93, pp. 256–8 and 2000, p. 531.

his administrative control, a wife could not dispose of her dowry as she wished. Only after his death was the dowry returned to the widow. Between marriage and death, however, 'the primary support came from her husband. But crucially, the goods the husband gave to his wife, such as clothing and jewellery, remained legally his.'[38] A wife accused of abandoning her husband and having adulterous affairs was therefore easily open to accusations of theft. In cases in which adultery resulted in the formation of a new couple, both partners were sued 'to make a restitution of all the things that have been stolen'.[39]

Adultery, as Antonia's case shows in an exemplary manner, was often committed in the absence of the marital partner, and contacts were made in the parish. A husband's long absence could cause economic problems, especially if he had not made sufficient provision before his departure. For example, Caterina, wife of Francesco Bergamin, who had a workshop, was forced to do the washing and sewing for their neighbour Giovanni Nuzio, whom she had met through her husband and with whom she would later engage in a sexual affair.[40] Other women who had to fend for themselves sometimes decided to work as domestic servants. In examining the archive materials it becomes apparent that parents, who appear frequently in separation suits as sources of redress and shelter, are noticeably absent in adultery trials – exceptions seem only to confirm the rule. Of course, they might have been dead,[41] or simply living outside Venice. But without a man providing the livelihood, women had to overcome economic pressure and, sometimes, extreme poverty. An example is Giovanna Grismondi, whose case is already familiar to us. Her husband Francesco Moretti had been exiled from Venice for 10 years by the Executors against Blasphemy. Soon after his return he accused his wife of having betrayed him in his absence. Giovanna argued in her defence that she was forced by extreme poverty to move into the house of another man: 'After he [Francesco] had been banished I was alone with four children and, because the *patroni* of my house intended to turn me out onto the streets, I begged my neighbour

---

38 Ruggiero, 1985, p. 51.

39 ASV, *Esecutori contro la Bestemmia*, b. 1, trial 3: Zuanne Bertelli contro Caterina sua moglie et Pietro Rigetti. Rigetti was accused of having stolen more than 700 lire, together with Bertelli's wife Caterina and his child. See also Derosas, 1980, especially p. 457.

40 ASV, A.d.C., Misc. pen. 339.5: Zane Nuzio, ratto della moglie di Francesco Bergamin, 1624.

41 Olwen Hufton reports that for European areas 'before the eldest child reached the age of marriage [about 24–26], one parent was likely to be dead'. See Hufton, 1995, p. 11.

Pietro Fastidiosi to let me stay in his attic ... and I paid four ducats a year.'[42]

This time the neighbourhood was split in its perception of Giovanna Grismondi. Some neighbours testified to her dishonest conduct of living in the same flat as Pietro Fastidiosi, 'so that one is forced to believe that they live in adultery'.[43] Others were more cautious in their moral judgement and stated that they had not actually witnessed the adulterous act itself. A certain Bortolo even testified in favour of Giovanna, emphasising the material constraints caused by her husband's absence:

> I have seen how this woman with four children lived in misery, since she had nothing to eat and never ... when I was in the house of the said Fastidiosi ... did I see anything scandalous or any indecent act and I know that this woman ... lives with the help of God.[44]

This case, then, points to a fundamental problem: the economic dependence of women on their husbands. Although dowered, they had only a limited authority over their property (dowry), and they seldom had an income. Some women held wealth or property in their own right, but this was only a minority.[45] When husbands had left their wives without making provision for the future and these wives were not property-holders, the women managed survival only by relying on the help of others. But if distressed wives could not count on the support of neighbours, and especially of parents, their situation could become pitiful. Some even relied on supernatural aids, hoping that the husband's behaviour would improve through the help of magic.[46] One such wife was Domenica Manini, who accused her husband of being responsible for her miserable marital life, alleging that

> He is a man who has never ruled properly and he has always dissipated everything he could find at home and I could no longer support his cruelty ... and he has beaten me and has injured me and has carried away the clothes ... and he did not even let me have a shirt ... and then he abandoned me, as I said, and left me alone with three creatures without any material help.[47]

The allegation of desertion centred on the husband's cruelty, both

---

42 ASV, A.d.C., Misc. pen. 82.9: Grismondi, Giovanna, adulterio, 4 April 1696.

43 Ibid.

44 Ibid., witness Bortolo, 6 April 1996.

45 Chojnacka, 2001, p. 46.

46 I am referring here to especially fascinating trials, held before the Venetian Holy Office, in which wives used love-magic 'in order to make my husband a good husband'. ASV, Sant'Ufficio, b. 82: September 1626, Donna Orsola.

47 ASV, Sant'Ufficio, b. 66: Domenica Manini, June 1590.

physical and mental. With the abandonment of the conjugal household, Domenica complained, her husband also had abandoned shared responsibilities and cared neither for her nor for their children. The abuse of patriarchal authority – in the form of domestic violence, economic mismanagement and lack of respect and care – was central to separation suits, but it acquired added significance in adultery trials.

Adultery and authority

Beside the connection drawn between adultery and theft, the one between domestic violence and sexual misconduct is most striking. Excessive corporal violence, financial mistreatment and harshness towards one's own wife were central in these lawsuits. Whereas men accused women of marital infidelity, wives argued in their defence that it was their husbands who had failed first by abusing their authority. Caterina Tesser, the young daughter of the deceased tailor Giovanni di Bogoli, was married to Francesco, also a tailor, living in S. Giacomo dall'Orio. In 1592 he accused her of having an affair with Nicolò da Elia, whom she allegedly had met through the bawd Caterina Tagiapietra from S. Zuan Degolà. Caterina, however, retorted in her defence that she had left her husband only because she 'could no longer endure my husband's blows', not because she had betrayed holy matrimony.[48] And Bartolomia Ferrari, who in 1683 was accused in Vicenza, a city under Venetian rule, of being an adulteress, complained in her defence about her husband's life-threatening cruelty and his dissipation of the property.[49] Although wives initiating legal proceedings on grounds of severe cruelty made use of the legal agency that canon law accorded them, the female protagonists in this chaper resolved their private conflicts informally, without relying on the Patriarchal Court.

In the context of accusations of adultery, allegations of ill-tempered and unruly husbands were investigated seriously. When husbands abused their authority they threatened conjugality, domestic harmony and, finally, household order and neighbourhood peace. The Avogadori di Comun, by listening to witness depositions, tested the truth of these allegations. Marital infidelity was judged in the broader context of the conduct of both wife and husband: domestic violence, then, was contextualised, as was adultery. A good example is the case of Lucia

---

[48] ASV, A.d.C., Misc. pen. 391.16: Tagliapietra, Caterina, per ruffianerino verso Tesser Francesca, 1592, fols 12r–v.

[49] ASV, A.d.C., Misc. pen. 177.13: Branditio, Bartolomeo, adulterio, 1682, fols 58r–v and 4r–v, respectively.

Bressana. In 1608 or so she had been living with her husband Giovanni Filareto in S. Stin. When she had been seen at a *luogo infame* (dishonest place)[50], Giovanni put her in the custody of Paola, daughter of the deceased Giacomo Parisotto, in Castello. She was staying in the houses of the priests in the parish of S. Martino together with her host Paola. After a few weeks Lucia had told Paola that she wished to leave. Without her husband's knowledge she had taken a gondola during the night and had disappeared, observed by some neighbours. Giovanni soon caught her in the house of some 'foreigners', where she was leading a 'bad life'.[51]

Witnesses summoned to the secular magistracy were encouraged to testify to the nature of the marital relationship and, especially, to the husband's government. The Avogadori di Comun sought the underlying causes of the immediate issue that had brought the pair to court; they inquired into conjugality and companionship. Husbands drew attention to their wise and careful government, emphasising that they had only 'corrected' female misbehaviour. Hence, the means undertaken were expressions of male authority, an argument already familiar to us. Witnesses also made moral judgements on the grounds of patriarchal rule. Paola was questioned about Giovanni's household government, especially about 'whether [he] had provided everything for [his wife's] well-being and had been an appropriate companion for her'. Paola had to express her vision of male authority and comment on the specific circumstances of marital disruption. She decided to recall Giovanni's words to his wife when he had brought her into custody, portraying him as a reasonable and mild husband. In Paola's presence he had said to his wife in an assuaging way, 'although you have done me injustice you will not suffer the lack of anything.'[52] Other neighbours also testified to his benevolence and mildness in governing his wife: one Alessandro reported that Giovanni had cared well for his wife and had provided everything for her when he was absent from Venice. Lucia's misconduct was thus portrayed as entirely unjustifiable, particularly because her husband was always a responsible household ruler. In his opinion Lucia had no reason to abandon cohabitation. That she was not 'content' with her husband was no argument to mitigate or explain her guilt; on the contrary, it demonstrated female assertiveness and the transgression of proper female conduct, such as female modesty and restraint. The

---

[50] This is not specified in the trial, but it might have been a place where the sexes mixed, where people danced and drank.

[51] ASV, A.d.C., Misc. pen. 276.4, Filareto Lucia moglie di Giovanni, 1609, witness Paola, 18 March 1609.

[52] Ibid.

widow Prudentia, who had rented a room in S. Stin from Giovanni, therefore expressed her disregard for Lucia by explaining the wife's motivation in abandoning the conjugal household as an intention to *far mal* – to lead a bad life.[53]

This case, however, ends in a comforting way. Lucia, who had not followed the order of appearance that was read against her on the steps of the Rialto by the Avogador Giovanni Maria Moldi on 7 May 1609, presented a supplication. She pleaded to be allowed to return to her husband, promising that she would live as 'honourable' matrimony demanded and be obedient to her husband as commanded by God. Because her husband apparently was willing to take her back, and because she stressed that she was remorseful and penitent, Lucia was *per ora* (for the time being) freed from the proclamation. The Avogadori, however, ordered her to return to her husband, to obey him and to lead an honourable life, otherwise she would be prosecuted again. Because Lucia was remorseful and willing to reform, she gained from the flexibility of the Venetian justice system and the government's intention to restore matrimonial, household and social order when possible.

Case study: Margherita Romani-Muti

The following case is an excellent illustration of female assertiveness.[54] Margherita, the daughter of Giovanni Battista Romani, a spice-seller with a workshop in S. Fosca, had lived in her father's household. Together with her mother and sisters, she had supported the household economy by making the ribbons often used in love-magic rituals. She was then married to Giovanni Muti, who was 75 years old and superior socially, as he claimed. Father and prospective husband most likely had met through their shared profession and the proximity of their workplaces. The match was settled and the wedding took place in October 1670. Marital fidelity, it seems, did not last long. The next month Muti turned to the Avogaria di Comun, accusing his wife of sexual misconduct and theft. In the Calle del Tollo in the parish of S. Simeon, he claimed, he had caught his wife in flagrante delicto. He had forced his way into a room and had discovered his half-naked wife hidden in a chest, with her lover sitting on it.

Giovanni Muti initially provided three witnesses and added more later, during the legal proceedings. Tragically, Margherita's allies proved to be her deepest enemies when it came to testifying against her in court. Marietta Valesana, Giovanni's niece, and Magdalena, a domestic

---

[53] Ibid., witness Prudentia q. Batta de Bernardo Tentor, 19 March 1609.
[54] ASV, A.d.C., Misc. pen. 268. 21, Romani-Muti, Margherita, adulterio 1670.

servant, both had especially detailed insights into Margherita's extramarital activities. They provided part of Margherita's alibi, accompanying her through the city on the way to her appointments. Like an 'honourable' woman she first had asked her husband for permission, claiming that she was on her way to church or to visit a relative – in this respect Margherita cautiously observed the rules laid out for married women. On the day Margherita was discovered in the chest she had left home as usual with Marietta and the servant Magdalena. According to Marietta they had taken a gondola, and the boatman Mosea first had taken them to a palazzo in the parish of S. Pantalon, where the three women had left the gondola. Margherita had disappeared into a room, leaving the two other women waiting in the *portico*, and had returned not long after. They then had continued to the parish of S. Marcuola. Unable to find a specific boatman named Matteo, with whom they had an appointment, they hired another man to take them to the Rio (canal) Martin in S. Fosca. On arrival the three women entered a house and were received by Anna Maria, a woman reputed to be a bawd.[55] Margherita wished to see a certain *signor* Martin Calegher – her cousin, as she implausibly explained to her companions Marietta and Magdalena. When the man called Martin was unable to receive her, Margherita became angry. Donna Anna Maria suggested that she might see another man – *un grande* (perhaps a tall man). However, he did not suit Margherita's taste, and she hesitated to go with him, but finally was persuaded. Donna Anna warmed up the bed and shut the door. But only 30 minutes later Margherita's husband arrived and forced his way into the room.

Margherita was interrogated in the rooms of the Council of Forty on 12 February 1672. She was accused by the examiner of having given liberty to her sexual desires and of having had sex with various people. Her sexual conduct was equated with that of a prostitute. In fact Venetian legislation, as has been remarked, made no clear distinction between adultery and prostitution, and a woman who had sexual intercourse with various men was easily open to attacks of being a whore.[56] Margherita, however, opposed the accusation and alleged in her defence that she was the victim of a major conspiracy between a certain Antonio Bareta and the servant Magdalena. She claimed that they were in love and had an interest in eliminating her – and indeed already had tried to murder her – because of an inheritance. She furthermore attempted to destroy the credibility of the witnesses,

---

[55] There existed in Venice a number of old women who 'arranged' couples, matchmakers of sorts.

[56] Cf. Cibin, 1985, p. 81.

especially that of Magdalena, and denied every single accusation. Her denials, however, were not likely to be believed. Her husband presented strong evidence against her in the form of two letters, which proved that she had been lying when testifying that Martin Calegher was unknown to her. The first letter is a pragmatic message giving her careful instructions on how to reach the house where she later was caught by her husband:

> My very beloved *patrona*. If you could go immediately after lunch to S. Andrea there will be a [covered] gondola with one oar ... waiting for you so that nobody can observe you: the boatmen is called Matteo and he is a person who is not known in this neighbourhood and he is a judicious man ... So when you go in the direction of S. Andrea, take a slightly hidden ... canal and when you see a small garden there is a room nearby ... which belongs to a woman who is a good friend of mine; nobody will be there except me; I will leave home a bit earlier than you and expect you ... And if ill fortune hinders you from coming, give me a sign from your window. Please be careful when you read this letter so that no disorder arises. I confess to you only that these few hours appear years to me, so great is my desire to see you again. I am forever your servant and friend.[57]

Meeting a lover was a dangerous activity, and various cautious measures had to be taken. Hiring a gondola was safer than walking, for gondolas were covered in the early modern period and passengers were protected from curious looks, as Martin Calegher pointed out. The people involved were carefully chosen: the gondolier Matteo did not belong to Margherita's parish – and probably was without close contacts there – and the woman who owned the rented room was a close friend. Loyalty could be expected. Despite this prudence witnesses and evidence were still produced: Matteo, Anna Maria and the letter, which Margherita had kept, despite Calegher's advice to handle it carefully. Apparently, it had an emotional meaning for her. The second letter is interesting from a different point of view, as the author Steffano Gallo reveals contemporary notions of female lechery by stressing Margherita's seductive qualities:

> My highly respected Signora ... Since destiny has forced me to love you until I die, I have decided to reveal my misfortune to you in order to make you realise how great the power of your beauty is ... and to prevent that other hearts will be inflamed as well. I will die, my Signora, unable to receive consolation ... and in this extreme situation my only help is that you alone are the reason for my death ...; in order to lighten the pitiful feelings of a lover who is to die I end this letter and shortly also my life. While you give no hope that

---

[57] ASV, A.d.C., Misc. pen. 268. 21, Romani-Muti, Margherita, adulterio, fol. 23r.

I will receive an answer to my letter, I remain the one who adores you.[58]

This description of unrequited love owes much – as we may assume – to culturally approved patterns of how to express intimate feelings in writing. As the historian Elizabeth S. Cohen has shown, published collections of letters set models that were later standardised into manuals of types and phrases.[59] Ironically, although this letter proves that Margherita did not engage in any illicit sexual activity with the unfortunate Steffano Gallo (at least until the date of the letter), it nevertheless provided evidence of her extramarital contact with men. The letter is composed around the image of her beauty – witnesses had described her as 'a beautiful horse' (*una bella cavalla*) – and her seductiveness.[60] The testimonies that Giovanni Muti supplied to strengthen his case dwelt on her disorderly sexuality; they contributed a great deal to building up the image of her moral depravity. The witness Valerio Sandeis, for example, was seemingly well-informed about Margherita's contacts and movements through Venice, listing them in detail and even supplying the names of some of her lovers. The casualness of Margherita's moral behaviour had not gone unnoticed in the neighbourhood. Two or three times a week Sandeis had noticed a gondola waiting under her balcony while her husband was at work. One day, when she was on the way to the attending boat, she had been insulted by an old woman in the street, accused of being 'a besmirching woman, a swine and a slut' (*brutta, porca, poltrona*). Her words stressed a morality that Margherita had offended. Quickly, the witness reported, Margherita had boarded the boat in order to escape the eyes of the many witnesses to these insults.[61] This old woman was not the only one to emphasise her disapproval of Margherita's conduct. Gasparo, another neighbour, recalled in court how he had rebuked Margherita because of her immoral life. In turn Margherita had insulted him, retorting that it was her life to live as she pleased.

This case remains an exceptionally strong example of female self-determination, wilfulness and autonomy. It might have been based on an initial deep desperation due to the exceptional age gap between Margherita and her husband (possibly 40 years or more), but the marriage had been blighted ever after. Instead of being modest, obedient and honourable, Margherita was perceived as selfish and stubborn,

---

[58] Ibid., fol. 24r.
[59] See Cohen, 1993, pp. 181–201. The question of how writers acquired familiarity with these set models is, however, less easy to answer.
[60] ASV, A.d.C., Misc. pen. 268. 21, Romani-Muti, Margherita, adulterio 1670, fol. 5r.
[61] Ibid., fols 8r and 6r.

placing individual concerns over marital relationships. She put conjugal
stability at risk by violating the sacrament of matrimony, most likely
with more than one man. The neighbourhood and the court perceived
her conduct as 'unbound' with regard to both her behaviour as a wife
and her sexual appetite. She was 'voracious' and ungovernable – this
might have been the reason Giovanni Muti had refused to take her back
before criminal proceedings were initiated. Had he accepted her back
into his household and forgiven her, he would not have had the right to
sue her in court.[62] And so Margherita had been imprisoned. She pleaded
for mercy on the grounds that she was pregnant. She was allowed to give
birth outside prison but had to pay bail. All traces of her beyond that
time are lost.[63]

Power and community: the case of Caterina De Cleves

This last, fascinatingly detailed case offers a micro history that is rooted
in neighbourhood and community. It draws attention to aspects only
briefly discussed so far, such as people's willingness to use the court to
regulate their marital problems and the social structures that favoured
(or did not favour) such a decision. Through this case we gain insights
into power structures in a small rural community at the beginning of the
seventeenth century.

During Easter 1614 rumours spread in Pinguente, a village under
Venetian rule.[64] On the day that he had been preaching against sins and
sinners, the priest of the church of S. Francesco had been threatened and
insulted. The poor man was frightened, and in the days following he
would only go to bed with the protection of a guard sleeping on a
mattress near his door. The main characters directly or indirectly
involved in this public scandal were soon identified as Giovanni Bolzani,
his wife Caterina De Cleves and the *dottor* Giovanni Verci.[65] Their
contributions were very different, but the events had bound them
together more than they could have imagined.

It was due to the threat against the father of the Francescan order that
the Capitano di Raspo prosecuted ex officio against Giovanni Verci.[66]
The investigation began with the summoning of Giovanni Bolzani to
court, where he revealed the extraordinary relationship between the

---

[62] Priori, 1622, pp. 172–3.

[63] The verdict is not recorded in ASV, A.d.C., raspe 3723 and 3724.

[64] Pinguente was under the jurisdiction of Capodistria, now situated in Croatia.

[65] ASV, A.d.C., Misc. pen. 158. 6: Giovanni Verci, Cleves Caterina moglie di Bolzani,
adulterio, 1614.

[66] Ibid., fol. 13r.

three persons involved. About eight years earlier Giovanni Verci had had sex with Caterina De Cleves, before she was married to Bolzani. Verci had taken her virginity, and for a long period they had lived as husband and wife, though no marriage had ever been solemnised.[67] A daughter and son were born as proof of a sexually active relationship. However, after some years Giovanni Verci decided to arrange an honourable marriage for Caterina and chose Giovanni Bolzani, a *bottegaio* like Caterina's father, Daniel De Cleves. The marriage seemed suitable because the partners were social equals. Bolzani agreed and the banns were published in church. At this moment Caterina's father interfered with Verci's plans and countermanded the arranged marriage. He had two incentives for doing so. First, he insisted on a father's right to arrange his own daughter's marriage, or at least to be informed about it; and second, he wanted Verci to keep his marriage promise to Caterina. His intervention introduces an even more disturbing detail to this intricate case. He did not succeed. The marriage was solemnised despite his efforts, and Caterina and Giovanni Bolzani moved into their new home.

After only two months the marriage was proving to be a difficult one, and their interrogations revealed the impact of the past on their relationship. The union was tempestuous, and neither was content with the development of their so-called marriage, though for different reasons. Caterina had been married unexpectedly to a man with whom she had nothing in common except social background. He had not courted her over a long period, a time during which young people grew to know each other. The man with whom she was sharing a dwelling was virtually a stranger. And, above all, her feelings were already involved with others outside the marriage, with her children and their father Giovanni Verci.

Giovanni Bolzani could not claim to have been tricked into marrying Caterina De Cleves, as he was familiar with the situation: Caterina had been deflowered by another man (Verci) and had two children by him. But the dowry of 230 ducats was acceptable, and the *bottegaio* might have thought that Caterina would not get another chance to marry. So he accepted, but soon regretted agreeing to such a troublesome union. It was during Easter, when Bolzani went to confession while his wife stayed at home, that events escalated. After confession the priest asked Giovanni to send his wife because he would like to have some words with her. Giovanni did as he was asked. He went home, but his wife had left. He later would testify that he quickly realised where he might find

---

[67] Caterina's father testified that Caterina had been deflowered three years earlier, whereas Giovanni Bolzani stated that defloration took place seven or eight years prior.

her. And he was right: when Bolzani entered Verci's house he found them embracing in the kitchen.

Bolzani had then sent his wife home, and would later punish her moderately with four punches, correcting her dishonourable conduct. However, Bolzani's authority over his wife was contested thereafter, and the past proved to be his greatest enemy. The day he discovered his wife in the arms of Verci, he had an open word with his rival. He asked Verci to keep the promise he had made several months previously, supposedly, to end his relationship with Caterina.[68] But Caterina and Verci were bound through mutual affection and through their children, who were living with Verci. Originally Caterina had agreed to marry Giovanni Verci, but he claimed a marriage promise never had been expressed. Nevertheless they had lived together for quite a long time with their children, as if they were a proper Christian family. Presumably Verci had not legalised the union because Caterina was socially inferior to him. It would seem that he was finally ruled by his head and not his heart.

But Giovanni Verci's preoccupation with Caterina was still intense. As Bolzani testified, when he stepped into Verci's house and took the *dottor* to task, Verci reacted sharply in defending his ex-lover:

> The Signor *dottor* immediately got upset and asked me whether I intended to threaten her or to cause her worry; and he went on, claiming that I was not worthy even to touch my own wife. In short, he started to threaten me and was very unpleasant and, since I feared he could dishonour me, I left.[69]

Verci took steps to protect Caterina against the possible consequences of these events. As he knew perfectly well, it was Bolzani's right and duty to punish Caterina for what might be interpreted as an adulterous act. Every sensible husband in Bolzani's situation would try to restore his authority over his wife. But the authority that Bolzani had over Caterina was blurred and contested, a circumstance that is best illustrated by the counterattack that Verci launched against Bolzani. He exhorted him not to take any measures against Caterina, thus revealing his feelings of protectiveness and affection for the wife of another man. Jealousy might even have played an important role, for Verci even asserted that Bolzani was not worthy to touch his own wife.

The law, however, was clearly on Bolzani's side. Verci had had his chance to get the woman he wanted, but had let it pass. Legally the

---

[68] According to the *proclama* against Verci and Caterina De Cleves, Verci had promised Bolzani 'di non travagliar ... il sudetto Bolzani', that is, not to torment or to disturb him. ASV, A.d.C., Misc. pen. 158. 6: Giovanni Verci, Cleves Caterina moglie di Bolzani, adulterio, 1614, fol. 16r. See also fol. 1v.

[69] Ibid., fol. 1v.

situation was less intricate, and after the interrogation of 16 or so witnesses, a *proclama* was issued against Caterina De Cleves and Giovanni Verci on 16 May 1614. Both were given nine days to appear before the court. The charge against Verci did not focus on the suspicion of adultery alone, but included his earlier crimes as well: among them the seduction of an honourable woman, interference with the authority of her parents, the breaking of a marriage promise and premarital sex. Caterina De Cleves, who had abandoned her husband after having been discovered with Giovanni Verci, was accused of adultery, theft and an attempt to destroy holy matrimony.

Giovanni Verci promptly obeyed the state's orders and presented himself in court on 10 June 1614. He held the charges to be 'in part ... true, and for the most part lies, and misfortune'.[70] In his interrogation he presented himself as a compassionate man who had sheltered and rescued Caterina from the severe government of her parents and her husband. He stated that a marriage promise was never given, though he did not deny having deflowered Caterina – as compensation he had married her off with a good dowry, thus revealing that virginity was a material good that could be recompensed with money. Nor did he deny that the two children were theirs. In his version Caterina had left her parents against his express will because she complained about the 'miserable life' that her father, in particular, had caused her. In the end it was Verci's compassion that moved him to help her, not his own interests. He presented his role in the marital drama between Giovanni Bolzani and Caterina as equally caring. They had never betrayed Caterina's husband, he opposed, and Verci strictly denied having exchanged corporal signs of affection with her. Their meetings were motivated because of their children. Verci insisted that Caterina relied on him when her marital situation was so unbearable that she could no longer stay with her husband. Domestic violence and death threats had forced her to leave her husband and had moved Verci to support her with accommodation and 'friendship'.[71]

This case might not have come to the attention of the state if the negotiations carried out by various villagers had been successful, and Verci stated that he had been active in these attempts at reconciliation. When he sent Caterina back to her husband, the priest Giovanni Piero was asked to accompany her to prevent corporal punishment and to prevent her husband from causing her worries. But it seems Bolzani's patience had been exhausted and anger had replaced his positive feelings towards his wife: 'her husband was furious ... and swore that he did not

---

[70] Ibid., fol. 18r.
[71] Ibid., fols 19r and 22r.

care about her at all'.[72] In the end it was Bolzani who gave up his wife, a wife who never really had been under his government. In court this matter of contested authority over Caterina was taken up by the secular examiners, who reminded Verci that Caterina's marriage and well-being was none of his business. Bolzani's authority over his wife was blurred by Verci's involvement. Without Verci's support, the examiners reasoned, Caterina would have been forced to return to her husband. But this possible outcome is mere hypothesis; the reality was far more dramatic. Whereas the *dottor* Giovanni Verci was fined just 43 ducats, on 26 July 1614, in absentia, Caterina De Cleves was banished for 10 years from Pinguente and its surrounding areas. Exile was common punishment in the republic for defendants who ignored state orders to appear in court (*bando ad inquirendum*). They were banished temporarily in absentia, as the Venetian Senate had decreed in 1504, but could still prove their innocence because they were only presumed guilty after 16 months.[73]

Caterina, however, might have faced a far more moderate punishment if she had obeyed the summons, as Verci had done. Nevertheless she simply fled Pinguente, while Verci remained in the village and faced the trial. These different ways of dealing with the situation were not accidental, but had wider implications. As this case demonstrates, the willingness to use the court to regulate private conflicts could vary considerably according to the social background, educational level and degree of power held in the community of those involved. If we look at the case in terms of the potential use that Caterina and her family could have made of the local court, they passed up at least two possibilities. This is not mere speculation, but was addressed during the trial. First, as Daniel De Cleves revealed, he had thought about suing Verci for breaking a marriage promise. The secular authority was interested in all crimes committed under their jurisdiction, and in cases of broken marriage promises they relied on the participation of the populace and their willingness to use the local court. The chance that De Cleves would win his claim was comparably good: Caterina's reputation as an honourable woman was not contested in her community, and she had received a ring as a sign of betrothal, an important piece of evidence. But De Cleves had decided to not take legal measures because Verci was superior socially and a person of great authority in the village. In court witnesses often referred to him as the *dottor*, without mentioning his name. Daniel De Cleves would have been forced to find members of the community willing to testify against him. In addition, Daniel De Cleves

---

72 Ibid., fol. 19v.
73 Povolo, 1997, pp. 120–23 and Tirabosco, 1636, p. 39.

mentioned his fear of possible retribution as a major reason for not suing Verci: 'I would have turned to the court, but there are many of them here, and this *dottor* has authority; and I felt uncertain about my future life, for without doubt something terrible would have happened to me; and because I could do nothing, I waited for things to happen'.[74] If we take his deposition seriously, it would mean that a willingness to use the courts was connected to power structures within the community. Justice could be achieved only by some.

Caterina De Cleves and Giovanni Verci also illustrate variations in defendants' behaviour from another perspective. The *dottor*, an educated and learned person from a socially distinguished family in Pinguente, followed the secular authority's order promptly.[75] He knew that he could back up his version of events with a large number of witnesses because he was a respectable and powerful man in Pinguente. Caterina's situation was quite different. She had left her parents without their approval and moved in with a man without their knowledge. The community knew about her sexual involvement with Verci and about their children. Many could testify against her honourable behaviour, having witnessed her continuing contact with Verci while she was a married woman.[76] Caterina's situation was hopeless, in both economic and emotional terms. She had no one to turn to except Verci, but she was obliged to avoid him for moral reasons. The flight from her village was thus an emotionally motivated decision, and not a very sensible one. But who would have been willing to testify in her favour in court?

This case nevertheless ends on a relatively positive note. Three months after Caterina's exile her husband and father presented her supplication in court, petitioning for mercy and an allowance to return to her husband and children, as her innocence had been established after all. What had happened? It seems as though Caterina, while absent from the village, had somehow re-established ties with her parents and husband. In particular the support of her husband changed her legal position. Adultery, as Caterina's lawyer pointed out in her defence, was a private offence, and the female adulterer could only be accused by her

---

[74] ASV, A.d.C., Misc. pen. 158. 6: Giovanni Verci, Cleves Caterina moglie di Bolzani, adulterio, 1614, fol. 5v.

[75] On his social standing see Povolo, 2000, pp. 513–14.

[76] This appears to contradict earlier statements about Caterina's character, but in early modern societies a woman's reputation was always open to interpretation (unless she was properly married and had had sex only with her husband). Caterina's father could argue that she was honourable because she had received a ring from Verci, whereas Verci could argue that he had had sex with her without being properly married.

husband, father or brother.[77] As we already know, in cases of reconciliation and *remissioni* the secular court had no incentive to prosecute if the husband withdrew the accusation, and the state was equally interested in preserving marriages and families, especially if the woman in question was pregnant.[78] A *salvocondotto* (state escort) for Caterina was ordered, the case was reinvestigated and Caterina was interrogated. Her petition for mercy was finally accepted; she was released from exile and instead received the rather modest punishment of a 20-lire fine and was ordered to pay the costs for the trial. Caterina De Cleves and Giovanni Bolzani were fortunate enough to get a second chance at living peacefully as marital partners, not enemies.

What have, then, adultery trials taught us about marital conjugality, patriarchal authority and the functioning of early modern households? As this chapter has demonstrated with clarity, adultery, perceived as a predominatly female crime in early modern Venice, was a much more drastic measure that questioned marital conjugality, than male cruelty and violence. Whereas husbands could justify their behaviour by referring to their patriarchal authority over wives, adulteresses had no comparable argumentative framework at their disposal to lighten their guilt. Because spouses were bound together inescapably, when a woman was married to a man whom she disliked, or whose age exceeded the acceptable age gap or who was not a social equal, this might be occasionally grounds which made moral judgements of parish members less harsh but which, however, carried no legal weight. These unhappy women could not sue for a legal separation at the Patriarchal Court. Only when they could plausibly allege that 'unbound' cruelty and the abuse of patriarchal authority had made marital life unbearable was a lawsuit initiated at the ecclesiastical tribunal. If that was not the case (or the woman decided not to make her marital problems a legal case), the only possibility to change the unhappy domestic and marital cicumstances was an informal separation, a solution, as has been shown, which often raised financial problems, since women had no property on their own. To overcome financial hardship women, then, turned to other men who supported them economically, a decision that made them open to moral and legal attacks.

Beyond these structural problems, adultery cases have demonstrated that the infidelity of wives was perceived and debated, both in the Venetian communities and during legal proceedings, in the wider

---

[77] Because this trial was initiated ex officio, Caterina's legal advisor most probably felt the need to emphasise that adultery was a private crime (*delitto privato*).

[78] This would appear to be the case with Caterina.

context of the marital relationship, drawing a connection between disappointed marital expectations, hardship, domestic disputes and extramarital sexuality. The abuse of patriarchal authority was central to separation suits, but it acquired added significance in adultery trials. Whereas men accused women of marital infidelity, wives argued in their defence that it was their husbands who had failed first by abusing their authority. Although secular examiners considered the contextualising of adultery an important aspect of legal practice, because it destroyed conjugal economy and household and social order, the breaking of matrimonial vows and sacraments was held to be a punishable crime. Instead of being modest, obedient and honourable, adulteresses were perceived as selfish and stubborn, placing individual concerns over marital relationships. The sexual fidelity of a woman, as has been remarked, 'was thought to be more fundamental to the functioning of a marriage than love and respect.'[79]

In prosecuting their adulterous wives, husbands also defended their honour in court. The gendered morality of early modern societies connected failed conjugality with feeble household rule, since in offering their bodies to other men, women were destroying not only their reputation as an honourable wife but questioned, additionally, that of the man as being a potent household ruler – in both sexual and symbolical terms. Sexual prowess, so central to early modern notions of a legally valid marriage (through which a man acquired the social and legal position as a household ruler) was an issue indirectly addressed in adultery suits as well as one that carried emotional, social, cultural and, finally, legal weight. In the most drastic way, it testified to the loss of ownership over a wife. In this sense, adultery was a manifest threat to conjugal households and, ultimately, bore witness to its collapse.

---

[79] Rublack, 1999, p. 216.

Conclusion and Epilogue

The aim of this study has been to explore how women and men in early modern Venice made use of the city's civil magistracies and the Patriarchal Court in order to improve their personal and marital life circumstances, as well as how these authorities responded to the needs of the population. This perspective on people's private lives is dominated by the conflicts, disruptions and anxieties that led men to break their promises of marriage, parents to enforce their authority over disobedient daughters, husbands to beat their wives and married or adulterous women to abandon the conjugal household. Case studies have opened many and fascinating insights into the ways in which men and women appropriated dominant ideals of Christian marriage culture within the urban communities of early modern Venice. They show how crucial gender was to the perception of marital disorder and the way in which it was measured against stated ideals of properly gendered behaviour. The study has, moreover, shown that men were vulnerable in their authority: domestic patriarchy could be challenged by sexually assertive wives and by the loss of male sexual ownership. Men had to negotiate conflicting cultural demands to stabilise marital conjugality and, in particular, to protect their 'natural' superiority, while also allowing for emotional closeness. These gender conflicts have been placed in the broader context of power and hierarchy within early modern society.

Everyday respect between husband and wife was sometimes blurred in marriages between socially unequal partners, in marriages in which an extreme age gap existed or when one spouse was attracted to another person. Therefore, parents had to be careful in choosing a husband who would be socially and emotionally acceptable for their daughter, as respect was fundamental to the well-being of the married couple and the enforcement of male authority and female obedience. Only when the authority that Venetian patriarchal society accorded to the male head of the household was used with wisdom and care was his rule perceived as wise, just and sound. Early modern marriage culture demanded balanced household government, just as the stability of the Venetian republic was attributed to the prudence and judiciousness of its civic rulers. In political theory, as in Venetian society, prudent government was thought to stabilise social order, whereas patriarchal abuse could easily deteriorate into misrule and tyranny, which clearly threatened the stability of households and society alike.

The model of a Christian marriage was not always realised in practice. When the marriage failed, partners simply separated without legal permission, or remarried elsewhere. But abandonment did not always indicate household collapse, and distressed partners had scope for reconciliation, for example when husbands agreed to take remorseful wives back, thus preventing total domestic breakdown. The tensions that overshadowed married life therefore had to be confronted on a day-to-day basis, with relatives, neighbours or friends acting as mediators. Christian doctrine stressed conjugality between husband and wife; they had to manage the good and the bad times, side by side. Through an examination of contemporary court cases which places them in the context of their juridical culture, it has been possible to highlight the different approaches of the Church and the state towards marital dysfunction. These cases serve to elucidate the gender-specific ways in which ordinary men and women, and husbands and wives used the Venetian secular and ecclesiastical courts, and the different legal contexts in which they revealed their marital and sexual problems.

In the overall context of early modern Venetian society, women were consistently confronted with the means that patriarchy had bestowed on household rulers. Among these means, corrective violence was one of the rights that a husband had over his wife or a father or legal guardian had over his daughter. The focus of this study has been to reconstruct the different social, cultural, emotional and legal contexts in which women became the object of violence, as well as the responses of female and male neighbours to it. Because domestic violence was generally approved of as 'moderate correction' for controlling wayward wives and wilful daughters, violence – not tyrannical rule – was perceived as an expression of the male authority that was necessary to reinforce household hierarchy and, thus, social and gender order.

If attempts at restoring marital and familial order failed, households finally collapsed with the desertion of the shared dwelling. At this point spouses either considered legal means to end the unhappy marital relationship or simply resolved their problems privately without ever approaching the Patriarchal Court. An unauthorised separation, however, was a sin according to canon law, and desertion was a dramatic expression of the breakdown of the marital relationship and of the conjugal economy. In Christian marriage doctrine, it was a marital duty to live in and share one household, and only if the offended party had obtained a judicial authorisation were couples actually allowed to live separately. Canon law therefore clearly restricted people's possibilities, and annulment or separation of unhappy marriages was only allowed in exceptional cases. Remarriage, as the Council of Trent had decreed, was not permitted in cases of adultery or severe cruelty; only after the annulment of a marriage or after the death of a spouse might one remarry. Yet apparently the law could be circumvented, and hopes for future marriages could be realised in exceptional cases. Courts could be used strategically as ordinary people tried their best to resolve individual problems, finding different ways to achieve their aims or enforce their own interests. Although the individual motivations to instigate lawsuits, sometimes after years, are not entirely clear, they nevertheless draw attention to the way in which common people used the courts to solve their private problems. As we have learned from various depositions, ordinary women and men participated actively in the legal process and shaped the legal culture to a certain degree. By commenting on acts of infidelity or failed conjugality, they gave vivid testimony of their moral vision of the civic world and the ways in which marriages and households should work within the fascinatingly heterogeneous parishes of late sixteenth- and seventeenth-century Venice.

These centuries, as we have seen, were a time of growing secularization in Venice (as elsewhere). In this book the precise implications of the long-term transformation of control over marriage and sexuality by the state and the Church have been explored. In making marriage the only place for sexual relations, Venice's secular magistracies followed a marital policy that fostered the stability of post-Tridentine marriages at every level of society. In doing so, the local governmental authorities relied on the Tridentine reform movement's new concept of marriage, which supported the state in its battle against dishonourable sexual behaviour. In this respect, the aims of the Church and the state in terms of a reform of actual marital practice clearly intersected. However, local government authorities also strengthened the rights of parents and, in turn, thus secular interests in marriage conventions. In order to prevent ill-considered marriages contracted without parental knowledge from endangering the social, economic and political interests of Venetian families, civil law accorded parents the right to disinherit their children, thereby creating a considerable challenge to the norm of consensual marriage which the Catholic reform movement had reaffirmed.

Stricter moral legislation, as has been shown, was aimed at defending women's virginity and honour, ensuring the solemnisation of proper marriages according to Catholic doctrine and, thus, guaranteeing the legitimacy of children. Although the legislation served the interests of women (but also restricted their possibilities to sue honourable citizens), it has been shown that legal practice was far more complex: one consequence of the renewed moralism was the reforming and disciplining of women. Their chances of receiving favourable verdicts in court after having consented to premarital sex worsened during the age of the confessional – except towards the end of the seventeenth century. However, the Venetian secular government followed the moral policy of prosecuting men for enjoying women under the pretext of marriage, but did not prosecute women for fornication, for example. Secular legislation was not bound to respect the free will of spouses and could enforce the fulfilment of marriage, whereas canon law had to respect the sacrament of marriage. These legal limits of canon law ran counter to government interests, as broken marriage promises disturbed the balance of an ordered society based on civil harmony, valid marriages and the legitimacy of offspring. Although legislation was harsh and severe, it was not consistently applied. Legal practice was more flexible, with each case judged individually.

A similar policy was followed in cases of adultery, which was defined as a predominantly female offence. Sexually assertive wives endangered conjugal households and were considered to be a meaningful threat to male honour, civic peace and the well-being of the republic. The state's prime concern in prosecuting these women lay not in punishment, but in the attempt to make them internalise guilt: remorse and penitence were required. It was, however, still the husband who decided a wife's destiny; only when husbands were willing to take repentant wives back into the household did the state have no incentive to prosecute further. Whereas imprisonment or exile destroyed marriages and households, the flexibility of secular magistracies in judging cases of adultery was aimed at restoring families, household economies, neighbourhood harmony and, thus, Venice's broader social order.[1]

In order to foster morality during the age of the confessional, the Church and the state also tightened parochial control of parishioners through the enforcement of the principle of marriage as a public act, through midwives who were given an increased role in the surveillance of sexual activity and, finally, through confession. Father confessors were key mediators between the populace and the ecclesiastical authorities in communicating the moral values of a renewed Christian marriage culture. When wives sought help or advice clergymen discouraged them from taking legal action, particularly when they wished to end their unhappy marriages. By contrast, should the marriage be unconsummated, priests would stress the religious meaning of sex,

---

[1] A systematic investigation of the verdicts for this crime is still needed.

through which a union was turned into a sacrament. If no permanently binding marriage existed, they would urge these women to plead for an annulment at the Patriarchal Court. Both approaches served the same end: priests defended the sacrament of marriage by stressing its indissolubility and by preventing fruitless sexual endeavours from turning the union into a sacrament. They defended the principles of Catholic marriage doctrine in the attempt to guarantee procreation and impede fornication.

The approach of the Patriarchal Court towards marital litigation was, therefore, less appropriate to the needs of wives in particular, who brought the majority of annulment and separation cases to court. The sanctity of marriage – a union solemnised in the face of God – was the worst enemy of couples in crisis. When matrimonial conflicts reached the Patriarchal Court, only in exceptional cases were long-term separations granted or marriages annulled. One can only speculate as to how many warring couples resolved their problems privately, with the help of mediators or simply by abandoning the conjugal household, without recourse to legal action. It would be interesting to know what effect non-favourable verdicts had on the lives of litigant couples. Because we do not know about these couples' lives after their trials – whether husbands actually moderated their behaviour, or whether wives moved back to their original families or sought shelter in charitable institutions despite the obligation to cohabit – it is difficult to measure the impact of post-Tridentine ecclesiastical policy on the lives of women and on Venetian social stability. Arguably, in defending the sacramentality of Catholic marriages, the Patriarchal Court's verdicts were not particularly stabilising because they forced cohabitation on partners who had already gone through a series of legal reworkings of their intimate and emotional conflicts. Only when the ecclesiastical court annulled marriages that could not be consummated or that had taken place with the major impediment of 'fear and force' did they actually judge the case according to the emotional wishes of young women, albeit simultaneously undermining the interests of families in marital formation. Thus, in these cases the court made decisions that were more in line with the needs and expectations of female litigants, and, in annulling marriages that had broken down long ago, these sentences were apparently socially stabilising.

At the end of the eighteenth century it was the stability of society in particular that motivated the state to bring legal matters more clearly under its control. The Council of Ten's 1782 law on the 'issue of divorces' aimed to prevent the dissolution of patrician marriages without state notice and approval, which would result in the disruption and collapse of family economies and disturb the harmony of households and families.[2] Had it not been for the fall of the republic, these debates might have continued well into the nineteenth century. On 12 May 1797 the Great Council met for the last time and voted – under fervid pressure from Napoleon's army – for self-dissolution; the days of the serene republic of Venice were over. French rule lasted only months, and in October 1796 the former Venetian republic became part of the Austrian Habsburg empire until 1866 – except from January 1806 to May 1814, when the city was under French rule. Thereafter Venice was subject to the 1811 Austrian General Civil Code, whereby a civil court could grant divorces for non-Catholics, but only on serious grounds (*per gravi motivi*), for example when the wife's life was in danger. The procedure was complex and slow, and judges were to act as 'defenders of marriage'. Hence, nothing had really changed, as judges were to preserve marriages rather than grant divorces.[3]

When Venice joined the Italian kingdom in 1866 civil marriages were defined in a new civil code that did not provide for divorce. Once again marriage was considered indissoluble, and divorce was not legalised for almost a century. Despite ongoing debates during the nineteenth century, especially during the fascist period, the issue was first taken up again seriously by the Italian parliament in the 1960s.[4] The attempt to introduce a 'little divorce' (*divorzio piccolo*) – separation without permission to remarry – in cases of hardship, long-term imprisonment of one spouse and similar cases, which had been discussed in the 1950s, had failed. Finally, in November 1969 a divorce bill was approved by the government. It was signed by the president of the republic on 1 December 1970 and came into effect on 18 December 1970.[5] The history of marriage and the process of ascribing social, cultural and legal meaning to domestic violence and cruelty was thus a long battle that came to an end only during the late twentieth century.

---

2 Cozzi, 1981, pp. 322–3.
3 Phillips, 1988, p. 406; Lulli, 1974, p. 1242.
4 On the fascist divorce policy see Phillips, 1988, pp. 544–6.
5 Ibid., pp. 572–4.

Bibliography

Manuscript sources

Archivio di Stato, Venice

Esecutori contro la Bestemmia
processi, b. 1
b. 54, Capitolare (1523–1797)
b. 55, Notatorio 1
b. 56, Notatorio 2
b. 57, Notatorio 3, 4
b. 58, Notatorio, 95, 96
b. 59, Notatorio 97, 98
b. 61, Notatorio 1–3
b. 62, raspe 4–6
b. 63, raspe 9–11
b. 65, raspe 13–14
b. 68, raspe 1–2
b. 69, raspa 9

Consiglio dei Dieci
Parti Comuni, filza 448, (1636)
Parti Comuni, registro 33 (1577–78); registro 35 (1580–81)

Compilazione delle Leggi
b. 277 (Matrimonio)
b. 186 (Dote)
b. 177 (Delitti Generali)
b. 317 (Assicurazione di Dote)

Notarile Atti
4884, Nicolò Doglioni, Protocollo 1601
6654, Orlando Graciolo, 1660 usque 1668
11227, Giovanni Pezzi, 1683
1041, Pietro Antonio Bozini, 1702
5511, Giorgio Emo, Protocollo 1656–57
6121, Marco et Antonio Fratina, Protocollo

692, Francesco Beazino e Andrea Bronzini, 1658
10902, Gerolamo Paganuzzi, 1657

Senato, Deliberazioni Roma Ordinaria, Reg. 1 (1560–65)
Senato Terra, Reg. 107 (March–August 1632)

Consultori in Iure, filza 132

Provveditori alla Sanità, b. 569, 571 and 572

Sant'Uffizio, processi
b. 66, 74, 82

Avogaria di Comun, Miscellanea penale, processi
29.14, 45.4, 49.20, 56.11, 76.2, 78.5, 82.9, 97.13, 97. 21, 127.17,
128.14, 141.11, 141.16, 158.6, 172.15, 177.13, 178.3, 182.2, 186.22,
191.1, 195.15, 198.3, 200.29, 224.27, 238.3, 239.5, 240.3, 251.7,
252.18, 268.21, 276.4, 276.24, 278.4, 282.13, 310.4, 310.15, 321.10,
339.5, 342.13, 342.23, 347.13, 361.12, 366.5, 375.7, 376.17, 382.5,
391.16, 403.15, 416.6, 416.13, 448.13, 456.10

Archivio Storico della Curia Patriarchale, Venice

Curia, II, Causarum Matrimoniorum

Reg. 71 (1570) = 7	Reg. 72 (1571–74) = 13
Reg. 73 (1575–78) = 10	Reg. 74 (1579) = 8
Reg. 75 (1580–81) = 8	Reg. 76 (1582) = 5
Reg. 77 (1583) = 1	Reg. 78 (1583–84) = 8
Reg. 79 (1585) = 1	Reg. 80 (1585–86) = 4
Reg. 81 (1587–89) = 6	Reg. 82 (1590–95) = 9
Reg. 83 (1596–97) = 6	Reg. 84 (1601–10) = 6
Reg. 85 (1612–17) = 8	Reg. 86 (1618–21) = 8
Reg. 87 (1622–23) = 7	Reg. 88 (1624–26) = 8
Reg. 89 (1627) = 3	Reg. 90 (1628–30) = 9
Reg. 91 (1631–36) = 8	Reg. 92 (1637–49) = 12
Reg. 93 (1650–75) = 8	Reg. 94 (1675–1700) = 7

Curia, II, Filciae Causarum, processi varii

Curia, II, Actorum, Mandatorum
Liber Actorum et Mandatorum, Reg. 66 (1560–64)

Reg. 72 (1579–1580)
Reg. 79 (1591–1594)
Reg. 80 (1602–1605)
Reg. 82 (1611–13)
Reg. 87 (1620–1621)
Reg. 88 (1621–23)
Reg. 100 (1637–39)
Reg. 104 (1643–44)
Reg. 111 (1655–57)
Reg. 117 (1677–78)
Reg. 124 (1695–96)

Curia, II, Sententiarum
Reg. 4, Sententiarum 1500–1663
Reg. 6, Sententiarum 1600–07
Reg. 8, Theupoli liber sententiarum civilium incipiens die VII februarii
1620 a nativitate usque ad diem quintam maii 1631
Reg. 9, Sententiarum civilium 1647–51, 1663
Reg. 10 (1637–89), Sententiarum Baduarii et aliorum

Curia, II, Status Animarum, b. 1–3

Biblioteca Nazionale Marciana, Venice

*Parte sostantiale delli decreti del sacro et general Concilio di Trento, che
furono publicati nella sinodo Diocesana di Venetia di XVII di
Settembre* (Venice, 1564), Miscellanea 2689.7.
*Istruttione per la formazione de' processi sin al punto della loro
deliberazione* Manoscritto, IT VII 1638 (7982), sec. XVII–XVIII.
Diarii di Giolamo Priuli, Cod. PD 252.

Biblioteca del Museo Correr, Venice

Codice Cicogna 3287, no. 70, 13 July 1601, Clarissima Donna Lucietta
filias q. Clar.mi Joannis Geno *vs* Clarissimo Marco Dolphino filius q.
Joannis.
Raccolta Cicogna, Manoscritto, Miscellanea 2039, fols 505–17:
Catalogo di tutte le principal et più honorate cortigiane di Venezia.

Printed primary sources

Azpilcueta, M. de (1569), *Manuale de' Confessori, et penitenti*, Venice.

Barbaro, A. (1739), *Pratica criminale*, Venice.

Bianchini, A. (1786), *Il diritto ecclesiastico tratto dalle opere canoniche del Vanespen con aggiunta di materie e delle pratiche particolari della Serenissima Repubblica di Venezia*, Venice.

Bistort, G. (1912), *Il Magistrato alle Pompe nella Repubblica di Venezia*, Bologna.

Bronzini, C. (1622), *Della dignità, e nobiltà delle donne*, Florence.

The Canons and Decrees of the Council of Trent (1687), London.

Contarini, G. (1599), *The Commonwealth and Government of Venice*, trans. L. Lewkenor, Amsterdam/New York: Da Capo Press, 1969.

Coryat, T. (1611), *Coryat's Crudities. Reprinted from the Edition of 1611: with his Letters from India*, 3 vols, London, 1776.

Dolce, L. (1545), *Della institution delle donne. Secondo li tre stati, che cadono nella vita humana*, Venice.

Ferro, M. (1845), *Dizionario del diritto comune e veneto*, 2 vols, 1 edn, 1778–81, Venice.

Leggi criminali venete (1980), ed. E. della Giovanna and A. Sorgato, Venice.

Lorenzi, G.B. (1870–72), *Leggi e memorie venete sulla prostituzione fino alla caduta della Repubblica*, Venice.

Marinello, G. (1563), *Le medicine partenenti alle infermità delle Donne*, ed. M.L. Altieri Biagi, C. Mazzotta, A. Chiantera and P. Altieri, Turin, 1992.

Paruta, P. (1579), *Della perfezzione della vita politica, in Storici e politici veneti del Cinquecento e del Seicento*, ed. G. Benzoni and T. Zanato, Milan/Naples: Ricciardi, 1982, 491–642.

Passi, G. (1599), *I donneschi diffetti*, Venice.

Passi, G. (1602), *Dello stato maritale*, Venice.

Priori, L. (1622), *Prattica criminale secondo il ritto delle leggi della Serenissima Republica di Venezia*, Venice.

Sánchez, T. (1607), *Disputationum de Sancto Matrimonii Sacramento*, 3 vols, Antwerp.

Savelli, M.-A. (1715), *Pratica universale*, Venice.

Teobaldo, F. (1736), *Pratica criminale. A notizia di chi voglia istradarsi alle cariche di assessore, ò di cancelliere*, Venice.

Tirabosco, M.-A. (1636), *Ristretto di pratica criminale. Per la formazione di processi ad offesa*, Venice.

Volumen, statutorum, legum, … venetorum, cum amplissimo indice (1597), Venice.

Printed secondary sources

Alessi, G. (1989), 'L'onore riparato. Il riformismo del Settecento e le "ridicole leggi" contro lo stupro', in *Onore e storia nelle società mediterranee*, ed. G. Fiume, Palermo: La Luna, 129–42.

Alessi, G. (1990), 'Il gioco degli scambi: seduzione e risarcimento nella casistica cattolica del XVI e XVII secolo', *Quaderni storici*, 75, 805–31.

Allerston, P. (1998), 'Wedding Finery in Sixteenth-Century Venice', in *Marriage in Italy, 1300–1650*, ed. T. Dean and K. Lowe, Cambridge: Cambridge University Press, 25–40.

Allerston, P. (1999), 'Reconstructing the Second-Hand Clothes Trade in Sixteenth and Seventeenth-Century Venice', *Costume*, 33, 46–56.

Allerston, P. (2000), 'Clothing and Early Modern Venetian Society', *Continuity and Change*, 15, 367–90.

Amelang, J. (1993), 'People of the Ribera: Popular Politics and Neighbourhood Identity in Early Modern Barcelona', in *Culture and Identity in Early Modern Europe (1500–1800)*, ed. B. B. Diefendorf and C. Hesse, Ann Arbor: University of Michigan Press, 119–37.

Arru, A. (1992), 'Servi e serve: le particolarità del caso italiano', in *Storia della Famiglia italiana*, ed. M. Barbagli and D.I. Kertzer, Bologna: Il Mulino, 273–306.

Bachorski, H.-J., ed. (1991), *Ordnung und Lust. Bilder von Liebe, Ehe und Sexualität im Spätmittelalter und Früher Neuzeit*, Trier: Wissenschaftlicher Verlag Trier.

Bachrach, B.S. and Nicholas, D., eds (1990), *Law, Custom, and the Social Fabric in Medieval Europe. Essays in Honour of Bryce Lyon*, Kalamazoo: Western Michigan University.

Barbagli, M. (1988), *Sotto lo stesso tetto. Mutamenti della famiglia in Italia dal XV al XX secolo*, Bologna: Il Mulino.

Barbagli, M. (1991), 'Three Household Formation Systems in Eighteenth- and Nineteenth-Century Italy', in *The Family in Italy from Antiquity to the Present*, ed. D.I. Kertzer and R.P. Saller, New Haven/London: Yale University Press, 250–70.

Barbagli, M. and Kertzer, D.I., eds (1992), *Storia della famiglia italiana, 1750–1950*, Bologna: Il Mulino.

Barzaghi, A. (1980), *Donne o cortigiane? La prostituzione a Venezia, documenti di costume dal XVI al XVII secolo*, Verona: Bertani.

Beck, R. (1992), 'Frauen in Krise. Eheleben und Ehescheidung in der ländlichen Gesellschaft Bayerns während des Ancien Régime', in *Dynamik der Tradition. Studien zur historischen Kulturforschung*, ed. R. van Dülmen, Frankfurt/Main: Fischer Verlag, 137–212.

Bell, R.M. (1990), 'Telling Her Sins: Male Confessors and Female Penitents in Catholic Reformation Italy', in *That Gentle Strength*.

Historical Perspectives on Women in Christianity, ed. L.L Coon, K.J. Haldane and E.W. Sommer, Charlottesville/London: University Press of Virginia, 118–33.

Bell, R.M. (1999), *How to Do It. Guides to Good Living for Renaissance Italians*, Chicago/London: University of Chicago Press.

Beltrami, D. (1954), *Storia della popolazione di Venezia dalla fine del secolo XV alla caduta della Repubblica*, Padua: Milani.

Berlinguer, L. and Colao, F. eds (1989), *Crimine, giustizia e società veneta in età moderna*, Milan: Giuffrè.

Black, C.F. (1989), *Italian Confraternities in the Sixteenth Century*, Cambridge: Cambridge University Press.

Blastenbrei, P. (1995), *Kriminalität in Rom, 1560–1585*, Tübingen: Niemeyer.

Blok, A. (1981), 'Rams and Billy-Goats: A Key to the Mediterranean Code of Honour', *Man*, 16, 427–40.

Bossy, J. (1970), 'The Counter-Reformation and the People of Catholic Europe', *Past and Present*, 47, 51–70.

Bossy, J., ed. (1983), *Disputes and Settlements. Law and Human Relations in the West*, Cambridge: Cambridge University Press.

Bossy, J. (1985), *Christianity in the West, 1400–1700*, Oxford: Oxford University Press.

Brackett, J.K. (1992), *Criminal Justice and Crime in Late Renaissance Florence, 1537–1609*, Cambridge: Cambridge University Press.

Brandileone, F. (1906), *Saggi sulla storia della celebrazione del matrimonio in Italia*, Milan: Hoepli.

Bressan, L. (1973), *Il canone Tridentino sul divorzio per adulterio e l'interpretazione degli autori*, Rome: Università Gregoriana Editrice.

Brown, J.C. (1986), 'A Woman's Place was in the Home: Women's Work in Renaissance Tuscany', in *Rewriting the Renaissance. The Discourse of Sexual Difference in Early Modern Europe*, ed. M.W. Ferguson, M. Quilligan and N.J. Vickers, Chicago/London: University of Chicago Press, 206–24.

Brundage, J.A. (1982),'The Problem of Impotence', in *Sexual Practices and the Medieval Church*, ed. V.L Bullough and J. Brundage, Buffalo/NY: Prometheus Books, 135–40.

Brundage, J.A. (1984), 'Let Me Count the Ways. Canonists and Theologians Contemplate Coital Positions', *Journal of Medieval History*, 10, 81–93.

Brundage, J.A. (1987), *Law, Sex, and Christian Society in Medieval Europe*, Chicago: University of Chicago Press.

Brundage, J.A. (1993), *Sex, Law, and Marriage in the Middle Ages*, Great Yarmouth: Galliard Ltd.

Buganza, G. (1991), 'Il potere della parola. La forza e le responsabilità della deposizione testimoniale nel processo penale veneziano (secoli XVI–XVII)', in *La parola all'accusato*, ed. J.-C. Maire Vigueur and A. Paravicini Bagliani, Palermo: Sellerio, 124–38.

Bullough, V.L. and Brundage, J.A., eds (1982), *Sexual Practices and the Medieval Church*, Buffalo/NY: Prometheus Books.

Bullough, V.L. (1994), 'On Being a Male in the Middle Ages', in *Medieval Masculinities. Regarding Men in the Middle Ages*, ed. C.A. Lees, Minneapolis: University of Minnesota Press, 31–46.

Burghartz, S. (1992), 'Jungfräulichkeit oder Reinheit? Zur Änderung von Argumentationsmustern vor dem Baseler Ehegericht im 16. und 17. Jahrhundert', in *Dynamik der Tradition. Studien zur historischen Kulturforschung*, ed. R. van Dülmen, Frankfurt/Main: Fischer Verlag, 13–40.

Burghartz, S. (1999a), *Zeiten der Reinheit – Orte der Unzucht. Ehe und Sexualität im Basel der Frühen Neuzeit*, Paderborn/Munich/Vienna/Zürich: Ferdinand Schöningh.

Burghartz, S. (1999b), 'Tales of Seduction, Tales of Violence: Argumentative Strategies before the Basel Marriage Court', *German History* 17, 41–56.

Burke, P. (1987), *The Historical Anthropology of Early Modern Italy*, Cambridge: Cambridge University Press.

Burke, P. (2000), 'Early Modern Venice as a Center of Information', in *Venice Reconsidered. The History and Civilization of an Italian City-State, 1297–1797*, ed. J. Martin and D. Romano, Baltimore MD/London: Johns Hopkins University Press, 389–419.

Cadden, J. (1993), *Meanings of Sex Difference in the Middle Ages. Medicine, Science, and Culture*, Cambridge: Cambridge University Press.

Casey, J. (1983), 'Household Disputes and the Law in Early Modern Andalusia', in *Disputes and Settlements. Law and Human Relations in the West*, ed. J. Bossy, Cambridge: Cambridge University Press, 189–217.

Cavallo, S. and Cerutti, S. (1990), 'Female Honor and the Social Control of Reproduction', in *Sex and Gender in Historical Perspective (Selections from Quaderni storici)*, ed. E. Muir and G. Ruggiero, Baltimore MD/London: Johns Hopkins University Press, 73–109.

Chambers, D. and Pullan, B., eds (1993), *Venice. A Documentary History 1450–1630*, Cambridge, MA/Oxford: Blackwell.

Chaytor, M. (1995), 'Husband(ry): Narratives of Rape in the Seventeenth Century', *Gender and History*, 7, 378–407.

Chojnacka, M. (2001), *Working Women of Early Modern Venice*, Baltimore MD/London: Johns Hopkins University Press.

Chojnacki, S. (1998), Daughters and Oligarchs: Gender and the Early Renaissance State', in *Gender and Society in Renaissnce Italy*, ed. R.C. Davis and J.C. Brown, London/New York: Longman, 63–86.

Chojnacki, S. (2000a), *Women and Men in Renaissance Venice. Twelve Essays on Patrician Society*, Baltimore MD/London: Johns Hopkins University Press.

Chojnacki, S. (2000b), 'Il divorzio di Cateruzza: rappresentazione femminile ed esito processuale (Venezia 1465)', in *Coniugi nemici. La separazione in Italia dal XII al XVIII secolo*, ed. S. Seidel Menchi and D. Quaglioni, Bologna: Il Mulino, 371–416.

Chojnacki, S. (2000c), 'Identity and Ideology in Renaissance Venice', in *Venice Reconsidered. The History and Civilization of an Italian City-State, 1297–1797*, ed. J. Martin and D. Romano, Baltimore MD/London: Johns Hopkins University Press, 263–94.

Cibin, P. (1985), 'Meretrici e cortigiane a Venezia nel' 500', *DonnaWomanFemme*, **25/26**, 79–102.

Cohen, E.S. (1989), 'Asylums for Women in Counter-Reformation Italy', in *Women in Reformation and Counter-Reformation Europe: Public and Private Worlds*, ed. S. Marshall, Bloomington: Indiana University Press, 166–88.

Cohen, E.S. and Cohen, T.V. (1993), *Words and Deeds in Renaissance Rome*, Toronto/Buffalo/London: University of Toronto Press.

Cohen, E.S. (1993), 'Between Oral and Written Culture: The Social Meaning of an Illustrated Love Letter', in *Culture and Identity in Early Modern Europe (1500–1800)*, ed. B.B. Diefendorf and C. Hesse, Ann Arbor: University of Michigan Press, 181–201.

Cohn, S.K., Jr, (1996), *Women in the Streets. Essays on Sex and Power in Renaissance Italy*, Baltimore MD/London: Johns Hopkins University Press.

Conti Odorisio, G. (1979), *Donna e società nel Seicento. Lucrezia Marinelli e Arcangela Tarabotti*, Rome: Bulzoni.

Coon, L.L., Haldane, K.J. and Sommer, E.W., eds (1990), *That Gentle Strength. Historical Perspectives on Women in Christianity*, Charlottesville/London: University Press of Virginia.

Cowan, A. (1995), 'Love, Honour and the Avogaria di Comun in Early Modern Venice', *Archivio Veneto*, **179**, 5–19.

Cowan, A. (1999), 'Patricians and Partners in Early Modern Venice', in *Medieval and Renaissance Venice* ed. E.E. Kittell and Th.F. Madden, Urbana/Chicago: University of Illinois Press, 276–93.

Cox, V. (1995), 'The Single Self: Feminist Thought and the Marriage Market in Early Modern Venice', *Renaissance Quarterly*, **3**, 513–81.

Cox, V., ed. (1997), *The Worth of Women by Moderata Fonte*, Chicago/London: University of Chicago Press.

Cozzi, G. (1955), 'Note su tribunali e procedure penali a Venezia nel' 700', *Rivista storica italiana*, **77**, 931–52.

Cozzi, G. (1973), 'Authority and the Law in Renaissance Venice', in *Renaissance Venice*, ed. J.R. Hale, London: Faber & Faber, 293–345.

Cozzi, G. (1976), 'Padri, figli e matrimoni clandestini', *La cultura*, **14**, 169–213.

Cozzi, G., ed. (1980a), *Stato, società e giustizia nella Repubblica veneta (sec. XV–XVIII)*, Rome: Jouvence.

Cozzi, G. (1980b), ' La donna, l'amore e Tiziano', in *Tiziano e Venezia. Convegno internazionale di Studi*, Vicenza: Neri Pozza Editore, 47–63.

Cozzi, G. (1981), 'Note e documenti sulla questione del "divorzio" a Venezia (1782–1788)', *Annali dell'Istituto storico italo-germanico di Trento*, **7**, 275–360.

Cozzi, G. (1989), 'La difesa degli imputati nei processi celebrati col rito del Consiglio dei X', in *Crimine, giustizia e società veneta in età moderna*, ed. L. Berlinguer and E. Colao, Milan: Giuffrè, 1–87.

Cozzi, G. (1991), 'Religione, moralità e giustizia a Venezia: Vicende della magistratura degli Esecutori contro la Bestemmia (Secoli XVI–XVII)', *Ateneo veneto*, **178**, 7–96.

Cristellon, C. (2003), 'L'ufficio del giudice: Mediazione, inquisizione e confessione nei processi matrimoniali veneziani (1420–1532)', *Rivista storica italiana*, **115**, 851–98.

Darmon, P. (1985), *Trials by Impotence. Virility and Marriage in Pre-Revolutionary France*, trans. P. Keegan, London: Chatto and Windus.

Davidson, N. (1994), 'Theology, Nature and the Law: Sexual Sin and Sexual Crime in Italy from the Fourteenth to the Seventeenth Century', in *Crime, Society and the Law in Renaissance Italy*, ed. T. Dean and K. Lowe, 74–98.

Davis, J.C. (1975), *A Venetian Family and Its Fortune, 1500–1900: The Donà and the Conservation of their Wealth*, Philadelphia: American Philosophical Society.

Davis, N.Z (1987), *Fiction in the Archives: Pardon Tales and their Tellers in Sixteenth-Century France*, Stanford CA: Stanford University Press.

Davis, R.C. (1994), *The War of the Fists. Popular Culture and Public Violence in Late Renaissance Venice*, New York/Oxford: Oxford University Press.

Davis, R.C. (1991), *Shipbuilders of the Venetian Arsenal: Workers and Workplace in the Preindustrial City*, Baltimore MD/London: Johns Hopkins University Press.

Davis, R.C (1998), 'The Geography of Gender in the Renaissance', in *Gender and Society in Renaissance Italy*, ed. J.C. Brown and R.C. Davis. London/New York: Longman, 19–38.

Dean, T. and Lowe, K., eds (1994), *Crime, Society and the Law in Renaissance Italy*, Cambridge: Cambridge University Press.

Dean, T. and Lowe, K., eds (1998), *Marriage in Italy, 1300–1650*, Cambridge: Cambrige University Press.

Dean, T. (1998), 'Fathers and Daughters: Marriage Laws and Marriage Disputes in Bologna and Italy, 1200–1500', in *Marriage in Italy, 1300–1650*, ed. T. Dean and K. Lowe, Cambridge: Cambridge University Press, 85–106.

De Biase, L. (1981–82), 'Problemi ed osservazioni sul "divorzio" nel Patriziato veneziano del secolo XVIII. Un tentativo di analisi storica seriale', *Atti dell'Istituto veneto di scienze, lettere ed arti*, 140, 143–162.

Denley, P. and Elam, C., eds (1988), *Florence and Italy. Renaissance Studies in Honour of Nicolai Rubinstein*, London: Westfield College, University of London.

Derosas, R. (1980), 'Moralità e giustizia a Venezia nel' 500-'600. Gli Esecutori contro la Bestemmia', in *Stato, società e giustizia nella Repubblica veneta (sec. XV–XVIII)*, ed. G. Cozzi, Rome: Jouvence, 431–528.

Diefendorf, B.B. and Hesse, C., eds (1993), *Culture and Identity in Early Modern Europe (1500–1800)*, Ann Arbor: University of Michigan Press.

Di Simplicio, O. (1990), 'Violenza maritale e violenza sessuale nello stato senese di antico regime', in *Emarginazione, criminalità e devianza in Italia fra '600 e '900*, ed. A. Pastore and P. Sorcinelli, Milan: Angeli, 33–50.

Donahue, Ch. (1983), 'The Canon Law on the Formation of Marriage and Social Practice in the Later Middle Ages', *Journal of Family History*, 8, 144–58.

Dülmen, R. van, ed. (1992), *Dynamik der Tradition. Studien zur historischen Kulturforschung*, Frankfurt/Main: Fischer Verlag.

Erler, M. and Kowaleski, M., eds (1988), *Women and Power in the Middle Ages*, Athens/London: University of Georgia Press.

Esmein, A. (1891), *Mariage en droit canonique*, 2 vols, Paris: Adhémar.

Farge, A. and Foucault, M. (1989), *Familiäre Konflikte: Die "Lettres de cachet"*, Frankfurt/Main: Suhrkamp Verlag.

Farr, J. (1995), *Authority and Sexuality in Early Modern Burgundy*, New York/Oxford: Oxford University Press.

Favero, G., Moro, M., Spinelli, P., Trivellato, F. and Vianello, F. (1991), 'Le anime dei demografi. Fonti per la rivelazione dello stato della popolazione di Venezia nei secoli XVI e XVII', *Bollettino di demografia storica*, 15, 21–110.

Ferguson, M.W., Quilligan, M. and Vickers, N.J., eds (1986): *Rewriting the Renaissance. The Discourse of Sexual Difference in Early Modern Europe*, Chicago/London: University of Chicago Press.

Ferrante, L. (1990), 'Honour Regained: Women and the Casa del Soccorso di San Paolo in Sixteenth-Century Bologna', in *Sex and Gender in Historical Perspective (Selections from Quaderni storici)*, ed. E. Muir and G. Ruggiero. Baltimore MD/London: Johns Hopkins University Press, 46–72.

Ferrante, L. (1994), 'Il matrimonio disciplinato: processi matrimoniali a Bologna nel Cinquecento', in *Disciplina dell'anima, disciplina del corpo e disciplina della società tra medioevo e eta moderna*, ed. P. Prodi, Bologna: Il Mulino, 901–27.

Ferraro, J. (1995), 'The Power to Decide: Battered Wives in Early Modern Venice', *Renaissance Quarterly*, 3, 492–512.

Ferraro, J. (2000), 'Coniugi nemici: Orsetta, Annibale e il compito dello storico (Venezia 1634)', in *La separazione in Italia dal XII al XVIII secolo*, ed. S. Seidel Menchi and D. Quaglioni, Bologna: Il Mulino, 141–90.

Ferraro, J. (2001), *Marriage Wars in Late Renaissance Venice*, Oxford/New York: Oxford University Press.

Filippini, N.M. (1993), 'The Church, the State and Childbirth: The Midwife in Italy during the Eighteenth Century', in *The Art of Midwifery*, ed. H. Marland, London/New York: Routledge, 152–75.

Filippini, N.M. (1985), 'Levatrici e ostetricanti a Venezia tra sette e ottocento', *Quaderni storici*, 58, 149–80.

Finlay, R. (1980), *Politics in Renaissance Venice*, New Brunswick NJ: Rutgers University Press.

Fiume, G., ed. (1989), *Onore e storia nelle società mediterranee*, Palermo: La Luna.

Flandrin, J.-L. (1979), *Families in Former Times: Kinship, Household and Sexuality*, Cambridge: Cambridge University Press.

Flandrin, J.-L. (1984), 'Das Geschlechtsleben der Eheleute in der alten Gesellschaft: Von der kirchlichen Lehre zum realen Verhalten', in *Die Masken des Begehrens und die Metamorphosen der Sinnlichkeit. Zur Geschichte der Sexualität im Abendland*, ed. Ph. Ariès, A. Béjin and M. Foucault, Frankfurt/Main: Fischer Verlag, 147–64.

Fletcher, A. (1995), *Gender, Sex and Subordination in England 1500–1800*, New Haven CT: Yale University Press.

Fortini Brown, P. (2000), 'Behind the Walls. The Material Culture of Venetian Elites', in *Venice Reconsidered. The History and Civilization of an Italian City-State, 1297–1797*, ed. J. Martin and D. Romano, Baltimore MD/London: Johns Hopkins University Press, 295–338.

Foyster, E. (1999), *Manhood in Early Modern England. Honour, Sex and Marriage*, London/New York: Longman.

Frigo, D. (1983), 'Dal caos all'ordine: sulla questione del "prender moglie" nella trattatistica del sedicesimo secolo', in *Nel cerchio della luna. Figure di donna in alcuni testi del XVI secolo*, ed. M. Zancan, Venice: Marislio, 57–94.

Frigo, D. (1985), *Il padre di famiglia. Governo della casa e governo civile nella tradizione ell' "economica" tra Cinque e Seiceno*, Rome: Bulzoni.

Gaeta, F. (1961), 'Alcune considerazioni sul mito di Venezia', *Bibliothèque d'Humanisme*, **23**, 58–75.

Gambier, N. (1980), 'La donna e la giustizia penale veneziana nel XVIII secolo', in *Stato, società e giustizia nella Repubblica veneta (sec. XV–XVIII)*, ed. G. Cozzi, Rome: Jouvence, 529–75.

Gentilcore, D. (1992), *From Bishop to Witch. The System of the Sacred in Early Modern Terra d'Otranto*, Manchester/New York: Manchester University Press.

Gilmore, D. (1990), *Manhood in the Making. Cultural Concepts of Masculinity*, New Haven CT/London: Yale University Press.

Gilmore, M. (1973), 'Myth and Reality in Venetian Political Theory', in *Renaissance Venice*, ed. J.R. Hale, London: Faber & Faber, 431–44.

Glass D.V. and Eversley, D.E., eds (1965), *Population in History: Essays in Historical Demography*, London: Arnold.

Gleixner, U. (1994), *'Das Mensch' und 'der Kerl'. Die Konstruktion von Geschlecht in Unzuchtsverfahren der Frühen Neuzeit (1700–1760)*, Frankfurt/Main: Campus Verlag.

Gottlieb, B. (1980), 'The Meaning of Clandestine Marriage', in *Family and Sexuality in French History*, ed. R. Wheaton and T.K. Hareven, Philadelphia: University of Philadelphia Press, 49–83.

Gowing, L. (1996), *Domestic Dangers. Women, Words, and Sex in Early Modern London*, Oxford: Clarendon Press.

Grendi, E. (1987), 'Premessa a fonti criminali e storia sociale', *Quaderni storici*, **66**, 695–700.

Grendi, E. (1990), 'Sulla "storia criminale": risposta a Mario Sbriccoli', *Quaderni storici*, **73**, 269–75.

Grubb, J. (1986), 'When Myths Lose Power: Four Decades of Venetian Historiography', *Journal of Modern History*, **58**, 43–94.

Guzzetti, L. (1998a), 'Seperations and Seperated Living Couples in Venice in the 14th Century', in *Marriage in Italy 1300–1650*, ed. K. Lowe and T. Dean, Cambridge: Cambridge University Press, 249–74.

Guzzetti, L. (1998b), *Venezianische Vermächtnisse. Die soziale und wirtschaftliche Situation von Frauen im Spiegel mittelalterlicher Testamente*, Stuttgart/Weimar: Metzler Verlag.

Habermas, R. (1992), *'Frauen und Männer im Kampf um Leib, Ökonomie und Recht. Zur Beziehung der Geschlechter im Frankfurt der Frühen Neuzeit*', in *Dynamik der Tradition. Studien zur historischen Kulturforschung*, ed. R. van Dülmen, Frankfurt/Main: Fischer Verlag, 109–36.

Hacke, D. (2000), 'Gendering Men in Early Modern Venice', *Acta Histriae*, **8**, 49–68.

Hacke, D. (2001a), 'Non Lo Volevo Per Marito in Modo Alcuno: Forced Marriages, Generational Conflicts, and the Limits of Patriarchal Power in Early Modern Venice, c. 1580–1680', in *Time, Space, and Women's Lives in Early Modern Europe*, ed. A. Jacobson Schutte, Th. Kuehn and S. Seidel Menchi, Kirksville MO: Truman State University Press, 203–22.

Hacke, D., ed. (2001b), *Das Verdienst der Frauen von Moderata Fonte*, Munich: C.H. Beck Verlag.

Hacke, D. (2001c), 'Von der Wirkungsmächtigkeit des Heiligen: Magische Liebeszauberpraktiken und die religiöse Mentalität venezianischer Laien der Frühen Neuzeit', *Historische Anthropologie*, **3**, 311–32.

Hacke, D. (2002a), 'La promessa disattesa: Il caso di Perina Gabrieli (Venezia 1620)', in *Matrimoni in dubbio. Promesse disattese, legami incerti unioni clandestini*, ed. S. Seidel Menchi and D. Quaglioni, Bologna: Il Mulino, 395–413.

Hacke, D. (2002b), 'Zur Wahrnehmung häuslicher Gewalt und ehelicher Unordnung im Venedig der Frühen Neuzeit (16. und 17. Jahrhundert)', in *Wahrheit, Wissen, Erinnerung. Zeugenverhörprotokolle als Quellen für soziale Wissensbestände der Frühen Neuzeit*, ed. R.-P. Fuchs and W. Schulze, Münster/Hamburg/London: Lit Verlag, 317–55.

Hacke, D. (2002c), 'Aus Liebe und aus Not. Eine Geschichte des Gefühls anhand venezianischer Liebeszauberprozesse', *Zeitschrift für historische Forschung*, **3**, 359–82.

Hajnal, J. (1965), 'European Marriage Patterns in Perspective', in *Population in History: Essays in Historical Demography*, ed. D.V. Glass and D.E. Eversley, London: Arnold, 101–43.

Hale, J.R., ed. (1973), *Renaissance Venice*, London: Faber & Faber.

Hammerton, J. (1992), *Cruelty and Companionship. Conflict in Nineteenth- Century Married Life*, London/New York: Routledge.

Hanawalt, B.A.(1986), *The Ties That Bound: Peasant Families in Medieval England*, New York/Oxford: Oxford University Press.

Hanley, S. (1989), 'Engendering the State: Family Formation and State Building in Early Modern France', *French Historical Studies*, **16**, 4–27.

Harrington, J.F. (1995), *Reordering Marriage and Society in Reformation Germany*, Cambridge/New York/Melbourne: Cambridge University Press.

Heller, T.C., Sosna, M. and Wellbery, D.E., eds (1986), *Reconstructing*

Individualism: Autonomy, Individuality, and the Self in Western Thought, Stanford CA: Stanford University Press.

Helmholz, R.H.(1974), *Marriage Litigation in Medieval England*, London: Cambridge University Press.

Herlihy, D. (1972), 'Some Psychological Roots of Violence in Tuscan Cities', in *Violence and Civil Disorder in Italian Cities, 1200–1500*, ed. L. Martines, Berkeley/Los Angeles: University of California Press, 129–54.

Herlihy, D. and Klapisch-Zuber, Ch. (1985), *Tuscans and their Families. A Study of the Florentine Catasto of 1427*, New Haven CT/London: Yale University Press.

Houlbrooke, R. (1979), *Church Courts and the People during the English Reformation, 1520–1570*, Oxford: Oxford University Press.

Hughes, D.O. (1975), 'Urban Growth and Family Structure in Medieval Genoa', *Past and Present*, 66, 3–28.

Hughes, D.O.(1983), 'Sumptuary Law and Social Relations in Renaissance Italy', in *Disputes and Settlements. Law and Human Relations in the West*, ed. J. Bossy, Cambridge: Cambridge University Press, 69–99.

Hufton, O. (1995), *The Prospect Before Her. A History of Women in Western Europe, 1500–1800*, vol. 1, London: HarperCollins.

Hunecke, V. (1992), 'Kindsbett oder Kloster: Lebenswege venezianischer Patrizierinnen im 17. und 18. Jahrhundert', *Geschichte und Gesellschaft*, 18, 446–76.

Hunecke, V. (1995), *Der venezianische Adel am Ende der Republik 1646–1797. Demographie, Familie, Haushalt*, Tübingen: Niemeyer.

Hunt, M. (1992), 'Wife Beating. Domesticity and Woman's Independence in Eighteenth-Century London', *Gender and History*, 4, 10–33.

Ingram, M. (1990), *Church Courts, Sex and Marriage in England, 1570–1640*, Cambridge: Cambridge University Press.

Jedin, H. (1951–71), *Geschichte des Konzils von Trient*, 4 vols, Freiburg: Herder.

Jerouschek, G. (1991), '"Diabolus Habitat in Eis". Wo der Teufel zu Hause ist: Geschlechtlichkeit im rechtstheologischen Diskurs des ausgehenden Mittelalters und der Frühen Neuzeit', in *Ordnung und Lust. Bilder von Liebe, Ehe und Sexualität im Spätmittelalter und Früher Neuzeit*, ed. H.-J. Bachorski, Trier: Wissenschaftlicher Verlag Trier, 281–305.

Jordan, C. (1990), *Renaissance Feminism. Literary Texts and Political Models*, Ithaca/London: Cornell University Press.

Kelso, R. (1956), *Doctrine for the Lady of the Renaissance*, Urbana: University of Illinois Press.

Kertzer, D.I. and Saller, R.P., eds (1991), *The Family in Italy from*

Antiquity to the Present, New Haven CT/London: Yale University Press.

King, M.L. (1975), 'Personal, Domestic and Republican Values in the Moral Philosophy of Giovanni Caldiera', *Renaissance Quarterly*, 28, 535–74.

King, M.L (1976), 'Caldiera and the Barbaros on Marriage and the Family: Humanistic Reflections of Venetian Realities', *Journal of Medieval and Renaissance Studies*, 6, 19–50.

Kirshner, J. (1985), 'Wives' Claims against Insolvent Husbands in Late Medieval Italy', in *Women of the Medieval World. Essays in Honour of John H. Mundy*, ed. J. Kirshner and S.F. Wemple, Oxford/New York: Blackwell, 256–303.

Klapisch-Zuber, Ch. (1987), *Women, Family and Ritual in Renaissance Italy*, Chicago/London: University of Chicago Press.

Kuehn, Th. (1982), *Emancipation in Late Medieval Florence*, New Brunswick, NJ: Rutgers University Press.

Kuehn, Th. (1991), *Law, Family and Women. Towards a Legal Anthropology of Renaissance Italy*, Chicago/London: University of Chicago Press.

Labalme, P.H. (1981), 'Venetian Women on Women: Three Early Modern Feminists', *Archivio Veneto*, 5, 81–109.

Labalme, P.H. (1984), 'Sodomy and Venetian Justice in the Renaissance', *Tijdschrift voor Rechtsgeschiedenis*, 52, 217–54.

Lane, F.C. (1973), *Venice. A Maritime Republic*, Baltimore/London: Johns Hopkins University Press.

Laqueur, T. (1992), *Making Sex. Body and Gender from the Greeks to Freud*, Cambridge MA: Harvard University Press.

Laslett, P. (1977), *Family Life and Illicit Love in Earlier Generations: Essays in Historical Sociology*, Cambridge: Cambridge University Press.

Laven, M. (2002), *Virgins of Venice. Enclosed Lives and Broken Vows in the Renaissance Convent*, London et al: Viking/Penguin Books.

Lazzarini, V. (1910–11), 'L'avvocato dei carcerati poveri a Venezia', *Atti dell'Istituto veneto di scienze, lettere ed arti*, 70, 1471–1507.

Lees, C.A., ed. (1994), *Medieval Masculinities. Regarding Men in the Middle Ages*, Minneapolis/London: University of Minnesota Press.

Lombardi, D. (1994), 'Interventions by Church and State in Marriage Disputes in Sixteenth- and Seventeenth- Century Florence', in *Crime, Society and the Law in Renaissance Italy*, ed. T. Dean and K. Lowe, Cambridge: Cambridge University Press, 142–56.

Lombardi, D. (2001), *Matrimoni di antico regime*, Bologna: Il Mulino.

Lulli, M.G. (1974), 'Il problema del divorzio in Italia dal sec. XVIII al codice del 1865', *Il diritto di famiglia e delle persone*, 3, 594–666.

Macfarlane, A. (1986), *Marriage and Love in England: Modes of Reproduction, 1300–1840*, Oxford/New York: Blackwell.

Mackenney, R. (1987), *Tradesmen and Traders. The World of the Guilds in Venice and Europe, c. 1250–1650*, Totowa NJ: Barnes & Noble.

Maclean, I. (1980), *The Renaissance Notion of Women. A Study in the Fortunes of Scholarship and Medical Science in European Intellectual Life*, Cambridge: Cambridge University Press.

Makowski, E.M. (1977), 'The Conjugal Debt and Medieval Canon Law', *Journal of Medieval History*, 3, 99–114.

Marland, H., ed. (1993), *The Art of Midwifery. Early Modern Midwives in Europe*, London/New York: Routledge.

Martin, J. (1985), 'Out of a Shadow: Heretical and Catholic Women in Renaissance Venice', *Journal of Family History*, 10, 21–33.

Martin, J. (1987), 'L'inquisizione romana e la criminalizzazione del dissenso religioso a Venezia all'inizio dell'età moderna', *Quaderni storici*, 66, 772–802.

Martin, J. (1993), *Venice's Hidden Enemies. Italian Heretics in a Renaissance City*, Berkeley/Los Angeles/London: University of California Press.

Martin, J. and Romano, D., eds (2000), *Venice Reconsidered. The History and Civilization of an Italian City-State, 1297–1797*, Baltimore MD/London: Johns Hopkins University Press.

Martin, R. (1989), *Witchcraft and the Inquisition in Venice*, Oxford/New York: Blackwell.

Martines, L., ed. (1972), *Violence and Civil Disorder in Italian Cities, 1200–1500*, Berkeley/Los Angeles/London: University of California Press.

Martini, G. (1986), 'Rispetto dell'infanzia e violenza sui minori nella Venezia del Seicento', *Società e storia*, 34, 793–817.

Martini, G. (1986–87a), 'La Donna veneziana del'600. Tra sessualità legittima ed illegittima: Alcune riflessioni sul concubinato', *Atti dell'Istituto veneto di scienze, lettere ed arti*, 145, 301–39.

Martini, G. (1986–87b), 'Sodomia e discriminazione morale a Venezia nei secoli XV–XVII: Tendenze evolutive', *Atti dell'Istituto veneto di scienze, lettere ed arti*, 145, 341–66.

Medick, H. and Sabean, D.W., eds (1984), *Interest and Emotion. Essays on the Study of Family and Kinship*, Cambridge: Cambridge University Press.

Migiel, M. and Schiesari, J., eds (1991), *Refiguring Women. Perspectives on Gender and the Italian Renaissance*, Ithaca/London: Cornell University Press.

Molho, A. (1988), 'Deception and Marriage Strategy in Renaissance

Florence: The Case of Women's Age', *Renaissance Quarterly*, 2, 193–217.

Muir, E. (1981), *Civic Rituals in Renaisssance Venice*. Princeton, NJ: Princeton University Press.

Muir, E. (2000), 'Was there Republicanism in the Renaissance Republics? Venice after Agnadello', in *Venice Reconsidered. The History and Civilization of an Italian City-State, 1297–1797*, ed. J. Martin and D. Romano, Baltimore MD/London: Johns Hopkins University Press, 137–67.

Muir, E. and Ruggiero, G., eds (1990), *Sex and Gender in Historical Perspective (Selections from Quaderni storici)*, trans. M. Margret and C. Gallucci, Baltimore MD/London: Johns Hopkins University Press.

Muir, E. and Ruggiero, G., eds (1994), *History from Crime (Selections from Quaderni storici)*, Baltimore MD/London: Johns Hopkins University Press.

Nelli, S. (1976), *Lo scioglimento del matrimonio nella storia di diritto italiano*, Milan: Dott. A. Giuffrè Editore.

Niccoli, O. (1980), 'Menstruum quasi monstruum: Parti mostruosi e tabù menstruale nel'500', *Quaderni storici*, 44, 402–28.

Niccoli, O. (1988), 'Il corpo femminile nei trattati del Cinquecento', in *Il corpo delle donne*, ed. G. Bock and G. Nubili, Ancona: Transeuropa, 25–43.

Niero, A. (1961), *I patriarchi di Venezia: da Lorenzo Giustiniani ai nostri giorni*, Venice: Studium Cattolico Veneziano.

Noonan, J.T. (1986), *Contraception. A History of Its Treatment by the Catholic Theologians and Canonists*, Cambridge MA/London: Harvard University Press.

Nussdorfer, L. (1993), 'Writing and the Power of Speech: Notaries and Artisans in Baroque Rome', in *Culture and Identity in Early Modern Europe (1500–1800)*, ed. B.B. Diefendorf and C. Hesse. Ann Arbor: University of Michigan Press, 103–18.

Outhwaite, R.B., ed. (1981), *Marriage and Society. Studies in the Social History of Marriage*, London: Europa.

Ozment, S. (1983), *When Fathers Ruled. Family Life in Reformation Europe*, Cambridge MA: Harward University Press.

Paolin, G. (1984), 'Monache e donne nel Friuli del Cinquecento', *Società e cultura del Cinquecento nel Friuli occidentale*, 201–28.

Pastore, A. and Sorcinelli, P., eds (1990), *Emarginazione, criminalità e devianza in Italia fra '600 e '900*, Milan: Angeli.

Palumbo-Fossati, I. (1984), 'L'interno della casa dell'artigiano e dell'artista nella Venezia del Cinquecento', *Studi veneziani*, 8, 109–53.

Pavanini, P. (1981), 'Abitazioni popolari e borghesi nella Venezia Cinquecentesca', *Studi veneziani*, 5, 63–126.

Phillips, R. (1988), *Putting Asunder. The History of Divorce in Western Society*, Cambridge: Cambridge University Press.

Pillon, D. (1981–82), 'La comare istruita nel suo uffizio. Alcune notizie sulle levatrici tra il 600 e 700', *Atti dell'Istituto veneto di scienze, lettere ed arti*, **140**, 65–98.

Po-Chia Hsia, R. (1989), *Social Discipline in the Reformation: Central Europe 1550–1750*, London/New York: Routledge.

Pomata, G. (1995), 'Vollkommen oder verdorben? Der männliche Samen im frühneuzeitlichen Europa', *L'Homme*, **6**, 59–85.

Povolo, C. (1978–79), 'Note per uno studio dell'infanticidio nella Repubblica di Venezia nei secoli XV–XVIII', *Atti dell'Istituto veneto di scienze, lettere ed arti*, **137**, 115–31.

Povolo, C. (1979–80), 'Aspetti sociali e penali del reato d'infanticidio. Il caso di una contadina padovana nel'700', in *Atti dell'Istituto veneto di scienze, lettere ed arti*, **137**, 415–32.

Povolo, C. (1980), 'Aspetti e problemi dell'amministrazione della giustizia penale nella Repubblica di Venezia. Secoli XVI–XVII', in *Stato, società e giustizia nella Repubblica veneta (sec. XV–XVIII)*, ed. G. Cozzi, Rome: Jouvence, 53–258.

Povolo, C. (1989), 'Dal versante dell'illegittimità. Per una ricerca sulla storia della famiglia: infanticidio ed esposizione d'infante nel veneto nell'età moderna', in *Crimine, giustizia e società veneta in età moderna*, ed. L. Berlinguer and F. Colao, Milan: Giuffrè, 89–163.

Povolo, C. (1996), *Il processo Guarnieri. Buje-Capodistria 1771*, Capodistria: Società Storica del Litorale.

Povolo, C. (1997), *L'intrigo dell'onore. Poteri e istituzioni nella Repubblica di Venezia tra Cinquecento e Seicento*, Verona: Cierre Edizioni.

Povolo, C. (2000), 'Rappresentazioni dell'onore nel discorso processuale', *Acta Histriae*, **8**, 2, 513–34.

Prodi, P. (1973), 'The Structure and Organization of the Church in Renaissance Venice: Suggestions for Research', in *Renaissance Venice*, ed. J.R. Hale, London: Faber & Faber, 409–30.

Prodi, P., ed. (1994), *Disciplina dell'anima, disciplina del corpo e disciplina della società tra medioevo ed età moderna*, Bologna: Il Mulino.

Prosperi, A. (1996), *Tribunali della coscienza. Inquisitori, confessori, missionari*, Turin: Einaudi.

Pullan, B., ed. (1968), *Crisis and Change in the Venetian Economy in the Sixteenth and Seventeenth Centuries*, London: Methuen.

Pullan, B. (1971), *Rich and Poor in Renaissance Venice. The Social Institutions of a Catholic State, to 1620*, Oxford: Blackwell.

Puppi, L. (1988), 'Il mito e la trasgressione. Liturgia urbana delle esecuzioni capitali a Venezia tra il XVI e il XVII secolo', *Studi veneziani*, **15**, 107–30.

Quaglioni, D. (2000), '"Divortium a diversitate mentium". La separazione personale dei coniugi nelle dotrine di dirtto comune (appunti per una discussione)', in *Coniugi nemici. La separazione in Italia dal XII al XVIII secolo*, ed. S. Seidel Menchi and D. Quaglioni, Bologna: Il Mulino, 95–118.

Queller, D.E. and Madden, T.F. (1993), 'The Father of the Bride: Fathers, Daughters, and Dowries in Late Medieval and Early Renaissance Venice', *Renaissance Quarterly*, **4**, 685–711.

Raffaele, S. (1989), '"Essendo real volontà che le donne badino all'onore." Onore e status nella legislazione meridionale (secc. XVI–XVII)', in *Onore e storia nelle società mediterranee*, ed. G. Fiume, Palermo: La Luna, 143–54.

Rapp, R.T. (1976), *Industry and Economic Decline in Seventeenth-Century Venice*, Cambridge MA: Harvard University Press.

Rasi, P. (1941), 'L'applicazione delle norme del Concilio di Trento in materia matrimoniale', *Studi di storia e diritto in onore di A. Solmi*, Milan: Giuffrè, 235–81.

Rigo, A. (1992–93), 'Giudici del Procurator e donne "malmaritate". Interventi della giustizia secolare in materia matrimoniale a Venezia in epoca tridentina', *Atti dell'Istituto veneto di scienze, lettere ed arti*, **151**, 241–66.

Rigo, A. (2000), 'Interventi dello Stato veneziano nei casi di separazione: i Giudici del Procurator. Alcuni dati degli anni Cinquanta e Sessanta del XVI secolo', in *La separazione in Italia dal XII al XVIII secolo*, ed. S. Seidel Menchi and D. Quaglioni. Bologna: Il Mulino, 519–36.

Rocke, M. (1996), *Forbidden Friendships. Homosexuality and Male Culture in Renaissance Florence*, New York/Oxford: Oxford University Press.

Rocke, M. (1998), 'Gender and Sexual Culture in Renaissance Italy', in *Gender and Society in Renaissance Italy*, ed. R.C. Davis and J.C. Brown, London/New York: Longman.

Romano, D. (1983), '*Quod sibi fiat gratia*: Adjustments of Penalties and the Exercise of Influence in Early Renaissance Venice', *Journal of Medieval and Renaissance Studies*, **13**, 251–68.

Romano, D. (1987), *Patricians and Popolani: The Social Foundations of the Venetian Renaissance State*, Baltimore MD/London: Johns Hopkins University Press.

Romano, D. (1989), 'Gender and the Urban Geography of Renaissance Venice', *Journal of Social History*, **23**, 339–53.

Romano, D. (1996), *Housecraft and Statecraft. Domestic Service in*

Renaissance Venice, 1400–1600, Baltimore MD/London: Johns Hopkins University Press.

Romeo, G. (1998), *Esorcisti, confessori e sessualità femminile nell'Italia della Controriforma*, Florence: Le lettere.

Roodenburg, H. (1998), 'Ehre in einer pluralistischen Gesellschaft: Die Republik der Vereinigten Niederlande', in *Ehrkonzepte in der Frühen Neuzeit. Identitäten und Abgrenzungen*, ed. S. Backmann, H.-J. Künast and S. Ullmann, Berlin: Akademie Verlag, 366–87.

Roper, L. (1993), *The Holy Household. Women and Morals in Reformation Augsburg*, Oxford: Clarendon Press.

Roper, L. (1994), *Oedipus and the Devil. Witchcraft, Sexuality and Religion in Early Modern Europe*, London/New York: Routledge.

Rösch, G. (2000), 'The *Serrata* of the Great Council and Venetian Society, 1286–1323, in *Venice Reconsidered. The History and Civilization of an Italian City-State, 1297–1797*, ed. J. Martin and D. Romano, Baltimore MD/London: Johns Hopkins University Press, 67-88.

Rosenthal, E.G. (1988), 'The Position of Women in Renaissance Florence: Neither Autonomy nor Subjection', in *Florence and Italy. Renaissance Studies in Honour of Nicolai Rubinstein*, ed. P. Denley and C. Elam, London: Westfield College, 369–81.

Rublack, U. (1996), 'Pregnancy, Childbirth and the Female Body in Early Modern Germany', *Past and Present*, **150**, 84–110.

Rublack, U. (1999), *The Crimes of Women in Southwest Germany*, Oxford: Oxford University Press.

Ruggiero, G. (1978), 'Law and Punishment in Early Renaissance Venice', *The Journal of Criminal Law and Criminology*, **69**, 243–56.

Ruggiero, G. (1980), *Violence in Early Renaissance Venice*, New Brunswick NJ: Rutgers University Press.

Ruggiero, G. (1985), *The Boundaries of Eros. Sex Crime and Sexuality in Renaissance Venice*, New York/Oxford: Oxford University Press.

Ruggiero, G. (1993a), *Binding Passions. Tales of Magic, Marriage, and Power at the End of the Renaissance*, New York: Oxford University Press.

Ruggiero, G, (1993b), 'Marriage, Love, Sex, and Renaissance Civic Morality', in *Sexuality and Gender in Early Modern Europe. Institutions, Texts, Images*, ed. J.G. Turner, Cambridge: Cambridge University Press, 10–30.

Safley, T.M. (1984), *Let No Man Put Asunder. The Control of Marriage in the German Southwest: A Comparative Study, 1550–1600*, Kirksville MO: Sixteenth Century Journal Publishers.

Sbriccoli, M. (1988), 'Fonti giudiziarie e fonti giuridiche. Riflessioni sulla fase attuale degli studi di storia del crimine e della giustizia criminale', *Studi storici*, **29**, 491–501.

Scarabello, G. (1980a), 'La Pena del carcere. Aspetti della condizione carceraria a Venezia nei secoli XVI–XVII: L'assistenza e l'associazionismo', in *Stato, società e giustizia nella Repubblica veneta (sec. XV–XVIII)*, ed. G. Cozzi, Rome: Jouvence, 317–76.

Scarabello, G., (1980b), 'Devianza sessuale ed interventi di giustizia a Venezia nella prima metà del XVI secolo', in *Tiziano e Venezia*. Convegno internazionale di Studi, Vicenza: Neri Pozza Editore, 75–84.

Schmidt, F. (1990), 'Zur Genese kapitalistischer Konsumformen im Venedig der Frühen Neuzeit', in *Stadtgeschichte als Zivilisationsgeschichte. Beiträge zum Wandel städtischer Wirtschafts-, Lebens- und Wahrnehmungsweise*, ed. Jürgen Reulecke, Essen: Die Blaue Eule, 23–40.

Schmidt, H.R. (1998), 'Hausväter vor Gericht. Der Patriarchalismus als zweischneidiges Schwert', in *Hausväter, Priester, Kastraten. Zur Konstruktion von Männlichkeit im Spätmittelalter und Früher Neuzeit*, ed. M. Dinges, Göttingen: Vandenhoeck & Ruprecht, 213–36.

Schmugge, L., Hersprenger, P. and Wiggenhause, B., eds (1996), *Die Supplikenregister der päpstlichen Pönitentiare aus der Zeit Pius II (1458–1464)*, Tübingen: Niemeyer.

Schmugge, L. (2000), 'Female Petitioners in the Papal Penitentiary', *Gender and History*, **12**, 685–703.

Seed, P. (1988), *To Love, Honor, and Obey in Colonial Mexico. Conflicts over Marriage Choice, 1574–1821*, Stanford CA: Stanford University Press.

Seidel Menchi, S., and Quaglioni, D., eds (2000), *Coniugi nemici. La separazione in Italia dal XII al XVIII secolo*, Bologna: Il Mulino.

Seidel Menchi, S. and Quaglioni, D. eds (2001), *Matrimoni in dubbio. Unioni controverse e nozze claudestine in Italia dal XIV al XVII secolo*, Bologna: Il Mulino.

Simon, M. (1993), *Heilige Hexe Mutter. Der Wandel des Frauenbildes durch die Medizin im 16. Jahrhundert*, Berlin: Reimer Verlag.

Shorter, E. (1975), *The Making of the Modern Family*, New York: Basic Books.

Sommerville, M. (1995), *Sex and Subjection: Attitudes to Women in Early Modern Society*, London: Arnold.

Sperling, J. (1999), *Convents and the Body Politic in Late Renaissance Venice*, Chicago/London: University of Chicago Press.

Stolberg, M. (2000), 'An Unmanly Vice: Self-Pollution, Anxiety, and the Body in the Eighteenth Century', *Social History of Medicine*, **13**, 1–21.

Stone, L. (1977), *The Family, Sex and Marriage in England 1500–1800*, London: Weidenfeld and Nicolson.

Stone, L. (1990), *Road to Divorce. England 1530–1987*, Oxford: Oxford University Press.

Strasser, U. (1999a), 'Vom "Fall der Ehre" zum "Fall der Leichtfertigkeit": Geschlechtsspezifische Aspekte der Konfessionalisierung am Beispiel Münchner Eheversprechens- und Alimentationsklagen', in *Konfessionalisierung und Region*, ed. P. Frieß and R. Kießling, Konstanz: Universitätsverlag, 227–46.

Strasser, U. (1999b), 'Bones of Contention: Cloistered Nuns, Decorated Relics, and the Contest over Women's Place in the Public Sphere of Counter-Reformation Munich', *Archiv für Reformationsgeschichte*, 90, 255–88.

Tamassia, N. (1971), *La famiglia italiana nei secoli decimoquinto e decimosesto*, Rome: Multigrafica (reprint from 1911).

Tedoldi, L. (1999), *Del difendere. Avvocati, procuratori e giudici a Brescia e Verona tra la Repubblica di Venezia e l'età napoleonica*, Milan: Franco Angeli.

Thomas, K. (1959), 'The Double Standard', *Journal of the History of Ideas*, 20, 195–216.

Tramontin, S. (1965), 'Gli inizi dei due seminari di Venezia', *Studi veneziani*, 7, 363–77.

Tramontin, S. (1991), 'Venezia tra riforma cattolica e riforma protestante', in *Patriarcato di Venezia*, ed. S. Tramontin, Padua: Euganea Editoriale Comunicazioni, 91–130.

Tramontin, S. (1992), 'La diocesi nelle relazioni dei Patriarchi alla Santa Sede', in *La chiesa di Venezia nel Seicento*, ed. B. Bertoli, Venice: Edizioni Studium Cattolico Veneziano, 55–90.

Turner, G., ed. (1993), *Sexuality and Gender in Early Modern Europe. Institutions, Texts, Images*, Cambridge: Cambridge University Press.

Trivellato, F. (1998), 'Out of Women's Hands: Notes on Venetian Glass Beads, Female Labour and International Trades', in *Beads and Bead Makers. Gender, Material Culture and Meaning*, ed. L.D. Sciama and J.B. Eicher, Oxford/New York: Berg, 47–82.

Watt, J.R. (1992), *The Making of Modern Marriage. Matrimonial Control and the Rise of Sentiment in Neuchâtel, 1550–1800*, Ithaca/London: Cornell University Press.

Wheaton, R. and Hareven, T.K., eds (1980), *Family and Sexuality in French History*, Philadelphia: University of Philadelphia Press.

Wheeler, J. (2000), 'Neighbourhoods and Local Loyalties in Renaissance Venice', in *Mediterranean Urban Culture 1400–1700*, ed. A. Cowan, Exeter: University of Exeter Press, 31–42.

Wiesner, M.E. (1993), *Women and Gender in Early Modern Europe*, Cambridge: Cambridge University Press.

Wiesner, M.E. (1993), 'The Midwives of South Germany', in *The Art of Midwifery*, ed. H. Marland, London/New York: Routledge, 77–94.

Wiesner, M. E. (2000), *Christianity and Sexuality in the Early Modern World. Regulating Desire, Performing Practice*, London/New York: Routledge.

Zanette, E. (1960), *Suor Arcangela monaca del Seicento veneziano*, Venice/Rome: Istituto per la Collaborazione Culturale.

Zanetto, M. (1991), "Mito di Venezia" ed "antimito" negli scritti del Seicento veneziano, Venice: Editoria Universitaria.

Zarri, G. (1996), 'Il matrimonio tridentino', in *Il Concilio di Trento e il moderno* ed. P. Prodi and W. Reinhard, Bologna: Il Mulino, 437–84.

Index